-LIVING HOMES-

THOMAS J. ELPEL'S
FIELD GUIDE TO INTEGRATED
DESIGN & CONSTRUCTION

4th Edition

Dedicated to Renee,
my partner in Dreams

HOPS Press
Hollowtop Outdoor Primitive School, LLC
12 Quartz Street
Pony, Montana 59747
http://www.hollowtop.com

-LIVING HOMES-
THOMAS J. ELPEL'S FIELD GUIDE TO INTEGRATED DESIGN & CONSTRUCTION
4TH EDITION

ISBN: 1-892784-09-2

Copyright: May 1998
2nd Edition: May 1999   3rd Edition: May 2000
4th Edition (1st perfect bound edition): May 2001

Photos and illustrations are by the author or his family and friends, unless otherwise noted.

Publisher's Cataloging-in-Publication Data
Elpel, Thomas J. 1967-
    Living Homes: Thomas J. Elpel's Field Guide to Integrated Design & Construction / Thomas J. Elpel.
    —4th ed.

    Includes bibiliographical references and index.
    ISBN: 1-892784-09-2 $25.00 Pbk. (alk. paper)
    1. Dwellings—Environmental Engineering—Amateur's manuals. 2. Stone Masonry Construction. 3. Log House Construction. 4. Strawbale Construction.
    I. Elpel, Thomas J. II. Title.
    TH4815.E4   690.837   LCCN: 2001012345

Table of Contents

HOPS Press: Our Commitment to the Environment

How many books about sustainable living and alternative construction are printed on recycled paper? Surprisingly few. Fortunately, as both the author *and* the publisher, I am able to make decisions that other authors have little control over. This book has the highest recycled content of any book we have yet published.

All of the interior pages of *Living Homes* are printed on Envirographic 100% post-consumer fiber paper, bleached without chlorine, from **Badger Paper Mills** in Peshtigo, Wisconsin. The ink on these pages is soy-based. Only the cover is printed on virgin fibers with oil-based inks. Thanks to **United Graphics** in Mattoon, Illinois for being flexible to our special printing requests. Each time we push the bar a little bit higher. We are determined to set a new standard in the publishing business, printing what we preach. Remember to recycle your papers!

HOPS Press
Hollowtop Outdoor Primitive School
www.hollowtop.com

$1.00 from every copy of this book sold
is being donated to the
Institute for Solar Living

The mission of the Institute for Solar Living is to promote sustainable living through inspirational environmental education. For more information, please contact:

Institute for Solar Living
PO Box 836
Hopland, CA 95449
707-744-2017
isl@rgisl.org
www.solarliving.org

Introduction
Building a House on Limited Means
The Elimination of all that is Unnecessary to Achieve a Dream

We built our dream home on a shoe-string income. Photo by Will Brewster, Western Way Photography.

We are very goal-oriented in Western culture, and we often count our successes by how much we accomplish. Eastern cultures can be very goal-oriented as well, but sometimes with a very different approach. While a Westerner sits on his laurels at the end of the day and adds up what he did, an Easterner might sit on his laurels and add up what he eliminated having to do.

As a simple analogy, you might say that a western artist does sculpture with clay, assembling an entire work piece by piece, while an eastern artist does sculpture in stone, eliminating everything that is not part of the final goal. It is two fundamentally different approaches to a similar point. Yet, there is still more to this analogy than that. The western sculptor may shape clay all day long, but the eastern sculptor sits in front of his stone and meditates on it. Then, at the end of the day he picks up his chisel and hammer and makes one strategic hit, revealing all at once a whole portion of the art!

Our approach to achieving our dreams was more the eastern approach than the western one. With this approach Renee and I were able to completely build and pay for our dream home on a combined annual income of only $10,000 to $12,000 per year.

I pretty much grew up in the pages of the old *Mother Earth News* magazine. All through high-school I collected and read and reread every issue of *Mother* that I could find, accumulating a wealth of ideas and dreaming of how to someday assemble those ideas into a way of life. Over the years there were a number of articles on the Japanese farmer Masanobu Fukuoka, and his "no-plowing, no-fertilizing, no-weeding, no-pesticides, do-nothing method of natural farming". His approach was essentially to research, meditate, and eliminate all the unnecessary work in growing his crops. I did not really understand Fukuoka's approach at the time, but I connected with it on an subconscious level. In many ways I was already doing a similar thing— by picking out ideas that would allow me to eliminate all the obstacles on the way to my dreams.

June 1989. Our first home... with phone service!

There was a six-year old concrete slab and footings already on site.

In Zen it has been said that, "Reverence is the elimination of all that is unnecessary." I've never studied Zen, except what I've absorbed by accident. But in high-school I envisioned a life in harmony and reverence with nature, and researched ways to eliminate all that was in my way of that goal. I wanted to live close to nature each and every day, in a house that was comfortable and modern, yet seemed to grow right from the land. I had no interest in earning a living, only in taking care of my needs so that I would be free to contribute to making the world a better place. I wanted a home without a mortgage, without high energy bills, and without the need for much of an income. I wanted a home that would sustain me and give me the freedom to do whatever I wanted in life.

Financing the Dream

In high-school the teachers were always telling us that we had to study hard so that we could find good-paying careers as adults. I found it irritating that they would paint such a dismal picture of the future. I did not realize at the time that most of my classmates considered it normal. I had a lot of Dreams in life, and the idea of getting a job and working for the next forty years just plain scared the heck out of me. I was highly motivated to find a no-job path to success.

Renee and I started dating during our senior year of high-school and were already drawing house plans by time we graduated in June of 1986. We both tried different things for two years, then did a two-month, 500 mile walk across Montana in 1988. With that experience we decided we could do anything together, so we set a wedding date, got jobs and started saving money. Our financial strategy was simple.

Most people rent a house, have a lot of expenses, work real hard, and maybe put 5% of their income away towards their dreams. But you have to work an awfully long time to get anywhere that way. We took the opposite approach and lived on 5% of our incomes while we put 95% away into savings. We got jobs leading stone-age wilderness expeditions, so it was pretty easy to keep expenses down. We had a sizable nest-egg by the time we married in 1989, so we bought land, pitched a tent, and started building. Living in a tent and cooking rice and beans over the campfire allowed us to continue putting virtually all of our income into our Dream. Construction took a long time, since we paid for it just a little at a time. But in the years since, with a comfortable home and no mortgage payment or other big bills, we have been able to continue living our Dreams with little need for a big income to support us.

Our greenhouse serves as an "airlock" to buffer the main part of our house from the outside weather.

Over the years we have shared our home with many friends and visitors interested in checking out our "unique" place. I have noticed that the one thing that grabs their attention the most is Not the stonework or the log construction, or the warm and cheery greenhouse in the middle of the winter. The thing that seems to amaze people is simply that we lived our Dreams, instead of waiting until such things were more practical.

We put up rebar and started forming the back wall, with shade.

We rented metal forms and filled in with our wooden slipforms.

Designing our Home

Our art teacher in high-school told us that art is never finished, that you just have to pick a point to stop working on it. The same is true of architecture. You can never completely "perfect" a set of blue prints, but the more time you meditate on it, the better off you will be.

The most important point to understand is that everything happens "on paper". How much a house costs, how it looks, how comfortable it is, how energy-efficient it is—all these things occur on paper before you pick up even one tool. A little additional time in the planning stage can save you tens of thousands of dollars in construction and maintenance. That is time well spent.

Outdoor style decking in the sun room above the green-house allows heat and humidity to rise up between the boards.

Too often, however, builders simply draw a few boxes on a piece of paper, scoot them around until they are reasonably satisfied with the layout, and start building. The result is houses that end up being more costly and less energy-efficient than they should be. Proper planning can make the difference between whether or not you get the house you really want.

Starting in high-school, we spent four years researching and designing our home. Even so, we were still polishing details in our plans when we started building. We simply reached a point where we had to put down the pencil and "pick up the hammer" (actually a cement mixer).

Our approach to designing was simple. We stuck to the basics. We protected the house on the north and east sides by building into the hill. We covered the south face of the house with glass, and created the greenhouse as a sort of an "airlock" between the main part of the house and the outside, as illustrated in our house plans at the end of this chapter. Only the west side of our house had to be heavily insulated against the cold.

People expect a solar home to cost a lot more, but it does not have to. The main difference between a solar and non-solar home is that the solar home has most of the windows on one side. There are no more materials involved; it just takes longer to come up with a blueprint that aesthetically works inside and outside. Similarly, solar homes often have some fancy heat storage system, such as a wall of masonry, or a stack of water jugs just inches behind a wall of glass, or perhaps a gravel heat sink under the house with a system of pipes and blowers to store and retrieve the warmth. These are extras that are tacked onto a house, and there was no way we could afford such extravagance with our income—so we eliminated them as unnecessary. But we needed walls and floors, so we simply built the walls of stone, and the floors of tiled concrete, to get the advantages of thermal mass without sinking money into a specialized heat system. To eliminate the need for ducting, we put our wood cookstove in the middle of the house and created an open floor-plan for easy air circulation.

After pouring the concrete wall we started slipforming the front.

June 1990. We set up lifting poles to raise the log walls.

Everywhere in a house there are ways to eliminate complexity. For instance, when builders pour a concrete wall for an earth-bermed house they often build an insulated frame wall inside the house. This becomes the equivalent of building two walls—an extravagance we could not afford. So we used a sand-texture paint to give the concrete the appearance of a plastered wall. We coated the outside of the concrete wall with tar, then insulated it with rigid beadboard insulation and backfilled it with dirt. Putting the insulation on the outside kept the thermal mass on the inside. The west side of the house was added on last, and is the only part of the main level that is truly exposed to the weather. Thus it is the only part of the house with insulation sandwiched in the wall.

By simply arranging our building materials in an energy-efficient layout we were able to create a warm house without throwing a lot of money into sophisticated materials or insulation. This also enabled us to eliminate the need for thousands of dollars of central heating. At first our only source of heat was our wood cookstove in the kitchen.

We chose the cookstove not as a matter of economics, but as part of our quality of life. I grew up around my Grandma's wood stove, and simply would not settle for anything else. We have no backup heat when we leave, but the house temperature gradually drops to 50° and stays there.

Remarkably, we can cook all day on our wood stove right through the hottest parts of summer, without cooking ourselves out of the house. Creating an open loft above the kitchen area allows the heat to flow straight up, so we just let it out the upstairs door. We evacuate the heat from the greenhouse the same way. Our water system runs through the fire box of the stove, giving us near-scalding water at the faucet at no extra cost. On sunny days we get "automatic" hot water from our solar panel, also free. In the winter time we initially fill our hot tub with free hot water from the tap, then pay only a few dollars more per month to keep it hot with an electric element.

A small stone hot tub makes human habitat in the greenhouse.

Our house may look expensive, but the reality is that we only have about $10 a square foot into it. Yet I have seen some million dollar homes that looked like junk. Appearance, like energy efficiency, is more a product of design than of cost. You can take the same materials and arrange them poorly or arrange them well. This is where art comes into architecture. We both had a background in art from high-school, but it does not take much artistic skill to design a good-looking house, it just takes time. Believe me, our first house plans were pretty funky, but after four years they started looking pretty good. You may not have much artistic skill to begin with, but if you picked up a pencil and sketched your cat or dog for the next four years you would probably get pretty good at that too. We developed a sense of architecture by just doing it, and now we are much faster at it. Most importantly, however, the investment of time allowed us to meditate on our plans, so we could eliminate extra work and materials and save many thousands of dollars.

We drilled holes and pinned the logs together with rebar.

The log upper story went up in a hurry!

The Building Process

Our house was well researched and planned, yet there were still many unknowns. In particular, neither of us really had any building experience to give us a basis in reality. Our house plan was more of a house hypothesis. It seemed like a good idea, but would it work? There was only one way to find out. One thing we learned walking across Montana is that the only way to get anywhere is to take it one step at a time and see what comes next.

A previous owner once started development on the land we bought, so there was already a concrete slab on site, measuring approximately 30 X 95 feet. Coincidentally, our tentative plans fit one section of the slab, and its footings, to within a couple feet in each direction. We threw out our house plans and grabbed a box of crayons. After a couple days of gesturing and imagining, we had a final, life-sized plan, with every wall outlined right on the slab.

But first we buried 1,100 feet of plastic pipe from the spring and cistern to the house, put up a new temporary power pole, and had the phone company install a telephone in our tent. Then we had to set forms and pour a concrete wall on the north and east sides of the house, where it would later be backfilled with ten feet of earth. Our first masonry experience consisted of three cement trucks and 17 yards of concrete!

Doing our slipformed stone walls after that was considerably less intense. We used Steve Parsons' book, *Stone Houses: A Design and Construction Handbook* (out of print), as our primary guide in this department. We set forms along the crayon lines on the slab and started building. Through our research we had identified the

Our kitchen counters are built mostly with recycled lumber. The floor tiles are a cast-in-place mix of sand, cement, and dirt. 600 square feet of floor tile cost us $50.

slipform technique as an easy low-skill way for amateurs like us to put together straight, good-looking stone walls. We used simple forms, mostly 2 feet tall and 8 feet long, framed with 2 x 4's and faced with plywood. These are set on each side of the wall, wire-tied together, and braced apart. Stones are placed inside the forms with a good face against the plywood, and concrete is poured behind them. The walls can be faced with stone on one side, leaving a concrete wall on the other side, or faced on both sides. Most of our walls are faced on both sides. Reinforcing steel is placed horizontally and vertically throughout the concrete.

All along the way we strived to eliminate costs. We salvaged old lumber from the dump. We used old steel cables, barbed wire, and steel fence posts for much of our rebar. Our rocks were free from the local hills and fields. We did not have much money, but we found a lot of resources. Eventually the house became my full time project, and Renee earned the money to support us. Every time we had any money we would spend it all on some big project. Then she would go back to work, and I would go salvage a few boards somewhere and keep building. If we had the money all at once then I am sure the house would have ended up costing twice as much. But every time the money ran out we simply became more resourceful. Building without money causes a person to meditate a bit longer, to redesign individual projects to fit the available materials.

"Timber framing" supports rigdepole and future floors.

. We slipformed the cellar and filled in the gable ends of the logwork.

Our stairwell formed half of a hexagon in the wall. We just called it the "hex" for all the extra work it took to slipform it and to cut and fit the logs around it.

During our second summer we put up the logs for the upper story. Let me emphasize that it is generally not advisable to switch building materials in this kind of a project. It requires twice as many tools and twice as much knowledge.

In our case, this was the equivalent of a college education, and we did not have enough knowledge at this point to be able to do anything else with our lives anyway, so we had time on our hands. Fortunately Renee's parents attended a log-building class and learned about an exciting new low-skill, low-cost method of working with logs. I peeled all of our logs in a few days using a tool called a Log Wizard™. It is essentially a planar blade that mounts on the end of a chainsaw. With the help of Renee's family we put up the main part of the log work in about ten days. Later we helped them to build their 3000+ square foot log home.

This method of log building we used went fast because it was so simple. It eliminated a lot of the complexities involved in the process. We did not do any notching, and we did very little to make the logs fit together. In fact, there were 2 inch gaps between the logs in some places, yet that is okay with this method. We drilled holes and pounded 1/2 inch rebar through each set of logs, every four feet along the walls, as well as through the corners. This rebar schiscabobbing holds the logs together without notching, and actually prevents the logs from settling at all, so you can safely put in doors and windows without any special engineering. The spaces between the logs are later filled with strips of insulation and chinked with standard masonry mortar. Galvanized nails are first pounded in every three inches along the logs to give something for the mortar to anchor itself on. Vertical poles are set in place to support the ridge pole, so it does not put any weight on the walls. The roof is pretty much standard construction, with 2 x 10 rafters, R-30 fiberglass batts, skip sheathing, steel roofing. The ceiling is sheet-rocked.

The most challenging part was working around the stairwell which jutted out into the greenhouse, making half of a hexagon. We just called it the "hex" for all the extra work it took to slipform it and to cut and fit the logs around it.

Construction usually proceeded slowly throughout the process, due to our chronic lack of money. We moved into the house that second year, with no doors, few windows, and no insulation in the roof. When we were both home we took turns around the wood cookstove, with one of us sitting on the oven door, and the other standing behind the stove. Our frigid Montana winter stopped about three feet from the stove. Renee said she was warmer when she was at work, leading teenagers on wilderness expeditions for three weeks at a time in Idaho. This might all seem a little rough, but I later realized that we saved at least $150,000 in interest payments by eliminating the need for a loan. That is not a bad wage for a couple years of camping out! We kept working on the house and by spring it was quite survivable; by the next winter it was definitely livable.

Labor Day, 1990. We framed the greenhouse with logs.

Putting up the rafters.

One time, after we installed the greenhouse windows and more or less finished the front of the house, I overheard someone talking about our place. We were riding on a bus with state officials for a tour of the nearby gold mill that posed a cyanide threat to the community aquifer. This man pointed to our house as we went by and exclaimed, "Those people must have bucks!"

Of course it was just an illusion. We had no money, and the inside of our house looked just as you see it in this picture. We continued to tackle projects one-at-a-time as we could afford them. I gutted an antique refrigerator and rebuilt it with a surplus refrigeration unit for $70.

We moved into the house that second year, with no doors, few windows, and no insulation in the roof. Living in the middle of a cold construction site was difficult, but I later realized we saved about $150,000 in avoided interest payments on a loan.... not a bad wage for camping out!

To finish the concrete floor, we made our own "terra tiles" from sand, cement and dirt. We troweled the mortar smooth on the floor, then cut the tiles with forms we made ourselves from masonite. It only cost us about $50 to make 600 square feet of tile. The soil we used had little color of it's own, so the tiles took on the grey color of the cement. For later projects we bought plastic forms and started adding dye to the tile mix for color. We mop an acrylic sealer over the floors for protection and to make them shine.

At first we lived off of an extension cord, but gradually we wired the house to the best of our abilities and ran all the wires out the west end of the building. There they were tied together in a knot, fed by the single extension cord coming from the temporary power pole. Overloading the circuit wasn't a problem, since we only used it for lights and a few tools. Eventually we replaced that knot of wires with a breaker box. The breaker box was supposed to go on the inside, but we wanted it in the "addition", which was really more of a "completion" to our house. So we installed the breaker box outside on the west wall and weatherproofed it as much as possible, until we could add on to that end of the house. In the meantime, we continued to use an extension cord from the breaker box to the power pole, and lived with it that way for a couple years.

The pluming was slow in coming too. At first we hooked a hose to our kitchen faucet and carried the drain water out in a bucket. Gradually we ran the plumbing lines, first hooking up the kitchen sink and the hot tub in the greenhouse, both of which drain into a graywater system in the yard. In 1993 we installed a septic system and connected the bathroom sink, shower and toilet. What a thrill it was to have an indoor toilet! Years later we extended plumbing to the washing machine in the addition.

We took our time working on the addition, since we already had a house to live in and many other dreams to follow. Along the way we built and sold the stone house featured in the *Slipform Masonry* chapter. It took us all of 1994 to build that place from start to finish, but only a month to spend our income from it. Some of the money went to buy a newer car, and some to buy a computer for my writing. The rest went into the addition, mostly for the roof and windows. We had it closed in by the spring of 1995, and built a strawbale chickenhouse the same year.

Installing the metal roofing was fast and easy.

November 1990. Finished enough to use, we moved in.

In 1996 we adopted our three children and spent six months just growing together as a family, without working at all. We didn't build the fireplace until 1997. In 1998 we tiled the floor of the addition. Pictures of the floor with deer tracks in the tiles are shown in the *Terra Tiles* chapter. In 1999 we built a stone retaining wall around the patio, pictured in the chapter *Water Supply & Management*. After several failed attempts over the years, I finally got our solar panel working for producing hot water in 2000. We even put trim around the doors and windows of the addition.

One of the realities of an endeavor like this is that once you start, you never stop. There are always unfinished projects left to complete and new ones yet to start. There are sections of our house which we have never finished, such as carpeting the upstairs, and new projects yet to begin, like building furniture and bookshelves or constructing a storage shed for our outdoor gear. We even reupholstered our ugly old couch with some denim cloth that Renee bought on sale. For $20 and a couple days of our time, we got a brand new couch. When you develop skills like this you tend to use them forever afterwards.

A town pet stops by to visit.

Although our house was probably as energy efficient as most typical houses, it took several years to really make it comfortable. The cookstove was our only source of heat up until we built the fireplace in the family room. But the cookstove is not very efficient, we discovered, so most of the heat went up the chimney. If we left for a day then it would take two days of cranking wood into the stove when we returned to get the house warm again. Remember, we have no thermostat or furnace in the house.

I think it has been immensely helpful not having an automatic heat source, because we became much more attuned to the nature of the house. Instead of masking the leaks with heat from a furnace or boiler, we could feel without a doubt what parts of the house were cold and when and why. That helped us to focus on the source of the problems and systematically eliminate them one-by-one.

Building an efficient masonry fireplace in the family room actually reduced our fuel consumption *and* made the house warmer. But the most important step was diligently sealing up cracks and tightening up the house where ever we could. Much of the warmth was being lost through the mortar joints between the logs of the upper level. The cement chinking is porous, so the wind blew right through it. Troweling a thin coat of a caulk-like latex product called Log Jam™ over the mortar made a huge difference in the house. With other energy efficiency measures we only have to light the fireplace about once a week through the winters now. We spend less time than ever cutting and hauling firewood.

Still, we try to do at least one energy efficiency project every year—building the solar panel, upgrading inefficient doors and windows, or finding creative ways to better insulate certain sections of the house. Knowing the house as well as we do, I have little doubt that we will eventually reduce the need for the fireplace down to once or twice a month through the winters. We may not have a thermostat or furnace, but we don't need one either.

We tarred the back wall, insulated it, and backfilled it with soil.

Installing the greenhouse windows.

In Perspective

Economically, we were able to boost the value of our $10,000 income up to about $50,000 a year, tax free. We did this by adding value to the resources we purchased, and even more by avoiding interest payments on a loan.

I often wondered if we really made the best choices, when the stock market soared sky high with internet stocks. Could we have done better by putting our money in the stock market and allowing it to grow? But the answer is clearly "no". We could have invested in the market, but we still would have needed a place to live. Without a house of our own, we would have had to rent one, which meant that we would spent all the money we wanted to invest. Even with steady jobs we would have no doubt been struggling just to pay the monthly bills, with nothing left to invest for the future. Building our own home was definitely the better financial investment.

Also, building our own home was the equivalent of a college education for us. Our house was our diploma, built and paid for. We had few marketable skills when we started, but many skills by the time we finished. We even built and sold the other stone house along the way, and we plan to do more.

Most importantly, however, we have our Dream home, and the freedom to decide each day what we want to do. That freedom is important because we have a lot of interests. We are heavily immersed in the primitive, or stone-age skills, which we research, practice, publish, and

We moved in with secondhand furniture, but Georgie didn't mind.

teach through our own wilderness programs. That in itself is like going to school for a couple degrees—it takes a lot of time.

One of my Dreams was to write books, but it took me almost eight years of staring at the computer and trying to write before it all clicked together. Then it took me several more years to learn the ins and outs of the publishing business to make an income from my writing. I know now that I would have never succeeded as a writer if we had followed a more conventional path. I would have been too busy paying bills to focus on the dream of becoming a writer.

We also research and publish on environmental economics, and we are working on plan to be able to "prefab" high-efficiency houses, to make them economical for more people to own. Each of these areas of interest requires that we have the freedom to sit back and meditate, to take the time to find out what complexities we can eliminate, so we can pick up the chisel at the end of the day and make our one strategic hit, to achieve our goals smoothly and easily.

For all the benefits we gained out of building our own home, I would still not recommend it to every person. Building a home has a way of becoming an education and a career. Do not try building a house only because you think you will save money; it does not work that way. Focus directly on your Dreams and make them your reality. Do that and you will always be successful.

We added on, slipforming stone walls with insulation in the core.

We spread the work on the addition out over several years.

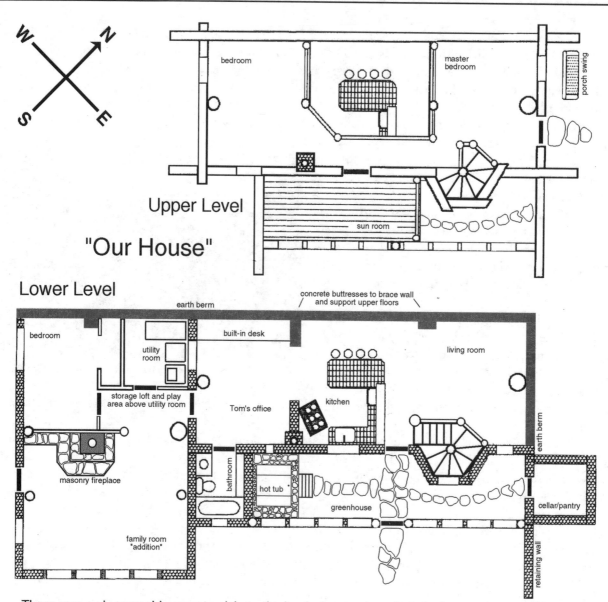

Upper Level

"Our House"

Lower Level

There was a six-year old concrete slab on the land when we bought it, facing southeast.   We adapted our plans to the slab, and called the front "south" for simplicity.   The main part of the house is protected by ten feet of earth fill on the north side,   eight feet of earth on the east side, and the greenhouse on the south side.   Each year we try to do at least one energy efficiency project. At first our house was too cold, but now we only have to light the masonry fireplace in the family room about ounce a week in the winter.

March 1995. Putting the roof on the addition.

We adopted our first three children and lots of pets "to fill up space".

Part I
Dreams, Goals
& Ecology

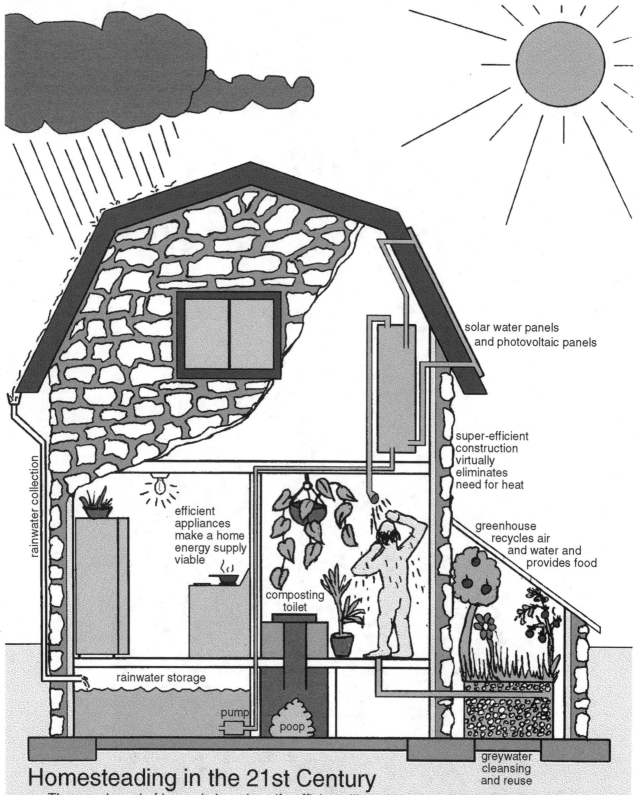

solar water panels
and photovoltaic panels

super-efficient
construction
virtually
eliminates
need for heat

greenhouse
recycles air
and water and
provides food

rainwater collection

efficient
appliances
make a home
energy supply
viable

composting
toilet

rainwater storage

pump

poop

greywater
cleansing
and reuse

Homesteading in the 21st Century

The new breed of home is largely self-sufficient, like a homestead, but also self-contained, like a biosphere. It is much like a homestead in a bottle—warmed by sunlight, with little need for supplementary heat. The household water supply may be partly or entirely provided from rain off the roof, while wastewater is cleansed and reused on site. Human waste and kitchen scraps are composted and used on the landscape. There is no need for a sewer connection. With hot water and electricity from sunshine, there is little need to connect to the power grid either. Even the air is partly recycled, cleansed by plants, which help to supplement the food supply.

Integrated Design & Construction
Homesteading in the 21st Century

Stop and think about all that houses consume, not merely in the initial construction, but in constant maintenance and repairs. Just the amount of fuel for heating and cooling is staggering, when multiplied by all the homes in America and beyond. Every winter hundreds of millions of people reach for the thermostat and turn up the heat. Gas furnaces, electric baseboards, wood stoves—hundreds of millions of heaters ignite in seeming unison, pumping heat into homes and offices, pouring pollution into the air, and sucking billions of dollars out of everyone's pocketbooks. But summer comes soon enough; the temperatures warm up outside and the heaters are all shut down. Then, air conditioners take their place, pumping heat out of homes and offices all across the country, pouring pollution into the air, and sucking billions of dollars out of everyone's pocketbooks.

Fuel for heating and cooling isn't the only resource consumed by poorly designed houses. Most of the appliances, from refrigerators to washers and dryers, hot water heaters, and light bulbs also consume much more energy than necessary to do the job, and besides working inefficiently, most of them do not last very long and have to be replaced. Houses often waste more energy every year than the amount consumed processing the materials used in the original construction. In addition, houses have to be repainted, recarpeted, and reshingled every few years, and the ragged old furniture needs to be thrown away for newer models. Eventually the moisture in the bathrooms covers everything in mold and rots out the studs, ruins the sheetrock, and by that time the showers are scratched and old-looking, so that the entire bathroom needs to be replaced. The amount of repairs and maintenance involved is roughly the equivalent of rebuilding every house in America several times per century. The need for eco-friendly homes is readily apparent in a culture that seems hell-bent on consuming the entire planet. If we can change the way houses are built then surely we can change the world!

The first step towards creating a sustainable future is to define what sustainable really means. How do people need to live in order to strike a balance with the earth's ability to provide? The popular assumption is that we need to reduce our standard of living to match the organic ecosystem's capacity for renewal. While this assumption is partly true, it is also mostly wrong.

Most animal species depend on the living ecosystem for essentially 100% of their sustenance, supplemented by small quantities of inorganic minerals acquired by licking or eating soil. Plants convert the sun's energy to starches, which are eaten by plant eaters like deer or cows, which are eaten by meat eaters like wolves or people. The amount of sunlight captured by plant life determines the number of plant eaters and meat eaters the system will support. The animal population cannot exceed its food supply, or there is mass starvation and a die-off to a sustainable level. Sound familiar?

Now, suppose that a certain species in this ecosystem discovered an additional energy source (i.e.: fossil fuels) to supplement the limited energy captured and stored by plant life each day. That species could greatly expand its population-or raise individual consumption-far beyond the ecosystem's capacity to provide. They could have a real party, at least up until the day the energy supply fizzled out. This has been the root message of the environmental movement since the 1970's—that we have artificially inflated our life-style beyond the ecosystem's ability to provide and we are about to suffer a "correction".

It seemed imminent then that we would exhaust our **nonrenewable energy resources** before the turn of the millennium. According to expert forecasts we should have been nearly or completely out of both oil and natural gas by now. The obvious solution, and the battle cry of the environmental movement, was that we would have to reduce our level of consumption and almost turn back the clock to live like the homesteaders of the 19th century.

Homesteading was largely a self-sufficient way of life. Almost everything a homesteader needed came from the land and was returned to it. Homesteaders grew their own crops and stored the roots, fruits, and vegetables away for the winter months, plus they raised their own meat. Kitchen scraps were recycled to the pigs or composted. Human wastes were recycled to the soil via the outhouse. Water came from a spring or well and was also returned to the land after use. Their fuel came from a private woodlot and the carbon and ashes were returned to the air and land to grow new trees. Homesteader's lives were deeply integrated with the cycles of the ecosystem and the renewal of resources on their land. In many cases, going to town was a once-a-year affair, to trade their surplus crops for coffee, sugar and other special wares to get through the coming cycle. It is easy to romanticize such a simple and balanced way of living.

I think it was this romantic notion of homestead life combined with the environmental concerns of our industrial culture that kicked off the back-to-the-land movement of the 1970's. People looked at the unnatural and unsustainable ways that industry took over our lives, heating and powering our homes and vehicles with petroleum, growing our food with petroleum, extracting vast resources from nature and polluting the environment with our wastes. People wanted to return to the pure simplicity of the past. They flocked to the country and tried the self-sufficient, homestead life-style—building their own homes, using wood heat, growing their own meat and vegetables, milking their own cows and doing their own canning. But homesteading, as it turns out, was a lot of work.

The back-to-the-land movement fizzled as the result of simple economics. As discussed in my book *Direct Pointing to Real Wealth*, it is highly impractical to live on the fringe of an industrial culture while trying to produce a living at a pre-industrial, agrarian level of technology. The simple agrarian life-style produces about 33 calories of energy per calorie expended while the industrial life-style produces about 300 calories per calorie of body energy expended. In essence, homesteading produces roughly one-tenth as much income as the same amount of work in the industrial world. People returned to the industrial work place simply to get decent-paying jobs. Unfortunately, it is difficult to hold a job while also trying to raise a small farm, milk the cows, can the vegetables, and make your own clothes. The 1970's simply proved that it is impossible to turn back the clock.

The industrial race never slowed down for a moment and has continued to build power and momentum ever since. The reason we haven't yet run out of fossil fuels is because new exploration and drilling technologies developed since the 1970's have put us into an energy glut that will last for decades to come—despite temporary ups and downs in the market. You might hear a lot about drilling in the Arctic National Wildlife Refuge to relieve the "energy crises" but the political pressure to do so comes mostly from special interests, such as the state of Alaska where the public gets paid a tax refund from oil industry profits every year. Oil industry insiders do not expect such a venture to be profitable while the price of oil is so low and is forecast to remain low for at least the next twenty years. We will wean ourselves off of oil long before we run out of it!

Ironically, our most urgent environmental problems today stem from the over use of "renewable" resources. Traditional homesteading might still be ecologically sustainable for a limited number of people, but it would not be sustainable if everyone tried to live that way. Even in a place as rural as Montana there are too many people still hunting for firewood, and in some communities there is too much air pollution from all the wood stoves.

Organic resources are becoming increasingly scarce worldwide. Rain forests are being cleared for agriculture. Old growth forests are being milled for lumber. Deforestation is destabilizing watersheds, causing flood and drought cycles. Fisheries on shore and in the ocean are being shut down. Habitats are disappearing, and exotic species are lost daily to extinction. The reality is that we truly did out grow the organic ecosystem's ability to provide, so it is no longer sustainable for every person to live directly off the earth. Fortunately we do not have to either.

Stop for a moment and imagine what it might be like to colonize the moon. First you would need an energy source, but obviously not firewood, methane, or any other kind of biofuel, since there is no life on the moon. By necessity you would choose a completely inorganic source of energy, such as photovoltaics (solar power) to power your colony. Then you would need to build shelters, but obviously you are not going to use wood, since there is none, so you would turn to minerals and metals to make completely inorganic structures to live in. You will also need to grow food and recycle a limited supply of air, water, and nutrients, but you cannot do that outside, so you will have to do it under glass. Of course it would be inefficient to try and glass in thousands of acres to farm with horses and plows, so you are logically going to develop factory-style farms to grow the most possible food in the least possible space-essentially hydroponically-fed with water and nutrients recycled from the colony's waste stream. Ultimately you would develop a completely sustainable way of life that is entirely independent of the organic ecosystem, only because there is no organic ecosystem there to depend on.

In short, this is exactly how we will one day achieve true sustainability on this planet too. We will have a booming civilization that no longer depends on the living ecosystem. That is a good thing too, because at the rate we are going, we are expected to wipe out half of all life on land by about the middle of this century. The faster that we can wean ourselves off of the living ecosystem, the more of it we will be able to save.

I am not suggesting that we should up and quit all use of our living products. It is possible to grow and harvest our organic resources sustainably, at a fixed level of use. But to sustain the massive human population and modern life-style we must increasingly substitute resources from outside the living ecosystem, so life can continue the process of renewal. The homesteads of the 21st century will be ever more like the sort of **biospheres** you might find on the moon, built of mostly inorganic resources, highly energy-efficient, and designed to recycle at least a portion of the air, water, and nutrients internally.

Today a new back-to-the-land movement is under way, marked by an effort to find a modern connection with nature. The emerging informational culture allows people to bring their work to the country, so they can earn a decent wage and live close to nature. These new homesteaders are returning to the land with computers, faxes, e-mail, the internet and teleconferencing-using their incomes to build large modern homes with natural woodwork, scenic vistas, and stone hearths and chimneys for fake fires.

The problem with the new back-to-the-land movement is that it is elitist—at least the part of the movement that is visible through the media. The magazine racks are full of "country" magazines with fancy new sprawling homes of adobe, or stone, or log, or straw. Some of the homes are natural only in design, while others showcase the latest eco-technologies for energy and water conservation, but in either case, they are expensive "eco-mansions" that lend the impression that you have to be rich to live close to the earth.

My own interest in "homesteading" and housing grew partly out of my interest in primitive survival skills. After all, it is the same process, the pursuit of basic necessities like shelter, food, clothing, water and fire. But I was also inspired by the *threat* of impending adulthood. I realized I would have to deal with the same basic needs in modern society. However, the idea of getting a meaningless job and walking the treadmill just plain scared the heck out of me!

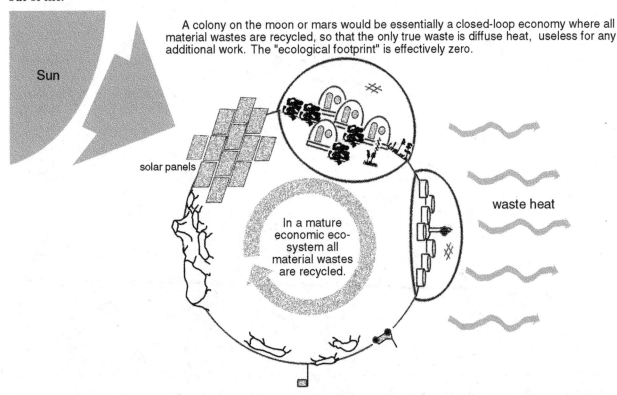

A colony on the moon or mars would be essentially a closed-loop economy where all material wastes are recycled, so that the only true waste is diffuse heat, useless for any additional work. The "ecological footprint" is effectively zero.

Sun

solar panels

In a mature economic eco-system all material wastes are recycled.

waste heat

A mature economic ecosystem functions as a closed-loop where all matter is recycled.
On planet earth we are developing a hybrid closed-loop economy, where some material wastes are recycled in nature and all other waste is recycled through industry. We are depending less and less on the natural ecosystem for waste management and more on the economic ecosystem. Adapted from Direct Pointing to Real Wealth

Beyond that, I have been highly motivated since I was a child to tackle social and environmental problems to find ways to make the world a better place. Many of our social and environmental problems are rooted in the human pursuit of basic needs like shelter, food, clothing, water and fire. The environmental harm from this massive energy and resource consumption is obvious. Yet, we must also acknowledge the societal unrest of people engaged in unrewarding jobs in the often hopeless effort to get ahead. If we could only provide sane alternatives for people to meet their basic needs, then we could certainly change the world.

I realized that if humanity were going to live in balance with nature then people would have to want to. There would have to be something about living with nature that people would perceive as being better than what they have now. The logical solution seemed to be to create a life-style for myself, cooperating with nature, that other people would desire to emulate for themselves. I wanted to demonstrate that it was economical to live an environmentally sound life-style, that it was not just for the elite who could afford to be ecologically hip, but for all people whether they had money or not.

The home that Renee and I built for ourselves was the first test of this idea, and we proved that it is still

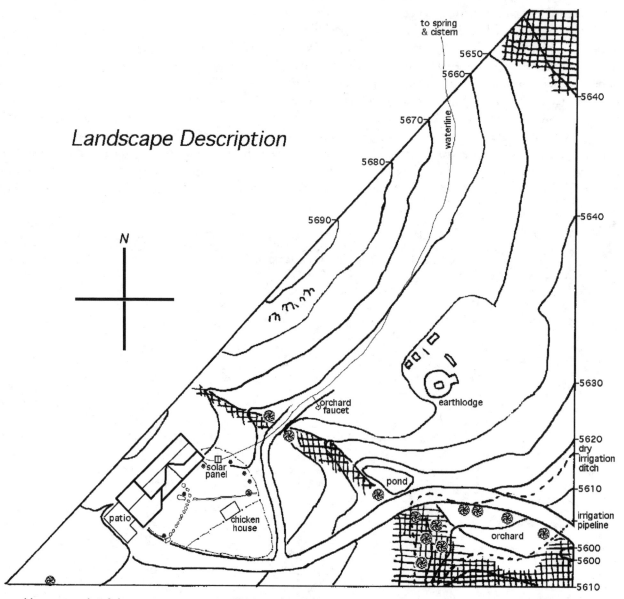

Landscape Description

Homesteads of the past were externally integrated with the world biosphere, dependent on the natural ecosystem for a fresh supply of fuel, air, water, or food. Homesteads of the 21st century are becoming more like biospheres— internally integrated ecosystems with little need for outside inputs of materials or energy. Our five-acre homestead represents a transitional phase, sharing characteristics of both the past and future.

possible to achieve the American Dream—to own a nice home, and that it can be done on surprisingly little income. I write this book especially for those of you who are like us, with big dreams, but few resources. It is my intention to provide you with the information you need to construct an elegant, but low-cost, long-lasting, low maintenance home that is at least as ecologically compatible as our own.

I must point out, however, that although our home, and the others we have built, may require fewer inputs of energy, materials, or chemicals to maintain than conventional homes, the truth is that they are still relatively high-maintenance houses, and they will require continuous time, money, and resources from the earth to keep them in good shape. These houses are a step up from conventional construction, but still primitive in terms of ecological integration and resource efficiency.

Through the pages of this book I have outlined the successes and the shortcomings of the structures we have built, and laid out the ideas we have for the next generation of low-cost, low-maintenance, "eco-homes". The information presented here will enable you to build a home that is less work, less-costly, and more resource-efficient than the ones we have so far built.

Proponents of renewable resources may object to some of my ideas, pointing out the **embodied energy** in construction materials, showing that organic materials like wood require relatively little energy to mill into usable building materials, while inorganics, like concrete and steel, require much more energy to process. Yet they ignore the fact that the amount of energy used to manufacture the average home is trivial compared to the amount wasted to heat and cool that home every single year. A well-built home of inorganic materials can ultimately consume far less energy over it's lifetime than a similar home built of "renewable" wood resources. Besides, the real problem is that most houses built from renewable resources have to be constantly repaired and rebuilt. As architect and visionary Buckminster Fuller once pointed out, biodegradability is not necessarily a desirable quality in a house!

Part of the confusion in the debate over renewables and nonrenewables comes from the habit of lumping organic resources together with solar energy and classifying them both equally as "renewables". Organic resources are renewable, but not necessarily sustainable, while solar energy is definitely sustainable, but not exactly "renewable", since it makes a one-way journey here from the sun.

We will ultimately wean ourselves off of fossil fuels sometime during this century, not because we will run out, but because solar and other alternative energy technologies are continuing to come down in price while the *environmental cost* of fossil fuels is continuing to rise. The switch to solar will be quite sudden and dramatic, driven by market forces, as explained in *Direct Pointing to Real Wealth*.

Although this guide is intended especially for the owner-builder, my personal focus has shifted in recent years towards the commercialization and **massproduction** of environmentally responsible housing. As a teenager I vowed to "change the world", and however impractical it may be, I have never lost sight of that goal. Along the way I have had to face the obvious reality that every person in the world is not going to go out and build their own home, nor should they. We may be able to change the lives of a few inspired owner-builders with the lessons we have learned, but in order to change the world, we must find a way to make eco-housing out-compete conventional construction on the market place.

Early in the formation of this new idea, Renee and I bought a city lot and built a stone house on speculation. I had envisioned building one stone house that first year, then two the next, growing a business that would soon employ many people building dozens of high-quality homes to compete with conventional construction. But ultimately we sold that house, made a modest profit, and have not built another house since.

The house that we built and sold was different from, but no more ecologically advanced, than our own. Besides that, it would have been highly impractical to hire and train a crew to do the specialized and labor-intensive work we were doing, and the labor cost would have no doubt wiped out most or all of the potential profit.

I realized that the fastest way to build the best homes at the least cost would be to build none at all, and to reevaluate the process from the ground up. We needed to design some simple, but aesthetic and ecologically advanced homes that could be easily mass-produced and mass-marketed. Some of the new ideas we have originated are applicable to the owner builder, and others are useful only to someone intent on building hundreds of houses. It is my intent to use profits from my writing career to one day jump back into the construction business and mass-produce "eco-homes".

It was probably **Buckminster Fuller** in the mid 1920's who first stated the need for low-cost, low-maintenance, mass-produced housing. Fuller observed that mass-production made automobiles affordable, and he reasoned that mass-production could make houses almost as inexpensive as cars. He developed prototypes over the coming decades that could be shipped in a cylinder and assembled on site in a day, and later disassembled and moved. He designed houses of aluminum and other advanced materials, that although unnatural in appearance, were at the very least low maintenance and impervious to insects, rodents, and rot. The houses were designed largely for solar heating and cooling, and included insulation, double-paned windows, and built-in wind generators for electricity, or gas-powered generators that at also captured and used waste heat. Fuller's houses were set up to collect rainwater, minimize water consumption and to recycle used water. His creations were intended to be ultra modern, with air filters and easy-to-clean surfaces to minimize dusting, plus electronic sensors to automatically open and close doors, washing machines that also dried and folded the clothes, and he even made space back in the 1920's for upcoming electronics devices like the television. Fuller was certainly decades ahead of his time.

Fuller had bids in the 1940's to mass-produce his houses at a cost that would be the equivalent of about $20,000 apiece today, but no one was willing to put forth the capital to tool up a factory to produce them-a cost that would be measured in billions now. Fuller had to return 3,700 unsolicited orders from people who liked the idea so much that they were willing to pay in advance.

Today the closest thing we have to Fuller's ideal of mass-produced housing is flimsy, inelegant and inefficient trailer houses that are expensive to operate and fall apart with a little time and a few gusts of wind. More recently there has been a trend towards modular houses that are trucked out in two or more sections and assembled on site on a poured foundation. These new modular homes are certainly better than trailer houses, but no better than conventional homes.

The real jewel of Fuller's house plans was the degree of synergy between the parts, and the self-sufficiency of the overall system, almost like a "homestead-in-a-can". Whereas the homesteads of the past were integrated externally, for example, relying on firewood for heat or a stand-alone wind turbine for electricity, Fuller's models were integrated internally, requiring little or no fuel for heating, and equipped with a built-in, wind or gas-powered generator for electricity.

Like Fuller, my interest is to mass-produce highly self-sufficient homes. I think of these dwellings as the homesteads of the 21st century. The difference from Fuller's ideas is that I believe houses should look and feel natural both inside and outside. Also, I think the biological component is an essential element of houses for the future, partly for food production, but also to help recycle the air. In effect, I envision mass-produced biospheres lining the streets of suburbia that are habitats as much as they are houses. I am not suggesting that these houses will look like glass bubbles, only that they will be designed to function as indoor ecosystems, recycling resources internally more than externally.

We made a giant leap towards building a biosphere with our own house, by including a large greenhouse with herbs and trees and vines and bugs and bees and toads. All that life helps to recycle air within our home, and it provides a small amount of food. Each year we make improvements to our home to further tighten the bottle, so that it requires fewer inputs of firewood or other fuels from the outside. Little by little our home becomes more like a biosphere, self-sufficient inside, independent of the outside world. That is the future of homesteading.

One of the challenges to building houses with this high-level of integration is that, like Fuller's washing machine that also dried and folded the clothes, there are certain technical components which are not readily available downtown. For example, the common refrigerator gives off a great deal of waste heat. A truly efficient, integrated house would capture that waste heat in a useful way, such as for heating water. Unfortunately there are not many refrigerator/water-heaters available on the market. Designing a truly integrated house must include designing the appliances that are used with it, and that means the future of superefficient ecological house-building will be more the domain of industry than of owner-builders.

Nevertheless, there is much that owner-builders can do right now to advance the yet primitive art of integrated design. It is my hope that you will document the successes, shortcoming, and the new ideas that you have in building your own home. I like hearing the experiences of individuals like yourself in pursuit of a Dream, and I hope you will share your stories and photos back with me.

Choosing a Location
Planning a Thousand Years into the Future

The face of the earth has taken shape over billions of years. It pains me to see how casually people alter the earth and make-over it's face according to their own puny whim and whimsy. In short, the houses you and I construct are little pimples on the beautiful face of the earth. Make sure that you give some consideration to where and how you build your pimple, and make your pimple so good that the earth will be proud to wear it.

Your house on the face of the earth will not last for forever. It will fade away as all pimples do, but it will be here for awhile so please give careful consideration to where you put it. Too often people want the most beautiful and pristine area on earth. They look all over the planet for just the right spot, and they say, "I want it for ME! ME! ME! ME!" They build their pimple right there on what was the most beautiful spot on earth. Housing developments, even a single home in the forest, often destroy wildlife habitat and threaten species with extinction. Each new house built without regard to the landscape cuts the face of the earth into little bits which become less usable to the rest of nature and humanity. One house sets off a chain reaction which can effect land use for generations to come.

Although family size has decreased to near equilibrium in America, the population is still exploding, due largely to continued immigration and their subsequent offspring. According to a range of estimates by the U.S. Census bureau, the population could double, triple, or quadruple between 2000 and 2100, a wave of growth that is hard to fathom. There is already discussion of Boston merging with Washington DC and all the cities in between to create one mega city. The Denver-Boulder metropolitan area, which now consists of 2.5 million people, is expected to grow by another million people just between 2000 and 2020. The Wasatch Front, including Salt Lake City and Ogden, is expected to explode from 1.7 million people in 2000 to 5 million people by 2050. As personal wealth continues to rise and people commute to work via the internet, they will have little incentive to stay in the cities. The suburban sprawl will hit the countryside like a swarm of locusts consuming the landscape. Scenic, rural communities can expect much more than a doubling, tripling, or quadrupling of the population. Places like the nearby Gallatin Valley will likely surge from under 100,000 people to more than a million in my children's lifetimes.

I am not at all opposed to immigration into this country or this state, as I think anyone else in the world has as much right to be here as I do. However, with a little farsighted planning we can make the future a lot more pleasant for all.

Too often people want to build in the most beautiful and pristine place on earth. But suburban sprawl destroys wildlife habitat, reduces hiking opportunities, and diminishes the scenic qualities and values that attracted people to begin with. Photo by Tim Crawford, courtesy of the Greater Yellowstone Coalition.

Cluster Development: Montana is often called the "Last Best Place", but it too has been discovered. In recent times, western Montana has become "chic" amongst movie stars and other wealthy, famous people. With their arrival it seems that everyone else wants to live here too. Instead of saving the last of its kind, we seem determined to develop this place to extinction before anyone else can, and we are succeeding. The countryside is being cut up in every direction with houses scattered here and there. Everyone is trying to get a piece of the wide open spaces, and pieces are all that are left over in the end. The popularity of this state is destroying the very thing that made it popular to begin with. Eighty thousand acres of biologically rich river banks and productive agricultural lands were lost to development in Montana between 1982 and 1992. The pace of development then accelerated, consuming another 123,000 acres in just the next five years.

Madison county, where we live here in southwest Montana is very rural, with only 7,000 people spread out over an area that is nearly as big as some northeastern states. A drive down any highway is like a drive through a picture book with grand, scenic vistas. But even in my short lifetime I've seen numerous subdivisions pop up at random across the land-scape, ruining the scenery. I am not opposed to development, and I know there is plenty of room for growth, but it has to be planned. The sad truth, however, is that enough land has already been subdivided on paper here to build 5,000 more homes. That will be enough new houses to triple the county population, yet virtually none of those subdivisions are in or any where near existing

Sprawl versus Planning

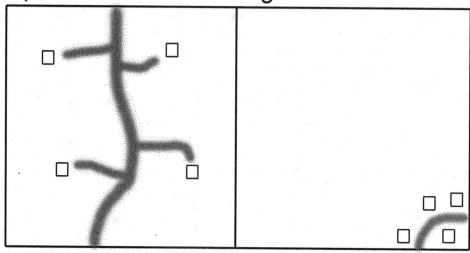

"Me, me, me development."   Cluster Development

communities. Besides ruining the scenic vistas that attract people here to begin with, these sprawling subdivisions are a tremendous tax burden, since there is a higher cost to maintain roads, bus kids to schools, and provide fire protection. The disturbed soils along the roads become a highway for noxious weeds to enter new lands, ultimately requiring massive chemical applications to control them.

When we cut the land into little chunks it is no longer usable as a whole. In the illustration shown here the land on the left has no more houses than the land on the right but you may sense that it feels more crowded. The cluster development on the right represents an area of community, openness and invitation. By locating in existing communities you can help preserve the qualities of open space that makes our land so beautiful. As an individual home-builder it is difficult to alter existing subdivision plans, but look around and you may be surprised to find good sites to build without significantly impacting the scenery or the wildlife of your region. I encourage you to consider the implications of your actions a thousand years into the future before you start anything.

For years I've been interested in becoming a real estate developer because I want the chance to design better communities to meet the needs of the people while preserving the qualities of the land. Interestingly, thoughtful land-use planning often results in higher real estate prices too, but few developers understand that.

Marginal or Abused Land: Too many people have staked out their place in the Garden of Eden and leveled it with a bulldozer. Rare and delightful species of plants, animals, insects and fungus all disappear when diverse and interesting habitats are leveled for home-building. But fortunately, it is possible to select a marginal piece of land and make it "better", rather than to select a piece of prime, productive land and plow it under for a house and driveway. It is possible to make the land more beautiful and more productive as a result of your living there.

I encourage you to seek building sites with nonproductive land where there is very little species diversity. In my area that means dry, grassy plains and hills. It is a shame to see productive farmland or diverse forest meadows and creek sides bulldozed to make new weed plots. There are many sites with only a handful of plant species and little use by animals. By building your home there and planting a yard you create habitat for a wider diversity of plant and animal species. Abused sites that have been bulldozed or trashed are especially good places to build a home and make a difference in the world. Build your own Garden and make the world bloom just a little bit more.

Landscape Architecture: Many people like to build their dream home on a peak where they can see everything, but then the rest of us are stuck looking at them. It is really annoying to see a house perched on top of a hill. It is some kind of an ego trip to build on the ridge where everyone else must look up at you. And if everyone builds on top of the peaks then that is all there is to see.

I encourage you to look around and design your place to fit the area. If you are in a flat prairie then design your house to hug the ground so it is not interrupting the skyline. And please do not ever build a tower on a hilltop that people will have to look at from miles in every direction. On the other hand, if you are in a neighborhood of two-story houses, then it would be silly to build a low or underground house. You would naturally design a home that would fit the neighborhood.

Keep in mind, most new construction is trash. Unfortunately it is trash that does not go away very quickly. When you build your home make it a good one. Make it worth keeping around for a few centuries, and make it so that everyone can be proud to have it in the neighborhood. In real estate everyone seems to say, "Me, me, me!", but I am asking you to go beyond that. When you design and build your home give some consideration to the environment and to the people around you, now and in the future. Build your house as if you are building it for the world, and not just for you—I encourage you to use your home as a means to make the world a better place to be.

The Cost of Hindsight

Every person wants the best piece of land with a view from the top of the hill. As a result, this is the view everyone gets.

Preserving Open Space

Whether you ever build your own house or not, it is useful to understand some of the available procedures for preserving open space, so that you can be informed and helpful in the process. There is much you can do to influence real estate development in your area, even if you do not own the land.

Zoning: Zoning is the best known, but least effective method of making sound development plans and preserving open space. Zoning works in highly urban environments where the majority who do not own open space can easily out-vote the minority who still do. But in rural environments the majority owns the open space, and they do not want to be told what they can and cannot do with it. It is extremely rare that a public official can get elected after mentioning the dreaded Z-word. However, in rare cases, farmers and ranchers have banded together with neighbors to voluntarily create their own open-space zones to preserve the rural way of life. Finding innovative ways to harness this power of free-will is the key to successfully making far-sighted development and preservation plans.

Conservation Easements: Conservation easements are a free-market idea that is catching on. A conservation easement is a legal agreement, usually between a landowner and a non-profit land trust, to protect a parcel of land from development for "forever" (whatever that means). The value of the property is assessed before and after the easement, and the landowner gets a tax deduction equal to the difference—essentially the cost of the lost development rights. Conservation easements have helped to preserve millions of acres of open space nationwide, but there are some problems and limitations to them.

The main limitation to conservation easements is that the farmers and ranchers who usually hold title to the land simply do not have enough income to need the tax deduction. It is more in their interest to sell the land for development and pocket the money. To remedy this problem, many non-profit groups and publicly supported open-space bonds have raised money to purchase conservation easements on certain parcels, so that the farmer makes money on the sale, but keeps the land and the right to farm it. Although these are essential steps in the right direction, they require a large population base to fund the projects. Most of the land must be developed before there are enough people to support preservation of what's left.

The key to igniting a conservation-easement revolution nationwide is to enable partnerships between the landowners who have no money and the wealthy individuals who desperately need tax deductions, in such as way that the former can make a real income and the latter can pay fewer taxes. For example, a millionaire might purchase a conservation easement on a ranch and donate it to a non-profit land trust, such that the land-owner gets the income, while the millionaire gets the tax deduction and use of an existing cabin on the land for hunting trips and vacation.

Another potential problem with conservation easements is that it is preservation at random. Many of the best sites are still lost to development, while a few parcels that are preserved probably shouldn't be. There are certain parcels of land that are ideal, ecologically and logistically, for development. Finally, the unknown part about conservation easements is that "forever" clause. Who will be there to police a parcel of land after it has changed hands a few times and the new landowner decides to do something new with it? Someone has to keep tabs on all those properties to make sure that they are not being developed anyway.

Transfer of Development Rights (TDR): The advantage to a Transfer of Development Rights program is it allows for open-space zoning, without financially penalizing landowners in the open space zones. Development rights are allotted equally across all land within the program, such as one house per twenty acres over a five square mile area—but some areas are zoned for open space while others are zoned for growth. The key to the success of these programs is that a developer can build more houses in a growth area by purchasing the development rights on the open market from other landowners. TDR programs are usually used near cities. The developer can save money on the cost to build and pave new streets, plus running power, sewer and water to each lot, by purchasing development rights to build more houses per acre. In this example, developing a 20 acre parcel into one-eighth acre lots, would require purchasing the development rights from 159 other parcels, thereby preserving 3,180 acres of open space. As with other approaches, TDR programs are less successful in rural areas, where people are opposed to any kind of control system, and wouldn't hesitate to develop twenty-acre lots anyway.

However, TDR programs have great potential in highly scenic rural places with a tourist economy. For example, the Upper Missouri Wild & Scenic River downstream from Fort Benton, Montana is bordered by mostly private land. Building subdivisions along the river would ruin the scenic characteristics and the economy. But a locally implemented TDR program could be used, such that builders could purchase development rights near the river to develop subdivisions far away from the water. That way landowners near the water could still take the profit their land is worth, but without selling it.

Disaster-Proofing Your Home
Preventing the Obvious. Preparing for the Inevitable.

Disasters happen. With all the earthquakes, tornadoes, hurricanes, fires, tidal waves, avalanches, floods, and industrial accidents, there is no spot on earth that is entirely safe. Disasters take human lives every year and cost hundreds of millions or billions of dollars in damages. But most of the damage is unnecessary. A little bit of common-sense preventative planning can let you ride through many otherwise devastating events. There is no need to be paranoiac in your planning—just consider the possible threats and take practical measures. Our own home is hardly perfect, but we have nevertheless taken many common sense steps to insure its longevity.

Communities in regions prone to floods or other recurrent disasters often use the terms "**100 year event**" or "**500 year event**" to signify the worst disaster that is expected to occur within those time periods. Thus, a one hundred year flood event is a major flood that is expected about one time per century, although it is impossible to predict when. When you build a home you should anticipate that it will last a minimum of one hundred years—although hopefully much longer. You should always prepare for the 100 year events, because they will come, and probably sooner than you think. Many homes are destroyed or badly damaged before the twenty or thirty year mortgages are paid off. The U.S. is big enough that we can expect several 100 year events across the country every year, and we do. Good planning could make those events merely anomalous weather, instead of major disasters. It is more difficult to think in terms of 500 year events, but keep in mind that the world is big enough that we must have disasters of that level just about every year. In the 1990's the flooding along the lower Missouri was considered a 500 year event. Disasters like that can and do come around, so take reasonable steps to prevent unnecessary damage.

Fires: More and more people are selfishly building their homes in the forests. Such recklessness diminishes the quality of the forest environment for all and reduces wildlife habitat, but it also raises everyone's taxes and home insurance rates. It is a law of nature that forests burn—especially in the West. People who opt to build in the forest cause everyone else to pay higher taxes for their fire protection, plus higher insurance rates because there is only so much that fire-fighters can do to stop a raging wildfire. Nationwide, more than 10,000 homes were lost to wildfires between 1985 and 2000.

This wildfire was reportedly started by an owner-builder grinding metal at his homesite. The fire missed the house, but scorched a few hundred acres of grass, hills and timber.

During the wildfire season of 2000, fire-fighting in Montana cost the state $52 million and the federal government $272 million. Many backcountry wildfires were largely ignored as fire fighters worked to save houses instead. The effort to save houses in just the Bitterroot Valley took nearly 700 fire fighters. Helicopters with water buckets hovered in the sky monitoring the advance of the fires, then dropped their loads on the houses immediately in the path of the flames. More than 50 houses were still lost inspite of heroic efforts to save them. We all pay higher costs for the selfish few.

If you choose to build in the forest anyway then you might consider cutting down all the trees around your home to create a fire break between you and the forest. Flames from a wildfire can jump hundreds of feet, even miles in the right conditions, but any space between you and the forest or brush will help when the time comes— and yes, that time will come.

Whether you build in the forest or not, you should still make fire prevention a priority in designing and building your home, starting at ground level. Construct nonflammable floors where possible. At ground level it is usually practical to pour some type of masonry floor. One local couple built a log house with a wooden floor and a crawl space. The pipes froze under the house soon after they moved in so the husband crawled under the house with a propane torch to thaw the pipes. I think you can guess the rest of the story. Had they routed the pipes elsewhere and poured a masonry floor then they would still be enjoying their home today.

Build walls of fireproof or fire-resistant materials as much as possible such as stone, rammed earth, adobe, stuccoed strawbale, and possibly cordwood. If you build a frame house then at least consider applying stucco to the walls to help make the structure more fire resistant. An earth home is probably the most fire-safe structure you can build because floors, walls, and roof are usually concrete.

Log walls can be surprisingly fireproof too, depending on how much kindling you put in and outside the building. There may be a lot of wood in the walls, but the big logs need an ample supply of kindling to burn all the way through. Eliminating some of the kindling, such as making a masonry floor instead of a wood floor, can prevent a fire from starting or limit the damage if one did start. A bad fire may gut the interior but leave the charred walls intact, so you could resurface them.

Sheetrock is preferable to wood for a flame-resistant ceiling. Long eves on a house tend to trap the heat underneath them, so short eves are preferable in areas of high fire risk. Use nonflammable materials on the roof, such as metal, slate, or tile. Please do not put wood shakes or wood shingles on the roof of your home. There is just no excuse to cover your whole home with kindling! Concrete roofs are very flame proof, but often impractical.

In our area there are many insulated, galvanized chimney pipes, usually in wood-frame "chimneys". Creosote builds up in the pipes and creates a fire hazard if it is not cleaned out on a regular basis. The creosote can catch fire in the chimney, and many houses burn down every year from chimney fires. Sometimes people die in the fires. A masonry chimney minimizes the risk, especially if used in conjunction with a nonflammable roof. The type of wood stove makes a difference too, since airtight stoves tend to choke the fire and send more particulate up the flue.

Also consider the types of insulation you use in your home. Foam insulations tend to be most flammable, fiberglass is less flammable, and cellulose (fluffed up bits of newspaper) is usually the least flammable because it is treated with fire retardant. What you put in your house makes a difference too. Often the most flammable part is not the house itself, but the furniture, draperies, carpets, and personal belongings.

Floods: People often build homes right on the bank of a river where it is obvious that at some point in time, either tomorrow or in the next century, there will be a flood or the bank will wash away. There is just no excuse for that. So do not try to defy mother nature. You will lose. In most regions of the country it is possible to make your house flood-proof just by building it well away from the river.

On the other hand, if you live in a county or state that is mostly or entirely in a flood plain then there are some steps you can take in construction to limit the damage from a flood. Raising the foundation, so the house if off the ground, will help for minor flooding. Houses are sometimes built on tall stilts, called pylons, in very wet areas.

Otherwise, it can be helpful to build masonry floors and masonry or log walls. These materials will be hurt the least in a flood. Sheetrock is useless around water. Most types of foam insulation are water resistant. Fiberglass or cellulose will pack down into soggy wet pulp. Ideally you should build your home so that you can let a flood in one door and out another without harming the house itself. During most floods you could theoretically move all your belongings upstairs during the high-water. Afterwards you could mop the floors, bring the furniture down and get on with your life.

Boulder rip-rap placed along the water's edge can only do so much to hold back the water. Ultimately this house will be destroyed by flood waters. On Montana's Yellowstone River. Photo courtesy of the Greater Yellowstone Coalition.

Be sure to research the soil type at your site to find out how the flooded, muddy conditions will affect the foundation of your home. Some soils will wash out beneath concrete footings and slabs, allowing the concrete to crack and collapse from it's own weight.

Earthquakes: People flee from California each time a major earthquake occurs, but that is really one of the safer places to experience a quake. Major quakes near metropolitan areas in California result in surprisingly few fatalities due to the strict construction standards. Earthquakes in other parts of the world frequently kill people by the tens of thousands, even in sparsely populated, rural areas. Fatalities are seldom caused by earthquakes; they are caused by poor quality construction. People outside of California are overly complacent about construction standards. Although most of the nation may not experience as much seismic activity, all parts of the country are periodically subject to major quakes.

All types of houses can be made more earthquake resistant if they are built on stable ground, preferably bedrock. Some of the worst earthquake damage in the 1989 quake in San Francisco occurred where buildings had been built over a dump. A house built on bedrock or stable ground is less likely to experience traumatic shifts and settling underneath it.

Another good precaution is to build partially, or wholly, underground. Earthquakes put severe strains on a building as the earth rocks back and forth and the structure above ground gains inertia in one direction, then gets yanked back the other way. Houses built into the earth are affected less because they move with the quakes.

When earthquakes kill thousands of people in foreign lands it is usually because the people are living in masonry homes that are not reinforced with steel. Masonry construction, including concrete, stone, adobe, mud, etc., are all very rigid. These types of materials do not flex with the shaking earth, so they break apart easily. Reinforcing bar, or "rebar" as it is commonly called, is simply a steel rod embedded in the concrete to tie all the masonry work together. Rebar helps protect your masonry work from cracking or breaking apart when the ground shifts under your house.

Log homes may be the most earthquake resistant type of contemporary construction there is. Log homes are woven together like a basket, where all the individual pieces can move around while the structure as a whole remains stable. There just is not too much that can happen to a log home, no matter how much it shakes. The chinking and windows may be broken out, but the walls should remain structurally sound.

Commonsense precautions can make a home damage-resistant through most earthquakes, but there is a certain threshold where conventional earthquake engineering principles become almost meaningless. The severity of an earthquake is measured on the "**Richter Scale**", where each higher whole number signifies a quake ten times as great as the previous whole number. Quakes with a magnitude of 3.0 or less are usually harmless. There are hundreds of such quakes every year and we rarely notice them. Earthquakes that register at around 4.0 are strong enough to make the lights sway a little, and those at about 5.0 can cause some damage. Magnitude 6.0 quakes are dangerous, and 7.0 quakes are deadly. The San Francisco quake in 1989 registered at 6.7 on the Richter scale. Quakes registering 8.0 are harder to classify because few have occurred in modern history, and no one is quite sure what would happen. The San Fransisco quake of 1906 was estimated at 8.3 on the Richter Scale. What is known is

Dome-shaped homes are much more resistant to earthquakes and many other natural disasters. This model was made with the kids using balloons and papier-mâché. A similar technique could be used to make a whole house, by anchoring room-sized balloons to the ground, then spraying them with insulation. The insulation would be stuccoed inside and out after the windows and doors are cut out.

that a quake of unknown magnitude killed some 830,000 people in China in the 1500's, and a quake in the 1700's killed 300,000 people in India. In those times there was only a fraction of the population that exists in those places today. A quake of equal magnitude today would kill far more people than that.

Major quakes in the United States occurred on the New Madrid fault in Missouri in 1811 and 1812. Three separate quakes exceeded 8.0 on the Richter Scale, forming new lakes and causing the Mississippi to flow backwards, but there were few buildings around to be damaged. At some point in time we will experience earthquakes of that magnitude again, both in the U.S. and abroad, and there will be millions of fatalities. Many of the buildings in California should be resistant to earthquakes registering less than 8.0, which is much better than the rest of the country, but even the best engineering is largely meaningless for quakes measuring much higher than 8.0 on the Richter Scale. One thing that is for certain is that we are in no way prepared to respond to such an event in any part of this country. The lives that will be lost could have been saved with more appropriate building technologies. Log homes, dome homes and huts are probably about the only buildings that could survive such quakes.

I've been interested in dome homes partly for disaster resistance, but also as a potential means to mass-produce low-cost, high-efficiency houses. A dome-shaped home, or a home that consists of many connected domes, might not be welcome in a neighborhood of conventional houses, but by itself in the country, or in a city of dome homes, it would look perfectly normal. Unfortunately, it is easy to get hung up on preconceived ideas of how a house should look, so most people would rather mortgage an extra decade or two of their lives away just to have a "house-shaped" house.

The reality though, is that, with the proper materials and design, dome-shaped homes can be more economical, more energy efficient and much more disaster-resistant to earthquakes, high-winds, fires, and just about anything else that comes along. Granted, round walls create all kinds of complications when it comes time to arrange furniture and hang pictures, but it is possible to straighten the lower walls of a dome, so that you can get most of the benefits of a dome-shaped house with few of the drawbacks. I know there are many rural folk who dream about having a quality home, but lack the money to do it. Much of rural America has been left out of the global economy, and people need realistic alternatives to survive on incomes much below the national average. Both owner-built and factory-built dome homes offer the promise of a future to many people who otherwise see none.

The exciting part about a dome is that the shape of the structure is inherently strong, so that the builder can select materials that would otherwise require additional support. The high cost of the roof in conventional construction is due in part to the need for an extensive support system. It doesn't matter whether you are building with stone, or log, or straw, or anything else—the roof of the house is usually the most expensive part. Dome houses can minimize or eliminate the need for structural support, resulting in a much less expensive structure.

One way to quickly produce a house of domes is illustrated here, using balloons as forms for each room in the house. The balloons are anchored to the ground with the aid of ropes and stakes, which can also squash the domes a little to manipulate the shape. Cardboard is wrapped around the base of the balloons to produce straight walls up to six or seven feet high. The balloons are sprayed with insulation, either from the inside or the outside, then the windows and doorways are cut out of the foam. (It may be possible to brace the windows and doors against the balloons and foam them right into place to eliminate the waste of cutting out the openings later.) Afterwards a footing is poured around the contour of the balloons and the entire surface is covered with wire and stuccoed.

Papercrete—a combination of paper fluff, sand, and cement—is a potentially very lowcost way to make a well insulated and structurally sound dome. Another alternative is to use polystyrene insulation and giant styrofoam-cup style molds to mass produce domes. The door and window frames should be made adjustable within the mold, so the domes could be easily customized. Also, with a series of molds it would be possible to make domes of many sizes, so the units could be packed inside of each other for transportation, then arranged on site, one dome for each room of the house. The domes would be anchored to circular foundations, the electrical work routered into the walls, and the surfaces stuccoed inside and out for protection. Plumbing could travel under the terra tiles, or some other kind of masonry floors. Of course there are additional details to work out yet, but that is the gist of the idea.

Avalanches & Mud Slides: Be sure to thoroughly investigate your building site for dangers from avalanches, landslides, or mud-slides. People often look for that hillside with a view, but some hills are composed of loose dirt or sand. During major rain storms the soil may become saturated and the entire side of the hill could slide, especially when human development has damaged the intricate system of tree and plant roots that holds the soil in place. If there is any danger at all, then choose another site. Many houses and lives are needlessly lost each year to mud slides in unusual wet weather. There is no excuse for it.

Houses destroyed by avalanches are less common, but during the winter of 1998-99, many villages in the Swiss Alps were devastated by avalanches thundering down from nearby mountains. Numerous lives were lost.

Hurricanes & Tornadoes: I remember watching the television shortly after Hurricane Hugo hit South Carolina in 1989. A fellow had his beach-front home blown away and was mad because the government forbid him from rebuilding on that site. He wanted to use the insurance money from his former home to rebuild. I guess it must be some type of an ego trip to build right in the face of mother nature when you know she will eventually sneeze and blow you away. Personally I think it would have been appropriate to fine that man for littering half of South Carolina with the remains of his house. Choosing a safe location is always the first step towards quality construction.

A hurricane or a tornado should be little more than an inconvenience if and when they strike. The devastation caused by Hurricane Andrew in Florida in 1992 is totally inexcusable. The amount of damage caused by tornados each year is also inexcusable. For that matter, trailer houses are inexcusable. In areas where major wind storms are a possibility houses should be built to ride through them virtually unscathed. A major windstorm should cause little more than an inconvenience in yard work; it should not tear apart peoples' entire lives. Billions of dollars have been spent cleaning up from major wind disasters. If that money had been spent on prevention in the first place then there would not have been any big disasters to clean up.

Even a frame house can be built to withstand most high winds. Hurricane Andrew entirely destroyed cheap frame houses, but other frame houses with better construction standards stood through the winds. Houses can and should be built to incur virtually no damage at all. Storm proofing the walls is the easy part— good frame construction, or any type of reinforced masonry or log walls should suffer little damage. The windows and doors are easy to protect with heavy duty plywood and screws. A conventional wood-framed roof can be built with big rafters, such as 4 x 10's, secured in place with 1/2" or larger bolts or spikes. Wind proofing the roofing material can be the biggest challenge. One possible candidate for roofing material would be the single-sheet membrane roofing, where you order a sheet of rubberlike stuff which is custom cut to fit your house with one "shingle".

Tornadoes may be more challenging to prepare for than hurricanes, since the storms are more focused, sometimes with stronger winds. The Category 5 tornado that struck Oklahoma City in 1999 left almost nothing standing in its path. Probably the best structures to resist that kind of a storm would be dome-shaped homes. Normal winds push down on dome-shaped structures, making them more secure. But tornado winds may pull up on the structure too, so more research needs to be done on this idea.

Human-made Disasters: There are many potential human-caused disasters such as chemical spills from train or truck accidents, toxic clouds from industrial accidents, radiation leaks from nuclear power plants, chronic pollution, plus crime and terrorism. While natural disasters can directly endanger your life and property, human-made disasters often endanger your health, poisoning your body and homesite for life. In rural areas we often assume we are safe from such things, but a recent train wreck and chemical spill in Alberton, Montana left many residents chronically ill, even after the spill area was "decontaminated". A vermiculite mine in Libby, Montana contaminated the local air with asbestos particles for fifty years—fully documented—before the EPA got around to doing anything about it. The Chernobyl nuclear accident in the former Soviet Union released toxic levels of radiation over an astonishing 200,000 square miles (imagine a square 450 miles each side). Our home is downwind from the closely related Hanford nuclear reactor in eastern Washington, nearly 300 miles away.

The year we bought land here in Pony, Montana the Chicago Mining Company broke ground on a millsite less than 1,000 feet upstream from town, where they used cyanide to extract gold from the ore. The mill only operated once before the company filed bankruptcy, but that was long enough to contaminate a small area of ground and one local well with cyanide. Terrorist bombings and biological terrorism are concerns in especially large cities. As with natural disasters, it is difficult to find a place that is completely safe from any kind of man-made disasters. But there is a difference.

There is little you can do to prevent an earthquake or a tornado, but lots you can do to help prevent man-made disasters. I do not advocate running for some place safe, but instead make a stand in the place you love and work to make it better and safer. Where ever you are you can get informed and be involved with the issues that affect your area, from pesticide use to pollution and poverty. Take a stand and make a difference. Vote for more conscientious politicians. Ask for better environmental protections. Volunteer to help impoverished families and neighborhoods make a change for the better.

Also, think about the world around you every time you shop. For example, approximately 86% of all gold mined from the earth is consumed for jewelry. When you purchase a piece of gold jewelry you are partly responsible for eighty-six percent of those homes where the wells have been contaminated by gold mining processes. You are responsible for the habitat loss and the flocks of ducks and geese and stray deer that have died in toxic tailings ponds at the gold mines. Every purchase, every action you make has some impact on the world. It can be paralyzing to try and change everything at once, but start today by thinking about the consequences of your purchases, and soon you too will begin to find positive alternatives.

Disasters in Slow Motion: Stop for a moment and consider how many tens of billions of dollars are spent in America every year for typical maintenance problems like painting houses, replacing rotten wood, putting on new shingles, or installing new carpeting, fumigating bugs and killing mice. Think about all the half-full paint cans and the piles of trashed building materials and consider the cost in human time to produce, use, and dispose of all those products. Mainstream construction is like a disaster in slow motion. Everything is always falling apart! Perhaps the world might be cleaner, and we all might be richer, if we took some common-sense steps at the outset to prevent the need for all that maintenance work. Perhaps if we saved ourselves from doing all that work then we would have more time to enjoy the beauty of that cleaner and wealthier world.

Eliminating Paints and Stains: I spent a good part of my childhood painting houses. We had a large house in Los Altos, California. Every year it seemed we painted part of the house or we painted the white picket fence that surrounded the property. If we were not painting our own home then we were painting the home of someone else in the family. In any case, I developed a definite dislike of painting (and other chores), and I knew for certain that I wanted my own home built in such a way that I would not have to spend my entire life mending it.

Today, with many years of construction experience, I have reached the conclusion that paint is a band-aid for wounded building materials. A log left whole does not need paint. The lignin in the outermost layer will turn gray, but in reasonable conditions the log will not rot. But when that perfectly good log is cut up into boards then it is susceptible to all kinds of ailments, and paint is applied to keep the wood from rotting, warping, or splitting.

You can save yourself a great deal of future cost and trouble if you design your home to minimize the need for paints and stains. The alternative methods of construction, like stone, log, strawbale, rammed earth, cordwood and adobe, are all good ways to reduce the amount of paint or stain needed. Optionally, vinyl or aluminum siding is a means to get a permanent paint job in a conventional frame house. Vinyl or aluminum frames are also a good choice for weather-proof windows in any kind of construction.

It is difficult to completely eliminate paint—even durable exterior stone walls can benefit from an occasional coat of clear acrylic sealer to prevent moisture damage, but any steps you take now to reduce the need for painting maintenance later will definitely give you more freedom later on.

Eliminating Rot: Probably half or more of the homes in America have rot in some part of their structures. The number one rot spot is typically the bathroom, and the number one cause is usually the shower. Other probable rot spots are the areas where wood is near the ground, such as floor joists under a house. Wood can also rot if moisture is condensing in the insulation.

Rot is easy to prevent, simply by building with rot-resistant materials. Masonry floors and walls are obviously an excellent way to prevent rot. Vinyl or aluminum window frames (and trim) should be a priority too. Good ventilation will help to dry out damp spots, and some houses can benefit from a dehumidifier to help pull moisture out of the air.

Also avoid building on especially damp ground. Some builders have the arrogance to think they can build anywhere and make the environment bend to their will, so there are many houses and apartments built on swampy soil with sump pumps working continuously to carry away the water. Besides being an absurd waste of energy resources to pump the water away, there is also the danger of excessive earthquake damage in any building that sits on top of unstable, waterlogged soils. The liquid-like soil can act as quicksand when vibrated by an earthquake. Building on stable, dry ground helps conserve resources, prevents major earthquake damage, and certainly helps to prevent rot problems.

Eliminating Varmints: Americans spend many billions of dollars every year to exterminate mice, termites, cockroaches and other creatures from our homes and to repair the damage they cause. But the creatures of the earth are just doing their job, and they move in wherever habitat exists. The key to controlling them is not to kill them, but to avoid creating habitat for them in the first place.

Termites love eating wood. Building with lumber in termite country is like eating a Thanksgiving dinner in front of a group of starving people—you are going to have guests, like it or not. Formosan termites, accidentally introduced from Asia to Louisiana in pallet wood after World War II, are especially voracious. A colony can completely destroy a wood frame house in three years. These super termites have already spread from Louisiana west to Texas and east to South Carolina. In 2000 the state of Louisiana nearly adopted regulations requiring homes to be framed entirely with treated lumber, but rejected the idea due to the health and environmental concerns of using so much treated wood.

Ultimately the key to deterring termites is to change the menu. A group of starving people will not mob you if you have a plate of rocks, and neither will termites. Any type of inorganic construction, such as stone, adobe, concrete, rammed earth, or steel framing will be your best termite insurance. Eliminate as much wood as possible from the structure. Note that log walls can be reasonably bug resistant since it is relatively easy to drill into the logs and insert boron rods, a natural mineral for repelling bugs. It is more practical to treat a few logs than to treat many 2 x 4's. Termites are not a problem in the north because they do not survive through the winters.

Mice are not often a problem in suburban areas where the ecosystem is managed as a series of uniform lawns. There is no habitat outside the home for them to launch an invasion from. But for people who live in the country as we do, mice are a fact of life. There can be hundreds of them within a hundred yards of the house. Eliminating the mouse problem is best done by eliminating the habitat within the house.

Framed walls and roofs create a safe haven for mice because there are cavities where nothing can get to them. A good defense strategy for mice is to build solid floors, walls and roofs. They will surely still find their way in the house through some small crack, but once inside there are a limited number of places they can safely hide. That makes it easy for a cat to do the rest.

As always, you have to balance many factors to come up with the best answer for your specific situation. You may not be able to completely eliminate paint or rot, insects or mice, but you can at least take common-sense steps to reduce these maintenance problems. In most cases you can greatly reduce future problems just through the process of thoughtful design and careful selection of materials, without adding extra expense.

Even our home has all of the above maintenance problems, but less than we would have had if we built this house and greenhouse with conventional frame construction. In fact, frame construction is the root cause of the problems we do have. Our mouse problems could have been largely prevented with a solid, rather than framed roof. Likewise, our painting and potential rot problems, mostly in the greenhouse, could have been prevented with aluminum or vinyl window frames and trim, rather than wood.

Keep in mind, you cannot prepare for every type of disaster, and it would be unhealthy to be too paranoiac anyway. Just understand the basic principles in this section and apply some of them that are most pertinent to your area. For example, tornados are possible here in western Montana, but highly unlikely compared to the plains states.

Earthquakes and fires can be expected, however, so we incorporated some basic precautions. Our home is far from earthquake-proof or fireproof, but we did take steps to make the house resistant to those disasters. We did this by choosing materials and a design that are integrally resistant. We did not add a significant amount of extra time or money to make our home disaster resistant. For instance, we had to put a roof on the house anyway, so we choose steel instead of shingles. That gave us a measure of fire resistance without a significant extra expense. That is the level of disaster preparation that I would suggest to you. Do what is practical and pertinent to your area without going overboard.

Let me also point out that another form of disaster insurance may lay beyond the laws of conventional physics. For instance, the quake of 1906 devastated San Francisco and nearby Santa Rosa, but did not crack even one window pane in the huge greenhouse owned by plant breeder Luther Burbank near Santa Rosa. Burbank was the world's most accomplished plant breeder. He recognized and worked intuitively with the energy and will of the plants. He was not particularly surprised about his good fortune through the quake. He surmised that his communing with the forces of nature may have protected his greenhouse. Whether he was correct, or just lucky and somewhat self-righteous, is a decision we each have to make for ourselves.

Defining Your Goals
A Blueprint is the Sum of the Criteria

People usually define houses according to the composition of the walls, for instance, that a house with stone walls is a "stone house". The prospective owner-builder therefore focuses his or her research on whichever medium they choose to use in the walls. That may be stone, log, adobe, strawbale, cordwood, rammed earth, tires, conventional frame construction, or one of many other possibilities. They may put three-fourths of their research into learning and planning how to build the walls, but the reality is that walls are a relatively minor aspect of any house.

The roof is typically much more expensive than the walls, no matter what you build with. Therefore every house could be called a "roof house". Yet there are also footings and floors to consider, plus heating, wiring, plumbing, windows, and doors. There is layout to think about, plus energy and resource efficiency, aesthetics, your labor, the cost and how to pay for it, and most importantly, your relationships with those around you. Put all of this together and the walls may amount to only a few percent of the total information and planning that goes into a structure. Thus there is a lot more involved in designing your home than merely choosing a medium for the walls and scooting boxes around on a piece of paper to find a workable floor plan.

Success at anything begins with well-formed goals, but forming clear goals is often the most difficult step in any accomplishment. Achieving a goal can be easier than defining it! Many owner-built homes fall short of their potential due to a lack of planning. A hastily built home may require more energy than it should, or more maintenance. The finished project may not turn out to be the Dream that you imagined it to be. In fact, many owner-builders sell out when they are done, and try again and again to build the house of their dreams. Proper planning ahead of time will help you to successfully build your Dream house the first time through.

A clearly defined goal always includes three parts: a *quality of life goal*, a *production goal*, and a *description goal*. The quality of life goal is a statement of what you value in life. The production goal is a statement of what you want to produce to achieve your quality of life goal, and the description goal is a plan of how to achieve it. Your goal does not need to be expressed in these exact terms, as long as all the parts are included one way or another.

You have to set your priorities straight from the beginning as to what is truly important; that is the purpose of the **quality of life goal**. Too many owner-builder projects end in divorce because the house itself is perceived as the ultimate goal. But even the nicest house is still just a box that holds you and those you love. You must not sacrifice the contents to build the container!

Your quality of life goal should encompass everything that really matters to you, such as "I want a loving and balanced relationship with my family, and I want to raise my children in a safe and healthy environment". Always keep your values in mind and you will be successful at whatever you do. Your goal should include your own values, but it should also be broad enough to extend out to your community. For instance, I value the freedom to do whatever I want whenever I want, but that does not mean that I will trample over other people to get what I want. I equally value the rights of others, and I value my responsibility to treat all people with respect. I appreciate being treated with respect, and I know the best way get that is to give it.

A **production goal** is a statement of what you want to produce—in this case a house. Start this goal with a broad statement, such as "I want to build a beautiful, low-cost, disaster-resistant, low-maintenance, and resource-efficient home in an appropriate location". Later, as you learn more about construction, you make a list of criteria to fit your production goals. After comparing different types of construction for instance, you might choose straw bale as the material of choice for producing your resource-efficient, low-cost home.

We especially liked stone masonry and chose that as part of our initial production goal, even though it was not the lowest-cost method for building. We added other criteria as we became more informed. For example, for fire resistance we chose masonry floors, a stone chimney, and a metal roof in addition to the stone walls.

As you add more and more criteria to your production goal you will find that you begin developing a detailed description of that goal. Thus the **description goal** is the blueprint of the criteria you have compiled. The list of criteria for our home may have totaled a hundred items or more, such as facing most of the windows south and having the kitchen sink positioned with a view next to the wood cookstove, which must be in the center of the house since it is also a heat source, which meant that the open loft had to be over the stove to distribute the heat around the house, etc., etc. Part of the reason we spent four years drawing house plans is because we had such specific criteria that it took us four years of drawing to come up with a plan that met all the criteria. One of my reasons for writing this book is to carefully review and consider every aspect of house-building to design a new generation of houses, before getting back into the construction business.

It may seem like a lot of specific criteria could be cumbersome, since we took four years to draw our house pans, but I disagree. Many owner-builders do not give proper consideration to all of their criteria. Their projects may be more expensive as a result, or they may not be satisfied with the final results. We took the time to meet our criteria and we feel good about that every day that we are in our home. Through the process of reading this book and brain-storming your own ideas, you will no doubt build a lengthy list of criteria too. When you integrate all or most of your criteria into one blueprint, then you are ready to build!

In the space below I have provided a sample checklist of criteria for a few of the concepts included in this book. Your goals will likely include many items from this list, plus unique items for your own situation. It would be impossible to list all criteria here, since one choice like a fireplace involves many specific criteria which impact the rest of the house. If you do not understand items on the list yet, that is okay, most are described throughout this book.

Sample Checklist of House Location & Design Criteria

Location
__ part of a community where you can be happy.
__ reasonably safe from natural or human disasters.
__ does not contribute to sprawl or habitat loss.
__ does not ruin someone else's view.
__ affordable for your budget.
__ water reasonably available to site.
__ grid or alternative power reasonably available.
__ clear title, access and zoning.
__ you are aware of permit requirements and costs.

Energy Efficiency
__ minimize exposure to wind.
__ berm into the ground, if practical.
__ lots of insulation.
__ few doorways to the outside.
__ enclosed entry ways with "airlock".
__ most windows face south.
__ solar heated mass in house.
__ active solar storage for extended cold weather.
__ heating system for backup, with appropriate fuel.
__ heating distribution through house.
__ projected zero or near zero heating bill.

Water Efficiency
__ composting or low-flush toilet.
__ water conserving showerhead and faucets.
__ water conserving appliances.
__ graywater reuse on landscape.
__ rainwater collection or swales to capture it.
__ appropriate vegetation, plus mulch.

General Construction
__ fire, insect, and rodent-resistant.
__ resistant to other localized disasters.
__ utilizes locally available materials.
__ frost-proof footing without wasting materials.
__ upper story walls, floor & roof have adequate support.
__ meets code or at least the intent of building codes.

Efficient Use of Space
__ eliminate crawl space and attic to maximize interior.
__ utilize short lofts or space under stairs for storage.
__ provide space for convenient recycling.
__ plan layout to minimize hallways.
__ minimize partitions between living/dining etc.
__ square layouts use less material than long rectangles.
__ a multistory house encloses more space under less roof.

Interior Aesthetics
__ backlighting with windows, skylights, white paint.
__ dining, sitting room and kitchen sink with a view.
__ cathedral ceilings add openness to small spaces.
__ windows and doors leave endough room for furniture.

Exterior Aesthetics
__ fits in the local neighborhood and/or landscape.
__ keep the design relatively simple and avoid odd angles.
__ don't mix too many mediums (bricks, log, siding, etc.)
__ minimize "light pollution" that outshines night stars.

Electrical & Plumbing
__ centralize wiring and plumbing to reduce costs.
__ consider future repairs and upgrades (fiber optics, etc.)

Part II
Principles of
Energy Efficiency

Principles of Energy Efficiency
Designing Warm Houses for Cold Climates

The challenge of the Biosphere II project in Arizona was to create an artificial, but sustainable indoor ecosystem, completely cut off from the outside world. Engineers endeavored to control the factors of solar input, heat loss, air infiltration, and air quality to maintain a healthy living environment inside. Building an efficient, healthy home for yourself is not much different from building a biosphere, except that you are allowed to come and go when you want to!

Creating a comfortable habitat for yourself is a matter of balancing the heat gain from the sun with the heat storage capability of the structure and the rate of heat loss through the insulation—while maintaining a healthy atmosphere and a sustainable budget.

The main reason that buildings are not more energy efficient than they are is because the heating and cooling systems are normally designed separately from the structures. The architect or builder draws up a floor plan, then passes it along to the heating contractor to determine the proper mechanical equipment to maintain a comfortable habitat inside. Technological fixes and fossil fuels are used to make up for the lack of smart design.

Using technological fixes to heat and cool poorly designed buildings is as expensive as it is inelegant. Think about your own average monthly power bill. Is it $50? $100? $200 or more? Now multiply that by twelve months and multiply that by the fifty years or so that you can expect to be living on your own and paying your own power bill. If your bill averages $100 / month then you can expect to spend $60,000 for power in 50 years. A little consideration given to energy efficiency up front can save you years worth of income in the future.

Efficiency is not a matter of technology, but of knowledge. You might hear that an efficient house costs more than a conventional home, but that is only true if you are making adaptations to the typical framed structure. There are so many inherent inefficiencies in conventional building methods that additional materials and technological gadgetry are required to upgrade an ordinary house to a reasonable and efficient habitat. It is easier and less costly to create a habitat by utilizing smart design from the ground up.

In other words, your personal biosphere does not have to be expensive; it requires thought more than money. For example, an energy efficient house may have exactly the same number of windows as an inefficient one, but most of the windows would be on the south face of the structure instead of on the north. Either house requires the same amount of materials, so the only added cost to building the efficient house is that you have to think a little bit longer to achieve balanced lighting and views throughout the house.

What would our world be like if we permanently removed every one of those heaters and air-conditioners? It is ironic that we despair over the cost of heating and cooling and worry about the implications of global warming, and yet we have the technology to simply and easily eliminate both problems. We have all the knowledge and resources we need right now to make comfortable houses completely without heaters or air-conditioners. In fact, there is no reasonable excuse to build another house that will require any outside source of energy, other than solar, to maintain an optimal temperature inside. That's a pretty bold statement to make, considering that I have yet to achieve that myself! Nevertheless, follow along, and I think you will understand my point.

There are hundreds of different ideas you can incorporate into your home to make it energy efficient, but many ideas require additional materials, labor, and money above and beyond the cost of your home. People are always inventing something new to build and maintain. That is easy to do. It is easy to throw money at the problem, to hook up a bunch of technical equipment and come up with something new that works. But it is a much greater challenge to invent something less—something that requires less materials, less labor, less money, but still achieves good performance. Energy efficiency should not be tacked on to your home—it should be inherent to the design.

Research into energy-efficient construction began in earnest after the 1973 oil crunch. Individuals in cold, cloudy climates experimented with "superinsulated" houses, while those in cold, but sunny climates experimented with solar house designs. Although my discussion is oriented towards staying warm in winter, many of the principles apply equally to staying cool in summer.

Superinsulated houses are based on the idea that a very thick blanket of insulation around a house can minimize heat loss so much that it can be kept warm with just the waste heat from living there. The few degrees of heat given off by the body, and from cooking or showering, etc., is enough warmth to replace that lost to the outside.

The first superinsulated houses were conventional frame buildings, except that the walls were made thicker to hold more insulation, and every square inch of floor, wall, and roof were carefully sealed with plastic and caulk to stop all air infiltration through the insulation. These airtight houses led to problems with dead and polluted air and the subsequent development of heat recovery ventilators.

Superinsulated houses were obviously more expensive with the extra materials and specialized labor, but they did prove it was feasible to keep a building warm with little or no heating system. Since then the entire construction industry has incrementally followed that lead—mostly due to changes in the national building standards—making tighter and tighter buildings. Fifty years from now super-insulated construction will no doubt be "standard".

Solar homes started out much more radical in appearance than the super-insulated homes. Solar architecture introduced strange new angles in construction—and lots of glass—for the purpose of capturing as much "free energy" from the sun as possible. Engineers experimented with "active solar", installing lots of gizmos to capture, store, and later circulate heat from the sun. The early models were warm enough, but there were plenty of problems, especially with temperature swings, mechanical parts breaking down, and the high maintenance to open or close window shades and pump valves every morning and night. Most of the fancy gizmos disappeared over time, and solar architects have since moved towards super-insulated homes with "passive solar" heating, where masonry floors and walls inside the home absorb sunlight directly and radiate it back into the air as the house cools.

Advancing technology has put new windows on the market that are insulated almost as much as walls. The windows reduce the amount of heat coming in, but more importantly, they greatly reduce heat loss to the outside. In effect, most of the new "solar" houses are essentially super-insulated structures with moderate solar gain and some thermal mass for heat storage. For good measure, simple active solar systems can also be added to collect and store extra energy from the sun for extended cold, cloudy spells.

Our own house became a hybrid of many different ideas, based largely on the literature available from the 1970's and early 1980's. We had little money, so we endeavored to bring diverse ideas together to achieve the greatest energy efficiency at the least cost. Based on the information available, we felt it would be relatively easy to make a house "95% passive solar", but doubted that we could achieve 100% solar without incurring much greater costs. We were also caught up in the ideology of the 1970's, to integrate our home with the external ecosystem, so we chose wood heat as a reasonable means to meet the remaining heating needs.

We read about the "earth home" builders who promoted building underground to escape the temperature swings above ground. Therefore, we at least built our house into the side of a hill, protecting the north side with ten feet of dirt and the east side with eight feet.

Other builders advocated "envelope" homes, where a house is double-framed for extra protection, basically a house-within-a-house. With that idea in mind, we enclosed the south-facing front of our home in a big greenhouse to function as a buffer zone and "air-lock" to the outside. We also incorporated solar design in the greenhouse, with lots of windows to let heat in, plus stone masonry to absorb and store that heat for later.

The west walls and the roof were insulated approximately at or slightly above the recommendations of the national building standards—with an R-value determined largely by the funds available at the time of construction.

With the combination of these ideas our project became a moderately-insulated-wood-heated-stone-and-log-passive-solar-earth-bermed-envelope-home. We achieved a very reasonable level of efficiency (although not quite "95%") at a truly modest cost.

The weakest link in the efficiency of our home is probably in the roof. Heat rises, so the roof always requires the most insulation. Unfortunately the roof is already the most expensive part of any kind of construction, much more expensive than the walls or floors. Besides that, a framed roof has the same problems as a framed wall, where the wood members cut through the insulation, allowing a channel for heat to escape—especially if the insulation settles away from the wood over time.

Sprayed-in foam may be the best way to insulate a framed roof or wall, but the cost is outrageously expensive Most people would be more than satisfied with the level of efficiency we achieved, but I have become consumed with the goal of eventually making the house 99 to 100% "passive solar". Every year we take additional steps, some small and some large, to make our house more efficient. It is a fun sport to see how much we can reduce our energy consumption each year!

Dodging the Point of Diminishing Returns

Insulation is a prime example of the "point of diminishing returns" in economics. In essence, the first layer of insulation you put on a home will hold in the most heat and save the most money, while each successive layer will provide less and less of a return for the same amount of investment. At some point it is more economical to pay a modest power bill than to buy additional insulation. This is the premise behind the insulation standards of the building industry, and the reason millions of people end up paying fifty to a hundred dollars or more every month of their lives for winter heating and summer cooling (I have yet to understand how this can be economical!).

Perhaps one reason it is considered cost effective to build poorly insulated homes is because it is too expensive and difficult to make conventional construction very efficient. Framed houses are relatively cheap and fast to build, but quite expensive when you try to design them for efficiency. A 2 x 4 wall has to be changed to a 2 x 6 wall, or even a 2 x 8 or 2 x 10 wall, to hold all the required insulation. The house has to be carefully sealed to make it airtight; and then an expensive ventilation system needs to be installed to exchange air with the outside while main-taining the temperature inside. Building an energy-efficient house in conventional construction requires more materials, specialized knowledge, and careful work. The law of diminishing returns does not yet clearly favor the extra expense to make frame houses truly efficient. The other problem, of course, is that contractors have no real incentive to build good houses in the first place.

As an owner-builder you can dodge the law of diminishing returns with the aid of alternative construction methods and innovative designs. It may not be economically feasible to make a house completely heat self-sufficient using just super-insulation or just solar design, but by integrating several different approaches you can still achieve the end goal of making a low-cost house that requires no heat source other than the sun. All it takes is a little knowledge and a lot of creative planning.

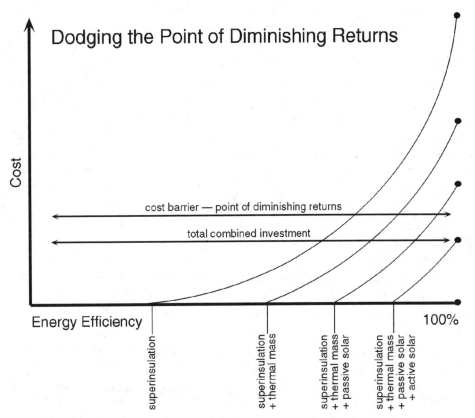

The first layer of insulation saves the most energy. Subsequent layers of insulation cost just as much, but make smaller gains in energy efficiency. Eventually you cross the point of diminishing returns where it is uneconomical to buy more insulation.

However, you can dodge the point of diminishing returns by using insulation combined with thermal mass, passive solar and active solar. For example, you could build a well-insulated house with masonry floors for thermal mass and south-facing windows for passive solar gain, plus active solar in the form of a solar collector producing hot water to pump through a radiant heat system in the floor. By integrating a little from each of these technologies into one plan you can achieve the end goal of making a house completely heat self-sufficient, while staying below the cost barrier.

Insulation & Insulation Systems
Many Choices, Most of them Bad

The most important key to building a warm house is insulation. Insulation on a house is like a down coat on your body. Tiny pockets of dead air space slow down the transfer of heat through the material. Warmth migrates very slowly from one air pocket to another, through hundreds of spaces before finally escaping out the other side. A house can be insulated so tight that it will stay warm using only waste heat from cooking and other normal activities.

The effectiveness of an insulation is measured as it's Resistance value or "**R-value**"—how well the material resists the transfer of heat. Dense materials like metal conduct heat very easily. That is why we use metal for frying pans. Concrete is also a very dense material. The R-value of concrete is only about 0.2 per inch of thickness.

Lighter materials have more air spaces inside to resist the transfer of heat. Wood is less dense than concrete and has an R-value of about 1.2 per inch (higher or lower according to the species). Fiberglass insulation has a resistance value of 3.2 per inch, while some types of foam insulation have resistance values as high as 6-8 per inch.

Resistance values are calculated under laboratory conditions and may vary considerably in real-world performance. A 3 1/2" fiberglass batt has a rating of R-19, but this figure does not show that additional heat is lost through the studs between the batts, or along the edge of the studs when there is a loose fit. Fiberglass batts have a loose, cotton-candy like consistency, so air travels more readily through the insulation on a windy day. A typical home loses 30 to 40% of its heat to air infiltration. Airtight insulation systems (usually foam) greatly reduce these losses.

Although R-values are determined in standardized tests at one temperature, the truth is that the performance of an insulation may fall dramatically when the R-values are tested at a lower temperature. Energy always moves towards equilibrium, so that the inside and outside of a structure are the same temperature. The greater the difference in temperature, the more pressure there is for the inside and outside to equalize. In other words, warmth can pass through the insulation more easily in extreme weather conditions.

The insulations table included in this chapter provides a comparison of different types of insulation and their approximate laboratory-based R-values. Comparing insulations is a little like trying to compare apples with eggs, so you will need to read individually about each type of insulation to better understand the differences between infiltration blockage, cost, versatility, water permeability, rodent resistance, ecological soundness and health issues.

I've spent a great deal of time exploring the various types of insulation and how they can be most effectively used. Mostly I have discovered that insulation is either impractical to use, too expensive, or environmentally a bad idea. Now that I've had some experience and lots of time to reflect on it, I feel ready to try some better ideas.

The key to successfully using insulation is to

Conduction, Convection and Radiation

Heat is transmitted in three distinct ways, through conduction, convection and radiation.

Conduction is the transfer of heat through a solid object, such as a frying pan. Insulation is made with microscopic air pockets that block conduction. The more air pockets, the better the insulation.

Convection is heat flow through a gas, essentially the flow of warm air out of or into a building. Convection losses increase on windy days, when the wind infiltrates a house, replacing the inside air with outside air.

Radiation is heat flow as a wave length of light (infrared) traveling through the air. When you feel heat from a wood stove you are feeling the infrared waves. Heat waves radiate right out through ordinary glass.

In the real world, heat losses are a combination of all the above. For example, heat from the stove might radiate across the room to a wall, where it conducts through the sheetrock into the insulation. Heat transfer is slow through the insulation, where it conducts through the solid matter, but convects across the microscopic air spaces. At the outside of the wall, convection carries the heat away, further cooling the wall.

choose a type of insulation and a type of construction where the insulation is continuous and easy-to-seal around and over the house. A professional could seal a conventional framed house and make it superinsulated, but there are too many separate parts to expect either amateurs or fast-paced construction crews to do that good of a job. Besides, there is always the chance the materials may shift and settle later, which would be a problem in a house with little or no heating system. Therefore, a person needs to use sprayed-in foam to achieve seamless insulation, or switch to a construction method that enables easy assembly of a continuous band of insulation around the house. Straw bale construction, papercrete, and polystyrene "beadboard" insulation show much promise among the currently available materials. These are ecologically friendly materials that enable a person to build a continuous wall of insulation without studs cutting through it.

About Vapor Barriers

I can think of no other part of the construction process that leads to more confusion than the topic of vapor barriers. A vapor barrier is simply a material like plastic that stops the flow of moist air through the insulation. But improper installation of the vapor barrier can lead to waterlogged insulation, rotten lumber, and disintegrating sheetrock.

The answer to using vapor barriers properly is really quite simple, but seldom will you hear the whole answer at once, so the information you get in bits and pieces may seem contradictory. Sometimes you will hear that the vapor barrier should be installed on the inside surface of the insulation, and sometimes it should be installed on the outside surface. Just when you get that part straight, then you might hear that you do not need a vapor barrier at all.

Houses of the past did not have vapor barriers, mostly because they did not have insulation. Moist air from inside the house easily migrated through small leaks in the walls and ceiling and vented to the outside.

Insulation made tighter, warmer houses, but created new problems for venting moist household air. The problem is that one side of the insulation stays warm while the other side stays cool, so moist air from the warm side migrates through and condenses on the cool side.

Heat and moisture always move towards equilibrium, so the vapor barrier must be used on the proper side of the insulation to stop air flow into it. Therefore, in most parts of the country, where the indoor environment is warmer than the outside, the vapor barrier must go on the inside surface of the insulation. In the deep south, however, where the outside air is warm and moist and the inside air is dry and air-conditioned, then the vapor barrier must go on the outside of the insulation to block air flow into the house.

It is helpful to understand that in physics there is no such thing as "cold". Cold can only be described as a lack of heat, much like a "vacuum" is a lack of air. Therefore, heat and moisture move towards equilibrium with cooler, drier air the same way air moves to fill a vacuum. The direction of flow is always from the warm, moist side towards the cool, dry side.

Of course many parts of the country have both cold and hot seasons, so what happens then? Basically any place with real winters should put the vapor barrier on the inside. Even in places with hot summers, the greatest risk of condensation is in the winter when the house is sealed up tight and the inside air is moist from showers, cooking and breathing. The moisture must be stopped from moving through the insulation. The same is true for the desert southwest, even where the weather is almost always hot, because the outside air is too dry to cause problems with condensation. You only need to worry about moist indoor air migrating out.

The strange thing is that you might work very diligently to create a flawless vapor barrier around all the walls, only to hear that you do not need to put a vapor barrier on the ceiling at all. Is that weird or what?

The difference between the walls and ceiling is that ceilings are usually designed for airflow over the top of the insulation to dry out any moisture that migrates through. Most walls are not built to be ventilated, so the moisture has to be stopped from entering the insulation to begin with.

Strawbale construction is one of a few exceptions, where moist air can safely migrate out through the walls. Note that superinsulated homes normally have vapor barriers on both the walls and ceilings, plus ventilating systems to remove the stale, moist air. The whole discussion of vapor barriers becomes simpler if you switch from fiberglass or cellulose to some form of airtight foam insulation. Airtight insulation stops all moisture and air from migrating through in either direction, like a plastic bag. With airtight insulation you can easily build a high-efficiency house, but like a biosphere, you have to deal with the new complications of managing your own air supply, as discussed in a later chapter.

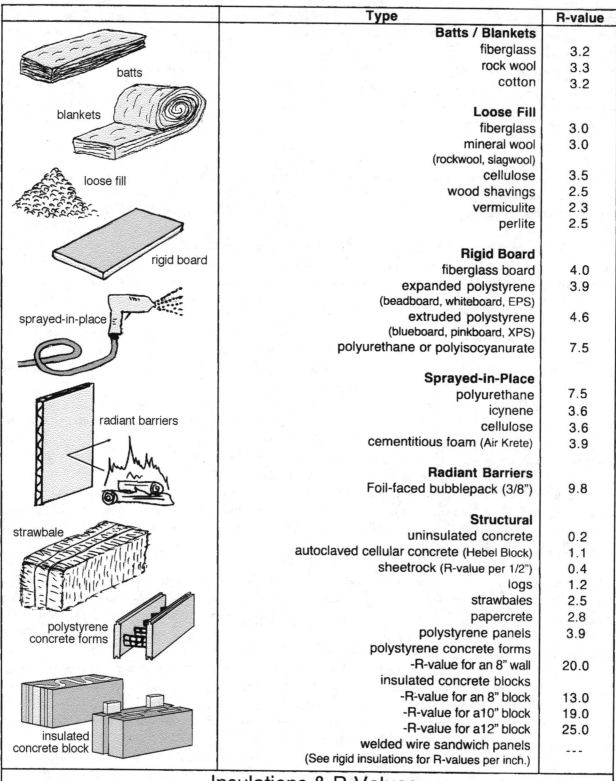

Type	R-value
Batts / Blankets	
fiberglass	3.2
rock wool	3.3
cotton	3.2
Loose Fill	
fiberglass	3.0
mineral wool	3.0
(rockwool, slagwool)	
cellulose	3.5
wood shavings	2.5
vermiculite	2.3
perlite	2.5
Rigid Board	
fiberglass board	4.0
expanded polystyrene	3.9
(beadboard, whiteboard, EPS)	
extruded polystyrene	4.6
(blueboard, pinkboard, XPS)	
polyurethane or polyisocyanurate	7.5
Sprayed-in-Place	
polyurethane	7.5
icynene	3.6
cellulose	3.6
cementitious foam (Air Krete)	3.9
Radiant Barriers	
Foil-faced bubblepack (3/8")	9.8
Structural	
uninsulated concrete	0.2
autoclaved cellular concrete (Hebel Block)	1.1
sheetrock (R-value per 1/2")	0.4
logs	1.2
strawbales	2.5
papercrete	2.8
polystyrene panels	3.9
polystyrene concrete forms	
-R-value for an 8" wall	20.0
insulated concrete blocks	
-R-value for an 8" block	13.0
-R-value for a10" block	19.0
-R-value for a12" block	25.0
welded wire sandwich panels	---
(See rigid insulations for R-values per inch.)	

Insulations & R-Values

R-values are listed per inch of thickness, unless otherwise noted. R-values are always approximate and different in every text. Please note that radiant barriers only reflect heat waves traveling through the air. There must be an air space for the reflective property to work. Heat conducts easily through the material if it is sandwiched in a wall.

Insulation Types

Cellulose: Cellulose insulation is a recycled product made from pulverized newspaper pulp. It is the about the least expensive, least energy intensive, least toxic, most environmentally benign form of insulation available on the market. The natural mineral boron is added as a fire retardant (usually in the form of boric acid) to make the insulation one of the least combustible forms of insulation. Cellulose has a respectable R-value of about 3.7 per inch, and cuts air infiltration better than fiberglass insulation.

With a resume like that you may wonder why a person would bother with any other type of insulation. The reason is versatility. Cellulose is ideal for insulating framed wall cavities and flat ceilings where there is access to the attic, but is not suited for other uses. You can purchase bags of loose cellulose insulation to do your own attic installation, but you will need to hire a contractor to install the insulation in wall cavities. When retrofitting older homes you can drill holes in the walls and blow in the dry insulation, but in new construction the cellulose is mixed with water and sprayed in the walls before the sheetrock goes on. Hiring a contractor raises the price, but not unreasonably so in comparison to other types of insulation.

I have never used cellulose for two simple reasons. First, we build with stone and log, so there are no framed walls on the exterior to insulate. We could build a framed wall along the inside of the masonry walls, but this would be an unnecessary duplication of the structural wall, and besides, heat would still conduct out through the studs in the frame work. Second, we prefer spacious cathedral ceilings rather than flat ceilings. Cathedral ceilings are usually insulated from underneath after the roofing goes on, but before the plasterboard. Air flow must be maintained over the top of the insulation to evaporate moisture away, so you cannot spray the entire cavity full of insulation, and the insulation cannot be allowed to slide or slump in any way that it blocks the flow of air over it. In the past we have reluctantly chosen fiberglass batts as the available alternative. Someone could probably make a lot of money if they invented cellulose batts. Also be sure to read about papercrete, near the end of this chapter.

Fiberglass: Fiberglass insulation is made from melted sand, and some manufacturers use recycled glass for up to 30% of the content. The R-value ranges from 3.2 to 3.7, depending on density, although real-world performance can be much lower due to air-infiltration and improper installation.

Fiberglass is nasty stuff. It is energy intensive to produce, outgasses some formaldehyde, and the asbestos-like particles are physical irritants to the skin, eyes and lungs. Keep in mind that unsealed passages may allow the microscopic fibers to continue blowing into the household air long after the construction is completed.

Like asbestos, fiberglass is a suspected carcinogen, but studies with rats revealed that the glass disappears from the lungs within a year, whereas asbestos stays there. That comes as a relief to me, as I inhaled more fiberglass than I should have before I took the warning label seriously and put on a mask. For awhile I feared that I might be among the living dead: alive now, but dead of cancer long before my natural time. Now I like to think I still have a chance for a long and healthy life.

I periodically vow that I will never use fiberglass insulation again in my life, but it is such a versatile material and so abundant that I have yet to escape it. It is inexpensive, easy to install, and available everywhere. Most of the fiberglass we used went between the rafters, but it is also easy to rip off a hunk and stuff it into any odd nooks and crannies, especially in log construction. (loosely, so it does not lose it's insulating properties).

Sprayed-in foam would be the better alternative in a cathedral ceiling, but foam is excessively expensive. Once a cathedral ceiling is framed, fiberglass becomes the least-cost option for finishing the job, particularly when the owner-builder is paying out-of-pocket and wants a warm house right away. Clearly the path to building without fiberglass is to eliminate the conventional rafter system. Therefore we are evaluating other roofing alternatives for future projects, as discussed in the chapter on roofing.

Fiberglass insulation is available as loosefill for attics, and also as batts or blankets, in various thicknesses. **Batts** are sections four or eight feet long, sold in compressed bundles. **Blankets** are longer than batts, sold in rolls, usually with an aluminum-paper backing on one side. The backing serves two purposes; it reflects heat back from the wall, and it functions as a vapor barrier. The paper backing can be used in a wall or as the first layer in the ceiling, but should never be placed over other insulation where moisture could be trapped underneath.

Rockwool is much like fiberglass, but made from basalt rock or wastes from steel mills. It has a similar R-value to fiberglass, but apparently without the irritating qualities. **Cotton insulation** is another alternative to fiberglass batts. Cotton batts are recycled pre-consumer waste from denim mills. The batts have an R-value of 3.2 per inch and are very colorful. Neither rockwool nor cotton insulation are widely available, but they can be ordered.

Polystyrene: If you look for the recycling symbol on the bottom of a foam egg carton, or on the bottom of many clear plastic food packages, you will see the letters "PS", with the number "6" in the little triangle. Those items are made of polystyrene, and they can be recycled into building materials, except that many regions do not yet accept polystyrene in their recycling programs. For the purposes of construction, polystyrene is typically manufactured as a rigid board insulation by one of two processes.

Blueboard or **pinkboard** are the popular names for extruded polystyrene or "XPS board". Chlorofluorocarbons (CFCs) were used as "blowing agents" in the manufacturing process until CFCs were banned in 1993 because of the harmful effects to the earth's ozone layer. The hydrochlorofluorocarbons (HCFCs) now in use diminish, but do not completely eliminate the harmful effects. Unfortunately, both CFCs and HCFCs are potent greenhouse gases. CFC-11 traps heat 1,600 times more effectively than carbon dioxide per unit of weight. Extruded polystyrene has an R-value of about 4.5 to 5 per inch of thickness.

Beadboard is the popular name for expanded polystyrene or EPS board, which could also be called **whiteboard** Beadboard is made by expanding polystyrene granules (carbon and hydrogen) with steam and pentane gas. It is the same process used to make disposable foam coffee cups. EPS is also commonly molded as a packing material for electronics. Fire retardants are added to beadboard for use in construction. Beadboard may be the most environmentally benign of the rigid board insulations, but it does release carbon monoxide when burned—an added

Beadboard can be custom-cut at the factory. Tom's brother Nick had these forms made for casting concrete trim. The curved unit was made by cutting a straight form lengthwise into narrow, more flexible pieces, then gluing the pieces back together around a curved wooded form.

risk if you are in a burning building. An industry fact sheet claims that fewer toxins are released from beadboard than from a similar *volume* of firewood—which suggests that it probably releases more toxins per unit of *weight*. Beadboard scraps can be ground up and used as loosefill insulation in concrete block walls, or mixed with sand and cement to make a lightweight, moderately insulating mortar.

Beadboard is made in 1 to 2 pound densities per cubic foot. One pound density is the most commonly available, with an R-value of approximately 3.6 per inch. High density beadboard is used where greater strength is needed, such as for hot tub covers; the gain in R-value is negligible.

There are two advantages to beadboard that make it especially usable in alternative construction. First, beadboard can be custom-cut to just about any size and shape you want. There is a manufacturer within an hour of our home, and certainly many other manufacturers around the country, probably within a few hundred miles of your home. The factories routinely cut channels and press-glue wood furring strips into the insulation, or laminate sheets of oriented strand board (OSB) to one or both sides (discussed in more detail in the chapter on roofing). Please note, however, that I've heard from one reader who said that their local factory would not custom-cut anything.

Secondly, because beadboard can be custom-cut, it can be used in thick enough pieces to be "semi-structural", with little need for reinforcement in the right applications. Beadboard panels are often used in hot tub covers for this reason.

The greatest potential for beadboard is in innovative new roofing systems to reduce the need for so much lumber, as discussed in the chapter *Putting the Roof On: The Search for Better Solutions*. Also be sure to read about welded wire sandwich panels in this chapter.

Concrete trim for the garage door was later laid in with rocks in the wall.

Polyurethane and Polyisocyanurate: Urea-formaldehyde foam was a popular insulator in the sixties and seventies, but homes eventually became unsalable as people became educated about the problem of outgassing formaldehyde. The insulation wasn't very stable over the long-term either. I have seen old foam insulation separate from the framing and decompose into powder!

Polyurethane and polyisocyanurate apparently eliminated the problems of urea-formaldehyde, but I wonder if anyone really knows how the insulations will perform twenty-five years down the road. Polyurethane and polyiso are both a dull yellow in color. They are popularly sold in rigid board form, usually with foil backing, but they can also be foamed in place. Rigid board is expensive enough, but the foamed-in process is really expensive. The resin expands about 30 times in thickness when applied. The R-values range from 6.0 to 9.0 per inch of thickness, depending on what source you read, but probably averages around R- 7 or 8.

CFCs were once used in the foaming process, but they have been replaced by HCFCs, which are less damaging to the ozone layer. Unfortunately both CFCs and HCFCs are potent greenhouse gases. An average home with one inch of polyiso board on the exterior contributes to the greenhouse effect the equivalent of 22 tons of carbon dioxide—the same as two years energy consumption in the home. We used polyiso board extensively in our stone walls in the past to achieve a high R-value without making the walls excessively thick, but we are now switching to the more benign beadboard.

Icynene: Polycynene insulation uses a modified urethane chemically related to the foam used in mattresses. Polycynene resin reacts with water to form carbon dioxide bubbles that expand the resin into a foam. There are no CFC's or HCFC's used in the foaming process. Icynene is believed to be much more stable than its urethane cousins over time, so it doesn't drop in R-value decades after you move in. A spray-paint thin application expands up to 100 times as thick to fill wall cavities in a matter of seconds. Usually the foam is applied thick enough to overflow the wall or ceiling cavities. The cured insulation is cut off flush with the framing. It has an R-value of 3.6 per inch. A slightly different formulation of icynene can be sprayed through small holes into closed wall cavities to retrofit uninsulated buildings, giving an R-value of about 4 per inch.

Icynene is an open-cell insulation which allows the resin to quickly outgas all chemicals within a few weeks, whereas closed-cell urethane insulations outgas over many years. Icynene is favored for people with chemical sensitivities since there is no detectable outgassing after 30 days. Also, the cured insulation is hydrophobic, meaning that it repels water, so it does not become damp and encourage mold in humid environments.

My brother Nick hired an icynene contractor to insulate the ceiling and certain sections of wall in his tilt-up stone house. He was less than satisfied with the application because it was uneven and there were some large voids in the insulation. I think the foam may not always expand evenly since it expands so much and so fast. This application may have been better if the entire cavity were filled between rafters and the excess trimmed off.

Cementitious Foam Insulation (Air Krete): Air Krete might best be described as concrete with the consistency of angel food cake. It is made from silicates and magnesium oxide extracted from sea water and expanded with compressed air. The insulation is completely inert, fireproof, nontoxic, and neither expands nor shrinks after it leaves the applicator nozzle. Air Krete has an R-value of 3.9 per inch. Unlike other foam insulations, cementitious foam is

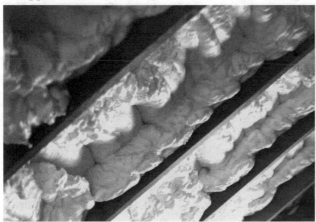

In this partially filled cavity the icynene insulation is very uneven.   *It is better to completely fill the cavity and cut away the extra.*

air-permeable like fiberglass or cellulose. It is more expensive than most other types of insulation, but the price may come down as it becomes more common.

An ideal house should have lots of insulation, but still be able to breathe without special ventilating systems. Unfortunately, superinsulated houses usually have to be sealed airtight with plastic to control infiltration. Plastic vapor barriers are used with fiberglass or cellulose insulation to achieve airtight construction, while conventional plastic foams are inherently airtight as applied. The permeability of Air Krete offers some exciting new possibilities to create superinsulated houses that breathe without ventilating equipment. Like other foams, Air Krete eliminates infiltration gaps that plague fiberglass installations, but unlike other foams, Air Krete allows air to slowly migrate directly through the insulation. More research needs to be done with Air Krete to study the feasibility of making superinsulated homes without ventilating equipment.

Vermiculite & Perlite Beads: The white, airy beads of perlite look like polystyrene beads, but instead perlite is made from expanded volcanic ash. Vermiculite, on the other hand, is made of little bits of mica. The insulating beads are usually poured into the hollow cavities of cinder-block walls. Polystyrene beads may be used similarly. The R-value of such walls isn't very high because heat conducts out through the masonry, but it is better than nothing. Vermiculite and perlite are water resistant but not totally water proof. The beads can be used to replace a portion of the gravel in concrete to make a lightweight, insulating mortar, but there is a significant loss of strength.

Radiant Barriers: It is easy to get excited when you first learn that foil-faced bubblepack has an R-value of 9.8 for only 3/8" of thickness. At that rate it would appear that you could sandwich a single inch of insulation in the wall and have a very warm house. Unfortunately, radiant barriers do not work that way. Radiant barriers function like mirrors: they reflect heat waves traveling through the air. In stores where the material is sold you will sometimes see a reflective tube for demonstration purposes. Put your hand inside, and almost immediately you will feel the heat from your hand reflected off the walls of the tube back on to your skin. Reflective barriers are very good at reflecting heat waves traveling through the air, but there has to be an air space for the insulation to work. Touch the surface of the barrier and the heat from your hand will easily conduct through the material. Reflective barriers are therefore used with frame construction where the material can be stretched from stud to stud without touching anything in between. It is often stapled across the bottom of floor joists to reflect heat back up into the house.

Some fiberglass blankets have foil-faced backing to combine the reflective property of the foil with the insulating property of the fiberglass. In order to function properly, the foil-faced blankets should be pushed gently back from the wall face, so there is an air space between the sheetrock and the foil.

Structural Insulation Systems

Autoclaved Cellular Concrete (Hebel Block): Autoclaved cellular concrete (ACC), also known as aerated autoclaved concrete (AAC) is a form of lightweight, foam-like masonry. It is a cement mortar made with extremely fine particles of sand, plus a foaming agent to make it rise like a loaf of bread. It is poured as a slab, then cut into sheets or blocks. ACC originated in Europe before World War II. It is widely used in other parts of the world.

ACC has been introduced to the southeastern states in recent years as a product called Hebel Block, intended for both exterior and interior walls. The R-value is only about 1.1 per inch, so it would be impractical for exterior walls in colder climates. However, ACC does have a high potential for interior walls, especially in the sheet or slab form. Labor and wood consumption could be reduced if whole walls of this lightweight masonry could be set in place at once, or large sections of it snapped together. The foamy masonry can be cut and drilled with conventional tools. Electrical and plumbing lines are routered in, then patched. Hopefully this material will become more widely available in the near future.

Insulated Concrete Blocks: Insulated concrete blocks are like regular cinder blocks, except that the concrete may include up to 60% polystyrene beads in place of the gravel, and rigid polystyrene is inserted in the cavities. Adding beads to the concrete reduces the strength, but the blocks are still strong enough for most building purposes. A typical 8" block has an R-value of about 13, a figure which varies according to how well the blocks are designed to minimize conduction through the concrete. Thicker blocks have higher R-values. Availability of these products is still limited and expensive.

Mortaring the blocks together creates thermal leaks around every one, so it is better to dry-stack the blocks and use "surface bonding cement" to structurally join the blocks together. Larger blocks include voids big enough for rebar and concrete fill.

Insulated concrete blocks are a good do-it-yourself product for beginners, but more expensive than other alternatives. The biggest drawback is that the R-values are insufficient for northern climates, so extra insulation would have to be attached to the blocks for increased efficiency.

Polystyrene Concrete Forms: Polystyrene concrete forms are available from several manufacturers now, some with stackable, Lego-like forms, and others with 4' x 8' panels. The forms are made with either extruded or expanded polystyrene insulation, usually two inches per side, for a total of four inches and an R-value near 20.

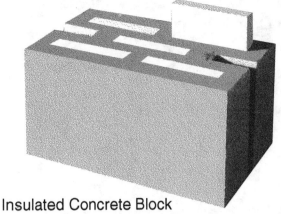

Insulated Concrete Block

Polystyrene foam beads replace some of the sand and gravel used in the mortar mix of insulated block. Beadboard insulation is inserted into the openings to increase the thermal efficiency. The block pictured here is Sparfil™ brand. Similar blocks with different insert patterns are manufactured under other brand names.

Real-world performance is higher than for frame construction of similar R-value because the seamless walls virtually eliminate all air infiltration.

There are several advantages to polystyrene concrete forms. Mostly, it is a labor-saving method of construction. The forms are lightweight and easy to install, plus they require less bracing than conventional concrete forms during the pour, and you do not need to remove the forms afterwards. The poured wall is effectively insulated and waterproofed. Electrical wires can be routed into the insulation after the pour, and plastic or metal plates are already embedded to attach sheetrock or siding.

One disadvantage to these lightweight forms is their cost. Although prices are continuing to fall, the do-it-yourselfer can still save money by taking the extra time to set and remove conventional concrete forms. If the wall is to be insulated and waterproofed then it might be worth the extra expense. Polystyrene concrete forms are probably the most useful for foundation walls, especially under frame or log construction. Some contractors are building whole houses with the forms, due to the virtually airtight construction, but the drawback is that the walls still have to be finished inside and out with siding, sheetrock, or expensive latex or acrylic based stuccos.

Welded-Wire Sandwich Panels: Welded-wire panels are like polystyrene concrete forms (see above) turned inside-out. The welded-wire sheets are connected by rigid wires through the insulation. Cement mortar is applied as shotcrete 1" to 1 1/2" thick to both the inside and outside of the walls. The standard panel includes 2 1/2" of

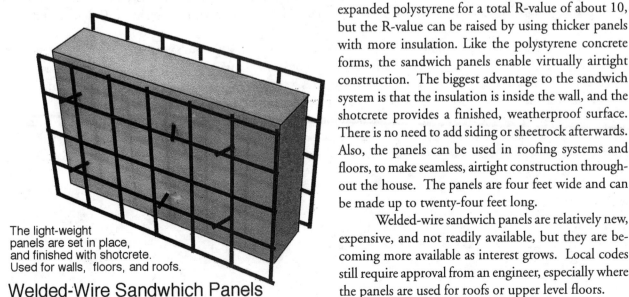

The light-weight panels are set in place, and finished with shotcrete. Used for walls, floors, and roofs.

Welded-Wire Sandwhich Panels

expanded polystyrene for a total R-value of about 10, but the R-value can be raised by using thicker panels with more insulation. Like the polystyrene concrete forms, the sandwich panels enable virtually airtight construction. The biggest advantage to the sandwich system is that the insulation is inside the wall, and the shotcrete provides a finished, weatherproof surface. There is no need to add siding or sheetrock afterwards. Also, the panels can be used in roofing systems and floors, to make seamless, airtight construction throughout the house. The panels are four feet wide and can be made up to twenty-four feet long.

Welded-wire sandwich panels are relatively new, expensive, and not readily available, but they are becoming more available as interest grows. Local codes still require approval from an engineer, especially where the panels are used for roofs or upper level floors.

We built our chicken house with strawbales.

Straw bales: Construction with strawbales originated over a hundred years ago in the plains where there were no trees. Strawbale homes are more popular today than ever before, and with good reason. Strawbale construction is one of the least expensive and most environmentally friendly building methods there are.

The orientation of the straw in the bales makes some difference in the **insulation value**. Bales laid flat (with strings running around the top and bottom) rate about R-2.4 per inch while those laid on edge (with strings running around the sides) rate R-3 per inch. However, the bales are usually wider when laid flat than on edge, giving a higher overall R-value. The bales are slightly stronger too, when laid flat.

Bale size varies according to the equipment it is produced on. A typical 3-string bale is 23 inches wide by 16 inches tall, with an R-value of 54.7 when laid flat or R-49.5 on edge. A typical 2-string bale is 18 inches wide by 14 inches tall, with an R-value of 42.8 when laid flat or R-32.1 on edge. Bale sizes in my area run about 18 inches in width and height.

Stucco wire is wrapped over the surface of the bales and cement mortar is troweled over the wire. We built our chickenhouse with this method. Wood frame construction is usually used on large structures so the roof load is not placed on the bales. Be sure to read the chapter *Building with Bales* for more information.

Papercrete: Papercrete is essentially cellulose insulation with a small amount of sand and cement mixed into it to make a structural building material. The typical ratio is about 60% paper, 30% sand, and 10% cement. Houses have been built from papercrete for almost nothing, some for less than $1.00 per square foot. The labor factor is surprisingly low.

The typical method is to build an oversized blender with a lawn mower blade for a cutter. Water, wastepaper, sand, and cement are added to the blender, which shreds the paper and mixes the ingredients. The resulting goop is allowed to drain for a period of time to get rid of the excess moisture, then the mortar is poured into wall forms, made into bricks, or applied like paper maché over stuccowire.

The sand and cement content makes papercrete semi-structural, with a compressive strength of 260 psi (pounds of pressure per square inch), yet the material is mostly air, with an R-value estimated at 2.8 per inch. Increasing the sand and cement ratio makes a stronger material, but also reduces the insulation value.

Papercrete was patented in 1928, but it was one of those technologies that was so cheap that nobody could make any money off of it. It is also known as fibrous cement. The material was reinvented in the 1990s, and has been used to build a number of structures, including conventional walls as well as domes, in Colorado and New Mexico.

Papercrete shows great promise so far, although there have been a few problems. Papercrete soaks up water like a sponge, and some of the structures were never waterproofed. In wet weather they became completely saturated, and then froze solid in cold weather. Most of the structures were remarkably resilient to this treatment, but others mildewed, and one collapsed. In other words, if you build with papercrete, it must be waterproofed.

I think papercrete has the greatest potential for building dome homes, like those pictured in the chapter *Disaster Proofing Your Home*. Papercrete also has the potential to be used in innovative new roofing systems, discussed more in the chapter *Putting the Roof On*, as well as in precast solar panels, as discussed in the chapter *Solar Input*.

Thermal Mass
How to Capture, Store and Release Heat

The second most important key to building a warm home is thermal mass. Thermal mass is any material dense enough to absorb, store and release a usable amount of heat. Adobe houses of the Southwest have dense walls which absorb heat in the day while the air is warm and release it at night when the air is cool, effectively moderating house temperatures. Log walls have a certain amount of both mass and R-value, so a house with eight or ten inch diameter logs may perform similarly to a conventional house with little mass, but more insulation.

Earth homes (houses built into the ground) take advantage of the thermal mass of the ground for protection from the elements. The temperature fluctuates from season to season in the first few feet of soil, but below that level the ground maintains a constant temperature. The ground temperature is obviously warmer in the south and cooler in the north, but it is relatively consistent in any given location. Across the frost belt of the continental U.S. the ground temperature is roughly 50° Fahrenheit, plus or minus 5 degrees. A house buried into the thermal mass of the ground only has to contend with the 50° temperature of the earth, rather than the -40° to 100°+ temperatures that may be encountered above ground. It doesn't take much insulation to protect a house against a constant 50º.

Earth homes also take advantage of free solar heat and masonry construction to maintain reasonable day-to-day house temperatures. One innovative builder in Montana built a "passive annual solar" home with enough mass to store the warmth of summer so that it would heat the house through an entire winter. He built a dome-shaped underground home for extra strength and smartly laid the insulation out like an umbrella a few feet under the soil surface, so that there were many tons of earth between the walls of the house and the insulation. The 70° temperatures of summer slowly heats up the entire mass, effectively raising the ground temperature around the house. Then the warmth radiates back inside all winter long.

Early solar architects relied heavily on thermal mass schemes to capture, store, and later release the warmth of the sunshine. In some cases they used brick walls or black barrels full of water as "heat sinks" and built walls of glass immediately in front of them. The sun shone through the glass and warmed the masonry or water all day. Then, as the air cooled at night, the warmth radiated into the house. This combination of solar and thermal mass worked okay, but there were some problems with temperature swings where the houses overheated in hot weather and cooled off too much in long cold, cloudy spells. Besides that, it was just a waste of a good view and valuable floor space to install a heat sink right behind the glass. Over the years solar architects have relied less on this combination of solar and thermal mass and more on insulation for warmth.

Lots of insulation is certainly the most important key in building a warm house, but thermal mass and solar input can still make a big difference. In fact, one problem with stick-framed, superinsulated homes is that there is no real thermal mass for heat storage. The heat is entirely contained in the air, so the houses can quickly overheat if the sun is shining in—or the heat will all escape outside if the door is left open for a few minutes. Thermal mass has a sort of balancing effect by absorbing heat any time the air is warmer than the mass and releasing heat when the air is cooler.

Without thermal mass, superinsulated construction alone can make a house so tight that a toaster will keep it warm, but the point of diminishing returns becomes a serious obstacle at that level, since each additional layer of insulation costs the same as the one before, yet saves less energy. In other words it is cost effective to make a house mostly energy-efficient, but potentially very expensive to achieve the final few percent. You can get around the point of diminishing returns by adding thermal mass and solar, or some other low-grade, "free" heat source. Thermal mass can be used to increase the effectiveness of a superinsulated house, so that the house will stay warm even if the construction or management of the house is less than perfect.

Thermal mass works best in a well-insulated house where it is used to modify only a few degrees of temperature. An almost superinsulated house can operate like a totally superinsulated one if it includes a heat sink—like masonry floors or walls—combined with a few strategically placed windows to let in the warmth of the sun.

Thermal mass will absorb and release warmth anywhere inside of a house, but it is most effective when directly exposed to the heat source. For instance, a masonry wall or floor absorbs heat more effectively if the sun shines directly on it through a window, rather than if the mass is positioned where the sun cannot reach it. A shaded mass still absorbs heat from warm air passing by, but not very efficiently.

Likewise a massive stove or masonry fireplace (covered in a later chapter) efficiently captures heat and releases it long after the fire is out. A thin-walled stove heats only the air, often making the house excessively warm while the fire is going. The hot air flows through the house, but doesn't transfer very effectively from the air into a mass in another part of the house.

One thermal mass system is the **thermal rock bed**. Air is warmed in a solar panel and blown through a rock bed beneath the house. This is essentially the "forced air" method of solar heat, where the warmth is stored until needed, then blown inside the house. Although effective, the same amount of capital might be better spent on additional insulation.

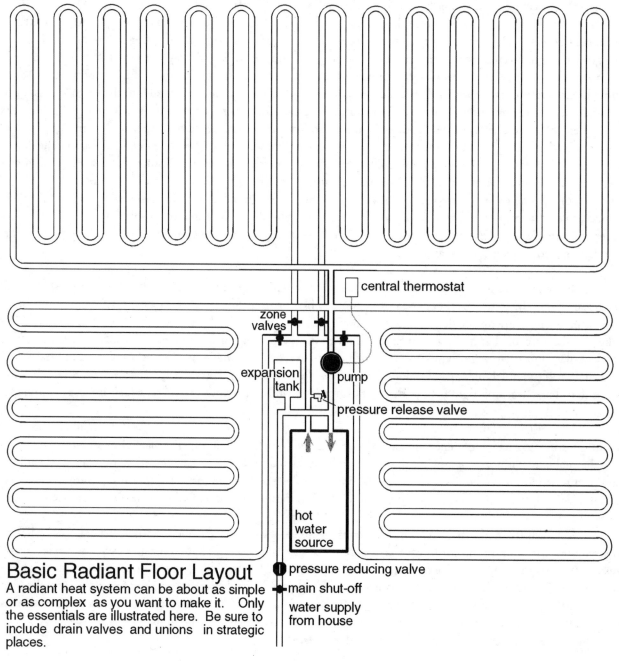

Basic Radiant Floor Layout

A radiant heat system can be about as simple or as complex as you want to make it. Only the essentials are illustrated here. Be sure to include drain valves and unions in strategic places.

Thermal rock beds may be most economical if used in situations where the main floor of the house has to be raised above ground level anyway. For example, in a flood plain or otherwise very flat place where there is little drainage for rainwater, you may need to raise the floor level by just a couple of feet to prevent possible flooding. The space under the floor could be filled with big rocks for thermal mass, then covered with insulation to trap the heat in, and capped with a concrete slab to make the floor. On the other hand, the rock bed must remain completely dry to avoid blowing mold into the house.

One of the best ways to use thermal mass is in the form of a **radiant floor**. A radiant slab is any masonry floor with embedded pipes for hot water heating. Most other heating systems warm only the air, leaving cool surfaces throughout the house that feel like they are sucking heat away from you. Comparatively, a warm slab underfoot gently releases a steady flow of heat, so the atmosphere feels comfortable even when the air is slightly cooler than normal. Besides, heat rises, so putting it in the slab gives the best sense of balance from floor to ceiling. Radiant slabs are especially helpful in superinsulated solar homes. Water is heated in a solar panel and circulated through the slab on nice days, so that the warm mass of the floor helps keep the house comfortable through cloudy spells. The water can also be heated with wood, gas, or electricity, which are covered later in more detail.

Radiant floors are about the nicest heating systems available, but they fell out of favor decades ago due to problems with the copper piping corroding in the concrete. The leaks were difficult and messy to fix. Today there are many new, long-lasting alternatives to copper, so there is a resurging interest in radiant floor heat.

A radiant heat system can be as simple or as complex as you want it to be. A simple system, like the one illustrated here, includes plastic tubing, a few valves, a pump, a source of hot water, and a centralized household thermostat. The expansion tank and pressure relief valve are critical for safe operation of the system. The pressure reducing valve is helpful if the household water pressure is high, but may not be necessary in low pressure systems.

Plastic tubing for radiant floors varies in size from 3/8" up to 3/4", but 1/2" diameter tubing is the most common. Keep in mind that friction increases with smaller diameter pipes, requiring more pump energy to move the fluid. In the past we used a cheap gray tubing "rated to 180 F°", called polybutylene. Later there were questions about the longevity of the material, and a class-action lawsuit was filed against the manufacturer, mostly on behalf of homeowners who had polybutylene piping for all of their household plumbing. We are not sure what will happen with the radiant floors we installed, but if the tubing ever failed it would be easy enough to disconnect and switch to radiant baseboard heaters.

The most popular types of tubing for radiant systems today are PEX™ and Entran 3™ polyethylene. The latter has three layers for maximum strength, including DuPont plastics and Goodyear rubber, with rayon or aramid mesh for reinforcing. The tubing resists freezing and abrasion, and may be warranted for up to twenty-five years, although realistically it should last much, much longer. Similar tubing can be used for household plumbing. The key difference is that floor tubing usually includes an oxygen barrier to prevent possible decay from the air in the water. Be to read more about tubing systems in the chapter *Practical Plumbing*.

Before a concrete or soil-cement floor is poured, the tubing is laid out in loops spaced no more than 12 inches apart. The length of each run or "zone" should be relatively equal in size. The tubing can be tied to the rebar or wire reinforcing to hold it in place for a concrete pour or temporarily weighted down with large rocks if you are pouring an unreinforced soil cement floor. Hot water from a solar panel or tank comes through a "header" made with copper pipe, where the flow is split to each of the zones. Each zone should have its own control valve, preferably a brass ball valve, before connecting to the rubber tubing. The pump is placed at the end of the run where the water is coolest to avoid problems with overheating. A radiant floor with a gas or electric boiler system is controlled by a centralized household thermostat. Typically the boiler has it's own thermostat, so there is always hot water available. The household thermostat turns the pump on to circulate the hot water through the floor. Swing check valves may be needed if the system is cycling water from one floor level to another.

This radiant system consists of three zones, with the return lines next to the out-going hot lines.

If one room seems too hot or too cool, then you can simply adjust the valves to let more or less water through each zone. Once the valves are set you will rarely, if ever, have to touch them again. Radiant heat systems can be made more complicated and expensive by installing separate thermostats and pumps for each zone, but there is little need for such extravagance, unless you are living off the grid and generating your own electricity. Then the cost of the additional thermostats and high-efficiency pumps is less than the cost of buying more power-generating capacity.

In a solar heated system the pump can be powered by a photovoltaic panel, without the need for a thermostat. If the sun is shining bright enough to produce hot water in the solar panel, then it is also bright enough to generate the electricity to run the pump that circulates the water through the floor.

Ideally the mass of the floor should accumulate enough heat during sunny weather to keep the house warm

This manifold serves radiant baseboard heaters on two floors. Each zone includes a small, high-efficiency pump with its own thermostat, plus a ball valve and a swing check valve to prevent backflowing. Notice the unions that were installed before and after the pump and after the check valves to facilitate future repairs. 3/4" polyethelene tubing runs from the manifold to the heaters. Sage Mountain Center (www.sagemountain.org).

through cold cloudy spells, without the need for additional heat. The problem is that the house may warm up too much when the sun shines, and cool off too much during those long cloudy spells when you need the heat the most. Burying the tubing deeper into the floor—even two feet down—will help to minimize temperature swings since it takes longer to charge the bigger mass, and it will radiate heat for a longer time afterwards. A second layer of tubing may be desirable close to the surface for more immediate heating when the sunshine returns. A system with a solar panel may require an antifreeze solution instead of water to prevent freezing in the panel.

Homeowners connected to the grid should include a tank with an electric element in the system for backup heat, with it's own household thermostat and pump. Normally the thermostat is turned all the way off, but it can be turned on as needed in extreme weather when the solar panel is unable to provide enough heat. Equally important, the electric backup makes the system legitimate according to building codes.

Some builders add radiant heat systems to the upper floors to equalize heat distribution throughout the house. There is little need for this extra expense if the house is sufficiently insulated and somewhat open to allow heat to migrate up from down below. If heating is desired on the upper levels then the tubing is stapled up underneath the wooden floors, or placed on top of wood floors and encased in thin-slab gypsum-based mortar.

Always keep in mind that radiant floors and other thermal mass systems are not substitutes for insulation but compliments to it. The most comfortable house will be the one that has the most insulation, the most thermal mass and the most solar input, but real world economics dictates that we must find an optimal balance of each at the least overall cost.

Solar Input

Passive and Active Solar Heating

The third key in designing a warm home is to take advantage of the available solar input in the area. A region with cold, cloudy winters requires more insulation to trap heat in, while a location with sunny winters allows more window space. The warmth from the sun "recharges" the mass of the house no matter how cold the weather is outside. Ideally, a house should be able to absorb enough heat when the sun shines to keep the occupants comfortable through the longest anticipated cold, cloudy spells. New high-tech windows allow more flexibility in this equation than in the past.

Windows and doors account for a fifth to a quarter of the heat loss from the typical home. In a superinsulated structure the heat loss may be proportionally higher, since the rest of the structure is so well insulated. Therefore, if you have taken due care to build

The Earth on its Axis

The tilt of the earth towards or away from the sun alters the amount of solar radiation absorbed, and causes our seasons. Likewise, the angle of the windows in your home also alters the amount of solar radiation absorbed.

energy-efficient walls and a roof for your home, then it is important to follow through with high-quality windows and doors too. Building a well-insulated shell without good windows and doors would be like trying to keep chicken soup hot in a thermos with no lid—the insulation of the shell is useless if the openings are not also sealed.

Maximizing Solar Gain

One of the most basic but controversial elements of solar architecture is the use of slanted windows to better capture sunlight in winter. The tilt of the earth's axis affects the absorption of the sun's energy enough to cause our seasons. The angle of the windows in your home has a similar influence on the amount of solar radiation absorbed or reflected through the glass.

Surface Area and Reflection

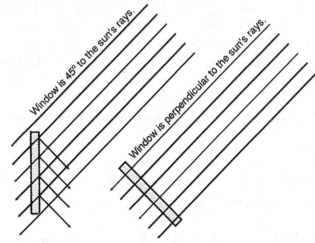

Solar radiation is lost to a reduced surface area AND to increased reflection when windows are not perpendicular to the sun's rays.

As illustrated here, the performance of a window changes significantly depending on how it is oriented to the sun. Windows absorb the most energy when positioned exactly perpendicular to the sun's rays. Performance drops geometrically as the window is tilted away from perpendicular. The surface area is effectively reduced and much of the light is reflected off the glass surface.

There is no mistaking a solar home with its slanted windows. The angles are difficult to work with architecturally, so solar homes are often not very pretty. Also, the tilted windows are more exposed to the weather, requiring more maintenance work. Architects today rely less on angled windows, only because the emphasis has switched to superinsulated structures and insulated glass, rather than solar gain and storage. Nevertheless, you should still evaluate the pros and cons of tilting windows in your home for maximum solar gain.

In order to position your windows at the correct angle you need to compensate for both the tilt of the earth and your latitude. Basically, the sun is lower in the winter sky as you travel farther north, so windows are set closer to vertical. Just add the latitude and the earth's tilt together and that is about the right angle for the glass. For example, at 40° north latitude, plus 23 1/2° for the earth's tilt, the sun rises to only 26 1/2° above the horizon on December 21st, the shortest day of the year. Therefore, windows should be at a 63 1/2° slant to absorb the most heat at noon of that day.

Unfortunately, the preceding equation is more complicated than it seems. First of all, the shortest day of the year is not the coldest part of the winter, because the earth has a slightly elliptical orbit around the sun. January is usually colder than December, even though the sun is higher in the sky and the days are longer, only because the planet is farther away at that time. Therefore, it is more accurate in the above example to round off the tilt of the earth to 20° and slant the windows at 60°. It is also necessary for ease of construction.

Another factor to add to the equation is that the sun is only at it's highest point for a short time in the middle of the day. The day is cooler before and after that when the sun is lower because the light must travel farther through the atmosphere. Just like the illustration of the tilted windows, there is effectively less surface area and more reflection, but in this case, much of the energy is also absorbed by air molecules.

The equation changes as you position the windows to either side of due south. For example, the windows in our greenhouse face southeast, only because that was the way the concrete slab was laid out when we bought the place. We did not slant the windows, but that was ideal since the winter sun rises just about exactly perpendicular to the face of the glass. There is not as much heat potential at that time of day, but it is enough to warm the house when it needs it most. Thus, for the sake of maximum solar gain, a house should have slanted windows on the south side, vertical windows on the southeast and southwest, and none on the north!

Of course, there is also the problem of taking in too much solar heat, especially in the summer time. The objective is to build a solar home, not a solar oven. The summer sun is much higher in the sky at noon, which can be figured as your latitude plus the tilt of the earth. Windows that are slanted for optimum solar gain in winter will deflect some of the summer heat, but a fully vertical window deflects more. With slanted windows you may ultimately consume more energy trying to stay cool in summer than you saved on winter heating.

summer sun

winter sun

Adjust the length of the eaves to block out the sun in summer, while letting it through in winter.

Blocking Summer Heat

The remedy for summer overheating is simple enough. Eaves over the windows will block the high summer sun, yet still allow the lower winter sun to pass under. You can use a piece of graph paper to determine the right length for the eaves. Just draw the windows and eaves in proportion, then figure the angle of the sun and draw light rays in at that angle. Adjust the eaves shorter or longer on paper to optimize them for both summer and winter conditions. Slanted windows will obviously require longer eaves than vertical windows.

Utilizing Smart Glass Technology

The single-pane windows of yesteryear had an R-value of slightly less than 1. In cold weather the moist, warm house air condensed on the glass forming a sheet of ice. Newer "double-glazed" windows have an air space between two panes of glass and bump the R-value up to 1.75— not great in itself, but a huge step up from single-pane windows.

Early solar architects had to contend with these double-paned windows as the best resources available. The windows let in more than enough heat on sunny days, but then they let it all back out on cold nights and cloudy days. To gain any efficiency the houses required extra large thermal heat sinks to store enough energy to offset the loss through the glass. Insulated shutters were often placed over the windows, but this meant they had to be opened and closed every day.

Double-pane windows have since been dramatically improved with the aid of invisible "low-emissivity" (low-e) films that block infrared waves (heat) from bouncing out the glass. This raises the R-value of the window up to about 4.75— or 270% better than a standard double-pane unit. We had low-e windows custom made for our greenhouse to fit against the angle of the roof line. Those windows are installed beside standard double pane units we acquired used. The temperature difference between the windows is dramatic when you put a hand on each. Thirty percent of new windows sold today contain low-e films; it is about the best value you can get for your money.

One caution, however, is that high-tech windows can over heat and crack very easily if the heat is trapped in between the panes of glass. I've broken three windows this way over the years, one with a silver-colored plastic bag leaning against the glass, one with a blanket leaning against the glass, and one with the kids' bulletin board, which was also leaning against the glass. Despite the cost and annoyance of replacing the windows, I still consider them very worthwhile for the extra efficiency.

Additional efficiency can be gained in a window by removing the air between the panes and pumping in an inert, low-conductivity gas like **argon** or **krypton**. Temperature differences between the inside and outside of a window creates turbulence inside the unit. Air molecules absorb warmth and rise along the inside pane, then descend along the cold pane, releasing heat to the cold glass. Argon and krypton gas are bigger than ordinary air molecules, so they are not able to move as freely inside the windows; this minimizes turbulence and achieves a modest gain in R-value at little or no extra cost. It is a worthwhile investment, even though the gas tends to escape over time.

"Superinsulated" windows are triple- or quadruple-glazed, usually with two panes of glass and one or two low-e films suspended inside. Argon or krypton gas is added between each layer. These improvements can raise the R-value of a window up to 10 or 12— the equivalent of a 2 x 4 wall insulated with 3 1/2 inches of fiberglass!

The biggest problem with high-tech windows, even double-pane windows, is that the parts are sealed together with silicone caulk which eventually leaks. You will often see windows with a white filmy substance in the middle. Moist air works its way in through cracks in the silicone then evaporates, leaving minerals behind where you cannot clean them off. Twenty or thirty years is about the maximum life-span on any kind of window before mineralization leaves the glass permanently stained. The energy conserved in that time far outweighs the energy expended to replace the units, so high-tech windows are still a good investment, but it is something you might want to think about before you build a house with an extra large number of windows.

Ultimately the ideal window would have all the air vacuumed out between the panes, like a true thermos bottle. A thermos bottle rates about R-75 (except through the lid) because there is no air or gas to transfer heat across between the panes. Thermos bottles are made of one continuous piece of glass, so there is no silicone seal to give out down the road. The reason we do not yet have true vacuum-paned windows is partly because the machinery would have to be customized for every size of window, but also because the windows would have to be relatively small for strength. Vacuuming out the air creates inverse pressure, like sucking the

Window Glazings

Image Source: Warm Places: A sampling of energy-efficient Montana homes. Montana Department of Natural Resources & Conservation. Spring 1988.

air out of a plastic soda bottle, so the windows would collapse inward if the area was too large. Perhaps the best solution would be numerous little vacuum-paned window squares pieced together in one decorative frame, similar to the way windows were made in the past, but much more efficient. We will have to work on that for a future generation of houses.

In any case, selecting the right type of window for your home is not quite as simple as merely choosing between what you can afford to pay for windows now versus what you can afford to pay in a power bill later. There are many types of low-e films; those that let the most heat in also tend to block more of the sun's heat out, and vice-versa. On the south wall of a house you want a low-e film that allows for maximum solar gain, while on the north face you want a film to minimize heat loss.

Another factor to consider is that each manufacturer's material and design choices affect the amount of heat conducted away through the window framing. Therefore the window industry uses it's own system for measuring the efficiency of the whole unit. **Unit values** or **U-values** run inverse to R-values—a low U-value is good, while a high U-value is bad. A single pane window has a U-value of .90, while a superinsulated window may rate around .21, with all other windows ranking in between.

The most important point to keep in mind is that a properly insulated house doesn't need much solar input, and your best investment is usually the windows that retain the most existing heat inside the house. That way you can have a superinsulated house with some solar input, and none of the temperature swings that were associated with early solar houses.

Solar Hot Water Systems

A discussion on solar input must also include the topic of solar hot water. Hot water from a solar system can be used to capture and store extra heat in a radiant slab to keep a house cozy and warm through cold, cloudy spells. The hot water can also be used for domestic purposes—dishes, laundry and bathing, etc.

One problem with solar hot water systems is that if you install enough capacity to meet most of your needs for hot water in winter, then you will have far more than you can possibly use in summer. You pay more for the extra

Black Polypipe Solar Water Preheater

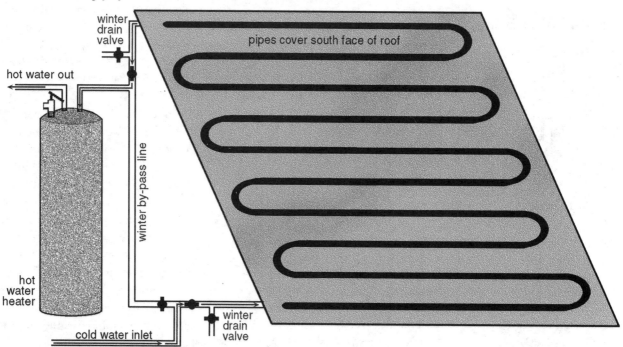

Large diameter (~1 1/2") polypipe, rated for drinking water, is looped back and forth across the roof. Hot water stays in the pipes until a faucet is turned on, drawing the prewarmed water into an automatic water heater. If necessary, the water heater will turn on to boost the temperature of incoming water.
The system must be drained in winter in northern climates. Note that the polypipes could prevent snow loads from sliding off the roof.

capacity, but use it only part of the year. The **point of diminishing returns** kicks in, and most people subsequently under-install and make up the difference with energy from fossil fuels.

There are many, many varieties of solar water heater designs, with varying degrees of cost and sophistication, from less than $100 up to several thousand dollars. If you take the time to do some research and planning before you build then you may be able to integrate a solar panel into your house plans at virtually no extra cost. The problem is that people often do not take that extra time up front, so the solar system is ultimately tacked on to the house later on at a much greater expense for materials and labor. I know, because this is one aspect of our house that was not well researched or properly integrated into our plans, so our solar panel cost many times more than it needed to. Granted, $700 is still cheap compared to most commercial solar panels— but it also took nearly seven years of trial and error to get it operational! If I had a chance to do it all over again, I would take a much different approach, incorporating the panel into our home instead of separately.

The best solar panels are often very simple, most of which are built in the southern states where there is little danger of freezing. Even a coil of **black plastic polypipe** laid out on the roof works remarkably well for generating hot water. With enough piping and some sunshine, this type of water heater will provide plenty of hot water for domestic purposes, even without a tank— provided you can wait on the bathing and dishes until the sun is out. Even better, use a polypipe system as a "preheater" to warm the water before sending it to a conventional water heater tank. Then you will always have hot water, yet you will save money on energy bills whenever the sun is shining. This combination can work in the northern states too, provided the polypipe can be easily drained each winter. Note that there are different grades of polypipe. The cheapest black pipe is not necessarily intended for drinking water. The higher grade pipe for drinking water usually includes a white plastic inner liner.

Another simple solar water heater is the "**batch heater**." A typical batch heater consists of a water tank painted black inside a wood frame lined with aluminum foil or aluminum printing plates to reflect light onto the tank. Ask at a local newspaper for their used printing plates. A window over the front, usually from a used patio door, helps trap in the heat and prevents losses to convection.

The batch heater preheats the water. The warmed water stays in the tank until a faucet is turned on, drawing the warmed water into a conventional water heater. If necessary, the gas or electricity will kick on and warm the water up to the desired temperature.

If the solar panel is separate from the house then it must be drained in the winter. However, if the house is designed with a section of wall or roof at the proper angle, then the panel can be built into the house where it won't freeze. An insulated shutter over the front of the panel will help retain the heat at night, but shouldn't be required to keep the system from freezing. There is nothing worse than being far away from home and realizing that you need to rush back to cover up the solar panel before it freezes and bursts the pipes! A new superinsulated window could be a wise investment in northern climates to better retain heat and prevent freezing without the need for insulated shutters.

hot outlet

aluminum foil or printing plates

window to trap heat in

cold inlet

Batch-Style Solar Water Heater

A simple "batch heater" can be made by painting a water tank black and placing it in a frame lined with aluminum foil or aluminum printing plates. A window over the front traps in the heat and prevents losses to convection.

Solar Water Heater with Thermosiphon

Thermosiphoning circulates water through the solar panel. Water expands as it warms, becoming lighter per volume. The lighter water rises up through the panel to the tank, pulling cold water from the tank back to the panel. The tank must be positioned higher than the solar panel for thermosiphoning to work.

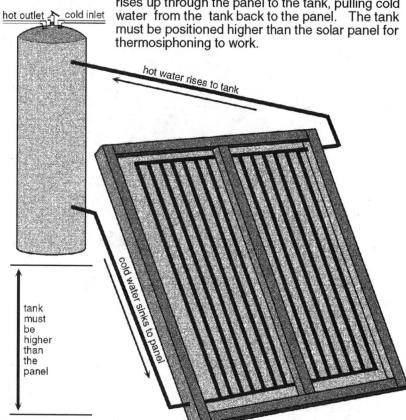

hot outlet   cold inlet

hot water rises to tank

cold water sinks to panel

tank must be higher than the panel

The most expensive part of a batch heater is usually the tank, but most solar hot water systems require a tank anyway. The cost of the tank could become more of an obstacle if you were building a series of solar panels along one side of the house and needed multiple water tanks. Be sure to check with local plumbers for good used tanks. Most water heaters are replaced after rusting through and leaking, but sometimes good electric water heaters are replaced with gas models to lower the home energy bill. You may get a secondhand tank free.

A slightly more complex, but also more versatile design is a **solar water heater with a thermosiphon** to a separate tank. "Thermosiphoning" circulates water automatically between the solar panel and the tank. Water expands as it warms, becoming lighter per volume. The lighter, warmer water rises up through the panel to the tank, pulling cold water from the tank back to the panel. The tank must be positioned at least two feet higher than the solar panel for thermosiphoning to work.

There are several advantages to this type of system. First, the solar panel is scalable, so you can add more surface area to collect heat without needing additional tanks. The system can also work with a very large tank to store hundreds of gallons of hot water. Second, a thermosiphon system tends to collect hotter water at the top of the tank right away, instead of slowly warming the whole tank, as in a polypipe or batch-style water heater. That gives you a small but useful supply of hot water very quickly. Over time the tank warms from the top all the way to the bottom. Third, a thermosiphon system eliminates the need for a costly pump, thermostat, or electricity. And finally, a **heat exchanger** can be added to the tank, with a glycol solution circulating through the system to prevent freezing in cold climates.

We used a pump and themostat with our solar water heater, plus a home-made heat-exchanger for the glycol solution.

Commercial tanks with heat exchangers are often very expensive, but also very high quality. However, you can also innovate your own. One simple method is to disassemble a gas water heater and weld plumbing fittings to the top and bottom of the exhaust pipe that runs through the tank. The inside of the tank is lined with glass, so be careful to avoid coming to close to the tank with the welder. Hot glycol circulates from the panel through the exhaust stack of the water tank, transferring heat into the water tank. Unfortunately it is hard to justify disassembling a new water heater for this purpose, and most discarded gas water heaters were junked because of leaks in the bottom, due to corrosive chemicals in the gas. It is unfortunate that such poorly made tanks are still being manufactured.

Another way to make a heat exchanger is to insert a coil of copper pipes into a water tank, as shown in the photo. The coil is made with 5/8" soft-copper "Refrigeration tubing", which is just the right diameter to fit standard 1/2" copper fittings (Read more about that in the chapter *Practical Plumbing*.) Soft copper kinks easily, so you have to work very carefully with it. I hoped to corkscrew the coil right through the tank, in one opening and out another, but ultimately I had to cut the lid off the tank to put the coil in. Cutting and welding this otherwise very durable tank will no doubt encourage rust and shorten the life of the tank, but we should be able to get many years of use out of it first. The coil enters and exits the tank through existing threaded holes. On each end of the coil I added a 3/4" threaded fitting with a reducer to 1/2" copper. After drilling out a stop inside the copper fitting, the coil slid right through. The piece was threaded tightly into the tank before soldering it to the coil. Ideally the heat exchanger should enter the tank a few inches below the top, so water can thermosiphon up to the tank, instead of diving down through the top of the tank. Optionally, a tank can be laid on its side to facilitate thermosiphoning through the end.

Keep in mind that the glycol solution must have room for expansion. A fill pipe at the highest point in the system can be left open, provided there is sufficient capacity for the glycol to expand without overflowing. A sealed system with a pressure relief valve can also work. Since the volume of glycol is relatively low, the expansion isn't that great either. For lack of room at the top of our system, I installed an expansion pipe extending straight up from the bottom. The pipe is always full of air, but the air is compressed by the expanding glycol to get the extra space.

The biggest drawback to a thermosiphon system is the design limitations, since the tank must be placed above the panel to work properly. With or without a heat exchanger, a thermosiphon system should be designed into a home from the beginning. For example, the panel can be built into a slanted wall on the lower floor with the tank situated upstairs. If the solar panel is not integrated into the design of the home, then it can cost a lot more to add it on afterwards.

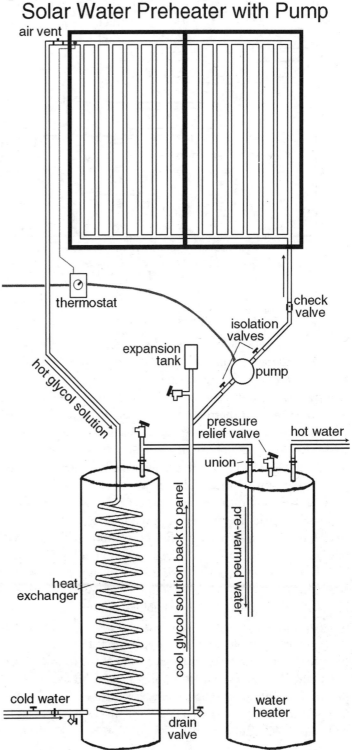

Solar Water Preheater with Pump

air vent

thermostat

check valve

isolation valves

expansion tank

pump

hot glycol solution

pressure relief valve

hot water

union

cool glycol solution back to panel

pre-warmed water

heat exchanger

cold water

drain valve

water heater

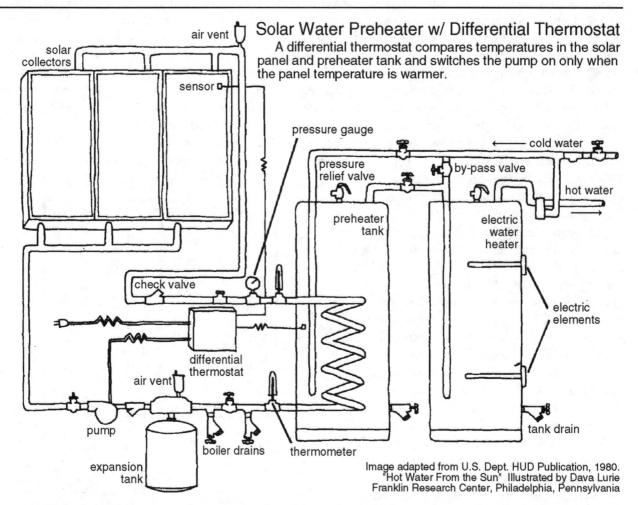

Solar Water Preheater w/ Differential Thermostat

A differential thermostat compares temperatures in the solar panel and preheater tank and switches the pump on only when the panel temperature is warmer.

Image adapted from U.S. Dept. HUD Publication, 1980.
"Hot Water From the Sun" Illustrated by Dava Lurie
Franklin Research Center, Philadelphia, Pennsylvania

We had to build a stone and concrete bunker in the yard to hold the our water tank and to support the panel. For aesthetic reasons, the tank ended up a few inches lower than the solar panel. I hoped that the effect of the glycol warming and rising in the panel would be enough to initiate flow through the system, reasoning that if it started moving at one point, then it would have to move throughout the system, but it didn't work that way. I had to had to add a **pump and thermostat** to circulate the glycol solution, similar to the system shown on the previous page. Our solar panel prewarms the water, which is additionally heated by the boiler system in our antique wood-fired cookstove. A more sophisticated system utilizes a differential thermostat to compare the temperatures in the solar panel and the water tank, as illustrated here. The pump only turns on when the solar panel is warmer than the tank.

One way to place a solar panel above the tank, but without a pump, is to utilize a **geyser pumping** technique. As water boils and turns to steam the gas bubbles rise up through the liquid creating a powerful pump that lifts the water right up out of the ground in spectacular displays. Old fashioned coffee pots work the same way, creating a small fountain that brings water from the bottom of the pot to the top where the coffee grounds are. The principles of geyser pumping can be harnessed to pump hot liquid downward to a tank positioned below the solar panel.

Geyser-pump solar panels use a methanol-water solution in a vacuum-sealed system to make the liquid boil at relatively low temperatures. For the geyser-pumping technique to work there must be nucleation sites, such as air bubbles in the liquid, for the gas bubbles to form. But since the air dissolves into the water with use each day, there are fewer and fewer nucleation sites and the liquid becomes superheated (hotter than boiling), without turning to vapor. Inventors of the patented Copper Cricket™ solar panel solved the nucleation dilemma by inserting a smaller tube inside the riser pipes for about a third of the length. A small amount of liquid becomes stagnant between the inner and outer tubes, quickly turning to superheated steam. The steam merges with the flow in the open pipes, providing a continuous supply of nucleation sites. With the aid of a nine inch high header at the top of the panel, the Copper Cricket™ is able to pump hot liquid as much as 36 feet downstairs to a hot water tank fitted with a heat exchanger. The Copper Cricket™ gets its name from the faintly audible chirping noise it makes while operating. The system is reasonably priced compared to other commercially available systems.

Dodging the Point of Diminishing Returns

A commercial solar panel like the Copper Cricket™ can be a good investment if you only plan to install a single solar panel to reduce your gas or electric bill. The up-front cost may be higher, but it will save you much time and labor compared to designing, building and troubleshooting a solar panel of your own design. How much energy you save depends largely on the climate where you live. A single panel will reduce your domestic hot water bill by an estimated 43% in Boston, Massachusetts; 54% in Columbia, Missouri; 55% in Medford, Oregon; 82% in Tampa, Florida; and 91% in Phoenix, Arizona (based on a 3.4 person household with an insulated water heater set to 120 F°). The greatest benefit is obviously in the hotter, sunnier climates.

The economics are much different if you plan to install multiple panels to increase your hot water supply for either domestic use and/or to charge a radiant slab that will keep the house warm through cold, cloudy spells. The cumulative cost of several commercial solar panels makes the do-it-yourself alternative much more attractive. If you take the time to design a house with the optimal angles in a section of wall or roof then you can integrate a solar system at relatively low cost. However, much of the cost in labor and materials is still spent to build the frames that support the piping and glass. If you can integrate the framing into the house structure to eliminate that cost and

Solar Panels Precast in a Papercrete Wall or Roof Panel

Much of the high labor and materials cost to build a solar panel is in the frame that supports the piping and glass. A series of solar collectors can be built faster and cheaper by casting them in a papercrete wall or roof panel. The panel must be fully waterproofed to protect the papercrete. Pipes can be drilled through the papercrete between the windows to connect each panel into one big one. The windows are dropped into place on pre-notched edges.

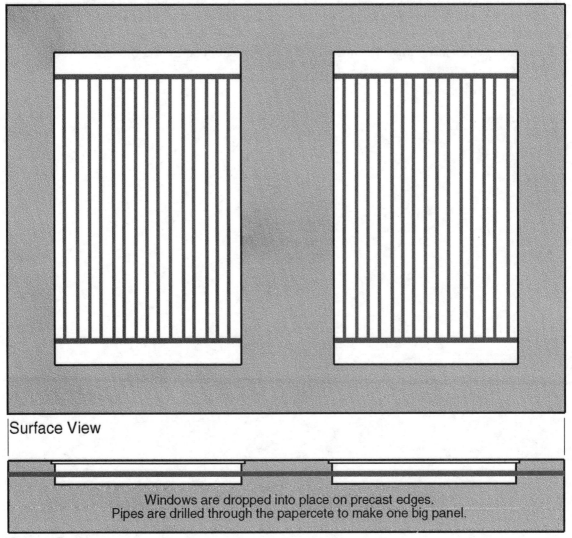

Surface View

Windows are dropped into place on precast edges.
Pipes are drilled through the papercete to make one big panel.

Cross-Section

work, then you can make a really big solar collector for relatively little cost.

In the past I proposed custom-cutting solar panels from EPS beadboard roof panels at the factory. The insulation is photodegradable, so it has to be coated with Dry-vit or some other medium to protect it from the sun. With the frames cut into the insulation, one would only have to install the piping and set the glass in place. But there is one flaw to this scheme: beadboard melts and surprisingly low temperatures. I installed some beadboard insulation behind our solar panel, protected by a 1/2" sheet of OSB board. But the panel absorbed so much heat while the pump was accidentally turned off that it melted two inches of the beadboard insulation. Beadboard solar panels, I realized, would be a lousy idea, especially if they melted a hole right through the roof of your house.

A better medium might be papercrete, as discussed in the chapter *Insulation & Insulation Systems*. Solar panels could be precast from papercrete, either in a section of wall or roof. Then it would just be a matter of waterproofing the papercrete, adding plumbing and setting the glass in place. The windows would be dropped into pre-notched edges in the insulation, so the surface of the glass is flush with the wall or roofing. The openings should be made to fit standard patio door sizes (76" high X 32", 34" or 36" wide). Also read about papercrete in the chapter *Putting the Roof On*.

With enough solar panels tied into one unit and a glycol solution and heat exchanger to prevent problems with freezing, this kind of system could easily provide enough hot water for domestic uses *and* a radiant slab. A pump and controls is a necessity, so that the hot glycol solution is always directed to the heat exchanger in the domestic water supply first. When that tank is completely warmed then the controls would direct all excess heat into the radiant slab until the household thermostat kicked it off. If the house is properly insulated then the heat stored in the slab will radiate plenty of heat through any cold, cloudy days to come. Excess heat might be directed to a hot tub or to some other creative use, especially in summer when the heat is not wanted in the slab.

With the aid of careful planning and integrated design work, it is possible to build houses that require no other central heating system, beyond a simple electric element in the radiant system to meet the building codes and insurance requirements. Just because you install an electric element doesn't mean you have to turn it on!

Heating Systems
For Backup Heat and Hot Water

Superinsulation is the biggest factor in making an energy-efficient house, but it is helpful to combine it with thermal mass and solar to optimize performance at the least possible cost. A well-insulated thermal mass home with passive solar input will be functionally 100% energy efficient... on most days.

Active solar systems, such as solar water heaters used to charge a radiant slab, can boost the performance of such an efficient house to keep it warm even through the extended cold, cloudy spells. Properly built, such systems are intended for overkill, to make a house warm enough to handle real world situations where kids leave the door open for an hour in the middle of January, or a future homeowner cuts a hole in the door for the cat or dog to pass through. Over time the weather stripping on the doors will falter anyway, and not every homeowner will jump up immediately to do something about it. A well designed house must allow some room for human error.

Also keep in mind that unusual circumstances may dramatically decrease the performance of your house. For example, if a burglar breaks a window and plunders your house while you are away on vacation, then the house may be a little on the cold side when you return. Natural phenomena may also influence performance. The 1815 eruption of Tambora in Indonesia spewed so much ash into the upper atmosphere (blocking out the sun) that the following year was described as the "year without a summer" as frost and snow fell across New England and northern Europe through June and July.

For these reasons, even the most well-designed home needs additional heat once in awhile, so heating systems must be included. Producing hot water for domestic purposes is a related topic, so it is covered in this chapter too. Potential sources of heat include wood, gas and electricity, or various combinations of these.

If you doubt the level of efficiency in your house designs, then you would be wise to install a gas or wood-heated backup system, or at least leave room to install a system later. Wood heat seems like the obvious choice for those who are interested in self-sufficiency, except that it is not a "valid heat source", at least according to code.

I think the purpose of the code is to insure that a person can turn on the thermostat and leave the house whenever they want to, without being a slave to the wood pile in cold weather. The unfortunate result is that in an emergency situation, such as the massive ice storms that knock out power lines, hundreds of thousands of people can be stuck in freezing houses with heaters that don't work.

Wood Stoves & Boilers

Wood heat is both a luxury and a nuisance. It is especially appreciated when you are chilled to the bone from being outside, because there are times when even a warm house isn't warm enough. Sometimes you might want the option of making your house hot. Wood heat is also a luxury if you happen to have your own fuel supply. A wood stove is simply a great way to clean the yard of broken branches and wood scraps.

On the other hand, wood stoves are very messy, and ours is the single biggest contributor of dirt and dust in our home. The next time I build a house with a stove or fireplace I would make it loadable from outside, with heavily insulated doors to hold the heat in, and only a viewing window from inside the house.

Also keep in mind that when you install a woodstove or fireplace you have to put a big hole in the roof to ventilate it, ultimately defeating the purpose of a high-efficiency house. Once the stove and chimney is installed you have to light the fire just to offset the heat loss through the roof.

Probably one of the worst crimes in conventional construction today is to install decorative fireplaces inapartmetns and condominiums. The fireplaces are very inefficient when in use, but most of the time they sit idle, drafting warm house air up the chimney. If you have one already, then I would recommend stuffing an old rag up the pipe to stop the heat loss. (Just remember to take it out if you ever light the fire.) The other problem with decorative fireplaces is that some people try using them to generate real heat to lower their power bills. They carry big piles of wood up the stairs (or on the elevator) and crank out the heat, jeopardizing their own and their neighbor's lives.

If you design a high-efficiency house with a radiant slab charged by solar water heaters, then it makes little sense to add any kind of fireplace or stove. However, if you have a radiant slab, but no solar system, then a wood-fired boiler can be a good way to keep the floor warm. If you do not have a radiant slab either, then a masonry stove, as described later in the book, can be the way to go.

Wood-fired boilers are relatively easy to make, provided you include space for them in your building plans. Our boiler system, as illustrated here, cost only $70 to construct, including $40 for a used, heavy-duty galvanized tank and $30 for all other plumbing parts. The heating coil is made of 1/2" copper pipe. Our main house line into and out of the tank is 3/4" copper pipe. The boiler is built into our antique wood-fired cookstove, which we use every day for cooking, so we have hot water every day without electric backup—but we do have to plan our dishwashing, showers and baths around the hot water supply.

A wood-fired cookstove like ours is a great waste-to-energy converter. Plastic is about the only kind of trash we ever take to the landfill, because we burn every scrap of waste paper, junk mail, old lumber and branches that we can find, and we recycle everything else. Granted, a wood-fired cookstove is not a realistic option for most home-owners, but there is a potential mass-market for a system that chips yard waste and automatically feeds the chips into a boiler as needed to generate hot water. Such a system could even be made to generate electricity, producing hot water as a by-product.

At present the most likely application of boiler technology for the typical home-builder is to produce hot water to recharge the thermal mass of a radiant slab during extended cold, cloudy spells. A boiler system can replace the need for solar water heaters to charge the slab. If your house is sufficiently insulated and you have quite a few trees in the yard, then you may be able to generate all the supplementary heat you need just from tree trimmings and scrap lumber, without the need to buy or cut an annual supply of firewood. You can add a boiler system to just about any kind of fireplace or woodstove, provided you make space for it in the houseplans.

A simple wood-fired boiler does not require a pump, thermostat, or any other fancy controls. Water circulates on its own through the pipes in the firebox due to "thermosiphoning". Hot water expands and thus becomes

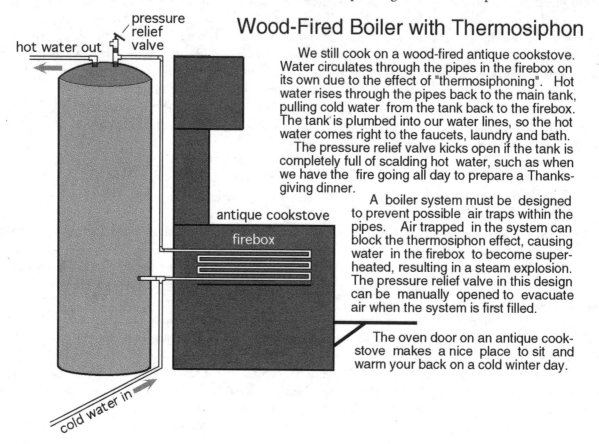

Wood-Fired Boiler with Thermosiphon

hot water out

pressure relief valve

We still cook on a wood-fired antique cookstove. Water circulates through the pipes in the firebox on its own due to the effect of "thermosiphoning". Hot water rises through the pipes back to the main tank, pulling cold water from the tank back to the firebox. The tank is plumbed into our water lines, so the hot water comes right to the faucets, laundry and bath.

The pressure relief valve kicks open if the tank is completely full of scalding hot water, such as when we have the fire going all day to prepare a Thanksgiving dinner.

antique cookstove

firebox

A boiler system must be designed to prevent possible air traps within the pipes. Air trapped in the system can block the thermosiphon effect, causing water in the firebox to become superheated, resulting in a steam explosion. The pressure relief valve in this design can be manually opened to evacuate air when the system is first filled.

The oven door on an antique cookstove makes a nice place to sit and warm your back on a cold winter day.

cold water in

lighter per volume, rising through the pipes to the main tank, pulling cold water from the tank back to the firebox.

At the temperatures generated in a fire the copper pipes will soften and the solder will melt, except that the water circulating in the pipes prevents them from ever getting that hot. The fireplace or stove must NOT be started unless the boiler system is completely operational. An air pocket in the pipes or insufficient water to allow thermosiphoning could result in a steam explosion.

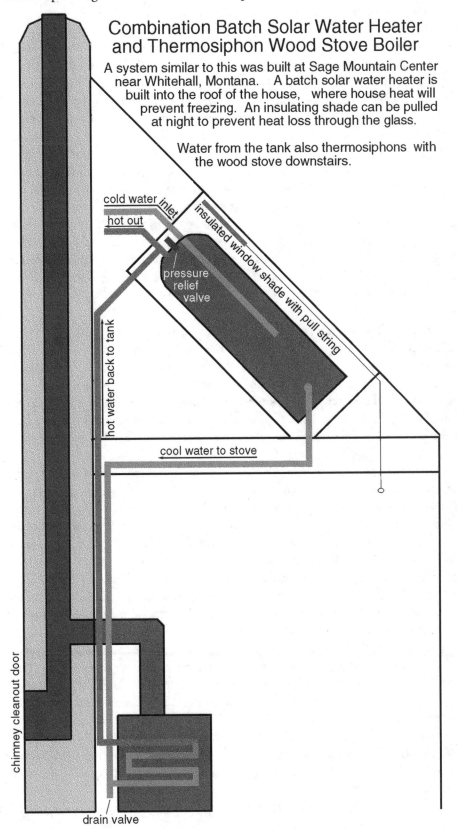

Combination Batch Solar Water Heater and Thermosiphon Wood Stove Boiler

A system similar to this was built at Sage Mountain Center near Whitehall, Montana. A batch solar water heater is built into the roof of the house, where house heat will prevent freezing. An insulating shade can be pulled at night to prevent heat loss through the glass.

Water from the tank also thermosiphons with the wood stove downstairs.

cold water inlet

hot out

insulated window shade with pull string

pressure relief valve

hot water back to tank

cool water to stove

chimney cleanout door

drain valve

One draw back to a wood-fired boiler is that it really sucks the heat out of the fire, reducing the amount of heat thrown into the room and killing hot coals that might otherwise burn through until morning. Our boiler system requires that we use more kindling to generate the temperatures we need for cooking. Fortunately, the boiler pipes also help cool the side of our stove that faces our cabinetry, which might otherwise be too hot.

The most challenging part to building a boiler system is to find a clean, high quality tank with the right openings that will fit into the space you have available. A stainless steel or heavy duty galvanized tank is ideal, but even a regular water heater tank can work, provided it doesn't leak. Ask around plumbing shops for a good secondhand tank. The galvanized tank we have was once a part of a compressed-air system at the county courthouse. Ideally, there should be an opening for the hot water to come in a few inches below the top of the tank, but many different configurations will work, as long as the water can thermosiphon properly and the pressure relief valve is situated at the top where the water is hottest. Note that the water in a radiant heat system can become stale and polluted, so it needs to be separated from the domestic hot water supply.

Keep in mind that no matter how efficient your house is you will still need either gas or electric heat to make the house acceptable according to building codes, mortgage companies and insurance policies. The bureaucracy is not usually a problem out in the country, but it is something to think about if you plan to get a loan or insurance, or if you ever plan to sell your house.

Electric Heat

Surprisingly, the most economical source of backup heat in a high-efficiency house is often the most expensive kind to operate: electric heat. When a utility generates electricity it has to burn three units of a lower-grade energy, like coal or oil, to produce only one unit of high-grade electricity. Two-thirds of the potential energy is lost as waste heat in the conversion. This is why electric heat is so expensive. You have to burn three times as much fuel to generate enough electricity to heat your home or business as you would if you burned the coal or oil directly.

Electric heat is only economical in high-efficiency houses because the heating systems are so inexpensive to install. Natural gas or wood heat can cost many thousands of dollars fully installed, while electric heaters cost only a fraction of that. The money saved from not putting in a furnace can be spent on extra insulation and better windows and doors and an active solar system to achieve the last few percents of energy efficiency. If your house is built efficiently enough, then you may only use the heater a few days over the course of an entire winter, at a negligible cost. Electric baseboard heaters are the most common form of electric heat and very easy to install. However, if you have a solar-heated radiant floor system already, then it is relatively easy to add an electric element and thermostat to the plumbing for backup heat. Just because you have electric heat doesn't mean you have to turn it on!

The biggest danger in building a high-efficiency solar home and installing electric heat is that you might be wrong in your estimations of how efficient the house is. You could end up paying fifty or a hundred or more dollars every month for heat when you were expecting to spend less than that for an entire winter. If you have any doubts about the efficiency of your house, then you should consider wood or gas as your primary heat source.

Gas Heat

If natural gas is available at your building site, then you should definitely connect to it, or retain the option of connecting to it later, no matter how efficient your house is without it. The cost of natural gas varies considerably over time and may even exceed the cost of electricity at times, but it is good to keep your options open. You may not need the gas for space heating, but it might come in handy to heat the domestic hot water supply on cloudy, cold days. Gas is also usually better and cheaper than electricity for the kitchen stove and the dryer. Besides, with fuel cell technology becoming more available, you will soon be able to generate electricity from a home-scale power plant. New cars outfitted with fuel cells will also generate electricity from the natural gas supply when parked, generating electricity for the home, or to rewind the meter on the utility grid.

If natural gas is not available at your site then you should at least consider installing a propane tank, especially if you intend to install photovoltaic panels to generate your own electricity. Photovoltaic power is still very expensive, but you can make it affordable by designing a superefficient house that also substitutes gas appliances for electric ones where ever possible— for hot water, the dryer, the kitchen range, even the refrigerator. If you reduce the electric demand to the few fixtures and appliances that cannot reasonably be run without it (lights, computers, radios, etc.), then it is much more economical to install photovoltaics to meet that demand.

For the purposes of space heating, you can install a furnace for forced air heat or a boiler for radiant heat. Personally, I do not like forced air heat. Most forced air heaters are noisy and only heat the air. Radiant systems are usually much quieter. Boilers with a radiant slab also have enough thermal mass to maintain the temperature of the house for longer periods of time so they are not constantly turning on or off.

Note that the water circulating through the floor can become stagnant and polluted, so you do not want it to mix with your drinking and bathing water. Fortunately, most new boilers on the market have separate loops built in, so you can heat water for the floor and the faucet separately within one unit. Typically the boiler heats the water for the radiant system. A heat exchanger built into the boiler tank is used to transfer heat to the domestic water supply. Most boiler systems provide hot water "on demand", producing hot water about as fast as you can use it.

These high-tech systems typically operate at 85-90+% efficiency, compared to only about 60% efficiency in a conventional gas water heater. What this means is that water heaters lose more heat out the exhaust than the new boilers do. For this reason, the relatively cool boiler exhaust can usually be vented out of a thermoplastic pipe right through the wall. There is no need for a metal chimney.

Unfortunately, boiler systems are also very expensive. A gas water heater costs a fraction of a boiler system, so it can be more cost effective upfront to run two gas water heaters at 60% efficiency (one for the radiant system and one for the domestic hot water supply) than to operate one very expensive boiler at 90% efficiency. But before you get excited about the possibility of saving money with two gas hot water heaters, consider that boilers are available with sealed combustion, whereas cheap water heaters are probably not. Most boiler systems will also out last conventional gas water heaters by decades, so there is a definite savings over the long haul.

There are certainly many other kinds of heating systems as well, and the more research you do before hand the better. Just keep in mind that the money saved by not buying a heater can be enough to pay for the materials to ensure that your home is warm enough without one.

Rethinking Appliances
Passive Cold Refrigerators & Other Gizmos

Building a comfortable home and energy-efficient biosphere requires thoughtful planning and design from the ground up. Household heating and cooling are the biggest energy users in the average home, followed by hot water production, so these topics were heavily emphasized in the previous chapters. By following the principles outlined through this book you can virtually eliminate the need for supplementary heating and greatly reduce the cost of generating hot water. Now we can move on to the other energy consuming appliances in the typical home—including refrigerators and freezers, washers and dryers, lighting and all the rest. The focus of this chapter is the steps you can take to buy or build better appliances that will conserve energy and dollars.

To begin with, note that there is a significant difference in the decision-making process for homes connected to the utility grid, versus those that are not. The cost of solar, wind and other home power systems is dropping rapidly, but it is still cheaper for the home power producer to purchase high-efficiency appliances that use little or no electricity, than it is to purchase the power-generating capacity to run inefficient models. For example, a gas cookstove and the propane to fuel it costs much less than the photovoltaic panels and batteries needed to power an electric stove—even if the electric stove is free.

In other words, the cost-effective way to generate all your own electricity is to find extremely efficient appliances or substitutes that do not use electricity, and produce only enough power to run what's left over. In the early 1990's I visited one home that generated 100% of their electricity from less than $1,000 worth of solar panels, but they also used it for little more than a few direct-current lights (like those from an RV) and a radio!

If you are connected to the grid and purchasing new appliances, then it is also desirable to get the most efficient models on the market. The higher cost upfront, if any, will quickly be repaid by lower energy bills.

However, if you are like us—connected to the grid and building on a shoe-string budget, unable to afford new appliances—then it is still cheaper over the long haul to buy less efficient secondhand appliances and simply pay for the extra power. But that doesn't mean you have to pay high power bills.

On the grid or off the grid, with a little forethought and sometimes a little tinkering, you can make a fully functioning house with little need for power at all. The greatest emphasis in this chapter is on the appliances that use the most power, such as refrigerators and freezers, the washing machine and dryer, and lighting. Smaller power loads are covered in less detail at the end.

Refrigerators & Freezers

According to basic physics, cold doesn't exist except as a lack of heat. You cannot generate cold, you can only remove heat. Refrigerators use heat pumps to extract warmth from inside the box, then radiate that heat away through the plate on the back of the unit. The electricity used in the pump is transformed into low-grade waste heat that must also be radiated away. Early refrigerators had the pump on top where the waste heat would rise away from the box, but it was later moved below for aesthetic reasons. Now the pump must work even more to get rid of the heat it is contributing. All that heat could be pumped into a water tank to prewarm the water supply, but that would require designing a house around the refrigerator-water heater system.

The funny thing about refrigeration is that much of North America is already thoroughly chilled for up to six months of the year. People turn up the thermostat and pump heat in the house, ultimately warming up the refrigerator and freezer which must then consume even more energy to keep all that heat out of the food. Clearly there could be some advantage to working with nature to utilize free refrigeration!

The reason we live with such inefficiencies is because it is simple to mass-produce millions of refrigerators and freezers that are exactly alike, and you can put them anywhere and plug them in. We use fossil fuel power as a substitute for brain power and intelligent design. High-efficiency refrigerators are built the same way; they just have more efficient pumps and lots of insulation. Even the most energy conscientious people usually choose these brainless conventional refrigerators, only because they are readily available and few people realistically have the time to design and build their own. Be sure to check out the *Real Goods Solar Living Sourcebook* for more information on the most energy efficient refrigerators and freezers on the market. Also, read on, and consider some of the stimulating alternatives to conventional refrigeration.

Seasonal Cooling: Grocery stores often spend hundreds of dollars each month to refrigerate all their milk, eggs, cheese, meet and vegetables. A few innovative stores have installed pipes, sensors, fans and valves to monitor the outside temperature and to circulate it through the refrigeration units when it is cold enough, saving hundreds, even thousands of dollars each year. A similar system can save energy in your own home, shaving up to ten or fifteen dollars a month off of your power bill through the winter. It would be sensible to design the home so the refrigerator is against a north wall. This is yet one more piece of criteria to factor into the floor plan! Keep in mind that this type of experimentation will void the warranty on a new refrigerator or freezer, so you would be wise to obtain them secondhand.

A very simple approach to a similar end is simply to build the refrigerator into the wall, with the radiator plate and most of the box outside the house. The original ice boxes were often built that way. In this case the refrigerator must be placed on the north side of the house and completely protected from the sun. Note that older refrigerators could work really well in this application, but newer models may have more sensitive parts that would fail in severe weather. After all, they are designed and built to be used indoors. Also keep in mind that rodents could be a problem nesting in the equipment or chewing on the wires. A vermin-proof screen would be required.

A third approach to seasonal cooling is simply to set out jugs of water to freeze, then put them in the refrigerator to reduce the work of the pump. It works well, but it is an easy chore to neglect for people who are already too busy trying to keep up with life.

Annual Cooling: Before the invention and popularization of the refrigerator, the most common form of cooling in northern climates was natural ice. Near urban areas, workers cut blocks of ice from frozen lakes by the hundreds of thousands of tons. The ice was stored in insulated buildings and sold to individuals for their ice boxes all year long. Homesteaders used a similar approach, often building double-framed sheds with a foot of sawdust insulation in the walls and roof. A well-insulated, fully-stocked shed could provide ice enough to last through the summer.

For practical reasons, any ice box strategies used today must be extremely low maintenance, so that you do not have to cut and haul ice in the winter, or deal with transferring small chunks of it to the household icebox the rest of the time. One simple approach would be to build a well-insulated, cone-shaped pond and freeze it solid during the winter, with tubing to circulate a glycol solution to and from the ice box. Freezing water expands harmlessly upward in a cone-shaped pool, rather than outward where it would cause damage. To make a passive cold refrigerator, the pool would be ferrocemented in place with cooling tubes protectively encased inside the cement. The pool would need to be heavily insulated from below, with a removable cover like strawbales on top. Remove the bales in winter and allow the entire pond to freeze solid, then cover it up for the summer. To facilitate freezing, the water may need to be applied in layers, freezing a few inches at a time.

With our house built into the hill, we could have easily built this sort of system so that the warmth of the icebox would thermosiphon uphill beneath the frozen pool, returning cold fluid back to the unit without the need for pumps at all. I hoped to build a system much like that, but in this case, intelligent design work suffered from a very unintelligent mistake during installation.

There are ten feet of earth against the north wall of our house, so I drilled through the concrete about seven feet up, such that the cooling tubes would be low enough to run underneath a pond behind the house. We were not actually ready to build the refrigerator, but we rented a hammerdrill and did as many jobs as we could while we had it. We backfilled everything else, but left a pit right behind the wall to work in.

One rainy night we came home from a wedding, puzzled to discover the entire downstairs pooled in water and mud. All the water off the roof and the hill channeled into that pit and poured through the holes in the wall! The water did no real damage—except to my ego—since the walls and floor are all cement work anyway. Besides the house was empty because we just finished making the terra tile floors. We were just waiting for the tiles to cure and dry completely before grouting them.

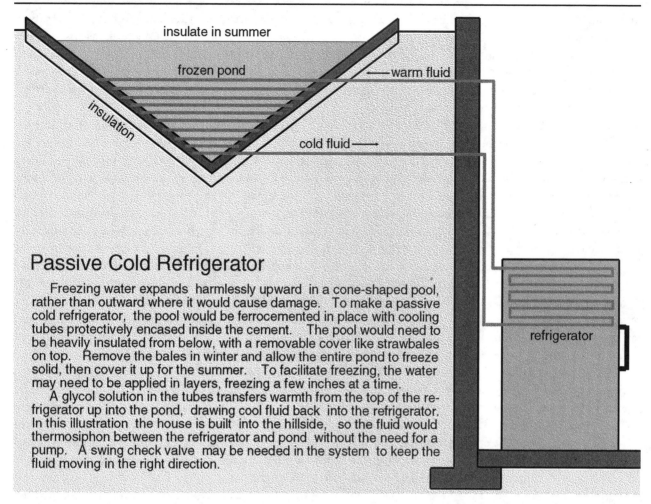

Passive Cold Refrigerator

Freezing water expands harmlessly upward in a cone-shaped pool, rather than outward where it would cause damage. To make a passive cold refrigerator, the pool would be ferrocemented in place with cooling tubes protectively encased inside the cement. The pool would need to be heavily insulated from below, with a removable cover like strawbales on top. Remove the bales in winter and allow the entire pond to freeze solid, then cover it up for the summer. To facilitate freezing, the water may need to be applied in layers, freezing a few inches at a time.

A glycol solution in the tubes transfers warmth from the top of the refrigerator up into the pond, drawing cool fluid back into the refrigerator. In this illustration the house is built into the hillside, so the fluid would thermosiphon between the refrigerator and pond without the need for a pump. A swing check valve may be needed in the system to keep the fluid moving in the right direction.

Drying took a bit longer due to the flood, and we had to clean the mud off all the tiles and out of the joints before we could apply the grout. We immediately mortared over the holes in the wall and backfilled the pit to channel rainwater away from the house. We buried the idea of a passive cold refrigerator right then and there.

Instead we were given an old-style refrigerator, which I completely gutted and rebuilt. I ordered a refrigeration unit from a surplus catalog and adapted it to fit our box, then put in all new foam insulation. Although it lacks some modern amenities, it has worked well enough for the $70 it cost to put it together. Later we bought a second-hand chest-style freezer for $50 to compliment the fridge. But every now and then I find myself dreaming about that passive cold refrigerator. Maybe, just maybe it will still happen.

Evaporative Coolers: Liquids absorb heat from the surrounding air as they evaporate. In the coils of a refrigerator a liquid is released into a partial vacuum, causing instant evaporation which absorbs heat from the box. The heated gas is then pumped outside the box and condensed into a liquid to force the heat off into the surrounding air. This is a closed system, so the liquid ammonia, Freon, or other refrigerant liquid is recycled again and again. An evaporative cooler uses a similar process, but it is exceedingly simple.

One common method of refrigeration in the past was to hang food from a branch in a tree, covered by a wet cloth. Evaporation from the wet cloth absorbed heat and was carried away with the breeze. No doubt you have experienced a similar phenomenon after putting on a wet shirt in a breezy day. Chilling, isn't it?

A Nigerian teacher, Mohammed Bah Abba, invented a simple water-powered refrigerator consisting of two porous clay pots with a layer of wet sand in between them. You could make it out of terra cotta pots from the garden store. Moisture evaporates out through the porous clay, cooling the pots. Nigerian potters have manufactured hundreds of thousands of these "Pot-in-Pot" refrigerators at a cost of about 30¢ each, preserving fresh food where people don't even have electricity. For his contribution, Abba was awarded a $75,000 Rolex Award for Enterprise.

A Pot-in-Pot cooler may be especially handy for people living on the job site where it is impractical to set up a refrigerator. With a little tinkering it should also be possible to design an evaporative cooler completely encased in a box, like a conventional refrigerator. The difference is that it would have a hollow chamber around the box with an air inlet and outlet, with water misted inside. With a bigger and higher air outlet than inlet the system could harness the Venturi effect, sucking the air through without the need for a fan. A project like this would require some research and development, but wouldn't it be a thrill to have a water powered refrigerator? Keep in mind that evaporative coolers work best in arid climates where water evaporates most quickly and easily.

Realistically, most people will purchase conventional refrigerators or their more efficient cousins, but it is still beneficial to consider these other alternatives. At the least, it helps to stimulate the type of creative thinking needed in integrated design work.

Washers & Dryers

Most of the energy used by a washing machine is used to heat the water. Saving water therefore saves energy. The most efficient washing machines are the horizontal-axis models like those found in many laundromats. Now there are top-loading, horizontal axis washing machines available for the home. The tumbling action cleans better with less detergent, using about 2/3 less water, 3/4 less detergent, and 1/2 as much water as conventional washing machines. Be sure to check out the Real Goods *Solar Living Sourcebook* for up-to-date product information. Installing a solar water heating system also helps to reduce the energy consumption of a washing machine.

Finding an energy-efficient dryer is a bigger problem, since it takes heat to dry the clothes. One point to keep in mind is that energy is always lost when low-grade fossil fuels are converted to high-grade electricity. Usually it takes about three units of coal, oil, or gas energy to produce one unit of electricity, although some new technologies are reducing the loss. Therefore, it is more energy efficient to use a gas clothes dryer than to convert that gas to electricity and run an electric dryer.

With that principle in mind, we planned to install a gas clothes dryer in our home, possibly fueled by home-generated biogas, discussed more in the chapter *Wastewater Management and Reuse*. However, we also installed a 240 volt outlet for an electric dryer, just to keep our options open.

For several years we did not install a dryer at all, since there was just the two of us. We waited until sunny weather and hung our clothes out on the line. That strategy worked fine until we adopted our three children. Then the laundry piled up so much during the bad weather that it was difficult to catch up when the sunshine returned. Doing laundry in the winter was the worst, because the good weather was often windy. Our laundry blew all over the yard and it seemed that we constantly had to go dig it out of the snow. The socks sometimes disappeared until spring. Then one day Renee picked up an electric dryer at a garage sale for $30. I seriously resisted the notion of jacking up our nice low electric bills, since I enjoy the sport of seeing how low we can keep the bill each month. But even I had to face reality eventually, that drying clothes on the line wasn't working!

Finally I agreed to hook the electric dryer up temporarily, figuring we could replace it with a gas model later. A gas model would have to be exhausted to the outside, so I ran a pipe up through the roof, the shortest route out. But to increase the efficiency of the system, I built a heat exchanger in my adjacent office by snaking the flexible dryer tubing back and forth along the wall, then encasing it all in concrete. The masonry radiator absorbs some of the heat as the exhaust passes by on the way outside.

It wasn't until I finished building the contraption that I realized my blunder. If the masonry radiator recovered an optimistic one-third of the waste heat and vented the other two-thirds of the heat outside, that would be no more efficient than running an electric clothes dryer and venting 100% of the warm air back inside the house. Worse, a gas clothes dryer would suck cold air in through every little crack in the house to replace all the warm air being pumped outside.

In an arid climate where extra moisture is needed indoors, it just makes more sense to vent the dryer inside, or to have valves to switch it back and forth at will, than to exhaust it outside. You can purchase filtered attachments for a dryer at many hardware stores or build your own with the aid of furnace filters. Be sure to give some consideration to where in the house the dryer is venting to. The humidity could be locally damaging to electronics or woodwork. Venting into a greenhouse, or into a rock bed below a house or greenhouse may be ideal. Keep in mind that too much humidity can be a serious problem in a tight house. I saw a new boiler system badly rusting in one house after the owners vented their dryer in the utility room, *and* plugged in a humidifier for extra humidity. Use of fabric softeners is discouraged in such systems because the chemicals are circulated into the indoor atmosphere.

Note that with home power sources it is still far more efficient to install a gas dryer operated on propane, than to install the extra solar or wind generating capacity to run an electric dryer.

Lighting

Lighting accounts for about 17% of the electrical load of the typical house. Cheap incandescent light bulbs produce good light, but also lots of waste heat. For that reason, light bulbs are often used as a substitute for a mother hen, to keep newborn chicks warm. Compact fluorescent lights are significantly more expensive upfront, but they last much longer and use only about 30% as much electricity to produce the same amount of light. Compact flourescents save more than enough energy over their lifetimes to recover the extra expense. The lightbulbs are best used in fixtures that are on for several hours at a time, such as in the living areas. Compact flourescents work best in moderate temperatures. They are not suited for outdoor fixtures in cold climates. We have also had poor results with the bulbs a kitchen light fixture which is in the path of the hot air from our wood cookstove.

Compact flourescent lightbulbs, like the ones in this fixture, use less than one-third the energy of incandescent bulbs to put out the same amount of light.

The newest lighting innovation is the white LED lights, which should soon replace all others, including compact flourescents. LED lights first appeared many years ago as the glowing red and green lights on computers and other electronics. These lights are extremely useful for the tasks they perform, and they consume almost zero electricity, but they could not be improved for household lighting use. However, the more recently invented white LED light is much brighter and it is quickly revolutionizing the lighting industry. White LED lights first appeared in flashlights, using so little power that the batteries now last an incredible 100 times longer than with incandescent bulbs. For the first time in my life I actually like having a flashlight!

At this writing, white LED lights are being manufactured for RV applications, especially useful for solar powered homes with direct current. LED lights adapted to standard light sockets cannot be too far behind, though it may take a few years for the cost to come down.

Keep in mind that the most energy efficient approach to lighting is to design your home to utilize natural light as much as possible. Sky lighting can be especially helpful to brighten up the interior, but conventional skylights also radiate away the warmth of the house. A much more efficient skylight is the "sky domes" where a small domed window is placed in the roof, with a reflective tube channeling the light into the room below. The light can even be piped down to a lower level of the house. Painting the walls a light color also helps to brighten up the home.

Note that indirect lighting is better to equalize light distribution and to reduce glare. Instead of aiming the light at your workspace, for example, you should aim it at the ceiling so it is distributed more gently. That is a tip I wish I knew when installing lighting in our home. The light in my office has caused the most trouble, reflecting off the computer screen so that I was always looking at a bright spot on the glass. I just ignored it until I realized that bright spot was doing serious damage to my eyes. Turning off my light and working in the dark helped my eyesight to quickly recover, but no one else likes my dungeon! An anti-glare screen for the computer might be an intelligent investment too.

Miscellaneous & Ghost Loads

When you build a house so efficient that it needs little or no auxiliary heating, and install a non-electric water heating system, purchase the most efficient refrigerator, freezer and washing machine, and resolve the issues with drying clothes, then all the remaining electrical loads become exceedingly minor in comparison.

Sure, there are still a few bigger appliances like microwaves, sucking up 1500 watts of power, but products like this are switched off 99% of the time anyway. Computers, televisions, radios and clocks also use power, but it would be difficult to measure any savings in your power bill, if you left one of them unplugged for an entire month. Nevertheless, it is still wise to shop for the most efficient appliances you can get. Although the savings may be negligible in your own home, the cumulative effect of many people making similar decisions can be considerable.

For example, televisions with remote controls still draw current when they are switched off. This is called a "ghost load". The electricity powers a sensor that detects the signal from the remote control to turn the television on. Although the electrical draw for one television is minute, there are so many televisions nationwide that it takes a 500 megawatt power plant running full time just to power all them all when they are turned off! Switching the television off on the set, such that the remote cannot turn it back on, helps to conserve energy.

Other ghost loads include all those portable CD players, battery rechargers, and battery-powered tools that use a transformer to convert a small amount of alternating current to direct current. The transformer draws current as long as it is plugged into an outlet, whether it is in use or not. Be sure to unplug them any time they are not in use.

If you take time to integrate the most energy efficient technologies into your home, then your power bills will always be low, no matter how expensive energy becomes. If you plan to install solar, wind, or some other alternative power source, then these conservation steps

Solar power and other alternative energies become reasonably affordable after you eliminate most of the need for them. This solar array tracks the sun at Sage Mountain Center (www.sagemountain.org).

are even more essential to reduce the cost to produce the necessary electricity. It would be cost prohibitive to buy enough solar cells to power a conventional energy-wasting home, but solar and other alternative power sources are surprisingly affordable when you greatly reduce the need for them! Be sure to consult the *Real Goods Solar Living Sourcebook* for more information on choosing an appropriate power system for your situation.

Air Quality
Finding Fresh Air in an Airtight House

Indoor air quality was an unknown problem in the past when drafty houses continuously let in a supply of fresh air. However, increasingly airtight construction in recent times has created all kinds of problems with stale air, molds and viruses, radon, backdrafting appliances and outgassing volatile organic compounds (VOC's).

For example, particle board, ceiling tiles, adhesives, caulking, paints, stains and varnishes all contain formaldehyde, xylene and toluene, benzene, and alcohols. Chlorinated tap water puts chloroform into the household air, while carpets outgas alcohol. Nail polish remover contributes acetone. Trichloroethylene is outgassed from photocopy machines along with ammonia, which is also present in many household cleaners. Mundane household items, such as draperies, upholstery, paper towels and paper grocery bags and facial tissues outgas formaldehyde. Even our natural body functions outgas significant quantities of many potentially harmful volatile compounds: ethyl and methyl alcohol, acetone, ethyl acetate, xylene, toluene, ammonia and hydrogen sulfide to name a few.

Prolonged exposure to indoor pollutants has led to allergies in many people, ranging from mild irritation to hypersensitivity. Sometimes called "sick building syndrome", common symptoms include allergies, asthma, irritation of the eyes, nose and throat, fatigue, headache, nervous-system disorders, plus respiratory and sinus congestion. At the extreme, there are people who lived without allergies for years only to suddenly reach a certain threshold where their bodies could take no more. A condition called "multiple chemical sensitivity", there is little the doctors can do to help. I have talked with a number of people who can no longer survive indoors. They have been forced to move into tents, often in the backyard, while the rest of the family continues to occupy the house.

Young babies and small children can be especially susceptible to chemical sensitivity, leading to allergies and asthma at an early age. Newborn infants are often brought home to a freshly remodeled nursery complete with new paint, new carpet, a new crib and mattress, plus new blankets, clothing and toys— all of which are outgassing a soup of chemical toxins for the developing baby to inhale.

For the health of your entire family, it is important to create a clean indoor atmosphere—your own personal biosphere. This need to manage the air supply was first addressed in superinsulated houses, which were roughly the equivalent of living in a plastic bag wrapped with insulation. New devices were developed to exchange the polluted air from inside with the fresh air from the outside. The machines were originally called "air-to-air heat exchangers" because the in and out pipes are interwoven so that the heat from the outgoing warm air out transfers to the incoming cool air. The gadgets are known today as "heat recovery ventilators" or HRV's.

Of course, the difference between an air tight house and a true biosphere is that in a biosphere you would recycle your air, rather than swap it for a fresh supply. As you will see, it is possible to do some of both, recycling much of your own air, while continuing to exchange the rest with the outside world.

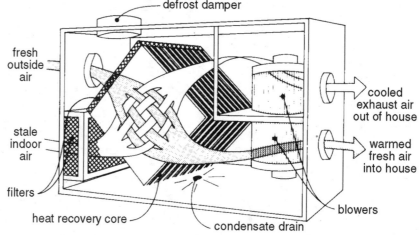

Heat Recovery Ventilator

- defrost damper
- fresh outside air
- cooled exhaust air out of house
- stale indoor air
- warmed fresh air into house
- filters
- blowers
- heat recovery core
- condensate drain

Image Source: Warm Places: A sampling of energy-efficient Montana homes. Montana Department of Natural Resources & Conservation. Spring 1988.

The first key to maintaining good indoor air quality is **prevention**— avoid polluting it in the first place. The greatest danger is from fuel-burning appliances that either vent inside or outside, but take air from the inside. Appliances like furnaces, hot water heaters, gas cookstoves, and fireplaces that burn air from inside the house and vent it outside are especially dangerous because they create a partial vacuum, sometimes causing carbon monoxide to backdraft inside. People die every year because new houses are built tighter than in the past, but not quite tight enough to fully require the specialized appliances used in superinsulated homes.

The solution to the backdrafting problem is "sealed combustion" appliances. Sealed combustion simply means the air supply is piped to the appliance from the outside, and the exhaust is piped back outside. Sealed-combustion appliances became widely available during the 1990s, so you should not have to go too far out of the way to find them.

Incidentally, sealed combustion also increases the energy efficiency of any kind of a house, because fuel-burning appliances use and vent large quantities of air. Without sealed combustion, the only way to replace the air taken from the house (besides backdrafting), is to suck it in through every little leak in the house. In other words, a small leak in house functions like a much bigger leak when a fuel-burning appliance is sucking air through it.

Other types of indoor air pollution should also be minimized as much as practical, especially by using chemically stable products that will not outgas harmful products. Some of the worst products, like urea-formaldehyde foam insulation, were banned or discontinued years ago. Other new building materials, especially paints and carpets, are available today with reduced chemical emissions, but often at a significantly higher price. Sometimes the cost problem can be avoided by completely switching to other substitutes, such as tile floors in the place of carpeting, and stone or stuccoed walls in place of painted ones.

It is also helpful to give ample time for new products to outgas before sealing them in your biosphere, such as installing new carpet only in summer when the house can be ventilated, or assembling and leaving a new crib in the garage for a month or two before the baby is born. Purchasing second hand furniture is an excellent way to avoid the worst of the outgassing problems, while also reducing resource consumption. Any of these tactics will help prevent chemical problems at the source, reducing the amount of pollutants that must be removed from your indoor atmosphere.

The second key to maintaining air quality is to **exchange air with the outside**— which does not necessarily imply installing a heat recovery ventilator. A commercial-grade HRV can cost several thousand dollars by the time it is completely installed, and will ultimately need repairs, so I would encourage you to consider the alternatives.

Traditional superinsulated homes are completely sealed like a plastic bag, mostly to stop drafts through the insulation or around studs, piping, and wiring. But slightly permeable insulation systems, such as strawbale construction, allow a small amount of air to steadily pass through the walls. (Keep in mind that acrylic or latex products should not be used on strawbale walls, because that would reduce or stop the air flow and may potentially trap moisture in the bales.) The air exchange with the outside is slow enough that most of the heat is retained inside the structure. Cementitious foam, although expensive, is another kind of insulation that allows a house to breath without becoming drafty.

Another way to exchange air with the outside is to make the house "more than 100% energy efficient", so you have extra heat to vent to the outside. A superinsulated house with both passive and active solar input and extra thermal mass can offset the heat loss when a small amount of cold air is allowed to leak in. Likewise, a simple solar hot air panel can be used to produce warm air on sunny days, to replace stale air from inside. The extra cost of these projects can be less than the cost of a conventional HRV.

Of course, a heat recovery ventilator doesn't have to be either sophisticated or expensive. You can make a simple HRV with two concrete boxes full of gravel, some piping, fans, and valves. Warm house air is blown out through one bed of gravel, while cool outside air is sucked back through the other bed. The trick is to periodically switch the air flow back and forth, so that the warm house air is being blown out through the cold box, while the cold outside air is being sucked in through the warm box.

Another form of air exchange with the outside is to bury an air pipe deep in the ground, extending some distance from the house, with a stand pipe up to the soil surface. Cold outside air is warmed somewhat by the temperature of the ground on its way into the house. Stale house air can be released elsewhere from the home. The ground pipe must remain dry and free from vermin or mold, or the air supply could become contaminated.

The third key for maintaining air quality is to recycle it through **plant life** within your biosphere. NASA researchers helped to focus attention on the abilities of plants to scrub the air clean of contaminants, especially to maintain air quality on extended missions. Remember—many hazardous indoor pollutants from building materials and other products are also outgassed by living beings. In nature the atmosphere is scrubbed by plants and the microorganisms associated with their root systems. Some chemicals are absorbed by the leaves and broken down into nutrients by the plants, while others are "translocated" (transported) down through the roots into the soil to feed microorganisms.

NASA researchers concentrated their studies on common house plants, typically tropical plants which adapt well to living indoors. Each of the fifty plants tested scrubbed the air of many chemicals, but specific plants were found to be more effective than others at removing certain toxins, according to B.C. Wolverton, author of *How To Grow Fresh Air*. For example, the areca palm (*Chrysalidocarpus lutescens*) removes more xylene and toluene than any other plant tested, while the lady palm (*Rhapis excelsa*) is the most effective at removing ammonia. The peace lily (*Spathiphyllum spp.*) scored highest at removing acetone. Of course there are several hundred thousand other species around the world that were not tested at all. The point is that you probably don't need to worry about which plants excel at removing which pollutants, just use a wide variety and make your house as green as possible.

Plants also release phytochemicals and humidity into the air which suppress airborne mold spores and bacteria, probably for their own self-defense. Studies show that rooms with ample plant life can reduce airborne mold and bacteria by fifty to sixty percent. Keep that thought in mind the next time you have a cold!

The part that is not as clear is the total amount of plant matter required to recycle all of the carbon dioxide you produce, to maintain a fresh supply of oxygen indoors. Studies show that astronauts consume about 2 pounds of oxygen per day, exhaling 2.4 pounds of carbon dioxide in return. It is also known that for every *dry* pound of plant matter produced, about 1.8 pounds of carbon dioxide are removed from the air and 1.4 pounds of oxygen are released. (Since water content varies widely in plants, it is necessary to dry them before figuring the weight.) That means it takes about 1.4 pounds of new dry plant matter each day to meet the oxygen requirements of one adult.

Since most house plants grow slowly, you would likely need a greenhouse stocked with higher growth plants—if you want to completely recycle the air supply of your biosphere. Probably a hybrid of some recycling and some air exchange with the outside would be the most practical. Also keep in mind that no matter how tight you try to make your house, there will always be some leaks, and you will get a blast of fresh air every time you open the door. In addition to providing fresh air, a greenhouse can be an economic asset, a net producer of fruits and vegetables.

The fourth key for maintaining air quality is to keep the **relative humidity** balanced within your biosphere, ideally between 35 and 65%. A lack of humidity can lead to irritation of membranes in the nose, causing increased susceptibility to pollutants and viruses. Too much humidity can cause mold and mildew problems to form. Most conventional houses are too dry in the winter, but in a very tight house it doesn't take long to create an indoor atmosphere that is dripping wet, generating mold cultures, rotting wood, and possibly making you very sick.

The remedy for insufficient humidity is simple: just add more plants and water them generously. Plants use the water and transpire it into the air, similar to the way that we breathe moisture into the air. The clothes dryer can also be converted to a heater and humidifier, by venting it indoors through a filter system that removes all the lint. Avoid using fabric softeners which would add more chemicals to your biosphere.

Excess humidity can be a bigger problem. During very cold weather our greenhouse windows condense large quantities of moisture on the glass at night,

What is relative humidity?

Warm air holds more moisture than cold air. If warm, moist air cools down then the moisture must condense out as precipitation. You can see this in a house on a cold winter day, where warm air chills on contact with cold windows, condensing its moisture load onto the glass. Opening the door of a moist greenhouse on a cold day is spectacular, as the cold air rushes in and condenses the moist greenhouse air into an instant cloud!

Note that in sub-freezing weather the outside air is extremely dry. When it enters the house it warms and expands, creating more capacity to hold moisture, and therefore decreasing the relative humidity even more. Heating systems, especially forced air, can dry the air even more.

Breathing, cooking, bathing, and watering plants all contribute water to the air. In very tight house the relative humidity can rise too high, leading to potential mold and mildew problems.

which subsequently runs down the glass onto the wood framing in the day time. To remedy this problem we water the greenhouse as little as possible during the winter. It is only during warm, sunny spells that we get out the hose and water the greenhouse, but never too much. I wait until spring to soak the entire mass of soil in the greenhouse. An underground drip irrigation system can help put the moisture where it is needed most—at the roots—instead of in the air.

More humid climates require different strategies to maintain a balanced indoor atmosphere. It is still possible to have an a lush greenhouse, but the open soil can contribute too mush moisture. The solution is to garden hydroponically, using containers where the water is always below the surface. The biosphere air treatment systems of the future are undoubtedly plant filters like these, which are also used to treat household wastewater. The nutrient-rich wastewater automatically flows beneath the plant beds, feeding and watering them, so that the plants cleanse the water and the air at the same time. Read more about these water and air filters in the chapter on wastewater management.

Note that especially humid environments may require either an HRV or a dehumidifier to condense out extra moisture, since the fresh air supply may be nearly as damp as the air going out. Any kind of air system that you do install should definitely have filters on it to remove dust and molds.

Radon Gas

Radon is a radioactive gas released from the natural decay of uranium. Radon is found in nearly all soils, although it is more prevalent in some locations than others, especially around granite rock. The naturally occurring level of radon gas in outside air is about 0.4 picoCuries per liter of air (0.4 pCi/L). But radon can seep into a home from the ground below, or to a lesser extent, through the water supply. Increasingly tight homes allow a buildup of radon gas, which would normally disperse in the atmosphere. The problem is exacerbated by fuel-burning appliances that exhaust air out of the house, creating negative pressure. Up to 20% of the replacement air supply can be sucked in from underground, greatly elevating radon levels in the home.

The radioactive particles are inhaled and trapped in the lungs. As it continues to decay, the radon releases small bursts of energy which can damage lung tissue and lead to lung cancer later in life. Any amount of radon is believed to be dangerous, but higher concentrations of the gas elevate the risk. Based on the available data, a lifetime exposure of 20pCi/L of radon gas would result in lung cancer in about 8 out of 1,000 people. Exposure to that level of radon gas, plus cigarette smoking increases the odds of getting lung cancer to an estimated 135 out of 1,000. The EPA recommends taking action to reduce radon levels if the radon level in your home averages 4 pCi/L or higher.

The radon level in a home fluctuates through the seasons, lowest when the windows are open, more when the house is tightly sealed, and the most when the wind blows, which creates negative pressure inside and sucks in replacement air from below ground. Radon test kits are available through most county extension services, or many hardware stores. Short-term tests are the least accurate, but useful to get an approximate measurement. A kit is opened, set out in a living area on a lower level of the house and left for several days or a week. Then it is sealed and mailed in for testing. Long-term kits are better to determine the household average over the course of the entire winter, or even a whole year.

Cosmic Beginnings

The Big Bang that started the universe produced only light elements like hydrogen and helium. These were the sole elements of the first stars. But as those stars grew old, collapsed and exploded as supernova, the light elements were transmuted—basically squashed together—to form the heavier elements that younger solar systems like ours are made of. Some of those heavier elements were radioactive materials with varying half lives, of which Uranium-238 is the most common. It has a half life of 4.5 billion years, meaning that there is half as much of the element left on our planet now, compared to what was here when the planet was first formed.

Uranium-238 decays into U-234 with a half life of 248,000 years, then into Thorium-230 with a half life of 80,000 years. The thorium breaks down into thoron-220 with a half-life of 54.5 seconds, then into Radium-226 with a half life of 1,620 years. Radium-226 breaks down into Radon-222 with a half-life of 3.823 days, resulting in lead, which is stable.

Radon gas is inhaled with the air and trapped in the lungs. As it continues to decay, the radon relieases small bursts of energy wich can damage lung tissue and lead to lung cancer later in life. The EPA estimates that 14,000 Americans die from lung cancer every year as the result of elevated levels of radon gas in homes.

The preferred method of reducing radon levels in a home is to ventilate the space underneath a slab or crawlspace to the outside, although this reduces the energy efficiency of the structure. Older homes with slab floors can be retrofitted by drilling through the concrete and installing a ventilation pipe through the roof. Active systems have a fan to help draw the gas out from under the floor, while passive systems do not. The number of vent pipes required depends on how easily air moves under the slab. A slab on a gravel base is easier to ventilate than one built on solid earth. In homes with a crawl space, a heavy layer of plastic can be rolled out on the floor and the space underneath it ventilated.

Knowing a little bit about radon gas, it would be sensible to take some basic precautions during construction. Some newer buildings have a system of perforated pipes under the floor to collect the gas and direct it outside. Using heavy plastic under the floor would help block the flow of radon gas into the house, making it easier to direct it outside without the need for a fan. To avoid ventilating precious heat from a radiant slab, it may be helpful to create a gravel bed and vent system a foot or two below the floor, or to insulate between the ventilated layer and the radiant floor. Building with earthen materials, including granite rock, is believed to contribute essentially zero radon to the home. The radioactive rock underneath the house is much bigger.

All homes new or old should be tested for radon gas, and retested after any major remodeling projects, especially those intended to make a tighter and more energy efficient structure. Homes with excessive radon levels *and* well or springwater should also have the water tested for radon levels. Additional information on radon gas and mitigation measures is readily available from your local extension service.

Part II
Water Supply
& Management

Water Supply & Management
Squeezing More Use out of Less Water

My interest in integrated house design can be traced back to one event more than any other—the California drought of 1975-1977. Like many other authors I have read, the drought made me conscious of the need for conservation, to get more mileage out of fewer resources. The need for water conservation was hammered in through film strips at school, through reminders at home, and most of all by Dad, when he cut the drain pipe from the shower and routed the waste water to an outside hose. We moved the hose around as needed to water plants and trees beside the house. From the vantage point of my sandbox, I think I saw just about every batch of sudsy water that came spilling out of the hose.

Today Renee and I live on a dry, south-facing hillside here in Montana. The sandy soil holds very little water, so even after a drenching rain it only takes one or two days of summer sunshine to dry the ground and wilt all our plants. Ironically, water conservation is rarely a concern here, thanks to a spring on the north side of the hill and 1100 feet of polypipe that wraps around the hill to our house, supplying us with gravity-fed water. We share the spring with a neighbor, but we still get close to 1500 gallons of water per day, which accumulates in our cistern until we turn on the spigot. Most of the time we leave the hose running a little bit in the yard, because any water that we do not use just spills down the other side of the hill.

The landscape is effectively dormant here for six months of the year in winter, followed by three months of cool, wet spring weather, so the annual water crunch lasts only from July through September, when we frantically race around with the hose, trying to water every tree and bush before they die. At that time of the year we really try to make every drop count.

We are working to reduce the swings in the water cycle with the aid of mulch to improve the water-holding capability of the soil. A simple greywater system helps keep a few bushes and a cattail/iris swamp alive and vigorous throughout the growing season. We are also putting gutters on the house for rainwater collection and we are building a storage pond (20' x 30' averaging about 3 feet deep) to store extra water during the winter and spring to use for irrigation during the dry season. The pond will give us an extra 13,000+ gallons of water to use as needed.

As you may sense here, our water situation is highly unique and we are customizing our solutions to fit the situation at hand. The same is true of most other houses. Retrofitting existing houses especially requires customized design work and many variables beyond the scope of this work, but this text will give you a good overview. Fortunately, for new construction there are fewer variables, so it is possible to make some generalizations that apply to most situations.

First, it is safe to assume for virtually every house that water is scarce. In our case the water supply is limited to what we get from our spring, plus whatever precipitation falls on our house and land. With a well there is a limitation of how fast it refills after all the available water is drawn out, plus the cost of the energy used to pump it out of the ground. For urban hookups there is usually a cost per volume of water used, so the supply is limited to your willingness to pay for it. Some cities still provide unmetered water at a flat-rate per month, but don't plan on that benefit sticking around forever. Installing meters is a cheap way to conserve city-wide water to provide for new homes without expanding the water supply. In all of the above cases there is a cost to heat the water for certain applications such as taking showers and washing dishes.

Second, it is safe to assume that if water is scarce then it is beneficial to conserve it. In our case water conservation gives us more of what we want—a greener, more abundant landscape. For you the advantage may also be a greener landscape and/or monetary savings on your water and energy bills. Good water conservation is simply a matter of thinking about where the water comes from and where it goes to, then closing the loop on waste, so that you get the most use out of the least water at the least cost.

The Water Supply

At most home sites the choices for a water supply are limited. In rural areas you typically have a choice between a well and/or rainwater collection. In the city you have a choice between the city system and/or rainwater, although wells for irrigation may also be permitted in some cities. Other home sites may offer different options, from surface waters such as rivers and ponds, to natural springs, or even desalinized sea water, but for the purposes of this book, only rainwater collection will be covered in any detail.

Rainwater collection systems are most common where rainfall is plentiful, such as in Hawaii where more than 25,000 people depend on the rain for their sole source of water. Only minimal storage capacity is needed in places like that, so rainwater collection often costs less up-front than any other water source. Rain is also about the highest quality source of water and purification is relatively simple.

In arid regions of the country rainwater collection can be much more expensive—if you plan to collect and store enough water during the wet season to extend through the dry season—but the water is also much more valuable. Before deciding to drill a well or hook up to the city supply you should compare the cost of that investment over the next twenty years versus the cost and capacity of a rainwater collection system over the same period of time.

A shallow well is relatively cheap, but in many regions of the country you will have to drill 100 to 200 or more feet to hit water, at a cost of more than $20 per foot. I've heard of household wells as deep as 600 feet, yet for all the expense there is no guarantee of hitting water or much of it. If you do strike water then you still have to pump it back to the surface, a cost which grows more expensive the deeper the well is. Some wells provide only a few gallons of water per minute, requiring the homeowner to supplement with rainwater anyway. The key is to ask your neighbors how deep they had to drill and how many gallons per minute they get from their wells. Ask everyone around, because hydrology is often hard to predict in certain substrates, so you may get widely different results from two neighbors a few hundred feet apart from each other.

If a city hookup is relatively cheap then you should take advantage of it, even if the cost of the water is expensive. You can use a rainwater collection system for the bulk of your supply, and just supplement as needed from the city. You can even have the city water turned off during the wet season, if there are significant fees to keeping it open. In other locations it may cost thousands of dollars to connect to the city supply—if the pipes need to be extended to your building site, or if the city charges an up-front fee for the cost of the existing infrastructure. In these situations it may be most economical to forgo the city water entirely (assuming that's legally possible) to depend solely on rainwater.

Also keep in mind that city or well water can be full of minerals that taste bad or stain your dishes and clothes. The cost of installing and maintaining a complicated filter and water softening system must be considered against the cost of using pure rainwater.

A supplementary rainwater system for irrigation purposes is the most simple to design and build because the capacity doesn't really matter if you are not depending on it. Even a garbage can under the spout of a gutter will capture and store water that can be used as needed. Larger storage facilities can be added to take advantage of available room like a crawl space. You can also build the house without the tank, but leave space to add it later, when you happen to find a good deal on a durable used one. In southern climates the tanks can be freestanding units outside, but in northern regions the tanks must be insulated, built into the house, or buried underground.

To get a rough estimate of the water potential simply consult local weather records for the average annual precipitation. Multiply that number by .62 to figure the gallons per square foot, and that number by the total square footage of the roof to determine the full potential. Measure the roof as if it were flat, since the sloped roof has a greater area, but collects no more water. For example, our house has approximately 1800 square feet of collector area and gets about 19" inches annual precipitation, which works out to 21,204 gallons per year (19 x .62 x 1800 = 21,204). Whether that is a lot of water or only a little depends on what it is used for.

This retaining wall prevents the hill from eroding onto our patio. The planter bed reinforces the base of the wall. A rainwater storage tank is buried behind the wall, with a faucet through the stonework.

For reference, the average household uses 40 or more gallons of water per person per day (excluding outside watering). A four-person household therefore uses at least 58,400 gallons of water per year, although water conserving appliances and a few less showers can dramatically reduce that figure. My family could probably survive off the rainwater from our roof, if we didn't like to water our yard so much. Still, the annual precipitation potential from our roof is the equivalent of two additional weeks worth of water from our spring. We could water a lot of trees with that.

Designing a rain water system as your only source of water is a bit more complicated, because you must also consider the frequency of the rain and calculate how much storage capacity you will need to get through the longest dry spells. The floor plan of the house, garage and other structures can be designed to increase roof area to favor

Water is gravity fed from the storage tank through the wall to the planter bed, shown here during installation. We leave the faucet open through the winter to drain the tank and prevent problems with freezing.

additional rainwater collection, if desired. It is a good idea to expect half as much rainwater and twice as much consumption when designing your system. If you do run out once in a while that is okay, because you can still call for a water truck to refill your tank. There are whole communities that depend on water hauled in by trucks, but it kind of defeats the purpose of a rainwater system if you have to do that too often.

Please note that we live in a very dry place and your region may get much more precipitation, even if it seems desert-like. Our part of the country stays relatively green only because the ground is frozen for half of every year, so the landscape uses 19" of precipitation in six months rather than twelve. You may be surprised at how much water you can collect off of a roof in your neck of the woods.

Rainwater storage systems vary widely and include fiberglass tanks, plastic water bags, galvanized tanks, poured on-site concrete tanks, precast concrete tanks, or even open ponds lined with plastic or concrete. The ideal storage tank should be closed to prevent evaporation and opaque to prevent the sunlight from growing algae in the water. A plastic water bag in the crawl space supported by the foundation walls of the house is one of the cheapest

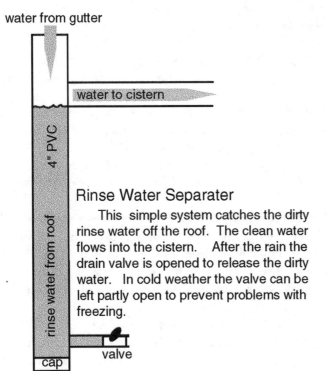

water from gutter

water to cistern

4" PVC

rinse water from roof

cap

valve

Rinse Water Separater

This simple system catches the dirty rinse water off the roof. The clean water flows into the cistern. After the rain the drain valve is opened to release the dirty water. In cold weather the valve can be left partly open to prevent problems with freezing.

ways to store water. Galvanized tanks are relatively cheap up-front, but have limited life-spans. Fiberglass tanks are the most expensive, but also long lasting. The tanks must be made from ATLAC 400 or a comparable resin which is approved by the FDA as inert and safe for drinking water.

Concrete tanks can be relatively affordable, especially if you build your own. A plastic-lined or ferrocement pond will lose water to evaporation and encourage algae and mosquitoes, but a pond is less expensive and more attractive than some of the other alternatives, if the water is for irrigation rather than household use. Special disks called "mosquito dunks" can be added to the water to kill the larvae without contaminating the water. The disks slowly release *bacillus thuringiensis* bacteria to infect and kill the developing larvae.

A smooth and inert roof like sheetmetal is ideal for household rainwater collection. Caution is advised with rainwater from an asphalt roof, which can accumulate enough petrochemicals to feel and taste in the water—enough to be lethal to fish. You definitely do not want to drink that! The water would be fine for irrigating any nonfood plants, but it might be wiser to pick an alternative roofing material. Any rainwater that is used for human consumption should be treated with a sediment filter to remove particulates. Be sure to install an ultraviolet light to kill microorganisms.

You must also consider the placement of the tanks and the need for pumps. The ideal situation is to place the tanks so that they can be filled and used without the need for a pump. For rainwater collection systems it is relatively simple to place a water tank below the downspout but above the yard. For household use it is possible to place the tank lower than second-story downspouts, but higher than the first floor plumbing, however it is probably not economical to do so in most cases. Usually the tank is placed out-of-site beneath the house and a pump and pressurization tank is used to deliver the water at the proper pressure.

Water Efficient Appliances

No matter where your water comes from, you can almost always save money and get more mileage out of the water and energy you use by installing water-efficient appliances. The most obvious water wasters are toilets, showerheads and faucets. Older toilets, for example, used 5-7 gallons of water per flush, while virtually all new models use 1.6 gallons per flush, thanks to more stringent regulations. Ultra low-flush toilets use as little as a quart or pint of water per flush, with the assistance of compressed air. The problem with these miserly toilets is that there may not be enough water to move the solids through the pipes, if there is a long run to the septic or sewer system. Composting toilets use zero water and will be covered in more detail shortly.

The cheap toilet we bought uses only 1.6 gallons per flush, but it doesn't always flush properly, so we sometimes have to flush it two or three times to clear the bowl. A higher quality toilet would have cost more up-front, but saved more water and a certain amount of time!

Older showerheads used 4-6 gallons of water per minute while new ones typically use 2.5 gallons or less. Installing a more efficient showerhead saves water, but it also saves energy, typically $20 or more per year with a gas hot water heater and $50 or more per year with an electric hot water heater. Cheap low-flow showerheads simply restrict the water flow while fancier models aerate the water and send it in pulses to increase the sense of volume.

Kitchen and bathroom faucets also come with aerators (the small screens at the end of the faucet) to restrict water flow while filling it with air bubbles for greater volume. Water-efficient appliances are now standard, but it is still a good idea to check the ratings and ask some questions when you buy. Some models conserve more water and perform better than others. Note that low pressure systems like our gravity-fed water supply may not work well with low-flow devices like faucet aerators. The aerators restrict the water flow so much that it can take forever to fill the sink. We had to remove the faucet aerators (a 30-second job) to increase the flow rate up to the low-flow rate.

Also be sure to check the water and energy efficiency on washing machines and dishwashers. Top-loading washers for laundry use more water, while newer side-loading machines use less water and clean the laundry better. The energy savings from reduced hot water use will easily recover the extra up-front cost of the side-loading machines.

Additional water savings can be attained by channeling waste water from a sink or washing machine into a secondary use, like flushing the toilet, provided there is a small storage reservoir to hold the water until needed. The system must include an overflow outlet to drain excess waste water if the storage tank is full.

Water saving appliances like these can easily save costly water and energy for any household, but the savings are most important if you depend on a minimal water supply from your spring, well or rainwater collection system.

Water Efficient Landscaping

Efficient water use in the house must also be matched by efficient water use outside to get the most of the landscape you want with the least possible water. Cool season grasses like Kentucky bluegrass thrive in cold climates with little water, but there are better alternatives for yards in southern climates. Buffalo grass, crested wheat grass and other species stay greener with much less watering. Reducing the total lawn area in favor of herbs, shrubs, and trees that require little water will make a nice yard with little need for expensive water or maintenance. Ask at your local nursery for shrubs and trees that require the least water. Plant moisture loving species only on the shady side of the house. Also keep in mind that a few carefully selected fruit trees and vegetables will produce a real asset from your landscape, to save you money at the grocery store. Most importantly, preserve as much of the native vegetation as possible when you build your house. Don't level everything in sight when you build. It only creates more work later to replace it all.

Mulch also helps to trap water in the soil and prevent evaporation. Some of our bushes were seriously languishing far from the hose until we started covering the ground with catalogs and magazines for mulch. We covered the magazines with wood chips, lawn clippings or other organic matter to hide the mess. Now the ground is always damp around the bushes, even in the hottest, driest weather, so the bushes flourish with only a couple of waterings each summer. Keep in mind that most magazines and catalogs are printed with inks that include small amounts of toxic heavy metals, so they should not be used around garden vegetables. Still, you should never have to throw out any kind of organic matter, from a piece of paper to a Christmas tree; these are all valuable resources that can be put to use on the landscape. Paper can be used as mulch or compost and tree trimmings can always be used for fuel or chopped into smaller pieces and used for mulch. To save landfill space and get free organic matter, we established a community compost pile on our own property, so our neighbors bring us everything from yard waste to horse manure.

For lack of a rainwater collection system you can add dips or swales into the landscape to catch and hold the water while it soaks in. We dig ditches across our long and steep driveway to channel runoff water to our trees. Some rainstorms barely soak into the ground, but still send a flood of water down the driveway. Our simple ditches can capture an extra ten gallons or more of water per tree from a single storm.

Any actual watering should be done conscientiously to reduce losses to runoff or evaporation. Sprinklers especially lose a large portion of the water to evaporation on hot days before the water hits the ground. Using sprinklers at night for the lawn and drip irrigation for bushes and trees can maximize growth while minimizing water consumption. Drip systems do not have to be expensive. We've collected old garden hoses from the dump, fixed the connectors, and poked holes in where desired to create a permanent watering system.

Every step that you take to close the loop on water waste will give you more of the landscape you want from a limited or costly supply of water.

Important: Building sites with acreage beyond the watered yard can present significant landscape challenges, especially in arid climates. You may think it quaint to have a little bit of rangeland to look at, but it requires concentrated animal impact to recycle dead matter and shelter new seedlings. Cutting up the range with fences ended the historical pattern of grazing by the buffalo and other herd animals, causing a trend towards desertification across most of western North America. Desertification was slow at first, when there was plenty of tight ground cover to aid new seedlings. But with continued rest the bare ground has gradually spread to the point where new seedlings cannot establish on much of our rangeland. Places that I knew as grassy and beautiful as a kid have already turned to bare ground and weeds. For more information on the ecology, restoration and management of arid rangelands, be sure to visit our website (www.hollowtop.com).

Arid rangelands require concentrated animal impact to recycle dead matter and shelter new seedlings. This subdivided range is dying without hooves to work the soil.

Wastewater Management and Reuse
Closing the Loop on Water Waste

One way to make a house more water efficient is to utilize wastewater for irrigating in a greenhouse or yard. Channeling the wastewater from a single source is relatively easy, as my dad did with the shower when I was a kid. Making plans for whole house water recycling is a bit more complicated, mostly due to the sewer water from the toilet.

The toilet water is called "blackwater", whereas all other household water is considered "greywater". In some developing countries the outhouses are placed directly over farm-scale aquaculture ponds, so the nutrients can be utilized by warm water, algae-loving fish. Otherwise the wastes are processed in biogas plants for methane gas and fertilizer, or simply composted. This "night soil" is a very rich and often essential fertilizer. In places where people survive on a tight calorie budget, the loss of nutrients from human waste can seriously threaten future food harvests. I've even heard of one dispute in a developing country where the hosts of a party were accused of getting too much fertilizer benefit in their outhouse, which was eventually resolved by digging into the pile and sending some of it home with the guests!

In this country human wastes are considered a nuisance to be disposed of, but the process of disposal causes more problems. Dumping too much sewage into our waterways massively fertilizes the algae. Dead algae is decomposed by microbes which consume all the dissolved oxygen in the water, ultimately killing the fish. Billion dollar treatment plants remove most of the nutrients, but often the sludge is simply disposed of in landfills. We are still wasting precious resources that could be put to good use, and it is not sustainable. At some point in the future we will have to close the loop on waste so that our city sewers are pumped directly into farms, greenhouses, aquacultures, or even to vats of tissue cultures to grow future food crops.

For the purposes of integrated house design, the key to success is to consider all wastes as valuable resources and strive to get as much mileage from it as you ecologically and economically can—without jeopardizing anyone's health. From a purely technological perspective, the optimal combination for a single dwelling is probably a composting toilet combined with a greywater system. This combination eliminates the need for a septic system or city sewer connection. However, for a variety of cultural, design, regulatory, mortgage, resell, and other site specific reasons the optimal combination may be impractical. In order to make the optimal choice for your particular situation it helps to understand some of the details behind the choices, including septic systems, biogas plants, composting toilets, greywater, and biological treatment or swamp filters.

Septic Systems

After municipal sewer systems, individual septic systems are the most common form of household wastewater treatment in this country. Septic systems involve large storage tanks with internal dividing walls to break down wastes with the aid of **anaerobic** bacteria. Anaerobic bacteria are holdovers from when the planet was young and the atmosphere lacked oxygen. Oxygen is toxic to these microbes, so they survive only in septic systems, organic muds, and in the guts of animals. In a septic system our feces, toilet tissues, soap and kitchen wastes are digested by the microbes, converting most of the solids into a liquid slurry. Any pathogens are destroyed in the process, so the nutrient-rich water that runs out of the tank into the leach field is theoretically harmless. The leach field consists of perforated pipes buried in gravel that allow the water to disperse into the ground. The nutrients and any remaining pathogens are consumed by microbes and plant roots in the soil to keep from soaking into the ground water. Some solids accumulate in the bottom of the septic tank over time, so every few years you have to dig up the lid and hire a septic truck to pump the tank.

While the technology is very sound, septic systems are still responsible for about half of all groundwater contamination in the U.S., mostly due to improper siting of septic systems too close to wells or where the water table is high. The contamination is from nitrates, a form of nitrogen which leaches into the water. Nitrates are good for plants, but not for drinking water. Awareness of the problem has led to septic permits in most areas of the country, with varying levels of cost and red tape. Our rural county is required by the state to issue septic permits. The $40 permit usually involves a site visit (another fee) from the county sanitarian to do a percolation test, and requires a licensed contractor to install the system. However, homeowners can also obtain instructions from the county and perform their own percolation test and submit a site plan to the county. That is a common practice in many rural areas. The percolation test is simply a matter of digging a pit to a certain depth, than filling it with water and timing how long it takes the water to soak into the ground. This test helps determine how large of a septic field is necessary. Photos of the installed septic system (prior to covering it up) can often be submitted by mail to eliminate the need for an on-site inspection. A typical septic system in our area costs less than $1,500 for materials and labor (in 1999 dollars), but you can expect twice that fee in some parts of the country.

Although septic systems do not allow full use of the wastewater and nutrients, the technology is often the best low-cost, low-maintenance choice to treat household water. They are also nearly idiot-proof, so that anyone can operate them with few problems along the way. Most importantly, septic systems are accepted culturally and through regulatory agencies, while many of the alternatives are not. In other words, it can be much more difficult to get a permit or mortgage, or sell your house if you install a composting toilet and greywater system. From that standpoint, septic systems still make sense for wastewater treatment in many households beyond the city sewer system.

However, you should especially consider all the alternatives if you live in an area where septic installation costs are high, or simply not allowed due to a high water table, or if you never plan on moving anyway and you want to experiment with truly closing the loop to make use of all your wastes. Composting toilets, especially commercial models are becoming accepted in many parts of the country already where the water table is too high for septic fields.

There are also some hybrid options worth considering. The most simple option is to install a conventional septic system, but plant trees along the drain field to utilize the water and nutrients. Over time the roots will migrate into the perforated pipes and ultimately clog them, so it is important to install a 90° elbow extending above the soil

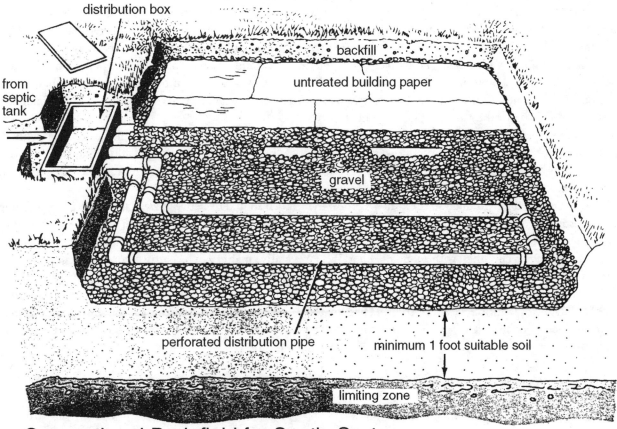

Conventional Drainfield for Septic System

Adapted from Mississippi Department of Health Form No. 309, "2.0 Regulation Governing Individual Onsite Wastewater Disposal." November 1992.

from the end of each drain pipe. Put a cap on the pipe for future access, so that a derooting service can cut out all the roots as necessary. Even with derooting, there is a likely chance that the pipes may become permanently clogged and you will eventually have to install a new drainfield. Another option is to install a conventional septic system for blackwater wastes, while utilizing some or all of your greywater wastes for irrigating, as discussed more in the section under greywater. A third option is to convert your septic system into a biogas plant, which has great potential, but also many complications.

Biogas Plants

In principle there is very little difference between a septic tank and a biogas plant, except that a biogas plant is designed to capture useful gas from the septic process. The annual waste from one person is enough to produce about $40 worth of gas, not including yard wastes, kitchen scraps, or other organic matter. Forty dollars person may not seem like a large amount of money, but worldwide it is a $240 billion asset virtually untapped. Add kitchen scraps and yard wastes to the mix and the gas potential can easily be doubled. If you drive by a city sewage plant and see a large gas torch burning uselessly in the air, it is the methane gas generated by thousands of your neighbors eating pizza and beer. Slowly those gas torches are disappearing as city planners realize how much money is going up in flame. The gas is being tapped to heat local buildings, or used to generate electricity.

For septic-scale biogas plants it would be best to not depend on the gas, but to use it as a supplementary fuel source. For example, you could use it to preheat water before sending it on to your primary water heater. That way you would benefit when you have a gas supply, but you would not run short of hot water if you ran out of gas.

Biogas consists of 60-70% methane (CH_4), 1% hydrogen sulfide (H_2S) and the rest carbon dioxide (CO_2). Natural gas is about 95% methane, so there is less energy value in biogas than in an equal volume of natural gas. Water vapor in the biogas should be removed with the aid of a condensation trap prior to use. The hydrogen sulfide can be removed by passing the gas through steel wool, or some other source of iron oxide. The carbon dioxide may be removed by running the gas through a lime-water solution, but this step is not necessary for most applications.

Most authorities consider home-scale biogas plants uneconomical, which is true, but if you have to install a septic system anyway, then the added cost of converting it into biogas production is almost nil. With some experimentation I believe it would be possible to mass-produce a modified septic tank that generates a usable amount of gas for home use from household and yard wastes. More than 200,000 similar digesters are already in use in India and more than 30 million Chinese depend on biogas for household use and farm equipment. The plants built in these countries are usually round in design, because that is the strongest shape that can be made with little money and poor quality materials. Our septic tanks are rectangular in shape only because we have different tools and materials at hand; they work just the same for biogas production.

Biogas plants fall into two categories: **batch plants** and **continuous plants**. Batch plants are filled with an optimal mix of organic matter and produce a single batch of gas before the tank is emptied and refilled every several weeks or months. Continuous plants take in a small amount of waste each day and produce steady flow of gas, much more desirable for our purposes.

For optimal gas production the ratio of carbon to nitrogen should be between 20:1 and 30:1, and this is one of the reasons we do not have household biogas plants in this country, since it takes a certain amount of thought to run them well. Human feces have a C/N ratio of about 8:1, so it is helpful to add other organic matter with more carbon, such as grass clippings, with a ratio of about 35:1. Vegetative matter can be partly composted first for greater efficiency, but uncomposted matter may work fine in converted septic tanks, which operate slowly anyway.

The digestion process proceeds in two phases. In the first phase protein, carbohydrates and fats are converted to fatty acids, amino acids and alcohol. These materials are converted to methane, carbon dioxide and ammonia in the second phase. The length of time to produce a batch of gas depends mostly on the temperature of the slurry. A hotter tank allows you to produce more gas in much less time:

-psychrophilic digestion takes place at 10-20 °C (50-68 °F) over 100 days
-mesophilic digestion takes place at 20-35 °C (68-95 °F) over 20 days
-thermophilic digestion takes place at 50-60 °C (122-140 °F) in as little as 8 days

As you can see the warmer temperatures are more desirable, but less practical. Hi-tech biogas plants are sometimes built to produce lots of gas from limited tank space by digesting it quickly at high temperatures. The

Septic Tank Converted to Biogas Plant

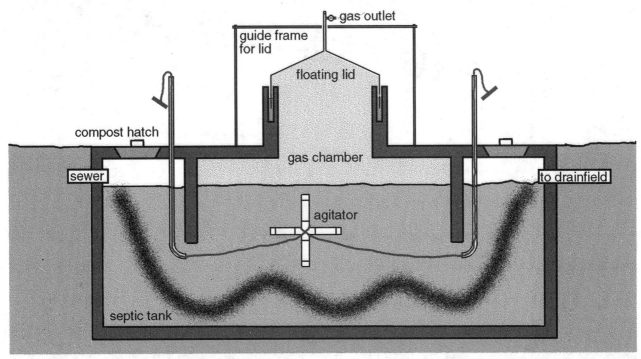

simple digesters in India and China take advantage of a warm climate to digest wastes in the mesophilic range, and that is a possibility across our southern states. At temperatures below 68° methane production is seriously inhibited, but still takes place slowly. Any little bit that the temperature of the tank can be raised will help speed gas production.

The septic tank biogas plant shown here would suffice for southern climates where the ground is always warm. Note that not all septic tanks come in the same configuration. This tank design is easily adapted for biogas production. Limited quantities of compost (kitchen scraps, lawn clippings, leaves, dog crap, organic kitty litter, etc.) could be added each day. The tank agitator helps mix the nutrients with the bacteria and breaks up surface scum so the gas can rise up. This simple agitator is made of 1 1/2" PVC pipe, using a 4-way "T", four short pieces of pipe and 4 end caps. The pieces are glued together to make a floatable cross and a tug on the rope agitates the tank. There are undoubtedly better agitator designs, but this one is certainly simple.

The floating lid is helpful to pressurize the gas; it rises and falls according to the volume of gas, delivering about five pounds of pressure to the appliances. This design is an adaptation from the round systems used in India, based on the work of Ludwig Sasse in his book, *Biogas Plants*. Be sure to refer to his work or others for additional details if you are seriously interested in biogas production. Also note that using your septic tank for biogas production will require more frequent pumping. You might want to get your own pump, so you can keep the nutrient-rich sludge for landscaping fertilizer. Local laws may require the sludge to be taken to a city sewer plant for additional treatment. Biogas production may also shorten the life of the drainfield, especially if the tank is not pumped regularly. Be sure to read about swamp filters as a potentially better alternative to drainfields for biogas plants.

Although our septic system is otherwise entirely conventional, we made some modest additions to enable future methane production here in our cold climate. We placed two inches of beadboard insulation around the outside of the tank before burying it to insulate it from our cold Montana ground. Then we built our solar/strawbale chickenhouse over the top of the tank to help keep it warm and to provide an extra source of organic matter in the form of chicken manure and straw. The idea is to sweep a small amount of matter off the floor each day into the tank. Our chickenhouse has a concrete floor with three access lids to the chambers below. I mopped fiberglass resin over the whole floor to keep gas from seeping up through the concrete into the chickenhouse.

Some important cautions are in order for dealing with biogas. First of all, the gas is very explosive in the air. If it leaked into a room and you flipped a light switch, the spark on the switch could blow the room apart. There must also be a stop in the gas line to prevent the flame from running down the line and blasting the tank apart. A wad of steel wool in the pipe (also used to scrub out the hydrogen sulfide) is supposed to be sufficient.

Septic Tank Converted to Biogas Plant with Chickenhouse

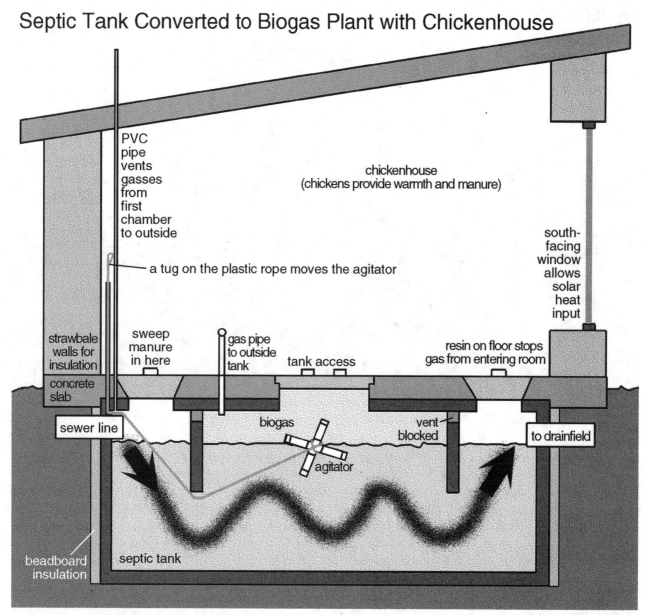

PVC pipe vents gasses from first chamber to outside

chickenhouse
(chickens provide warmth and manure)

south-facing window allows solar heat input

a tug on the plastic rope moves the agitator

strawbale walls for insulation

sweep manure in here

gas pipe to outside tank

tank access

resin on floor stops gas from entering room

concrete slab

sewer line

biogas

vent blocked

to drainfield

agitator

beadboard insulation

septic tank

Finally, hydrogen sulfide, which you will recognize by its rotten-egg smell, is a deadly gas in sufficient concentrations. As I understand it, a person would drop dead or unconscious immediately if there is enough of it in the air. Supposedly, some individuals have died when they jumped down into a septic tank (for inspection?) after the tank was pumped dry, but while there was still gas inside. Precautions must be taken to prevent serious accidents when working with biogas. It is for these reasons, and the fact that I am extremely busy already, that I have not yet finished our own biogas plant, even though it is 95% complete. I will consult with several experts in the field prior to finishing our system.

Keep in mind that these kind of modifications to a septic system are not likely to be embraced by your county sanitarian. In our case, we got a septic permit and installed the system entirely according to specifications... then we added a few extra parts. Technically speaking, we did not take away from the septic system at all, we only added to it. In other words, we are operating in a gray area of the law. That may be the best you can hope for, until there is a proven and standard system for converting septic systems into biogas plants.

Whether or not septic-biogas plants prove to be economical for a single dwelling, the technology is definitely sound for larger facilities, such as a residential development. A centralized biogas plant can economically provide gas for a community center, providing all the fuel needed to heat a community spa. Although it would require some engineering, it is probably easier to get a permit for a community-scale biogas plant—involving about the same amount of effort as it would take to permit any other sewage treatment system of similar size.

Composting Toilets

If you stop and think about it, it is a shame to spend so billions of dollars building dams and water treatment facilities to make safe, drinkable water, which we then defecate in and flush down the toilet to another treatment plant where we spend billions more dollars trying to unpollute the effluent as much as possible before discharging it into a beautiful river. If whole communities switched to composting toilets it would save enough water to serve many more households without building any new dams, or it would greatly reduce the amount of energy now used in pumping and treating that water. Composting toilets can reduce household water use by 20-50%.

The key difference between a composting toilet and a septic system is that composting is an **aerobic** process utilizing microorganisms that breathe oxygen. A composting system must have plenty of air to work properly. If the compost becomes saturated with liquids and unable to breathe, then it turns septic and starts to smell bad. The biggest challenge to making a good composting toilet is to separate out, or soak up the urine, to keep the pile properly aerated. There are many home-built composting toilets with serious shortcomings, but there are also many that work really well.

Composting toilets will decompose anything organic, including kitchen scraps, egg shells, paper, cardboard, lawn clippings, plus tampons (not the plastic part) and clothes or diapers made from natural fibers. Note that kitchen scraps may attract flies and other insects in some installations.

Composting generates heat, at least in warm climates, which kills pathogens and viruses, making the resulting humus safe to use in the yard and garden. In cool climates the composting process may slow down to the point where the pile does not perceptibly produce heat. However, with time it will compost, and the microbes will consume everything in the pile. If there is any doubt about how well it is composted, then the finished humus may be moved to an outside pile in summer and mixed with leaves or lawn clippings for additional composting. Heavily insulating the compost chamber, or using a completely indoor design, will help maintain compost pile temperatures. Supplying solar heat into the composting chamber can help to dry up the urine and warm the pile, but there is a risk of drying out the fecal matter too, creating an uncomposted stalagmite.

Like biogas plants, composting toilets come in two basic designs, batch systems and continuous feed systems. Batch systems are usually very simple, whereas continuous feed systems are often much more complex.

The most simple composting toilets consist of a seat over a five gallon bucket hidden inside a wooden box. The wooden box includes a ventilation pipe to the outside to carry away odors. The toilet seat should have an airtight lid over it to prevent any possible odors from entering the house. A fan should be installed in the ventilation pipe to automatically switch on and vacuum out odors when the lid is lifted. A handful of sawdust, peat moss, or other organic matter is thrown in each time the toilet is used to soak up urine and cover the pile. When the bucket is full (a "batch") it is removed and set aside to continue composting, and a new bucket is put in place. Small containers may not generate enough heat to kill all pathogens on their own, so it is helpful to put the "finished" compost into an outside compost pile with greater mass for insurance in killing all pathogens.

A variation of the bucket composter, but with greater capacity can be made in a house with a basement, by extending a pipe from the toilet straight down through the floor to a full-sized plastic garbage can on wheels. The lid

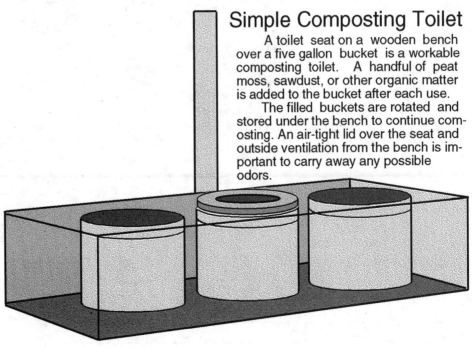

Simple Composting Toilet

A toilet seat on a wooden bench over a five gallon bucket is a workable composting toilet. A handful of peat moss, sawdust, or other organic matter is added to the bucket after each use.

The filled buckets are rotated and stored under the bench to continue composting. An air-tight lid over the seat and outside ventilation from the bench is important to carry away any possible odors.

of the garbage can is modified to make an air tight connection to the delivery pipe. A ventilation pipe to the outside is also connected into the garbage can lid. When the garbage can is full it is simply disconnected and wheeled out-of-the-way to continue composting, while another garbage can is put in its place. These bucket-style composters can be home-built very easily. There are also commercial models based on the same principles.

A slightly more sophisticated version of the bucket composter is a perforated bucket placed on a slightly sloping, watertight surface, so that the liquids drain out the holes and flow through a pipe outside into a miniature leach field or swamp filter. The holes also let air into the buckets, improving the composting process. The advantage

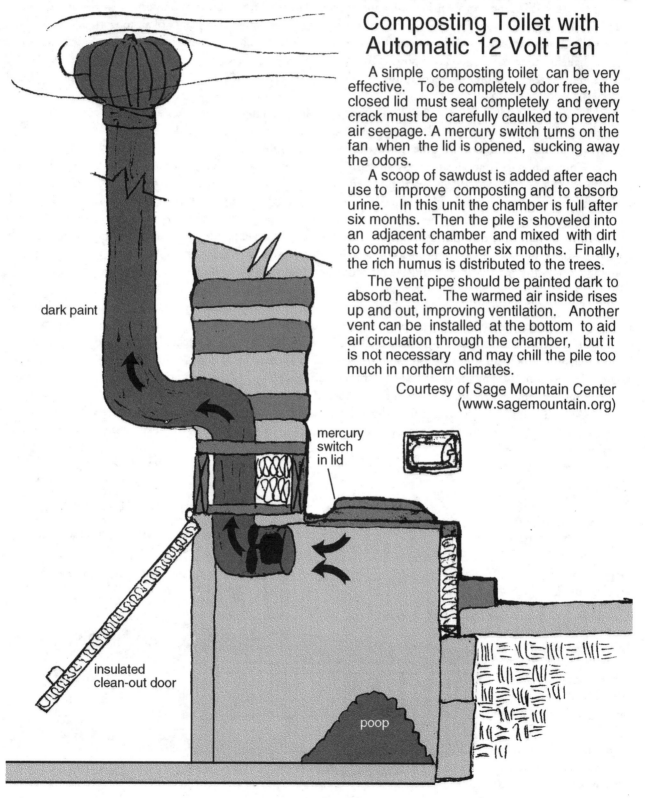

Composting Toilet with Automatic 12 Volt Fan

A simple composting toilet can be very effective. To be completely odor free, the closed lid must seal completely and every crack must be carefully caulked to prevent air seepage. A mercury switch turns on the fan when the lid is opened, sucking away the odors.

A scoop of sawdust is added after each use to improve composting and to absorb urine. In this unit the chamber is full after six months. Then the pile is shoveled into an adjacent chamber and mixed with dirt to compost for another six months. Finally, the rich humus is distributed to the trees.

The vent pipe should be painted dark to absorb heat. The warmed air inside rises up and out, improving ventilation. Another vent can be installed at the bottom to aid air circulation through the chamber, but it is not necessary and may chill the pile too much in northern climates.

Courtesy of Sage Mountain Center
(www.sagemountain.org)

dark paint

mercury switch in lid

insulated clean-out door

poop

to this improved version of the composter is that you do not have to add peat moss or other organic matter every time the toilet is used to sop up the liquids. Any peat moss, potato peels or other organic matter will improve the composting process, but you don't have too worry about creating a stench when you run out of peat moss for a few days. Note that the liquids drain may be prone to clogging.

A larger composter can be custom built into a house, as illustrated here. Use concrete block for as much of the construction as possible, or at least exterior grade plywood coated with floor paint. Do not use galvanized metal or aluminum to line the box, as it will be corroded by the urine. A scoop of sawdust is added with each use to improve composting and absorb urine, eliminating the need for the leachfield. To be completely odor free, the

A simple and inexpensive composting toilet. Sawdust is added after each use from the lidded bin beside the toilet. Courtesy of Sage Mountain Center (www.sagemountain.org).

closed lid must seal completely and every crack must be carefully caulked to prevent air seepage. A **mercury switch** turns on the fan when the lid is opened, sucking away the odors. The mercury switch consists of a small glass bubble with two wires protruding into the inside. When the bubble is tilted, a bead of mercury rolls back across the wires, making electrical contact between them.

When the unit is full, the partially composted matter is shoveled into another chamber and mixed with dirt and/or other organic matter for further composting. Finished humus is then distributed on the landscape, such as around the base of trees. We may have used this kind of composting toilet in our house, but the only designs I was familiar with at the time were the continuous feed systems which require more subfloor space than we had to work with. A unit like this can be built for very little expense.

The purpose of the more complicated (usually continuous feed) systems is to further reduce the level of thought required to properly maintain a clean composting process. Air baffles, injected air, and mixing tools help increase aeration of the pile to encourage thorough and odorless composting. Solar or electric heat is sometimes used to evaporate liquids (if there is no leachfield or swamp filter) or to raise the temperature of the pile to encourage composting and to destroy pathogens. Nonelectric models combined with leach fields or swamp filters are better in the long run to conserve energy. Worms can also be added to increase the quality of the composting process. Commercially available models like the well-known Clivus Multrum take material in at one end and deliver finished compost out the other, which must be emptied once or twice a year. Up-to-date information on commercial composters and plans for do-it-yourselfers can be found on the internet at http://www.compostingtoilet.org and other sites.

Note that **ultra low-flush toilets** (1 pint per flush) can be used with some composting toilets, which is helpful if there is a second toilet some distance from the composter. However, any time water is added to the pile it must be removed again, usually by solar or electric heating or a fan.

Most commercial units cost more up-front than a septic system, although they are usually built to last as long as your house, while most septic systems eventually require significant repairs or replacement. The best systems require at least four feet of accessible under floor space. Homemade units can usually be built for much less than the cost of a septic system.

Proper sizing of the composting toilet is very important. Many units are designed to handle the wastes of only a couple people. A composting toilet must have the capacity to handle the wastes of everyone now or expected in the household, plus it must be able to handle "shock loadings" of parties or company, without overloading the system and creating foul odors.

Be sure to research local codes before installing a composting toilet, if codes matter in your area. Commercial composters have a proven track record, so you can usually get a variance for them, provided you take time to work with the bureaucracy and provide all the printed information they need to be assured that the toilets are safe and effective. Note that many locations only require a permit for installing a septic system. If you are not installing a septic, then it may be better to avoid engaging the bureaucracy at all— assuming there is no one other agency to do a general household inspection. When you install a composting toilet and eliminate the need for a flush toilet, then it is quite easy to deal with all other household wastes through simple greywater or swamp filter systems.

Greywater Systems

Once you have formed a plan to handle sewage wastes then it is relatively easy to deal with all other household wastewater, called greywater. Greywater systems can be very simple, like the hose my dad attached to the shower drain, or more elaborate, such as a whole house drain to a centralized filter and underground distribution network. The best systems are those that treat the wastewater beneath the soil surface, away from human contact. But there is no need to make a greywater system too complicated. A low-cost greywater system can save you thousands of gallons of water every year, enabling you to produce a more beautiful yard with less expense for water.

All household greywater can be used for irrigation including showers, sinks, washing machines, dishwashers, and the kitchen sink. Some people do not like to use kitchen water because of all the gunk and grease that comes down the line. However, all that gunk is also full of valuable nutrients. As long as you do not have a diet that is too heavy on grease, then kitchen water can be very good for irrigating. Just be sure to use bigger rocks at the end of the drainpipe to make lots of open space for the water to discharge. Otherwise the gunk will back up and clog the pipe. Alternatively, you can install a simple nylon mesh filter and distribution box.

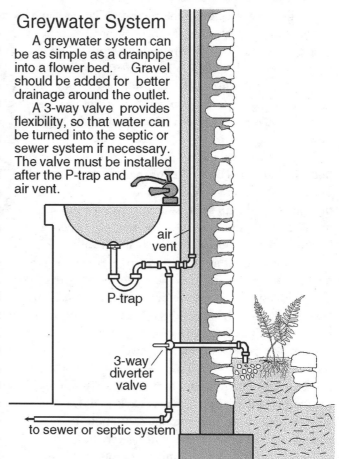

Greywater System

A greywater system can be as simple as a drainpipe into a flower bed. Gravel should be added for better drainage around the outlet.

A 3-way valve provides flexibility, so that water can be turned into the septic or sewer system if necessary. The valve must be installed after the P-trap and air vent.

air vent

P-trap

3-way diverter valve

to sewer or septic system

A distribution box is also helpful for large volumes of water, if you have greywater from several sources channeled into one pipe. The distribution box should not be used to store water for future use, as it will turn septic if the wastewater is allowed to sit. Instead the distribution box simply holds the overload until it can seep out through a series of perforated drainpipes. A 30 gallon plastic drum makes a good distribution box. Newspapers often order ink in 30 gallon drums, so you may be able to pick up the empty drums for free. The lid must be accessible and removable. The drum can be placed in a basement or outside, but it must be fully insulated in northern climates.

If you have a sewer or septic system then it is advisable to keep all options open by installing 3-way diverter valves in the drainpipes. That way you can run most greywater outside to the plants, but you can always choose to switch it to the sewer line if the need arises. For example, if someone in the house has an infectious disease, or if you plan to sell the house, then you should turn the wastewater back into the sewer line. This sort of greywater system is legalized in California and overlooked in most other states.

Three-way valves may not be readily available at plumbing supply shops, but you can usually order them through hot tub dealers. Installing two regular valves takes more spaces, but may cost less.

With a greywater system you have to be conscientious of what you put down the

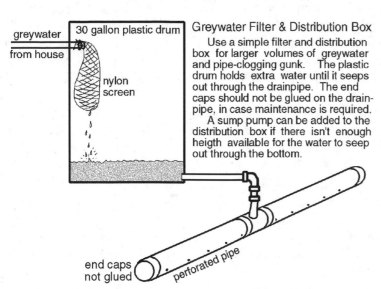

greywater from house

30 gallon plastic drum

nylon screen

Greywater Filter & Distribution Box

Use a simple filter and distribution box for larger volumes of greywater and pipe-clogging gunk. The plastic drum holds extra water until it seeps out through the drainpipe. The end caps should not be glued on the drainpipe, in case maintenance is required.

A sump pump can be added to the distribution box if there isn't enough heigth available for the water to seep out through the bottom.

end caps not glued

perforated pipe

drain, or you may kill your favorite plants. Any strong cleaners like bleach should be avoided or diverted to the septic or city sewer. But keep in mind that even septic systems rely on biological activity to function properly, and city sewers ultimately pour into rivers or lagoons. A greywater system reminds you that you need to always think more carefully about what goes down the drain.

Please note that greywater systems are best used in dry ground far above the water table. Contamination of the groundwater is possible if the greywater reaches it without being cleansed by plants and microbes. Be sure to read the booklet *Create an Oasis with Greywater* by Art Ludwig for additional details and ideas on greywater systems. More sophisticated greywater systems can be built using the closely related principles of biological treatment or swamp filters.

Biological Treatment Or Swamp Filters

Greywater systems apply wastewater to the land for plants and microbes to treat and use it. The water is both treated and dispersed through the process. Biological treatment or swamp filters also use plants and microbes to treat the water, but the difference is that the cleansed water is retained and may be used for subsequent irrigation or even recycled for household use. Even sewer water or "blackwater" can be fully cleansed for reuse.

Biological treatment utilizes a series of tall, clear tanks containing algae and other water loving plants and microbes, eventually becoming clean enough for tanks with fish and freshwater snails. Like swamp filters, the purified water is typically cleaner than the original fresh water source. Biological treatment can work well for a community, but may require more maintenance than is practical for the individual home owner. Thus the principle focus of this section is on swamp filters.

Swamp filters come in two different forms. One form is simply a swamp filled with water-loving plants. A swamp filter built in San Diego uses water hyacinth plants to purify a million gallons of water a day for reuse. A cattail swamp in Saskatchewan purifies wastewater from the 5,000 people of Humbolt, while providing critical waterfowl habitat. Much of the natural swamp land has been filled in for agriculture, so these artificial swamps are

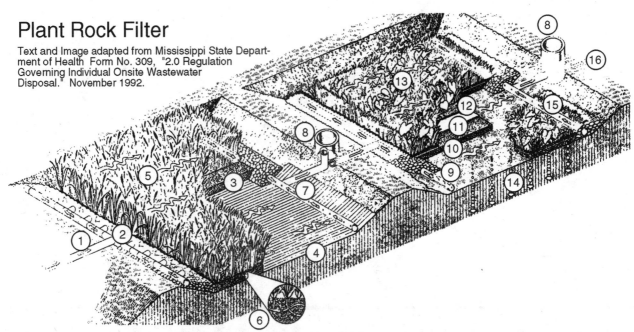

Plant Rock Filter

Text and Image adapted from Mississippi State Department of Health Form No. 309, "2.0 Regulation Governing Individual Onsite Wastewater Disposal." November 1992.

Wastewater enters the filter (1) where it is distributed evenly across the width of the first cell through a series of plastic PVC tees (2). The first cell contains gravel (3). A waterproof liner is used on the sides and bottom of the first cell to conserve water and provide more effective treatment (4). Cattails and bulrushes are usually planted in the first cell (5). The roots of these marsh plants form a dense mat among the gravel (6). Here chemical, biological and physical processes take place which purify the water. Water from the first cell passes into the second cell via a perforated pipe embedded in large stone (7). The water level within each cell is regulated by swivel standpipes located in concrete tanks at the end of each cell (8). Wastewater in the second cell is distributed evenly across this cell through another perforated pipe (9). Cell 2 has a layer of gravel (10) covered with topsoil (11) and then mulch (12). This cell is planted with a variety of ornamental wetland plants such as iris, elephant ear and arrowhead (13). The water in cell 2 eventually seeps into the soil below (14) or passes into another perforated pipe (15) where it is released into a drainfield or discharged over land.

helpful to replace what has been lost. Home-sized swamp filters can be built by making shallow ponds lined with heavy plastic and planted with water-loving plants. The main drawback to city-scale swamp filters is that they take a lot of land, and land is expensive in the city.

The other type of swamp filter is similar, but the water is hidden beneath a layer of coarse gravel or rock, and the swamp plants grow up through the gravel. It is usually called a **plant rock filter.** It is the most common type of swamp filter for household water treatment.

A plant rock filter can be made as a single trench lined with heavy plastic and filled with gravel and ornamental swamp plants. The trench should be a minimum of 100 feet long, but it can wrap around the borders of a yard for a decorative flower bed. The standard dimensions are 18" deep and 12" to 36" wide, filled with 1/2" to 1" gravel. There should be at least 300 square feet of filter bed for a house with three or fewer bedrooms and at least 400 square feet of filter bed for a house with four or more bedrooms. There should be at least four inches of fall from the outlet of the septic tank to the outlet from the end of the plant rock filter. The treated water may be discharged over land or used for other irrigating purposes. The swamp filter shown here is more complex and more compact.

But before you get too excited about treating wastewater with a swamp filter, please note that the technology is appropriate for greywater OR for the effluent from a septic tank, but it is NOT a substitute for the septic tank. Swamp filters can replace the drainfield of a septic system, but not the tank itself. Plastic-lined swamp filters are especially used in southeastern states like Mississippi where the water table may be too high for septic drainfields. Swamp filters may be used without the septic tank only if treating greywater.

In theory you could completely close the loop on wastewater with the aid of a swamp filter (except for water lost to evaporation or transpiration) so that you could run a household on a very limited water supply, such as rainwater in a very dry desert. However, few people have the need to completely recycle their wastewater, since there are always plants that need water too. It just makes more sense to "downcycle" wastewater from higher uses (showers, etc.) to lower uses (irrigating).

Part IV
The Nuts & Bolts
of Home-Building

Footings, Foundations and Floors
Starting From the Bottom Up

The footings and foundation support a house and anchor it to the ground. It is well worth the investment up-front to build a sure-footed house to withstand the test of time. But there are many different designs for footings and foundations and many cost variables, so how do you design a system that's best for your situation? In this chapter we will consider many variables, starting with standard footings used in frame construction, so that you will be able to weigh the options and make an informed decision.

Standard Footings are made as deep as the foundation wall is thick, and twice as wide. For example, a six-inch thick foundation wall has a footing six inches thick and twelve inches wide. An eight-inch foundation wall has a footing eight inches deep and sixteen inches wide. See the illustration on the next page.

Houses built on **soft soils**, including soft clay, fine sand, or soils deep and rich in organic matter may need wider footings, especially in very wet conditions. The footing must be wide enough for the house to "float" on the soft ground. The table shown here shows how much house weight each square foot of the footing will support. You do not need to consult the chart unless your building site seems especially soft or wet. Houses can also be built on **pylons** in wet or soft ground, useful for frame, log, or strawbale construction, but not realistic for masonry houses.

Most house-building books show footings that are

Soil Strength for Footings

Base	Supports Weight of:
solid rock	40 tons per square ft.
soft rock	8 tons per square ft.
coarse sand/gravel	4 tons per square ft.
hard, dry clay	3 tons per square ft.
fine clay/sand	2 tons per square ft..
soft clay	1 tons per square ft.

Adapted from *Low-Cost Energy Efficient Shelter*,
by Eugene Eccli. Rodale Press. 1976.

"keyed" to tie in with the wall and to help keep out water, but I have never yet seen a footing poured that way. Usually the footing is troweled off flat and short lengths of rebar are inserted into the wet concrete, protruding straight up. Stone or cement block have often been used for foundations in the past, but poured concrete is usually the best choice for strength and economics today, unless it is impractical to bring a cement truck into your location.

The footing should be placed below the maximum **frost line**, at least in theory. In Montana the maximum frost line is three to four feet below grade, but most footings here are buried only about 2 1/2 feet deep, unless local codes specify more. The danger is that water expands with tremendous force as it freezes; so wet soil can easily crack a foundation or lift one side of a house. Soils with a high clay content can also swell when wet, wreaking havoc with a house. However, in either case, there must be a significant quantity of moisture in the ground to cause problems. In regions with perennially dry or well-drained soils there is relatively little risk of heaving or settling. Also, there is always some warmth from the house entering the surrounding ground, so the frost line isn't as deep near the building.

Footings for Stone Walls: Footings for stone walls are similar to those used in frame construction, just bigger. We've always built our stone walls to the same thickness as dimensional lumber, so the door and window frames would fit right in the forms. For a stone wall faced on one side only, we used 2 x 10 lumber, which is really 9 1/4" wide. Based on the formula for footings in standard construction we used 2 x 10's for the formwork, so our footings were 9 1/4" deep and about 18 1/2" wide. (You may need to read the chapter on stone masonry for these figures to make sense.)

As the walls become bigger then the standard formula for footings becomes cumbersome. Within each house we often build stone walls of several different thicknesses, 9 1/4", 11 1/4" and 18 1/2". According to the formula the footings should be the same depth and twice as wide, but that would mean complicated formwork and many extra tons of concrete. As long as you are building only one story of stone (frame or logs may be added above that) on solid ground then there is little need to go overboard with the footings. On solid rock there is little need for

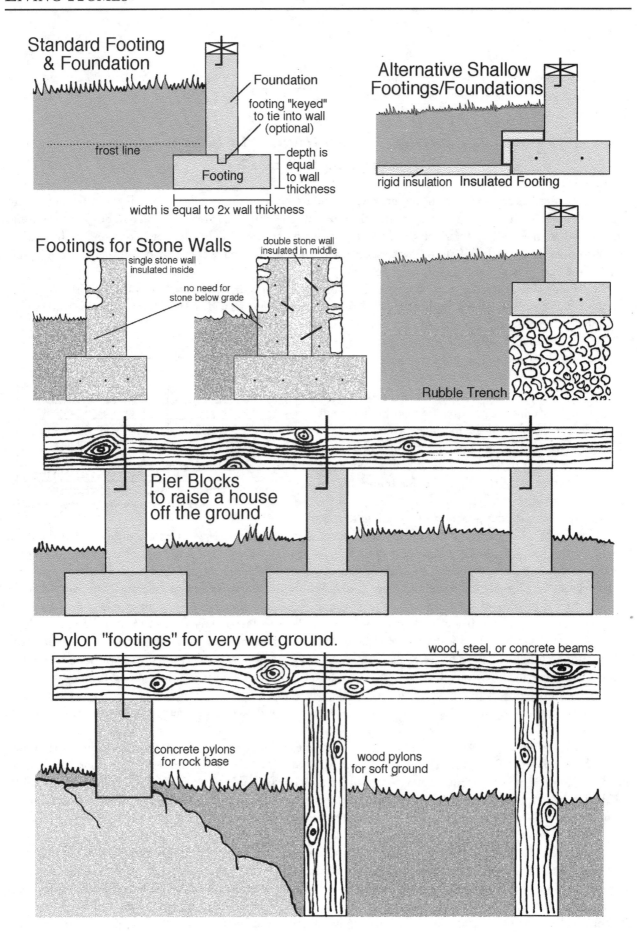

Standard Footing & Foundation

Foundation

footing "keyed" to tie into wall (optional)

frost line

Footing

depth is equal to wall thickness

width is equal to 2x wall thickness

Alternative Shallow Footings/Foundations

rigid insulation   Insulated Footing

Footings for Stone Walls

single stone wall insulated inside

double stone wall insulated in middle

no need for stone below grade

Rubble Trench

Pier Blocks to raise a house off the ground

Pylon "footings" for very wet ground.

wood, steel, or concrete beams

concrete pylons for rock base

wood pylons for soft ground

a footing at all, except that it provides a level surface for subsequent construction work. In most cases the footing will be sufficient if it is nine or ten inches deep and as wide as the wall with four or five inches extra on each side. You can always add extra heavy steel reinforcing if there is any doubt.

You can also consult a structural engineer for their opinion, and this will be required by law in some locations. The engineer will or should evaluate the soil base and mathematically figure the footing specifications for you. Then they will double all the figures for insurance against malpractice suits and multiply that by something else to figure out how much you owe them.

One and half levels are easily done in stone, especially if the first floor is a half basement. Stonework can also be done to the peak of a single story dwelling, but I do not advise building two or more full levels in stone. First, it is a lot of extra work to lift all the stones up that high. Second, tall stone buildings are more susceptible to earthquake damage, and third, you will need to make both the footings and the lower

Slipform Foundation for a Strawbale Wall

A slipformed stone wall is a low cost, functional way to put the footing below the frost line.

The stone masonry must rise high enough to keep the bales dry, but may go higher if you want. Stonework up to the bottoms of the windows may be especially nice, both inside and out, or the entire first floor may be stone.

A moisture barrier such as tarpaper should be placed under the first row of bales to prevent wicking problems or condensation.

A tamped sand base with concrete or tile pavers makes an elegant, low-cost floor.

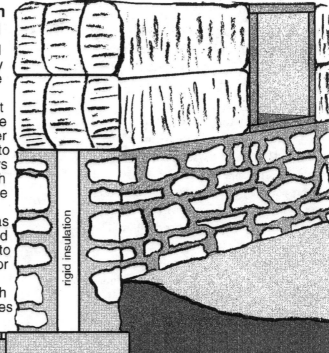

walls much heftier to support the extra weight on top. For taller buildings you might consider a hybrid of stone work and strawbale construction.

As illustrated here, a stone masonry foundation can also solve one of the biggest problems of straw bale construction—how to bury the foundation below frost line while keeping the strawbales up high and dry—without wasting tons of concrete in between.

Shallow Footing Alternatives: Many houses have deep footings and foundations which are simply buried and not utilized as house space. If you are building a house on a tight budget then you may not be able to afford such waste. Shallow footings are sometimes used to conserve concrete. One method is the insulated footing. Simply bury a two-inch thick sheet of rigid board insulation above the footing. The insulation should extend out horizontally from the wall. Heat escaping from the house helps keep the ground from freezing there. We used an insulated footing on the stone house featured in the slipforming chapter of this book. The disadvantage to an insulated footing is that you cannot plant any bushes or trees near the house, since there is not enough soil for their roots.

The **rubble trench** is another way to conserve concrete. A trench is dug below the frost-line and filled with rock or large gravel, then tamped down with a pneumatic tamper. The footing and house is then built on top of the rubble trench. This technique is intended for well-drained soils. The trench should not be allowed to fill with water. Architect Frank Lloyd Wright used the rubble trench with many of his houses.

Pier Blocks: Pier blocks are another way to conserve on concrete. Concrete blocks are placed below the frost line, with columns extending up to support the house. Obviously this technique would not work for masonry houses, but it is common in frame construction and ideal for log homes, at least in some climates. It may also work for strawbale homes. Pier blocks are especially useful in termite country to help lift a wooden structure up out harms way. But there are several disadvantages to building on pier blocks as well.

A house on pier blocks requires wooden floors, and that can be more expensive and more of a fire hazard than a concrete slab. Also, in cold climates it is usually advisable to burrow a shelter into the ground as much as possible to reduce exposure to the elements, especially where the wind blows. A house on blocks would require massive amounts of insulation under the floor to retain heat, plus specialized systems to protect the plumbing in and out of the structure.

Pier blocks are sometimes used to minimize impact with houses built in the forest. If the soil stays damp under the building and the plants are adapted to low light levels, then the ground will remain green under the house. The house is positioned between existing trees so the end effect seems as if you tiptoed into the forest and placed a house on stilts. Personally, I have a different sense of aesthetics and would rather blast a big hole in the ground and half-bury the house so it becomes part of the forest landscape instead of just a big block suspended in the air.

Flooring Systems

Before you can fully determine which footing and foundation system is best for your project, you must also consider the type of flooring you will use with it. Many houses have a footing down below the frost line and a crawlspace under a wood-framed floor. The crawl space makes it easy to access plumbing and wiring beneath a house, but it also seems like waste of resources to pour those foundation walls and not really use that space. Also, wood floors are more combustible and often more expensive than masonry floor alternatives. So in many cases it is worthwhile to take the time to design your home with at least a partial basement and a masonry floor. Wood floors are covered in more detail later in the book.

The most common masonry floor in this country is a **concrete slab**, preferably with lots of reinforcing bar, mesh, and/or fibers. Despite its aura of strength, concrete is a surprisingly weak and brittle material. It is difficult to pour a concrete floor that will not crack at some point. Usually the cracks are cosmetic, but I did see one house were there was an inch-high toe tripper along a crack in the floor. Extra care in the construction process will prevent most settling and cracking problems. Especially be careful in excavating the site. If one part of the structure rests on solid, undisturbed ground and another part is on loose fill, then there will likely be some settling. The ground under the slab itself should also be of an even consistency, and possibly tamped with a pneumatic tamper. The concrete floor will expand and contract with heat and cold inde-

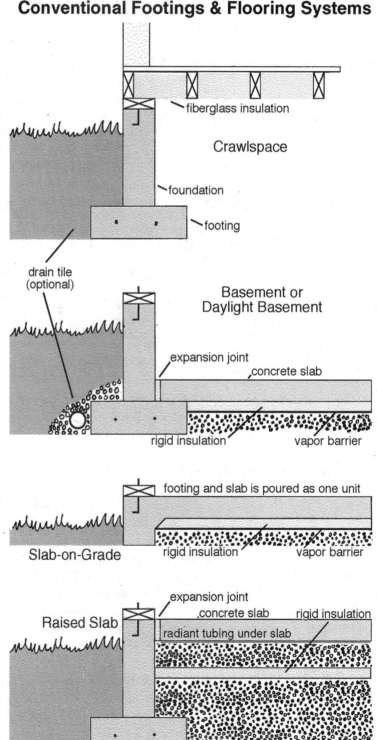

Conventional Footings & Flooring Systems

fiberglass insulation

Crawlspace

foundation

footing

drain tile (optional)

Basement or Daylight Basement

expansion joint

concrete slab

rigid insulation   vapor barrier

footing and slab is poured as one unit

Slab-on-Grade   rigid insulation   vapor barrier

Raised Slab

expansion joint

concrete slab   rigid insulation

radiant tubing under slab

pendently from the walls, so it is helpful to place a thin strip of insulation or fiberboard around the perimeter as an expansion joint before pouring the floor.

On damp ground the space between the footings should be filled with gravel and covered with a layer of heavy plastic to prevent soil moisture from wicking up into the floor. Rigid insulation can be used under the floor in northern climates, but if possible it is better to leave the insulation out and install piping for hot water heat in the floor. The heat loss downward is negligible and the mass of ground helps store surplus heat which may be needed in cold spells. Most concrete slabs are about four inches thick, but they can be five or six inches thick if a radiant hot water system is included, or if the footing and slab are poured together as a slab-on-grade.

A **slab-on-grade** is a means to reduce the materials and labor consumed by a footing and foundation system. The house site is first cleared and leveled. Six inches or more of drainage rock or coarse gravel is raked out on the site, if soil moisture is a concern. Insulation is also optional. The dirt or gravel base is mounded in the center, so that only the edges are poured thick. Footings may be run across the center of the house for additional strength. A single set of forms is used around the perimeter of the slab, and the whole job is poured at once, saving both materials and labor. The footings and slab should have ample reinforcement. In theory the combined footing and slab has extra strength to resist cracking, but the technique is probably best suited to well-drained soils where there is little chance of heaving. In many towns the slab-on-grade is only acceptable for utility buildings, not homes. However, the edge can be protected with insulation extending out beside the structure to make it more palatable to building inspectors.

The slab-on-grade system is especially ideal for **strawbale construction**, since it is hard to justify a strawbale-thick foundation wall buried several feet into the ground. A couple inches of "stem wall" can be added to keep the base of the bales above the slab surface, so that any potential plumbing disasters do not rot the walls.

Concrete slabs can be finished in a number of ways. In standard construction the concrete is often covered with carpet, tile, or even wood floors, but there are many alternatives. Concrete dye can be added before the floor is poured, or the finished floor can be stained. Dye can also be sprinkled loosely over the floor, giving a mottled appearance. Combined with a hand-troweled texture, a concrete floor can become absolutely gorgeous.

Alternative Masonry Floors: Although the concrete slab is by far the most common masonry floor system, there are numerous drawbacks to it. Concrete slabs usually cost less than wood floors, but still, they are not cheap, nor are they easy to construct. If you have no prior experience with forming, pouring, screeding and polishing a concrete floor, then you will definitely want to hire a professional to be in charge of the job. Also, concrete floors are very permanent, so any plumbing or wiring or settling problems that do arise are major to fix. Besides that, concrete is just plain hard underfoot.

One way to avoid problems with cracking across a slab is to use bricks or pavers, so that all the pieces of the floor can move independently. Concrete pavers three or four inches thick can be made with forms right in place or in a shop. The base should be leveled and tamped before setting the pavers, and the joints should be grouted. It is relatively easy to remove a few pavers if there are ever any plumbing, wiring or settling problems underfoot.

Earthen and adobe floors were common in the past, and are now regaining popularity. Special floor hardeners are used to protect the surface. *The Straw Bale House* by Steen and Bainbridge includes a useful discussion of these techniques. We've made soil-cement "terra tiles" on a tamped soil-cement base, with relatively good results. For more information, refer to the chapter on *Terra Tiles* later in the book.

For our own house we adapted to the footings and slab that were started by a previous owner. They intended to build an underground house, so the footings were especially hefty—one foot deep by three feet wide—to support the masonry walls and the earth load of the roof. The site was excavated deep into the hill, so the footings and slab were poured on broken rock. We adapted our house plans to the slab, utilizing the existing footings wherever possible. We added other footings as needed, although part of a later addition, including the most massive stone wall of the house, was built across the unreinforced 3 1/2 inch slab with no footing at all. We put extra reinforcement in the concrete and have not yet had any problems with it. Most importantly the soil is very grainy, so there is little chance of heaving.

The existing slab was cracked and heavily weathered from years of exposure, but it was easily covered with terra tiles. In hindsight we should have laid down plastic tubing for a radiant heating system and poured thicker tiles to cover it, but we have learned to like a floor that is always cool to the touch.

Excavating the House Site

When you are ready to dig in and start building your dream home, the first step in construction is to mark the site and excavate it. Some projects require little precision at this stage. For slab-on-grade construction you may only need to remove the topsoil and level the site. A few stakes outlining the area of excavation may be sufficient. Other projects, especially on city lots or hilly terrain, require more precise measuring and marking from the start. First it is helpful to know how to make square lines on a not-so-square landscape.

The easy method to make a square is to use **right triangles** to measure. A triangle that is 3 feet by 4 feet on the square sides will be exactly 5 feet across the angled side. For the illustration these numbers were multiplied by three to make 9, 12, and 15 feet. For the best accuracy you should use the largest right triangle possible on your site, such as 18, 24, and 30 feet (multiplied by 6). Simply follow the instructions in the illustration. After you have made a complete box you can check your work by measuring the diagonals. The diagonal measurements from corner to corner across a square or rectangle are always exactly the same.

For some projects you can make-do with just corner stakes for the excavation and later a separate set of corner stakes for the house itself. However, using a system of "batter boards", as illustrated here will give much better accuracy and minimize the amount of time spent remeasuring the site. The string-lines should be leveled with the aid of a **string level**, a small and lightweight level that can be hung right on the string. As shown in the illustration, a **plumb bob** can be used to mark from the strings straight down to the ground. Hilly terrain simply requires taller stakes to determine what's level.

Extensive measuring should be done during excavation to insure that the house site is very level before the equipment leaves. Even on terrain that appears level to the eye, the ground can easily slope six inches from one side of the house to the other. Take the extra time to make the site level and square, and the rest of the building process will be made much easier.

A backhoe is probably the most versatile tool for excavating typical house sites. Backhoes usually have a front-end loader attached to one end and the backhoe scoop attached to the other. For large excavation projects it is

Use a right triangle to make two perpendicular lines.

A. Hold the tape at the corner, measure 9 feet out, approximately perpendicular to the corner and make an arc on the ground.

B. Measure 12 feet from the corner on the main line.

C. From that point measure 15 feet back across the triangle and make another arc on the ground. The point where both arcs cross is perpendicular to the corner.

9 feet

15 feet

12 feet

A
B

C

main line

Staking the house site with batter boards.

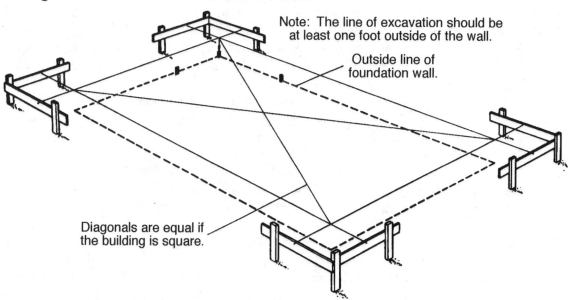

Note: The line of excavation should be at least one foot outside of the wall.

Outside line of foundation wall.

Diagonals are equal if the building is square.

Image Source: USDA Ag Handbook No. 73: Wood-Frame House Construction. April 1975

important to get one with a large front-end loader; smaller equipment will eat up many extra hours transporting dirt by little scoops.

Footings Formwork

The footing of a house is almost always buried out of sight. It doesn't matter what the footing looks like, as long as the top surface is level and straight enough to put a wall on it. Formwork for the footings usually consumes a lot of lumber and labor. Some straw-house builders have shortcut the cost and labor by using strawbales as forms. It would be difficult to make a truly level footing this way, but the technique would suffice for many strawbale building projects.

In recent years a system of squared plastic drain pipe has been invented for footings formwork. The pipes are easy to install, then left in place after the pour to drain moisture away from the footing and to ventilate radon gas away from the house. It is a good idea, but certainly more expensive than traditional options. Hopefully competition and recycled plastic will increase the viability of this method in the near future.

Another way to reduce material costs is to use an excavated ditch as the form for the footing. You will still need lumber to level the top, but you can get by with 2 x 4's versus 2 x 8's, or other larger boards.

Wooden or metal stakes should be driven into the ground along the edges of the formwork. The forms are leveled with the aid of the lines on the batter boards. Additional leveling can be done by pulling a string level across different points on the formwork, or with a four-foot level across short sections.

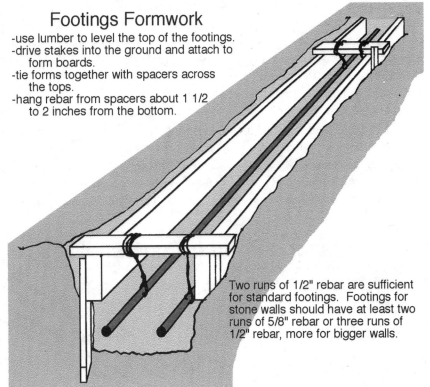

Footings Formwork
-use lumber to level the top of the footings.
-drive stakes into the ground and attach to form boards.
-tie forms together with spacers across the tops.
-hang rebar from spacers about 1 1/2 to 2 inches from the bottom.

Two runs of 1/2" rebar are sufficient for standard footings. Footings for stone walls should have at least two runs of 5/8" rebar or three runs of 1/2" rebar, more for bigger walls.

Keep in mind that you may need to lay pipes through the footing, so plumbing and electrical lines can pass through later. Be sure to read the *Cement Mixing and Measuring Guide* in this book for instructions on calculating the volume and ordering a load.

Help is always a good idea when you are pouring concrete. You may be able to pour a footing with just two people, but it is a good idea to have extra bodies on hand. As the concrete is poured it should be vibrated to help it settle and fill air pockets. A shovel repeatedly jabbed into the wet mortar should suffice. Next, use a 2 x 4 to screed across the top of the footings. Slide the screed back and forth as you drag it along the footing. The vibration will help settle and smooth the surface. When the pour is done and the footings are screeded, then you can jab short lengths of rebar straight down into the footings to attach the stone, log, or straw bale walls, or a foundation wall if needed. The rebar should not extend all the way through the concrete into the soil, or it will be more susceptible to rusting.

Basements & Foundation Walls

Poured concrete is used for the foundation walls or basements under most conventional wood frame homes. A similar strategy works well under log homes, using an eight-inch thick concrete wall to support logs that may be twelve inches or more in diameter. However, pouring a foundation wall or basement under a stone or strawbale wall can be cost-prohibitive, since it takes so much more concrete to pour a wall that is ten, twelve or more inches thick, rather than the standard eight. The entire wall can be built in stone—using lots of reinforcement if it is a full basement with many tons of earth load against it—but that is a lot of work if you are just going to bury it anyway.

Of course, the walls can be faced with stone on the inside only, but that may be more stonework than you really want inside. Due to this cost and labor factor, many slipformed stone homes are redesigned to eliminate foundation walls and basements. Using a partial basement, such as the stone/straw hybrid shown earlier in the chapter, is an economical alternative to avoid burying lots of concrete. Our own home is bermed into the hill, so we used stone walls along the visible front and poured eight-inch concrete walls along the back, which is hidden below ground. The log work of the upper story is supported equally well by the concrete or stone walls.

There are many different types of forms for pouring concrete walls. The best systems are the insulated, snap-together forms you leave in place (described more in the chapter on insulation), but those are also the most expensive. Most people on a budget will have to rent concrete forms, much like the ones pictured here. The 2 x 4's in the photo are called "whalers", used to keep the wall from bulging or "blowing out". The **spacers** used in this system emerge between the whalers, and the metal **wedge clamps** are knocked in place over the ends to tie the wall together.

You can usually rent forms and purchase the spacers from the ready-mix company that will pour your walls. They will give you instructions for the type of forms they have.

Rented forms and whalers for a poured concrete wall.

Formwork for a Poured Concrete Wall
Image Source: USDA Ag Handbook No. 73.
Wood-Frame House Construction. April 1975.

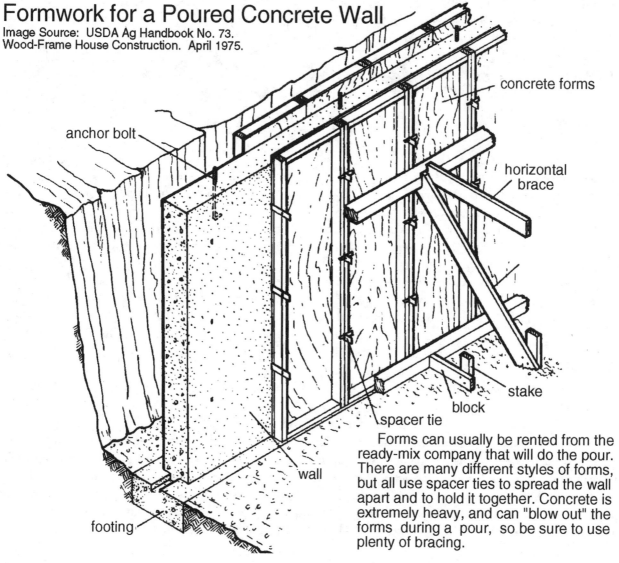

concrete forms

anchor bolt

horizontal brace

stake

block

spacer tie

wall

footing

Forms can usually be rented from the ready-mix company that will do the pour. There are many different styles of forms, but all use spacer ties to spread the wall apart and to hold it together. Concrete is extremely heavy, and can "blow out" the forms during a pour, so be sure to use plenty of bracing.

Cement Mixing & Measuring Guide
Including Aggregates, Additives, and Reinforcement

Cement is the magic ingredient in many alternative house-building methods, especially stone masonry, but also strawbale, log, cordwood, papercrete, and rammed earth construction. In this chapter we will examine this multipurpose substance in detail, including it's history and development, many useful cement formulas and additives and how to measure a volume of space when ordering concrete.

The Origins of Cement

The earliest known use of cement materials was in Egyptian times. Burnt gypsum and/or lime was crushed and mixed with water to make a cement paste. It was used as a bonding agent between the stone blocks of the pyramids. Later the Greeks used burnt lime mixed with crushed sea shells. The Romans used a mixture of burnt lime and volcanic ash.

Knowledge of cement-making was nearly lost after Roman times until 1756, when the English engineer John Smeaton made a thorough study of cement technology to build the Eddystone lighthouse. He produced cement by baking limestone that included part clay. In 1824, Joseph Aspdin, a builder in Leeds, England patented the basic formula that is used today, called **portland cement**. The color of the cement was similar to the rocks from the island of Portland, off the coast of England, hence the name.

Portland cement includes some form of calcium, alumina and silica. The calcium comes from limestone or chalk, while the alumina and silica comes from clay or shale. The main ingredients are tricalcium silicate—55%, dicalcium silicate—25%, tricalcium aluminate—10%, and tetracalcium aluminoferrite—8%. Bottles from recycling programs are sometimes used as a source of silicate. The materials are ground, mixed in the right proportions, and burned in a large, rotating kiln at about 2500°F (1350°C). In the kiln it fuses into chunks called clinker. It is cooled, ground into a fine powder, and gypsum is added to control how fast it sets. The formula can be altered in many subtle ways for specialized projects, such as fast-setting cements for well-drilling.

The only formula you really need to know is called Type I & II portland cement. Just ask for **Type I & II** when you order. The cement must be kept absolutely dry; even humid air will make it set over time. So it is a good idea to buy it in small batches, no more than 10 or 15 sacks at once. Besides, at about 94 pounds apiece, it doesn't take too many sacks to overload a truck. One sack is approximately a cubic foot of cement.

Adding water to the cement starts the **chemical reaction** that binds the minerals together to make artificial rock. The lime combines with the silica to make stone. However, at the surface the lime may combine with carbon dioxide from the atmosphere and reconvert to limestone. An **alternative form of cement** is to mix lime with silica-rich plant fibers like hemp, plus small proportions of sand and clay. Apparently the lime binds with the silica in the sand, clay and plant fibers to produce a low-tech, lightweight cement, sometimes referred to as "petrification".

The process of setting and hardening is called **curing**. Curing is different than drying. Water is included in the chemical reaction, and the molecules become bound in the end product. If cement is dried too quickly then it may not have to time cure and become hard. Working in cool weather, or keeping the masonry covered and damp in hot, dry weather, will produce stronger masonry.

Cement will begin to set in as little as five minutes, but it can be used for more than an hour before it starts seriously losing strength. Adding more water and **remixing** it does not help when the cement has begun to cure; it only weakens the end product. Mortar is still semisoft on the second day, although you can usually walk and work on it. After a week the new mortar will seem almost as hard as old mortar, but it is considered **fully cured** only after a month. Even then there is some residual hardening over the years to follow.

Aggregates

By itself cement is very weak. The powder hardens into clumps if wetted, but the particles are so fine that the clumps crack easily. Larger particles, called aggregates, like sand, gravel, sawdust, or straw, are mixed with the cement to give it strength. These aggregates do not react chemically with the cement. The different-sized particles interlock to produce a stronger **mortar**, highly resistant to cracking. If both sand and gravel is included in the mortar then it is called **concrete**.

Sand and gravel can be purchased in several different sizes. We used **washed sand** for most of our building projects. Washed sand includes bigger particles than **masonry sand**. The varied particle sizes in washed sand makes a stronger mortar, but I've come to prefer the smoother quality of the masonry sand for grouting stonework and other finish work.

Most **gravel** for concrete is 3/4" mesh, although **pea gravel**, or 3/8" mesh is easier to use in slipform masonry. The pea gravel flows between and bonds to the rocks better than the larger gravel, although the concrete itself may not be as strong. The cost can vary considerably depending on what is available.

Cement, sand, and **sawdust** are sometimes used together to make a lighter, partly insulated mortar. The sawdust weakens the mortar, but it is still strong enough if used in the right application. Our neighbors used a sawdust mortar in the construction of their cordwood home. **Straw** can be added to cement and sand mortars, both for it's insulating properties, and because the fibers function as reinforcement to tie the cured mortar together.

Polystyrene beads, **perlite**, or **vermiculite** can also be included to make lightweight, insulated mortar. These additives weaken the mortar, but it is still strong enough for certain applications. Cement building blocks have been made with these formulas. We added perlite to the mortar in our masonry fireplace to make it less brittle to better handle the expansion and contraction.

Additives

Most additives are powders or liquids that chemically react or bond with the cement, altering its properties. **Slaked lime** (calcium hydroxide) is the most common additive. It is used to help whiten the mortar and speed the drying time. Lime makes the mortar softer and weaker, but that can be desirable in some applications like fireplaces. The softer mortar is able to expand and contract more without cracking.

Calcium chloride is also used to speed the drying time. It is especially helpful for concrete pours in winter conditions. Cold weather really slows the chemical reaction necessary for the curing process. Calcium chloride stimulates that reaction. A little goes a long ways, and it can give you a chemical burn, so you have to be careful.

Chemical additives can also be used to make microscopic air pockets in the concrete. This **air-entrained concrete** is not as strong as regular concrete, but it is highly resistant to frost damage, even while curing. The air pockets provide space for the water to crystallize without damaging the cement.

Acrylic Bonding Agents are white, glue-like liquids used to strengthen cement. Acrylic is sometimes painted onto old, cured concrete to make a better bond with new concrete. The acrylic can also be mixed right into the mortar, but at $20 per gallon, it is very expensive. I sometimes add a little acrylic to the grouting mortar I use with stonework. When the mortar starts to set in the wheelbarrow the acrylic is used to keep the mix smooth and workable, without weakening it.

I've recycled old **latex paint** into cement and sand mortars to make a smoother mix for stucco work. Latex paint can contaminate the groundwater when half-full cans are landfilled. Using the paint in a cement mix is a safe way to dispose of it. Do not use alkyd paints—the oils do not mix or bond in the water-based mortar.

Mineral **pigments** can also be added to mortar. Just ask the local brickyard for a color sheet. There are many exciting colors to work with, but don't get too carried away. Also, keep in mind that the cement powder is gray and the sand and gravel is colored too, so it is difficult to control the final color of the mortar. The drying rate also strongly affects the color. It is helpful to make test samples before you take on a big project.

Caution: sugar is not an additive. Although I do not understand the chemistry of it, sugar blocks the curing process when added to the mortar. Sugar water can be sprayed on the surface of a concrete panel while the mortar is still fresh, to clean and expose the aggregate. I remember one story of a junior mason who "saved the day" when there was not enough water on the job site for a masonry project. He added lemonade to make up the difference and proudly told his boss, whom no doubt wanted to strangle him.

Also avoid minerals with **sulfur** (common in mine tailings), which may oxidize to form sulfuric acid that will disolve the cement.

Wire Mesh & Reinforcing Bar

I cannot understate the need for proper reinforcement. When earthquakes kill thousands of people in foreign lands it is usually because the people are living in masonry-type homes that do not have any form of reinforcing bar. Masonry construction, including concrete, stone, adobe, mud, etc., are all very rigid. These types of materials do not flex with the shaking earth, so they break apart. Reinforcing bar, or "rebar" as it is commonly called, is simply a steel rod embedded in the concrete to tie all the masonry work together. Rebar helps protect your work from cracking or breaking apart when the ground settles or shifts under your house.

Reinforcing bar is remarkably cheap, costing only about three dollars for a 20 foot length of 1/2" diameter rod, but it still adds up when you buy a lot of it. Fortunately you can use about any reasonably clean, skinny piece of steel for rebar. We tied all the walls together in our house above the door and window frames with 40 foot lengths of 1 inch diameter steel cables we found. Our walls and footings are full of all sorts of other cables, steel fence posts, and barbed wire. You may find that masonry work can be a constructive way to clean up your neighborhood!

Purchased rebar comes in many sizes, including 3/8", 1/2", 5/8", 3/4" 1" etc. You can order it by the diameter, but in the construction business it is also known as #3, #4, #5, etc. The number stands for eighths, so #4 rebar means 4/8" or 1/2" rebar. That is the standard sized used in most masonry work. Rebar comes in twenty-foot lengths. You can often have it custom cut when you buy it, but at an extra cost. It is just as easy to pick up a masonry blade for a circular saw and cut your own.

There are non-steel alternatives to rebar too. Some home-builders have become concerned about the long-term health effects of surrounding one's self in a metal cage. **Fiberglass rebar** is more expensive, but eliminates this concern.

Bamboo is another alternative to steel and it may be almost as strong. Bamboo is used extensively in China for masonry work. Even **straw** is sometimes added to mortar for reinforcement. Short **polypropylene** plastic fibers are also used to strengthen mortar; it is often called **"fiberglass fibers"** since that is what it looks like. I used real fiberglass fibers to strengthen the mortar in our masonry fireplace, since I was concerned the polypropylene fibers might melt or outgas fumes in the room as the masonry warmed. I used old fiberglass matting that was given to me, so I was recycling that too.

Welded wire mesh is commonly used to reinforce concrete slabs, but you can also use regular rebar. **Stuccowire** is used to reinforce stucco work, most notably on strawbale homes. It looks just like chickenwire. Other options for reinforcing masonry projects are as limitless as your imagination.

The important part to remember is to make sure you always include enough reinforcement, no matter where you are building. If you are using improvised reinforcement materials, then add extra just to be sure. More specific information on the proper amount of reinforcing bar is included the other parts of this text.

It is also important to consider the **placement of rebar** in the masonry. As illustrated, reinforcement provides the most strength if positioned opposite the load. In footings and beams that means the rebar is placed near the bottom.

An alternative method of reinforcement is used in **prestressed concrete**. Hold a length of rebar from both ends and you will notice that it sags in the middle. Concrete can be made much stronger if there is tension on the rebar so it is stretched as tight as possible. But it is easier to stretch steel cables than rebar. The cables extend out of the concrete forms and come-a-longs are

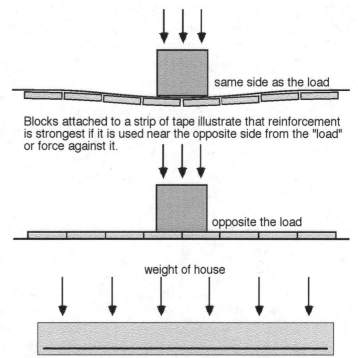

Placement of Reinforcing Bar

same side as the load

Blocks attached to a strip of tape illustrate that reinforcement is strongest if it is used near the opposite side from the "load" or force against it.

opposite the load

weight of house

Rebar should be placed within 1 1/2" or 2" of the bottom of footings and beams for maximum strength.

used to stretch them tight. The tension is released after the concrete cures, but the cables remain stretched. Pre-stressed concrete panels and beams can be made thinner than conventional concrete work. The panels are often used for concrete roofs.

Measuring Volume & Ordering Concrete

Ordering a load of concrete takes a bit of nerve the first couple times you do it, especially when you are working on big projects that require more than one truck for the pour. You need to measure the volume of the footings, walls, or slab you are pouring and order just the right amount. You have to be careful to order enough for the job, but not so much extra that you are wasting money and resources. Ideally, you should have other small projects ready to go, in case there is extra concrete. Then you won't be wasting any.

Concrete is ordered by cubic yards. One yard is like a cube 3' x 3' x 3'. You need to measure each section of the project you are working on and convert the figures to cubic yards. The measurements can be taken in feet, but I think it is easier to work in inches, to avoid working with fractions of a foot.

Simply measure each section in inches and multiply the **width x length x height**. The numbers are astronomical in inches, but have some faith. As long as you don't hit the wrong numbers on the calculator, then it will work out. Add all the numbers together and then divide by 46,656—that's the number of cubic inches in a cubic yard (36" x 36" x 36"). Always have someone else double-check your figures. They should double check both the measuring and the calculating. You can order yards in fractions too, so an estimate of 7.6 yards could be ordered as 7 and 3/4 yards instead of eight.

Footings can be the most difficult to measure, since the concrete may flow out into odd cavities underneath the formwork. There is always some guesswork involved. That's why it is helpful to have other projects where you can use the extra concrete. At the very least, the concrete makes good driveway gravel. Just be sure and rake it out thin before it dries!

The standard mix delivered by trucks is **"five sack"**, meaning that five sacks of cement are included in each yard of concrete. A sack of cement is one cubic foot, and there are 27 cubic feet in a yard (3' x 3' x 3'), so there is about 1 part cement to 5 parts sand and gravel. You can also order **"six sack"**, if extra strength is desired.

Mixing Your Own Concrete

A **cement mixer** is a must for most alternative house building projects. Watch the classified ads in your local paper. You should be able to get a decent used cement mixer for $200 or less. We bought ours at an auction for $100. Electric mixers are definitely more pleasant to work with than gas powered mixers, unless you do not have electricity.

It is important to know that a cement mixer should turn slowly to mix properly. A slow mixer allows the ingredients to rise to the top and then fall back down as the drum turns. **Centrifugal force** in a fast mixer will hold the ingredients against the edges, so it doesn't mix. Our mixer was not geared correctly when we bought it, but we didn't know any better. We were able to mix concrete, just not very efficiently. We used it that way for several years before the motor burned out. Then we replaced it with a different motor which happened to turn slower. The difference was incredible. That motor soon burned out too, which was also an effect of improper gearing. With the third motor we installed an extra wheel and belt to reduce the rpm's of the drum. Mixing was a lot more fun after that.

A good **formula** for mixing your own concrete is about 1 part cement to 5 parts sand and gravel mix. The ingredients can be loaded into the mixer by the shovel full, but we've always preferred buckets. A five gallon bucket of sand plus a five gallon bucket of gravel, and a 2 gallon bucket of cement is just the right size for one load in our 3-cubic foot mixer. The size of your mixer may be

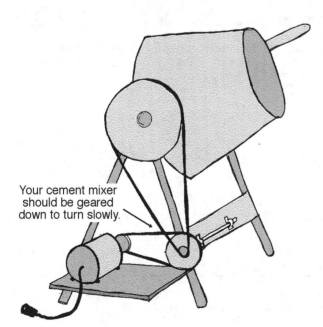

Your cement mixer should be geared down to turn slowly.

different. The five-gallon buckets are heavy, but I set them on my knee and use leg strength to lift them up to the mixer. Renee always lets me do the loading.

Water should be added until the mix is the consistency of oatmeal: thick and gooey. Most books say that you should mix all the ingredients dry before adding any water, but that only works good for the first batch. Once the drum is damp then the next batch starts sticking to the sides. An efficient way to work is to measure the amount of water needed to mix a batch, then use just that amount of water after each batch to clean the mixer. Use the cemented water for the next batch and add the new ingredients. We usually add gravel to the water first, then part of the sand, all of the cement, and the rest of the sand. The sand and cement particles work their way to the back and fill in the spaces between the gravel. You will always end up with less volume out of the mixer than what you put in!

Grouting Mortar

We've used many different mixes for grouting stone walls and tile floors. My preferred mix is now a ratio of **1 cement + 1/2 lime + 4 sand**. Sometimes I use 1 part lime if I want a whiter mortar.

For **grouting stonework** or **chinking logs** we prefer masonry sand, which is finer and smoother than washed sand. Chinking logs goes very fast, so it can be worthwhile to mix the mortar in the cement mixer. But grouting stonework is very slow, and the batches are small, so it is easier to mix the mortar in the wheelbarrow with a hoe, than to bother using and cleaning the cement mixer. We use coffee cans to measure the ingredients, and we usually make double batches. The ingredients should be thoroughly mixed dry, then water is added a little at a time until the mortar is creamy, yet thick. Read more about grouting stonework in the slipforming chapter of this book.

For **grouting floor tiles** we use a 30 mesh silica sand. It is a very fine white sand, and it can be purchased in 50 pound bags at the brickyard. We mix it in small batches with a hoe in the wheelbarrow. Commercial tile grouts include a great deal of latex, presumably to make the grout more flexible to resist cracking. You can add your own latex, if desired, by simply replacing some or all of the water in the mix with latex paint. White latex paint will turn gray from the cement. This is a good way to use up extra paint. A very thin mortar which includes latex paint is helpful to fill any cracks that do form in the grout lines. We've had cracks form in the grout lines when we grouted terra tile floors before the tiles finished curing and shrinking. Be sure to read more about tile grouting in the terra tiles chapter of this book.

Protecting Masonry Work from the Weather

In order for masonry work to cure properly, it must be protected from extreme hot or cold. If you are insistent, then you can always get the job done in extreme weather, but there is a cost to working against Mother Nature. In extreme hot or cold weather you are wisest to go find something else to do until the weather changes.

In moderately hot weather the masonry should be soaked with water repeatedly, or better yet, covered with wet blankets or burlap. We often use wet cement sacks. There are special additives available to slow down the set time if you insist on working with mortar in extremely hot conditions.

In moderately cold weather, just insulate the mortar with a few blankets or some straw. Warm days with freezing nights are fine for masonry work, as long as you keep it covered. The chemical reaction generates a small amount of heat, provided the ingredients are warm enough to activate the cement. In colder weather, with hard freezes at night, plus day time temperatures less than 40°F, you can still work with concrete, but you may have to add hot water and/or calcium chloride, plus lots of insulation to activate the cement and keep it warm. You can order concrete trucks any time during the winter, but you will have to pay extra for the hot water. For some projects you may need to build a tent and put in a space heater to keep it warm. There are always risks working under those kind of conditions, and winter days are so short anyway that it is seldom worth all the extra effort. A little patience can save you a lot of money.

Slipform Masonry Tools

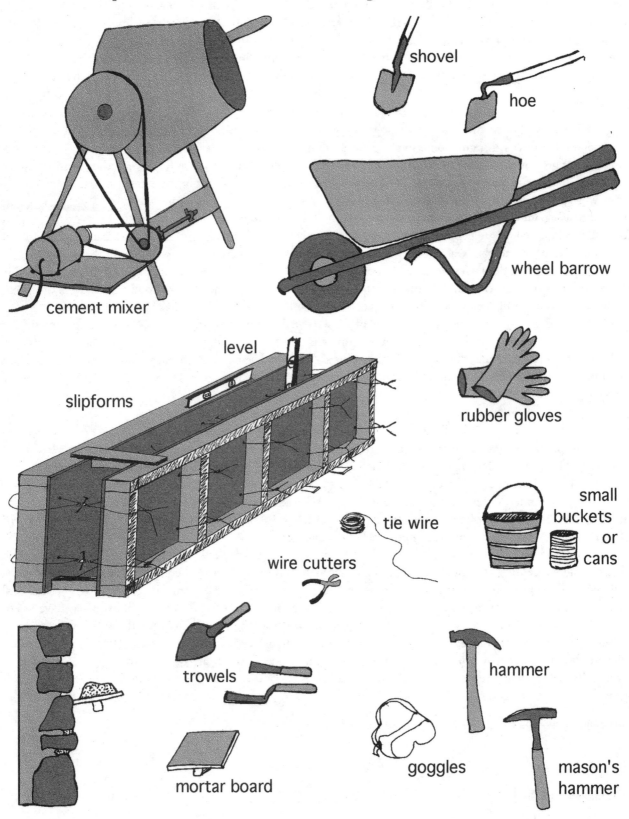

shovel

hoe

cement mixer

wheel barrow

level

slipforms

rubber gloves

tie wire

wire cutters

small buckets or cans

trowels

hammer

mortar board

goggles

mason's hammer

The Art of Slipforming
A Stone Masonry Primer

Of all the alternative building technologies, stone masonry is neither the cheapest nor the fastest. But there is a certain irresistible charm about a stone house, and I simply would not settle for anything less. Besides, a stone house can out-last any other kind of construction by hundreds of years.

Stone houses have both enduring and endearing qualities about them. There is an aura of timelessness about them, as if they have always been there and always will be. Perhaps this feeling of timelessness is exuded from the rocks themselves. Building with materials as old as nature makes a home seem as if it were part of the story of the land.

The method of stone masonry we use is called "slipforming". Short forms, up to two feet tall, are placed on both sides of the wall to serve as guides for the stone work. Stones are set in place with the best faces against the forms. Reinforcing bar is set in place behind the stones and concrete is poured in to fill the voids. After the concrete sets enough to hold the wall together, the forms are "slipped' up to pour the next level. Slipforming makes stone work easy even for the novice.

Slipforming is an old-fashioned style of masonry, resulting in a random or "rubble-stone" appearance, without the uniform joints or sharp, clean lines of most modern masonry. In fact, slipforming is comparatively messy, and you will often find cement drips permanently ad-

Slipforms make it easy to build straight stone walls.

hered to the face of the rocks when you remove the forms. But these stains also contribute to the "patina" of the stone work, giving it an "antiqued" appearance. We rarely remove the drips, even when we can.

Slipform stonemasonry was originally developed by the New York architect Ernest Flagg in 1920. He built a vertical framework as tall as the wall, then inserted 2 x 6 or 2 x 8 planks as forms to guide the stonework. When the masonry work reached the top of a plank, he simply added another one, simply adding more planks until he reached the top of the wall. Helen and Scott Nearing modified the technique in Vermont in the 1930's, using a system of forms and wire ties much like what you see in this chapter.

The footings... with lots of rebar to reinforce the walls.

Door frames are inserted in the forms

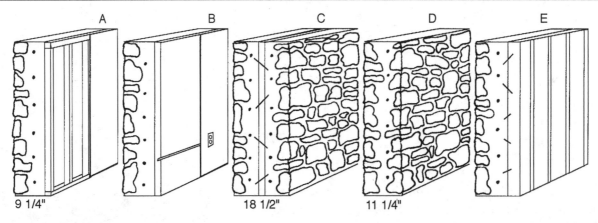

A   B   C   D   E

9 1/4"   18 1/2"   11 1/4"

Slipform Wall Options

Overview

Old-style stone work was done completely free-form, usually using poles with strings as guides. The stones were aligned with the string guides and placed on a bed of mortar. If the stone tilted forward or back into the soft mortar, then small stone shims had to be placed under the rocks to level them. I have done some freeform masonry (see the chapter *Revival of the Masonry Stove*), but the work is very slow and challenging. I could not have done it without years of slipform experience.

Most modern stone masonry today is attached as a veneer on the surface of concrete or block walls. The concrete offers plenty of strength to the structure, but the veneered stone sometimes separates from the wall. Slipforming may take a little longer than pouring a concrete wall and adding veneer, but the cost is a little lower and I believe the quality is higher.

Slipforming combines stone masonry and concrete work to form a wall that shares the attributes of both. The walls have the beauty and strength of stone with the additional reinforcement of concrete and steel. The final product is long lasting, low maintenance and virtually weather and fireproof.

When we started building, the available literature was for walls that were stone outside and concrete inside. These had frame walls built against the concrete for holding the insulation and attaching the sheetrock (A). This combination always seemed inefficient to us, partly due to the duplication of the structural wall, but also because the studs are conductive gaps in the insulation. We have avoided the need for the interior studs in some projects by using adhesives to glue rigid insulation and sheetrock directly to the concrete (B). (Any wiring or plumbing is routed into the insulation.)

We also like to build homes that feel as natural on the inside as on the outside, so we always build some walls with stone inside and outside, with rigid insulation in the core. To do this we form both walls at the same time and push short pieces of rebar horizontally through the insulation to tie the walls together (C). In our home some of the stone walls are completely inside the house, positioned to support the log upper story while being protected from the weather by the greenhouse in front. These walls have no insulation in them and are simply formed with stone on

Large stones can be propped up before the forms are put on.

The forms are "slipped" up the wall to make the second layer.

both sides and concrete in the core (D). This method uses more rocks and less concrete, often with the rocks from each side of the wall overlapping in the core. Wiring and plumbing can be placed in this type of wall, but I do not recommend it for the beginner.

The width of each wall in the drawings is determined first by the amount of room needed for the stone and concrete and secondly by the size of the dimensional lumber used for framing in the doors and windows. A "2 x 10", for instance is really 9 1/4 inches wide, so we make the walls that width and screw the slipforms directly onto the faces of the window or door frames.

For the next generation in slipform technology we recommend using EPS polystyrene beadboard "structural building panels" with 1 x 2 furring strips embedded in one face for attaching sheetrock (E). Cut out all the doors and windows and stand up the 4 x 8 foot sheets, boxing in the whole house with the insulation. This insulation serves as the form inside the house, thereby eliminating the need for half of the slipforms forms and half of the form-setting work. This also insures straight, plumb walls from the beginning. Our first test of this method is a small workshop and storage shed beside our house. Be sure to check our website for our *Slipform Stone Masonry* video of this project.

I originally proposed this method in an article in *The Mother Earth News* magazine, but had not yet tried it myself. Dani Gruber, an enthusiastic builder in western Colorado, was the first person I know of to test out the new method. The method worked very well, and I had the pleasure of touring the house when it was nearly complete.

The main problem, Gruber said, was the availability of the panels. The industry standard is a 5-1/2" thick panel with oriented strand board (OSB) glued to both sides. Her local manufacturer said it would be cost-prohibitive to manufacture thicker panels or to embed the furring strips I described, so she purchased the standard panels, but with the OSB board on only one side. The house is 32 x 64 feet and an incredible three stories tall! See the end of this chapter for photos.

Footings

The footings for stone walls are much like those in conventional construction, just bigger. For most stone-work I recommend framing the footings with 2 x 10's. Make the footings as wide as the walls, with enough extra width to set the forms on for the first layer of slipforming. Most importantly, use lots of steel reinforcing—at least three runs of 1/2" rebar in a footing 18" wide, preferably more. Footings of this size will be sufficient for stone walls up to about twelve feet tall. For higher walls you should consult an engineer. You should also consult an engineer if you are building on soils that seem perennially damp, contain significant amounts of sand or soft clay, or otherwise seem like there may be a potential for shifting. Be sure to read more in the *Footings, Foundations and Floors* chapter of this book.

In the house shown here the vertical lengths of rebar were jabbed through the wet concrete into the soil below. The technique saves work later on, but we've since learned that it is not accepted by code. Presumably the ends of the rebar will rust in the ground and eventually allow the rust to follow the rebar up through the concrete.

Our place had a concrete slab when we bought it, with no rebar sticking up out of the footings. We simply drilled through the slab and into the footing with a hammerdrill and stood the lengths of rebar up in the holes. The Grubers used a different approach to a similar end, by inserting 1/2" PVC plastic sleeves into the fresh concrete.

Insulation is inserted in the middle of a double wall.   *The wheelbarrow can be pushed through the door, below the forms.*

Later they hammered the tall lengths of rebar into the plastic sleeves.

Although these methods work well enough, and could not possibly allow shifting in an earthquake, codes seem to favor L-shaped rebar anchors firmly embedded in the footings. I would suggest using both methods, using L-shaped anchors to tie the walls to the footings, plus embedded PVC plastic sleeves to extend the rebar from the footings to the top of the stone walls.

Slipforms

Slipforms are easy to make. Simply screw 2 x 8 foot pieces of 1/2" plywood onto 2 x 4 frames, using a square to keep the frames straight. The plywood should be painted with used motor oil or a commercial form oil to keep the concrete from adhering to the wood. Slipforms are a multipurpose tool. We especially use them for scaffolding material, but one time we bolted all of them together to make a temporary storage shed for the winter.

Setting Slipforms

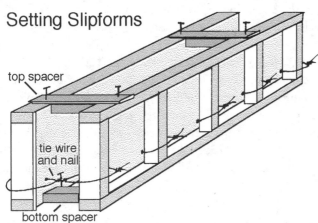

top spacer

tie wire
and nail

bottom spacer

To set the slipforms, start by snapping a chalk line on the footings for a guide and position the forms along the walls, inside and out; then nail them together end to end. Preferably, the studs on the back of the forms should line up between the inside and outside sets. Now make some temporary "spacers" from scraps of wood such as 2 x 2's. These should be cut to fit the width of the wall and dropped in between the forms to hold the bottoms apart. Spacers for the top of the forms are made similarly, but should be nailed onto a thinner piece of wood such as plywood or a 1 x 2 and placed across the tops of the forms. The 2 x 2 spacers hold the forms apart, while the longer 1 x 2's are nailed to the tops of the forms to tie the forms together. This eliminates the need for a wire tie near the top of the forms.

To tie the bottoms together, simply drill holes on both sides of the studs through the back of the forms. Purchase a roll of "tie wire" at the hardware store, and feed the wire through the forms, wrapping around the studs and twist the wire ends together outside the forms. Place a nail between the wires and twist the wires together to pull the forms snug against the wooden spacers. There should be a top and bottom spacer, and a wire tie for each stud on the back of the forms.

It is crucial to get the first form-setting straight and plumb. Fortunately the slipforms almost level themselves as you tighten the wire ties. A little bump here and there and a few shims are all that is usually needed to set the forms straight and level. For stubborn sections you may need to wedge a 2 x 4 against the ground to level the forms. Adjusting the forms across one section may jar all the others, so you have to go around again and again to check and recheck for level and plumb.

Keep in mind that if you frame the house with EPS beadboard panels first, then you will only have to set slipforms along one side of the wall. The wire ties through the foam panels should be left in place to help tie the beadboard panels to the slipformed wall.

There are large gaps between the stones that must be grouted.

Georgie. King of the sand pile.

Use your legs and not your back to lift all rocks, light or heavy.

Rebar

Reinforcing bar, or "rebar" as it is commonly called, is simply a steel rod embedded in the concrete to tie all the masonry work together. Rebar helps protect your masonry work from cracking or breaking apart if the ground shifts under your house. A small amount of shifting may occur from the weight of the house settling into the ground, but the greatest shifting is caused by earthquakes. Earthquakes put severe strains on a building as the earth rocks back and forth and the structure above ground builds inertia in one direction, then gets yanked back the other direction. Houses built into the earth are affected less because they tend to move with the quakes. Be sure to read more about rebar in the chapter on *Cement Mixing and Measuring*.

For slipform masonry we start with vertical lengths of 1/2 inch rebar spaced about every eighteen inches to two feet along the wall. We bend these up around the window frames as we come to them, so there is comparatively more reinforcement at these points. We lay a length of rebar in horizontally about every foot up the walls. This is especially important at the corners. The rebar should be bent at these points, extending for three or more feet in each direction. We always use whatever scrap steel we can find to reinforce the concrete as well. Our walls are full of steel cables, metal fence posts, and barbed wire. We fold the barb wire back on itself and twist it together for greater strength.

Structurally, slipformed stone walls have greater "compressive" strength compared to concrete walls, making them stronger for a weight load on top. However, slipformed walls are weaker against lateral forces, like a heavy earthload against the walls. If you have any concerns about the strength for the intended application, then increase the amount of rebar in the wall. You can also increase the width of the concrete portion of the wall, but the rebar will give you the most strength for the added investment. For added reinforcement in our larger retaining walls we've picked up the rails from abandoned mines that the ore carts used to run on. With these two-inch or larger metal rods running through the walls we feel very confident about their strength!

Rocks

Rocks can be purchased at almost any brickyard, but it is much better to get your own if you have a source. Brickyard rocks are expensive, partly because they are usually transported hundreds of miles from a quarry, but also because the rocks are selected for freehand masonry, with similar thicknesses and flat, brick-like platforms all the way around. Slipform masonry is much more forgiving than freehand work, and you can easily save $100 to $200 per hour of effort by driving around the countryside picking up almost any rocks you can find. Just be careful not to overload your vehicle. As a loose rule of thumb, a load of rocks a foot deep in a pickup bed is a cubic yard, weighing approximately 2000 pounds!

We set all the inside forms first, attaching them to window frames.

Concrete poured on a platform can be bucketed into the wall.

The rocks should be solid and not fractured or crumbly. There should be at least one good, flat face to place against the form. Avoid those tempting thin stones that are only an inch or two thick. These may ultimately pop off the wall, leaving an ugly patch of concrete exposed. The rocks should have an average thickness about 2/3 the width of the wall you are forming, but can vary from as much as 3 1/2 to 7 inches thick in a wall 9 1/4 inches wide. Do not use rocks that are as thick as the walls; the concrete backing is an essential part of the slipforming system.

Farms are often good sources of stone. Farmers pick rocks out of the fields and place them conveniently in a pile, ready to load. Usually they will let you have the piles as they have no use for them. We picked most of our rocks in the mountains within a mile of our house, but we also gathered river rocks for around the hot tub, and we brought back a few special rocks from picnics. The house in these photos was built with rocks we gathered at an abandoned quarry. There are 16 truckloads in it (25 x 40 feet outside dimensions), and probably twice that in our own home.

The Gruber house, shown at the end of the chapter, was built at what used to be a small gravel pit. It was full of rocks, so they didn't have to travel far for good building materials. Actually, the lot was a bit of an eyesore beforehand, and the owner didn't know what to do with it. So he reportedly sold it to Dani Gruber's father for two bales of hay, to see if he could come up with something better for the land. Dani bought the lot from her father and "offered to double the price". As you can see from the pictures, a stone house was the perfect use of the land.

Laying Stone

Start the first row by laying out a bed of concrete one to two inches thick and place your biggest rocks into it. Be sure to read more about concrete in the chapter on *Cement Mixing and Measuring*. Otherwise, for maximum efficiency I recommend laying in as much stone as you possibly can in all the forms. It is often possible to stack the stones several deep before filling in with concrete. Just make sure there is room to work the mortar in around each and every rock. Also work towards a "brick layered" effect, by bridging the joints between the rocks on every level. Staggering the joints this way will make a stronger and more beautiful wall. Place as many rocks as you can and then start mixing cement.

Note that in dry-stacked stonework a wall is made level and plumb with the aid of many small stone **shims**— flat pieces of rock inserted whereever necessary between the bigger rocks to make them level. In slipform masonry there is no need for shims because the concrete flows between the rocks, forming shims that fit the voids exactly. Sometimes you have to hold a rock flat against the forms while you work the concrete around and under it. We often use smaller stones or sticks braced against the rebar or the opposite slipform as temporary props to hold the rocks in place until the concrete is poured. Once the rocks are pressed against the form by the fresh concrete then the props can be removed.

Make the first batch of concrete by mixing the ingredients dry, then add the water. Ideally the mix should be gooey enough to slide in around each stone, but not so soupy that it runs out through the joints and down the rock faces. Measure the amount of water used in this first batch, then pour the same amount of water in the mixer to clean it. Save this water and add the gravel, cement, and sand—in that order—to the water to mix subsequent batches. Adding the sand last allows it to work down into the spaces between the gravel, instead of clumping up in the back.

The last form-setting must be very level to pour the sill plate.

A load of rocks one foot deep in the truck weighs about a ton.

You must wear rubber gloves to protect your hands from the cement. The cement will cause a mild chemical burn—basically drying out your hands and eating away at the first layer of your skin. It is not a powerful chemical reaction, but you may end up with small cuts and bleeding finger tips after a few days of work. The abrasiveness of the sand and gravel further eat away at the skin. Wear gloves as often as you can, and lather up with lotion after work each day.

Besides protecting your hands, rubber gloves are also useful as tools for working the mortar between the rocks. We use coffee cans to bucket concrete from the wheelbarrow into the walls, then plunge our gloved hands down into the wall to vibrate the concrete in between the rocks. Pour concrete to the top of your stone work, then place a new row of rocks in on the fresh mortar and continue stacking as before. It is okay if some of the rocks stick up above the forms, but tilt them back at least a 1/4 inch, otherwise they tend to bulge the forms out on the next level. Wash the gloves, or take them off, when you are laying stone, to avoid smearing concrete from the gloves onto the rocks.

At the end of a day you should **cover masonry work** with blankets or cement sacks, especially in hot, dry or freezing weather. And always soak old masonry work with the hose before you start adding to it again. Otherwise the dry mortar absorbs the moisture out of the new material before it properly cures. Note that every time you stop working at the end of the day you create a "**cold joint**" where the concrete sets and doesn't chemically bond to the new mortar added later. Certainly it would be better to eliminate all cold joints, but that just isn't possible with slipform work. Just try to stagger the joints, so each one is in a different part of the wall.

When Dani Gruber built her family's stone house, her 73 year-old father volunteered to mix the concrete. For three hours every morning for three months, he mixed concrete while she set the stones. They quit at mid day when it was too hot out, then Dani returned in the afternoon to set forms for the next level. When spectators stopped by to visit, he teased about the project, "Oh yeah, she think's she's going to build a rock house. We'll see. I bet when she gets a couple feet of rock done, she'll get smart." After the walls were up fourteen feet high and he was still mixing concrete, he kidded, "By God, she never did get smart!"

Moving Up the Walls

The simplest way to move the forms up the wall is to set new forms on top of the previous layer. However, it is usually more desirable to pull the old forms off and chip away any globs of concrete on the rock faces before they become too hard. Move the forms up and hold them in place with stilts. The stilts may be merely propped underneath, or screwed onto the sides of the forms. The forms are wobbly at first, until you clamp them tight against the walls with the wire ties. It is easier to move the forms up the wall in places where the door and window frames are already in place. Just hoist the forms up to the right height and screw them into the frames. You do not need wire ties or spacers at these points.

One problem you may encounter above the first form setting is that the wet concrete may drip down across the rock faces of all the layers below. Mixing thicker batches of mortar will help stop this problem. Another trick is to plug up any gaps at the bottom of the forms with scraps of the beadboard insulation. You can easily pull the bits and pieces of insulation off the wall when the forms are removed. Third, you can hose or scrub the stained stonework, being careful to avoid hosing the still-wet concrete in the top layer.

The foundation is coated with tar to keep moisture out.

Trusses are set in place to serve as a guide for stonework in the gable.

Windows & Doors

There are many ways to save money and recycle old resources while building your home, but you should be very careful about reusing windows and doors. We tend to think that it is economically and environmentally sensible to salvage windows and reuse them. But the cost and energy expended to manufacture a new window is trifling compared to the amount and cost of the energy that will leak through the glass over it's lifetime. Often the most sound course of action is to discard the old windows (recycle them if it is an option), especially single-panes, and replace them with double- or triple-glazed units.

Granted, there are always trade-offs, especially when you are paying cash-as-you-go. Sometimes it is more expedient to install old windows, and to simply accept higher fuel bills in the future. We installed used double-glazed sliding glass door panes in our greenhouse because they were virtually free, and we were building our house almost without money anyway. Our house is reasonably efficient with these windows, but in order to eventually achieve 100% passive solar heating we will have to replace these units with the new triple-glazed, low-E, Krypton gas windows.

Drive screws or nails part way into the window and door frames to anchor the wood into the concrete.

If you do install used windows and doors then you should at least make sure that the sizes are interchangeable with those on the market today. Otherwise, having the new windows custom made to fit odd-sized openings will at least double your costs when you do decide to "upgrade".

For installing new windows you should pick them out before you begin construction and build the frames according to the "rough size" specified for each unit. You may also want to build the frames extra large to insulate across the thermal gap that occurs through the stonework. We added three inches in width and height to the frames to leave room inside for rigid insulation and sheetrock. We nailed in 2 x 4's at the outside edge to attach the windows. Positioning the window in the middle of the wall, closer to the insulation, would also help to reduce the thermal leak through the wood. In our next project we will have the window frames custom cut from a high-density polystyrene beadboard to eliminate both the thermal leak and the wood framing. We will use windows that can be glued in place rather than nailed.

Build the window and door frames on the ground and put braces across the corners to keep them squared. Drill screws in part way all around the frames to anchor the wood to the concrete. Large frames should be temporarily braced inside so they do not bow inward from the sides or top while you are doing stonework.

The door frames are often installed directly on the footings, and you should leave a gap in the forms through at least one doorway so you can go in and out with a wheelbarrow. For symmetry we usually align the tops of the windows with the tops of the doors, even if the windows are of multiple sizes. Measure down from the top of a door frame to find the starting point to install the windows. Mark this with a level and a pencil on the inside of the forms.

Slipforms can be used for scaffoling material.

Temporary supports held up the floating rafter until the concrete set.

Bridging the Thermal Gap

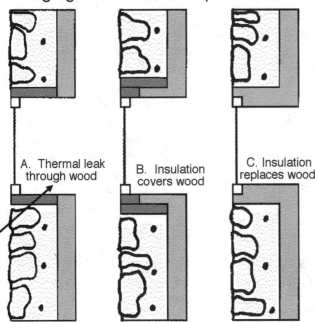

A. Thermal leak through wood

B. Insulation covers wood

C. Insulation replaces wood

Sometimes the hardest part is to remember to stop putting stones in before you rock in the whole opening!

The stonework should end 1 or 2 inches below the windows. Then lay in a thick bed of mortar and drop the window frame into the forms, tapping it into the mortar. Check with a level in all directions and recheck it as you work until the end of the day. Keep in mind that both your successes and your mistakes will be permanently "cast in stone".

Window and door frames up to about four feet wide can be spanned with stone by laying out multiple lengths of 1/2 inch rebar in a bed of mortar one-inch deep across the tops of the frames. Cover the rebar with more concrete, then add the stones. Longer spans may be bridged using 5/8 inch rebar or heavy I-beams or metal channel.

The Roof

The form-setting at the top of the wall must be very level. Fill the forms with stonework, but stop 1 to 2 inches below the top. Cap the top of the wall with a thick bed of mortar, but be careful to keep the mortar back from the outside edge so it does not run down the stonework. Trowel the mortar smooth with the tops of the walls, then tap L-shaped anchor bolts down into the fresh masonry, about every 4 feet along the walls. Attach a "**sill plate**" to the anchor bolts when the masonry is cured, and attach the roof system to the sill plate. A strip of fiberglass or foam "sill insulation" should be placed on top of the wall, sandwiched under the sill plate to separate the wood from the mortar. If moisture condenses on the cold concrete during the night, the insulation simply creates the necessary gap to prevent the wood from soaking it up and eventually rotting.

There are many different options for roofing systems, as covered in a later chapter. The method shown in these photos and illustrated on the next page is for a roof with conventional framed rafters or trusses. The gable ends are easy to fill in with stone once the rafters or trusses are in place. Just make sure you line up the rafters so that one set will be concreted into each gable, preferably along the inside edges of the walls. Then continue with the slipforming, using the rafters as a guide inside the forms. You will need to stop at the rafter bottoms, then pull the forms off and construct the floating rafters with supports resting on the stonework. Now finish the remaining stonework between the supports. This will be freehand work, without the use of forms.

Please note, when you are building a double stone wall with insulation in the core, then the inside wall should stop short enough to allow a continuous line of insulation from the wall into the roof.

We framed in the porch and grouted the walls.

Finished!

Grouting

Grouting is the process of filling in the joints between the rocks with a smooth sand, cement and lime mortar for a very finished appearance. Grouting the wall fills all the little spaces; it makes the rock work stronger and protects the wall from the weather. But first you need to use a hammer and a chisel or a rock pick to chip away the

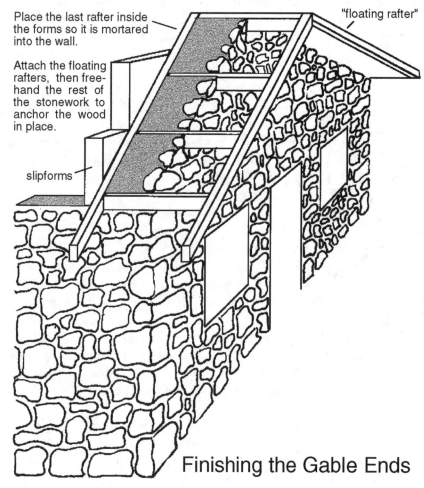

Place the last rafter inside the forms so it is mortared into the wall.

Attach the floating rafters, then free-hand the rest of the stonework to anchor the wood in place.

slipforms

"floating rafter"

Finishing the Gable Ends

concrete on the wall face. Chip the concrete back an inch or so in between the rocks; this will make enough space for the grouting mortar. Obviously it is best to chip away the concrete within a day or two of pouring it, before it becomes hard. Just be gentle around the stones. A bad hit can easily loosen a rock.

Note that many slipform stone homes are not grouted at all. The concrete is thoroughly worked into every joint during the slipforming phase, and any extra globs are removed immediately after the forms are removed. One builder I talked to simply drug the claws of his hammer around through all the semi-set mortar joints to create an even texture.

When working with round river rocks, as in the Gruber house, shown at the bottom of these two pages, it is usually necessary to use extra concrete to firmly grip the round surfaces of the rocks. In other words, it may not be possible to safely leave out or remove enough concrete to make room for grouting mortar.

However, with the sharply angular field stones that we usually work with, it is possible to bind them firmly in place while leaving deeply recessed joints to fill with grout later. Grouting does not need to be done right away, but it is good to do it while you still have momentum on the project. Besides, grouting brings out the beauty in your stone work. It is the masonry equivalent of framing a picture.

We have tried many different mixes for grouting work, and we now prefer a mix of 1 part lime to 2 parts cement (Type I & II), and 8 parts masonry sand. We measure this with coffee cans and mix it in the wheelbarrow

Pouring the footing for the Gruber house. (Dani Gruber photos.)

The house walls were framed with EPS beadboard building panels.

Mixing grout for the walls.

with a hoe. It could be mixed in a cement mixer, but the batches are usually too small and spaced too far apart to justify setting up and afterwards cleaning up the mixer. The mortar should be moist enough to easily work into the wall, without being so wet that it sags in the joints, or smears all over the rock faces. Hose down the wall before you start grouting, so the old concrete does not suck the moisture out of the fresh grout.

Additional tools you will need for grouting are a mortar board and small trowels. A mortar board can be made by attaching any kind of a handle to the middle of a 12 inch square piece of 1/2 inch plywood. Hold the board from underneath and pile the mortar on top. Then place the edge of the board against the wall where you are working and shove the mortar directly off the board into the mortar joints around the stones. There are many sizes of grouting or pointing trowels commercially available, but my favorite tool is still a cheap, flexible putty knife, about 1 1/4 inches wide.

Grouting finishes the wall.

It may seem odd to use such a wide trowel when so many of the mortar joints are less than an inch wide, but there are also wider joints, and this one tool works for them all. We fill the joints with cement, then press the trowels back in at an angle along the edges of the rocks; this highlights the individual stones while bulging out the center of the mortar joints. Of course there are many other styles of grouting, and you should practice on an out-of-the-way part of the wall until you come up with a technique you like.

Grouting can be an excruciatingly slow process, but it is a process I have learned to enjoy. To often we rush, rush, rush from one project to another, but grouting cannot be rushed. You may spend an entire day grouting an 8 foot by 10 foot section of wall, but it is meditative work. You will have time to reflect on your Dreams and how to continue achieving them in the most effortless ways. You may ultimately save more time on all your other projects than you actually spent staring at the wall doing the grouting! Then, at the end of the day, you may step back and blink, realizing that your castle walls are finished, and it really did not take all that long after all!

The stone walls were slipformed up against the insulation.

A very ambitious project, nearly complete!

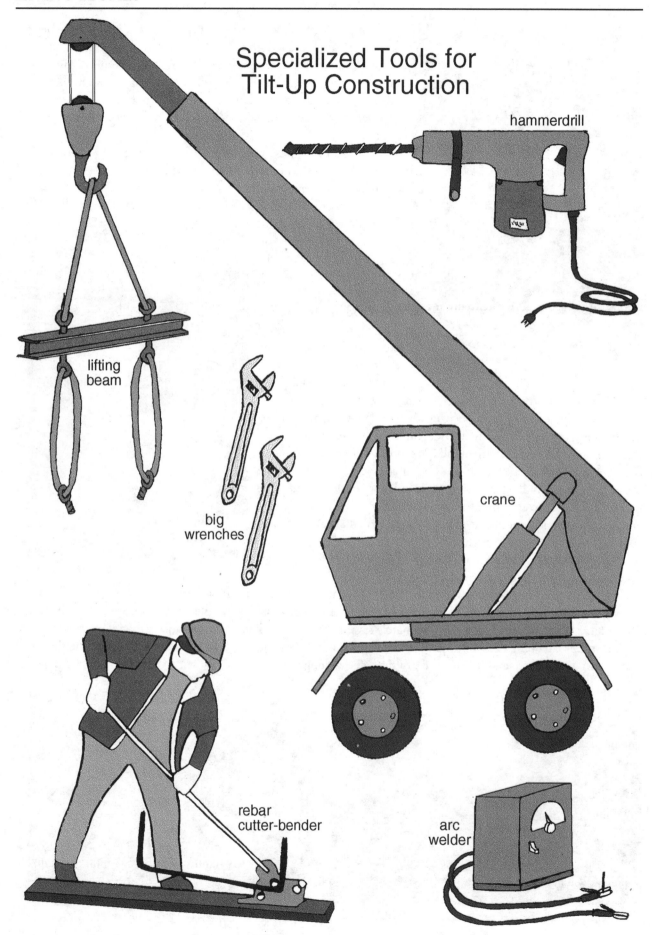

Specialized Tools for Tilt-Up Construction

hammerdrill

lifting beam

big wrenches

crane

rebar cutter-bender

arc welder

Tilt-Up Construction
Exploring Time-Saving Methods of Stone Construction

Tilt-up construction is the process of pouring masonry walls flat on the ground, then "tilting" them up into position. My interest in tilt-up construction developed out of the desire to mass-produce stone houses. Stone buildings can last for hundreds of years without falling apart the way most modern frame houses do. The environment would simply be better off if we took the time now to build quality houses that would last for generations. The only problem is that conventional stone masonry is too labor-intensive to compete with frame construction in the

market place. I turned to tilt-up construction as a way to minimize the labor and potentially mass-produce stone walls. The cost per house could be lowered substantially if a person made a single set of forms and made many duplicates. If the cost of a stone house compared favorably with the cost of a frame house, then I think many buyers would choose stone.

Tilt-up construction, I should point out, is definitely not for beginners. For one thing, you will not save any money on materials, because there is just as much concrete, and usually more rebar, in a tilt-up stone wall, versus a slipformed stone wall. In addition to the materials cost, you will need to hire an engineer to approve of the plans and a crane operator to lift the walls, which

We practiced tilt-up construction on Nick's garage first.

may cost several thousand dollars before you are done. Also keep in mind that moving concrete panels weighing thousands of pounds each is implicitly hazardous. In the event of an accident, your body may fit into a casket about an inch high. Tilt-up construction requires a high level of precision and advance planning, far beyond any practical level for beginners. Slipform masonry, on the other hand, is relatively forgiving and slow enough that you can catch many mistakes before you get there.

Nevertheless, for the experienced builder, or someone who wants to make numerous copies of a single structure, tilt-up construction may be the way to go. As for my own interests in tilt-up construction, the biggest problem was that I spent years mastering slipforming, and then had to start at "ground zero" learning the process of tilt-up construction. As you might know from my other books and our extensive website, I already have too many

Forms for interlocking corners, plus window frame and moulding.

House walls. Rocks and rebar are set in place. Ready for concrete.

"irons in the fire", so it is difficult to take the time to figure out a whole new construction method.

Fortunately, my brother Nick grew interested in the idea and decided to figure it out himself. Nick built and remodeled conventional frame homes for over fifteen years, then decided he wanted to construct permanent, low maintenance homes. Stone was an easy choice for that. He purchased a building lot a block away from our place and built a stone garage as the first test run with tilt-up construction. I worked with him during much of the project. Through the process we learned a lot about what Not to do, and gained some valuable insights for the next tilt-up project, his house.

Experimentation

Any kind of new process involves a "learning curve" where the job takes longer and costs more at first, then gets easier with experience. Coming from a background in conventional construction, the transition to stone masonry and tilt-up construction was especially torturous for Nick, since he was accustomed to working fast, efficiently, and with a high-level of quality on everything he built. He was also used to working in the city where he could run to the store for anything he needed. Our little town is an hour away from the city.

Rebar was wrapped around the beadboard cores in the interlocking corners. (The beadboard was later burned out.) After setting the walls in place, a rebar pin was dropped down through the hollow corner, followed by concrete to bind everything together.

The process was much less painful for me, obviously, since it was his place and not mine, but also because I was accustomed to tinkering around with prototype projects that take much longer than they should. In fact, I have never built anything fast or efficiently, so my expectations were really low! Besides, it simply isn't practical to run to town for unanticipated parts and materials. I've never known anything but the routine of country living. Most of the time it just works better to put the tools away and do something else for a week or two until you need to go to town for something else. I try not to be in too much of a hurry on any kind of a building project.

One particular complication was the season. Frame construction can be built in just about any kind of weather, but masonry work absolutely must be protected from freezing. Masonry work can be done any time of year, assuming you are willing to use enough plastic and lumber for tents and fuel for heat, but there is definitely a cost involved. We worked through one of the coldest, wettest winters in recent memory, often breathing diesel fumes and carbon monoxide under half-ventilated tents. We built a temporary wood-fired boiler with a pump and hoses to keep fresh masonry work warm under a layer of straw. We succeeded in building the garage in winter, but it cost a third more and took twice as long than it would have in summer.

Another major problem was the cramped workplace, a site dug into the side of a hill. There wasn't enough space to pour the panels separately. The walls had to be built in a stack on the site. When it came time to assemble the garage we had to move each of the panels out of the way first, then pick them up again and put them in the right

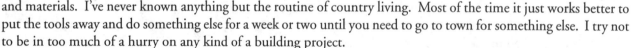

Pouring the Wall

Concrete fills the beadboard moulding around the windows.

places. Each panel had to be lifted at least twice, occasionally three times before the process was all over, more than doubling the cost of the crane work.

We made many improvements to the system before starting Nick's house, as illustrated through the photos and text of this chapter. I believe that with the appropriate building site and a set of plans optimized for that site, that there would be a definite savings with tilt-up stone work... especially if you made reusable forms and duplicated the house several times. That is a dream of mine for the near future.

This chapter provides an overview of the tilt-up process, but not too many details. I need to build some additional structures with the tilt-up method before I have the depth of experince needed to give step-by-step details. Be sure to watch for updates on our website.

Two styles of pickup points are shwon here, one for grabbing the top of the wall, the other for grabbing the side. Only the latter seemed to be necessary. Note that the legs are secured behind the rebar.

Footings

Tilt-up work is often used in large modern buildings. Some buildings are put together really well, while others look like they would fall down with the most gentle quaking of the earth. Coarse, decorative gravel is often used on the face of the wall, and there are usually bare patches where the stones have fallen out. Most tilt-up structures seem to rely on concrete or steel post and beam structures, using the panels as mere infill between the posts.

Bonding the walls to the footing is a unique challenge in tilt-up construction that virtually requires putting up the panels first, then pouring the footing underneath. The solution we found was to pour concrete pads at the corners or other joints where two panels come together. The pads should be big enough to support both panels, usually about two feet square. Rebar should extend out of the concrete pads into the future footing. Rebar should also extend out of the bottom of the wall panels, to bond into the footing.

The concrete pads should be poured in place on solid ground, never poured in forms and moved into place. We tried the latter with Nick's garage, since the wall panels were in the way. Leveling the pads on a gravel base was much like putting them on ball-bearings—it was very difficult to keep them in place long enough to assemble the building. Pouring the pads in place for the house greatly solidified the base and simplified the process.

Note that the footings should also be placed below the frost line. That wasn't an issue with Nick's place, since both the house and garage are nestled into the hill. However, on a flat building site, it would be advisable to design a floor plan where the main level is placed below frost line to avoid using any extra concrete. (See my draft plans for a tilt-up house in the *Conclusion*.)

When you pour the pads, you should also pour a "deadman" anchor in the center of the house. It should be a very solid and unmovable pad of concrete, so that you can bolt a temporary brace to it to support the wall, as shown on the following page.

A finished panel with interlocking corners.

Walls are lifted with a crane and set into place.

Forming the Walls

Bonding tilt-up panels to the footing is only half the challenge. The walls must also be bonded to each other, to look and function as a single unit. Weld plates should be pressed into the wet concrete to connect the wall panels together at the joints, but this is only a temporary fix. For true bonding the walls must be permanently connected.

The **garage** consisted of many small panels—seventeen in all— two for each side of the building, three inside the garage, plus six roof panels. The concrete roof served as a load-bearing surface which was covered with earth to make the yard. The panels were bonded together with the footing at the bottom and a bond beam at the top. Rebar was left protruding from the roof and the wall panels and intertwined to join them together. We set forms and poured concrete to make a bond beam around three sides of the building. To hide the joints between the panels, we simply left out a few stones in the beginning and filled them in by hand afterwards, bridging the gap in the process. The stones hid the joints while the bond beam tied the panels together, but this project was both labor intensive and very expensive. The specialized roof panels were especially costly. While we saved time on the stone panels, we realized it would be cheaper and easier to pour the concrete walls in the back with conventional concrete forms.

The first wall was secured with a temporary metal prop bolted to the wall and to a concrete block buried in the floor, thus freeing the crane to pickup the next wall.

Putting the **house** together was much easier, partly because it did not have a concrete roof, but also because the wall panels interlocked without the need for custom stonework to cover the joints. As you can see in the picture series, Nick built wood forms to make interlocking corners. The beadboard columns cast into the concrete created a round void (after drilling out the beadboard) to drop a one inch-diameter rebar pin down through the corners. With the rebar also wrapped around the columns, it was much like an interlocking hinge, except that mortar was poured down the hole and troweled between the joints to permanently bond the panels together. Leave a full inch for each mortar joint between the corner blocks, so you have plenty of room to maneuver the panels. Measure everything a hundred times if necessary to insure accuracy. You cannot afford to get the panels up in the air, only to find they do not fit together!

Keep in mind that the ground is part of the formwork, so it must be perfectly flat. Level the site as much as possible, then stake down the perimeter forms and level them. Next, rake the ground smooth inside, adding or removing dirt as necessary. Make a screed that fits inside the forms to check for level, and spread a thin layer of sand over the site to make a good surface to work from.

Window and door frames must be included in the formwork before the pour. Nick used wooden frames combined with ornate trim made with the aid of custom-cut beadboard molds. The beadboard factory is nearby, so Nick provided a profile of the trim, and the factory used a hot wire to cut that pattern from the insulation. The mold was placed around the window frame and simply filled with concrete to make permanent trim. The beadboard was

Note the four separate pick-up points used by the crane.

Panels were welded together inside. Ridgepole connects both ends.

removed after the walls were lifted. The mold left a beadboard texture on the trim. The beadboard is also easily injured, so it would be better in the long run to make reusable forms from sheet metal.

Another option to consider is the **beadboard window frames** I described in the chapter *The Art of Slipforming*, making them thick enough to serve as trim. An ornate pattern could be cut into the edge, if desired. Instead of concrete trim, the beadboard would be left in place and surfaced with a stucco-like finish, such as Log Jam or Dry-vit.

Structurally, keep in mind that the concrete and rebar holds this type of wall together as it is lifted and set in place. The panels should be at least seven inches thick, with only 2-3 inches of the total for stonework. Because the stones are thin, they should also have small faces, ideally less than 12 inches across, to bind them securely into the wall. Bigger stones may be prone to popping off of the wall, leaving ugly patches of concrete.

Nick used flat field **stone** for his projects. Each stone was placed carefully in the forms, leaving space for mortar joints all the way around. Although faster than slipform stone masonry, it was still a time-consuming process of sorting through the puzzle pieces to find just the right stones each step of the way. For the purpose of mass-production it may be necessary to use round stones which can be rolled into place with minimal fitting work. I would recommend doing a test panel with round rocks before attempting the real thing.

Lifting cables are bolted into the pickup points imbeded in the wall.

Note that on the garage we did the stonework (and the trim) face up on the panels, pouring the concrete first, then quickly adding the stonework on top. We did it that way to better control the mortar joints between the stones. However, it was difficult, fast-paced work to set the stones in the fresh cement, level them and fill the joints—without smearing mortar on the faces, and to do this before the concrete set. We decided to pour the house panels with the stonework face down on the ground, pouring the concrete slab over the top.

To make **recessed mortar joints**, Nick sprinkled a mix of sand and bentonite clay powder about half an inch deep between the rocks. The bentonite swells when damp, making a waterproof barrier so the cement slurry does not leak through the joints and stain the rock faces. Spread the sand/bentonite mix between the rocks, then sweep the back of the rocks clean. Mist over the site with a hose to dampen the bentonite and start the swelling. Then it is time for the reinforcing bar.

Make a grid of 1/2" or 5/8" **rebar** spaced one foot apart throughout the walls, with additional, thicker rebar around windows and doors. The rebar should be propped into the middle of the panel for maximum strength. Panels up to about twenty-four feet wide, tapering to a peaked roof of similar height can be lifted with a mid-sized crane. Larger panels would require more serious engineering and a much larger crane.

After the rebar, you must imbed **pickup points** for the crane to grab on to, as pictured earlier in this chapter. The legs of the pickup point should be placed behind a section of rebar to insure that the pickup point doesn't rip out of the wall in mid air. A plastic plug keeps the threaded hole free of concrete, so the lifting cable can be bolted right

Back walls were poured with conventional formwork.

A heavy tar coating keeps the moisture out.

to the wall. Note that in a large wall, as pictured back a couple pages, there are four pickup points to evenly spread the load. It is advisable to consult an engineer for optimal placement.

Pouring the concrete is much like pouring a slab. Six sack cement is advisable for optimal strength (refer to the *Cement Mixing and Measuring Guide*). Fill the forms and screed off the top. Then tap the **weld plates** into the mortar, positioned so that they will nearly touch when two walls come together. This is also the time to add metal brackets to attach floor joists, purlins, or a ridgepole, if those are included in your plans. The concrete must cure for at least two weeks before lifting, but three or four weeks would be better, just to be on the safe side.

The cast-in-place concrete trim gives the house a professional look.

Lifting the Walls

Lifting the walls is clearly the most exciting aspect of building a tilt-up house, both for the builder and for spectators. People may drive by for weeks not knowing what you are up to, but all of a sudden there are these massive stone walls standing there like they've always been there. Lifting the walls is also the most hazardous aspect of the work, so make safety your top priority.

Before you start a tilt-up house you will have to find out what types of **cranes** are available and how much they can lift. Each cubic yard of concrete and rock in the walls weighs about 2,000 pounds. (See the *Cement Mixing and Measuring Guide* to calculate volume.) Check the phone book, or simply watch for cranes at construction sites, and stop to ask questions. If they can't help you with your project, they can probably lead you to someone else who can. Note that a crane can lift more when the load is close to the rig, such that the boom is almost straight up and down. The lift capacity drops dramatically as the boom is lowered toward a horizontal position. In other words, a crane rated to carry the weight of your panels may not be able to reach far enough with the load to do any good. You will need to describe the panels you are working with and your job site, to make sure that the crane can lift the panels *and* put them where they belong.

Also note that the crane may not have the proper **attachments** to lift wall panels. A crane usually comes with a hook, and everything else is purchased or improvised as needed. If necessary, show them the pictures here, and they can tell you what they have or need. You may be able to purchase or make the attachments and give them to the operator as partial payment. Or you might want to keep them for your own future projects. Make sure that every little part is ready to go, before the crane shows up and starts billing you $200 or more per hour while you run to the hardware store for extra parts.

After the cables are bolted onto the wall, the lift is all crane work. If necessary, you can stand at the edge of the panel to guide it as it floats through the air. Avoid passing beside the panel, where it could flatten you like a pancake in an accident. Be sure to make guide marks ahead of time on the concrete pads, so that you know exactly

2 x 10 rafters makes for a sturdy roof.

1 x 4 skip sheathing makes a base for the steel roofing.

where to put the wall. As long as the crane is lifting some of the weight, it is relatively easy to pry the wall in any direction with a prybar. The wall must also be checked for square with the house and plumb along the face and the edges. There are special durable plastic shims available for tilt-up work, or you can cut some scraps of metal in varying thicknesses for the same purpose.

When the wall is exactly where it belongs, lock it in place with the aid of a brace bolted between the wall and a solid pad of concrete anchored in the floor. Have the crane slack the cables gradually, to make sure everything is okay. If nothing moves, then you can move on to the next panel. Keep in mind that a single panel could easily be blown over in a strong wind. Once you start this project you must finish it!

Subsequent panels can be set into place without the need for a brace. Again, check and recheck for level, plumb and square. Weld the panels together with the weld plates imbedded in the concrete at the corners. You will likely need to use metal scraps to bridge the gap between the plates. Make sure these are good welds, as that is the only thing that will be holding the house together until the footings and corners are poured with concrete.

Expect the panels to be quite messy when you first lift them off the ground. The sand and bentonite mixture really sticks to the wall, and you may have to scrape it out of every nook and cranny with a stick. Optionally, give it time to dry out and shrink, then sweep it out with a broom. Be patient and the remaining residue will crumble away over the months (possibly years), exposing your beautiful stonework.

Finishing Touches

After the walls are up, it is time to go back to the beginning and pour the footings. Use plenty of rebar and pour a wide footing, similar to

Nick poured concrete risers for the stairs from the house down to the garage. The stones were fitted into sand and gravel base without mortar.

those used in slipform construction. Also insert the rebar pin in the corners and pour the cores full of concrete. From that point the rest of the construction can be finished any way you choose.

Since Nick's place is built into the hill, he only tilted up three sides of the house, then used conventional concrete forms to pour the back walls. Rebar from the tilt-up panels extends into the poured concrete walls. Slipform masonry was used for the stonework on the porch.

Nick built a stone stairway from the house down to the garage, as pictured here. There is a curved concrete retaining wall (shown at the beginning of the chapter) and railing along the lower part of the stairs, but only part of the railing shows here. He poured concrete risers for the stairs, then set the stones into a sand and gravel base without mortar. Another innovative idea Nick worked with was a wood-fired boiler built into the side of the hill down by the garage. He never has to haul firewood into the house or clean up the mess of it later. Hot water from the boiler is circulated through a radiator in the garage and a radiant floor in the house. The house is insulated enough that the boiler only has to be used two or three days a week through the winter to keep it warm.

All closed in...

... and finished!

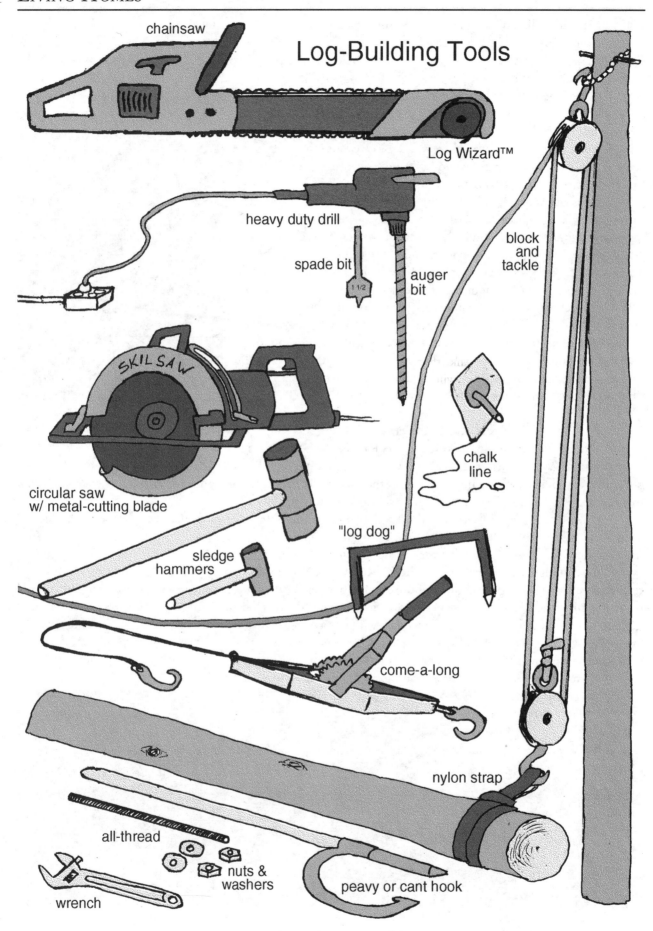

Log-Building Tools

chainsaw

Log Wizard™

heavy duty drill

spade bit

1 1/2

auger bit

block and tackle

SKILSAW

circular saw w/ metal-cutting blade

chalk line

"log dog"

sledge hammers

come-a-long

nylon strap

all-thread

nuts & washers

wrench

peavy or cant hook

Log Building Basics
For Builders with Little Time or Experience

There may be hundreds of methods of fitting logs together and hundreds of books on the subject of building log houses. Given the amount of information available on log house construction already, it seems like there should be no need for yet more coverage of the topic. However, most log-building techniques require a great deal of skill and much time to carefully scribe and notch the ends to fit together. Some methods include scribing and fitting the entire length of every log. But most people in today's world simply do not have the necessary craftsmanship background nor the requisite amount of time it takes to learn this art form. Fortunately you do not have to become a master craftsman to be able to build a high-quality log structure in relatively little time.

The traditional methods of log-building have been passed down from a time when people went out into the woods and built cabins with little more than an ax, a saw, and an adz. The logs had to be notched because it was the only way to tie the pieces together as a stable structure. Modern log home companies continue to do the scribing and notching in part because they have the big, automatic tools to easily shape and fit the logs together, but also because they can build a house at the factory, then take it apart and ship the parts to the home site for snap-together assembly.

Today there are inexpensive modern materials available that greatly simplify the process of log building so you can put up a house with very little in the way of skill, time, or money. Especially, the use of a big electric drill, lots of cheap reinforcing bar (otherwise known as "rebar"), and a sledge hammer, allows you to pin the logs together with essentially no scribing, no notching, and no close fitting. The final product is in fact stronger than a scribed and notched log home. As far as I know, this "butt-joint" method was originated by a man named Skip Ellsworth, who teaches log-building seminars in Washington state.

Structurally, there are many advantages to the butt-joint method versus original log-building techniques. For instance, the traditional scribing and notching immediately weakens the logs at the joints and creates vulnerable places for moisture and rot to set in. Also, traditional log houses tend to "settle" over time, potentially wreaking havoc with doors and windows. These log homes have to be carefully engineered with hidden spaces above doors and windows, so that the logs can settle without destroying the openings. On the other hand, the butt-joint method has no vulnerable notches for rot to start in, and all the pieces are so shiscabobbed together with rebar that there is no settling. The window and door frames can be nailed directly to the logs without worry. With the butt-joint method it is even possible, at least in theory, to build a house with green logs, rather than waiting six months or more for the logs to season. The only major reason why you would need to let the logs season is because green logs are very heavy and therefore more dangerous to work with than after they are dried.

Surveying the logs.

Bolting the lifting logs to the wall.

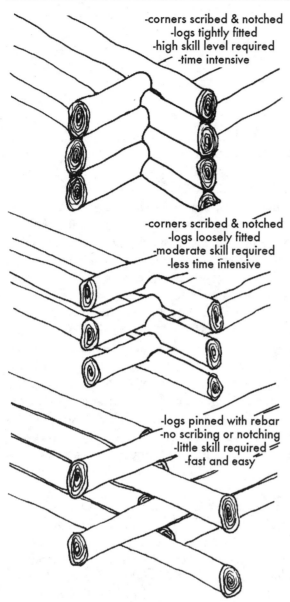

-corners scribed & notched
-logs tightly fitted
-high skill level required
-time intensive

-corners scribed & notched
-logs loosely fitted
-moderate skill required
-less time intensive

-logs pinned with rebar
-no scribing or notching
-little skill required
-fast and easy

Log Joints Comparison

Logs to Build With

The pioneers of this country were, for the most part, very practical people who made do with what they found at hand and log houses were the logical choice where there was an abundance of trees to work with. In an era when real estate was essentially free to anyone who chose to call it their own, the pioneers could both adapt their houses to the resources at hand, and choose a home site that was close to the materials they wanted to use. Acquiring the logs to build with often involved no more than cutting down the trees that grew immediately around the chosen home site. Today few of us have the luxury of a private woodlot at our disposal. Chances are you will need to purchase logs through a logger who has the necessary equipment to cut and haul logs from the timber site to your doorstep.

There are still many small-scale, independent loggers who bid on public or private timber sales; usually they cut the trees and resell them to lumber mills or they manufacture and sell their own log home kits. These independent loggers are the most flexible to work with, and you will usually save money buying directly from them, versus purchasing through a mill.

You can build with just about any kind of trees imaginable, as long as they are reasonably tall, halfway straight, and large enough in diameter. A few trees such as cottonwoods are rarely used in log homes, but with the increasing prices and pressure on conifer forests, cottonwoods should be considered as a reasonable substitute.

Ethically speaking, building with logs is a complicated question. Certainly there are plenty of trees in the world for building and for firewood, but the questions remain: which trees are they? where did they come from? how were they harvested?

You will sometimes hear from environmental organizations that only 10% of our original forests remain. That in itself is true. There are very few old-growth forests left, and they need to be protected. The other truth is that there are more trees in America today than ever before, mostly because fire control programs and urbanization have allowed trees to grow in places where they couldn't before.

Hoisting the first log into place.

Drilling through a log to pin it in place.

In most cases the process of logging is very destructive, with roads being gouged into the side of steep hills and all the trees "clear-cut", leaving bare soils susceptible to erosion and noxious weed infestation. Erosion depletes the forest soils and muddies nearby creeks, destroying fish habitat. Also, forests often have intricate relationships between the trees and fungus in the soil. Clear-cut logging can kill the fungus and greatly impede reforestation. (Note, however, that there are a few environments where clear-cut logging may be "beneficial".)

Some regions have recently switched from clear-cut to "selective" logging, where only the biggest trees in the forest are marked and cut, so the forest is thinned, rather than leveled. Selective cutting is almost always preferable to clear-cutting, but the question remains about the roads into the logging sites. Roads are notorious for erosion and they are often the cause of mud slides. Moreover, they allow hunters easy access to game animals, so that populations are reduced and ultimately more hunting restrictions (fewer permits and shorter seasons) must be put in place.

Ideally then, you should build with standing dead or green logs that have been selectively cut from a forest with preexisting, permanent roads, or where the roads are reclaimed afterwards. This concern obviously complicates the process of purchasing logs, just as it complicates the process of buying a board at the lumber yard, or a ream of paper for the copy machine-even subscribing to the daily newspaper. You are left with the options of either a) researching and buying only "ecologically friendly" wood products, b) finding wood alternatives, or c) putting the ethics out of your head as "somebody else's problem", not yours. The best choice might be a combination of all the above.

Obviously it would be difficult to find an alternative to wood if you are building a log house, and I do think that inorganic materials like stone and concrete are a better bet ecologically. If you were to do everything necessary to find and purchase genuinely eco-friendly logs you might end up paying ten times as much for them. Nevertheless, it doesn't hurt to politely ask questions and to express a generalized concern for the way the logs are harvested. Other than that, if you choose to build with timber of any kind, you just about have to put ethics aside and hope for a better way of timbering in the future. At the very least you can join an environmental organization and promote better logging practices.

The trees we used were killed in a forest fire, so the ecosystem was already reverting to grassland, and the heat split all the logs (called "checks"), so they were useless for milling lumber. Overall, I think that is about as eco-friendly as a person can find, although I have always wanted to see the site myself to better understand the impacts of building our home. In any case we do enjoy the little black spots in the knots and the other recessed places where charcoal is still visible. The charcoal spots help to tell the story about these trees and where they came from. I would enjoy building log houses commercially if I owned a woodlot to selectively harvest the trees from.

As for the quantity of logs, you should ideally order about 20% more than you need, so you can use the best logs and weed out the bad ones. Logs taper significantly over their length, so it is easiest to figure the quantity from the "average" or "middle" diameter of the logs. For instance, an eight-foot tall wall will require eight logs with an average or middle diameter of twelve inches. In some locations you may be able to find larger logs, while in other places you would have to use smaller material. Just make sure you are using the same language as the logger you work with, since some people use average diameter, while others use the butt or even the tip diameter when measuring logs. The logs should be at least three or four feet longer than the actual lengths needed.

A block and tackle and sling is used on each end of the logs.

The strap must be removed before pounding the rebar all the way in.

We paid $1,300 in 1990 for the 34 logs we used to construct the 15' x 40' upper story of our home, including the numerous logs we used to support the ridgepole, the floors, and to frame in the front of the greenhouse. Bob and Judy paid about $4,000 for the 101 logs used in their two story 32' x 32' log home (which also has a full basement). Logging and lumber prices have changed a lot since that time, so you may have to pay more than double that amount. The cost of logs is likely to vary significantly from one region to another, and you would be wise to shop around.

Seasoning and Peeling the Logs

If you start with green trees then it is best to cut them in the fall or winter when the sap is down. The logs will dry lighter and with less checking (cracking) than if they are cut during the growing season. The bark should be peeled off the logs at the home site.

Green logs can be peeled easily with a "peeling spud", a tool with a sharp blade, kind of like a hoe, but straight instead of hooked. In theory the logs could be used green, but it is preferable to season them. Two sacrificial logs are placed on the ground, and the rest are laid across, so the air can freely circulate around them. The logs are turned about every ten days for at least three months. The drying rack should be placed in the shade of a tree, or a tarp can be rigged to provide shade, but the tarp must not be laid directly on the logs. The circulation of air around the logs is important for proper curing.

Ellsworth says to "never" use a drawknife on the logs because the blade cuts across the layers, exposing the edge of the tree rings to the weather. In essence, logs with the least injury will be the most protected from future rot, a genuine concern in the wet Pacific Northwest. Drier parts of the country are certainly more forgiving.

A peeling spud would have been useless on the charcoal-black, fire-killed logs we used in our home. The bark was seared onto the logs. We tried a drawknife and peeled a strip about five feet long down one log and determined that the job would be nearly impossible that way too. Fortunately the logger we hired brought along an ingenious tool called a "Log Wizard™", essentially a planer blade in a casing that mounts on the end of a chain saw. The chain drives the blade and all the operator has to do is to walk backwards, dragging the Wizard down the log. Each pass peels off one narrow strip of bark. It takes several passes to peal one sides of a log. The log has to be turned three or four times to completely strip it. With practice I was able to peel a forty foot log, with an average diameter of twelve inches, in about twenty minutes. The finished appearance looks very similar to a log that has been peeled with a drawknife. The Log Wizard can also be used on green logs, but the sap tends to gum up the tool.

The Log Wizard retailed for $185-$200 in 1990. With inflation it will no doubt cost more when you purchase one for yourself. Ask for the Log Wizard at your local saw shop, or look for it at the hollowtop.com web site in the future.

The Essential Log Catalog

The most essential organizational step in building a log house, besides having well-designed house plans, is to make a written inventory of your log supply. First number each of the logs using bright spray paint or crayons then measure the diameter of the big and small ends and the length of each log. The catalog should also include a

A 2 x 4 nailed to the "overdangles" makes a ramp for the next log.

Almost up! A partial doorway allowed us to go in and out.

description of the characteristics of each log, for example, "slight bend", "lots of
knots" or "straight".

At this point you
should also pick out and label logs for specific projects.
For instance, even though
the ridgepole is one of the
last logs used, it should be
the first log chosen usually
the straightest log with the
biggest diameter and
marked in the description as
"ridgepole". Also pick out

Log Catalog					
Log No.	Large Diameter	Small Diameter	Length	Description	Location
1	26"	12"	42' 6"	slight double-twist	east side
2	17"	9"	39' 5"	straight	east side
3	19"	10"	40' 9"	good	east side
4	25"	14"	43' 1"	straight—ridgepole	south side
5	16"	8"	40' 2"	bad bend	south side
6	18"	12"	42' 8"	straight—cap log	east side
7	10"	6"	36' 5"	lifting log	east side
8	22"	13"	41' 7"	very good	east side
9	23"	10"	40'	good	south side

the "cap logs", which are the top logs on the walls, parallel to the ridgepole. The rafters sit right on the cap logs, so
the straighter the better. You can also choose the "**lifting logs**". The lifting logs are placed upright in each corner of
the house during construction, and a block-and-tackle (pulley system) is mounted on each pole to easily lift logs into
place. The lifting logs should be at least five feet higher than the finished walls, and preferably five feet higher than
the ridgepole too.

Note: if the logs are in separate piles, or positioned out of numerical order for any reason, then the catalog
should include a column for "location" as well. Once completed, your log catalog will make it easy to pick out the
best logs every step of the way.

Mounting the Lifting Poles

It is possible to build a small log cabin with very few tools at all, using short logs that can be hand-lifted, or
rolled up a ramp into place. To build a log house, however, you will no doubt use very large and heavy timbers, and
you will hoist many of them high above your head. Fortunately the use of "block-and-tackle" or pulley systems
makes it easy and safe to lift and position logs that are many times larger than yourself. The block-and-tackle is hung
from a "lifting pole" in each corner of the house. With four lifting poles you can tie on to both ends of the logs for
any wall and easily steer them into place. The cost of pulley systems, and all the rope that is used with them, adds up
quickly, but it is probably the best tool investment you can make when building a log house.

The lifting poles need to be at least five feet taller than the planned height of the wall, and preferably five
feet taller than the planned top of the ridgepole too. The lifting log can be secured against a foundation wall by
drilling and bolting through both the log and concrete. (Better yet, plan ahead and concrete a small pipe in place so
you can bolt through it later.) The poles may need to be spaced out a few inches from the concrete with wooden
blocks to make enough room for the width of the logs. If you are working off of pier blocks then you will need an
even longer lifting pole, so you can plant it four or five feet into the ground.

Ropes from the block and tackle to the trucks made log lifting easy.

We pounded rebar pins in at the corners into the butt ends.

Lifting pole with block-and-tackle attached.

The lifting logs should be reasonably small diameter and therefore lightweight, so that a few people, possibly with the aid of one or two ropes, can lift them into position. A 1/2" hole should be drilled through near the top of each pole beforehand, and a short length of rebar pounded through. The rebar will be used later as a stop to hold a loop of chain at the top of the pole, and the block-and-tackle is hung on the chain.

The lifting poles also need to be cross-braced with one another using come-alongs and steel cables to tie from the top of each pole to the bottom of the next, making an "X" between each of the poles. Put an extension ladder up to the top of the pole, and carry up the chain loop and the block-and-tackle. The block and tackle with all the rope can be very heavy, and the ladder unstable against the round lifting pole. Be sure to have lots of help holding the ladder steady. Hang all four pulley systems in place and you are ready for the fun part-putting up the walls.

Block and tackle.

Building the Walls: The First Layer

Putting up log walls is fast and fun with the butt-joint method, especially after the first layer of logs is up. The first layer is the most difficult, because holes must be pre-drilled and the logs carefully lowered onto the rebar that extends out of the foundation wall or pier blocks.

Start by snapping a chalk line down the center of the foundation wall or across the pier blocks. Leave enough width at the corner for another log to pass by, and mark the point where the butt-end of the first log begins. Then measure the distance to each length of rebar protruding from the concrete, and the amount of offset left or right from the chalk line. But, instead of using the terms "left" or "right", which are relative to your position, I recommend communicating in terms of the cardinal points, "north, south, east, and west".

With all the measurements taken, choose a log to begin with, and turn it slowly with a peavey. The log will be difficult to put in place if it is bowed towards the top or bottom, so turn it to determine which way the bow goes and place it to the outside of the wall. Placing the bend to the outside makes the room seem slightly bigger than if the bend is to the inside. Logs with excessive bows to them should be

We worked in teams, drilling and pounding.

Setting the RPSL on a concrete pad in the basement.

used on walls of lesser importance such as behind the closets.

With the top and bottom determined, turn the log over so you can work on the bottom. Snap a chalk line from end to end, then measure and mark the distance to each length of rebar and the offset from the chalk line. Remember to make the offsets in reverse, since the log is turned over.

Next use a 5/8" inch drill bit and drill clear through the log at each mark made for the rebar. Only the first layer of logs is drilled with the large drill bit, so the 1/2" rebar can slide easily through the loose holes. The upper layers are drilled with a 1/2" bit for a tight fit, and the rebar is sledge-hammered in.

The easiest way to move a log into position along the walls is to wrap a chain around it and drag it behind a truck to the correct spot. Release the chain and wrap the nylon straps around the log as close as possible to the points where the log will sit next to the lifting poles. Then hoist the log into position, either by hand, or by tying the pull ropes securely to the frames of two vehicles (not the bumpers), and driving slowly backwards. It helps to use a system of clearly defined and easily visible hand signals to communicate between those who are monitoring the action close-up, and those who are driving backwards pulling the logs into position. With the first layer, the logs must be slowly and carefully lowered onto the protruding spears of rebar. You may need to pound on the log to make it go down, if there is too much friction with the rebar in the holes.

When the log is fully lowered into position then release the block-and-tackle, take out the nylon straps, and finally use a sledge hammer to bend over the short stubs of rebar protruding through the top of the log. Ideally the rebar should stick out 2 or 3 inches. The bent-over rebar will secure the first row of logs in place.

Continue in this way, putting on the first row of logs all the way around. Be sure to match big ends to big ends and small ends to small ends at each of the corners. Use the log catalog to choose logs that match up nicely with each other. Ideally you should select logs four-at-a-time, so that you have one entire layer figured out before you put any in place.

Pinning the First Log

The positions of the rebar on the wall must be measured and transferred to the bottom of the first log. Drill through from the bottom so the log can be lowered on to the rebar. The cardinal points aid communication more than "left" and "right".

Continuing Up the Walls

Putting up the first layer of logs involved butting the big ends of the logs together at two corners diagonally across from each other, and butting the small ends together at the other two corners. The logs for the second layer should be positioned just the opposite to level out the height of the wall. After each layer you should measure the

Support logs around the front door will support the other RPSL

Moving the lifting poles. Note the beams to support upper floors.

height from the top of the foundation to the top of the logs at each corner, and make sure the height is reasonably level with every other set of logs you put on.

Once you get past that first layer of logs you will no doubt discover that the rest of the walls go up very quickly. Just pick out four logs at a time, drag them beside the house, and hoist them into place with the block and tackle. Try to position the straps on the logs so that the logs will end up right-side-up on the wall. Sometimes, however, you will need to set the weight of a log down on the wall and loosen the straps just a little to turn the log so it fits better. Do not allow too much slack though, in case the log slips off the wall-just a few inches of loose rope is all you need.

A House of Rebar

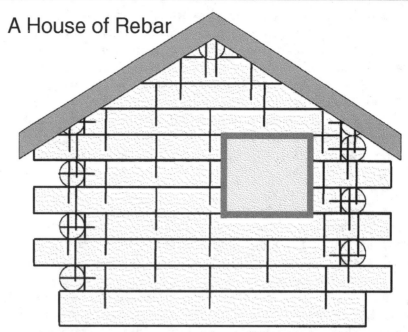

At the corners and every four feet along the walls rebar is hammered through one log and half way into the log below. Rebar is also pounded in horizontally at the corners.

Once a log is positioned the way you want it, you can temporarily hold it in place with a "log dog" at each corner. A log dog is basically an over-sized staple nail that is hammered across two logs to secure them together. A log dog will keep the log from rolling while you are perched on it drilling holes through and pounding in the rebar. Nevertheless, absolutely do not remove the ropes and straps until the log is pinned in place with rebar.

Use a 1/2" drill bit and drill all the way through the log you are putting in place, but not into the log below it. It is important to drill completely through the first log, or the rebar will make a big split in the wood when it is hammered out the bottom. However, it is best not to drill into the next log below, because you can hammer the rebar into it like a big nail.

Rebar	List
Quantity	**Length**
25	14"
40	16"
50	18"
35	20"
20	22"
10	24"

The rebar should be precut in lengths that go all the way through one log and half way into the one below. A good rebar cutter can cost hundreds of dollars, so it may be less expensive to have the brickyard cut the pins for you. Just submit an approximate list of what you need and let them do the work, but be sure to shop around, since some places charge a lot more for cutting than others. Be sure to specify 1/2" rebar. Optionally, a metal-cutting blade on a skill saw is a quick and inexpensive way to cut lots of rebar.

Lifting the ridgepole over the front wall.

Drilling and pinning the ridgepole to the RPSL

Drill a hole at each end of the log you are working with, then drive the rebar pins in with a sledgehammer. We used four pound sledge hammers to drive the pins in through the holes, then twelve pound sledgehammers to drive the pins into the logs below. You will build up some muscles with this job! But just before you give the final blows with the hammer, be sure to slack the rope and remove the straps, so they are not permanently sandwiched between the logs.

We found it most time-efficient to work this way, securing the logs with one pin at each end, until all four logs were in place. Then we climbed up and put in the rest of the pins. The first person in line drilled all the holes and scooted around the box, while the second person followed, hammering the pins part way in with the four pound sledge hammer, and the third person finished the job with the twelve pound hammer.

The rebar should be pinned in approximately every four feet along each log, with an additional pin hammered in horizontally at each corner. Ideally you should have all the windows and doors in mind ahead of time. Mark the openings out on the logs as you go, with about six inches of leeway on each side. Drive pins in at each side of the openings, but be sure to offset them from the pins in the layer below.

The **cap logs** must be very straight and level, because that is the part that holds up the roof. The cap logs are also longer than the other logs, because they "overdangle" past both ends of the house, instead of just one end.

The way to make the cap logs level is to plan ahead when choosing the previous layer or two. Try to make the last layer of logs out-of-level just enough so that adding cap logs will make the wall exactly level. It is tolerable, but not desirable if you have to shim up one end of a cap log to make it level. Obviously there will still be numerous little bumps and dips along the log, but make the log itself as level as possible, and your work will be much easier later when it is time to put the roof on.

The Ridgepole and Support Logs

The ridgepole and it's support system are as much for show as for function. Functionally, the system supports most of the weight of the roof and keeps that weight off the walls. It is an ingenious and simple system that makes exceptionally strong roofs without the need for trusses, so you can have open, "cathedral" style ceilings. The logs do not need to be very large to provide the desired strength, but they do become strong focal points inside a house, so it is kind of fun to use the biggest logs you have.

To determine the height of the ridgepole support logs (RPSLs), simply decide how high the peak of the roof should be above the walls, and measure from that point all the way down to the concrete slab or footing on the first floor or basement. Subtract the diameter of the ridgepole, and the measurement that is left is the proper height for the RPSLs. Just keep in mind that the ridgepole has a different diameter at each end, so one RPSL should be longer than the other to keep the top of the ridgepole level.

The RPSLs can be set in place using the existing lifting logs and block-and-tackle, but you might have to cut a doorway into the house to bring the logs inside. The lifting logs can also aid in dragging the logs through the door. Once inside, put the butt end of the RPSL in place against the wall, and use the two lifting logs from the same wall to raise the log in place. Stand the log up and turn it until it fits nicely against the wall.

The next step is to secure the RPSL with 5/8" "all-thread" bolts, nuts, and washers. The RPSLs should be bolted to the log wall and/or the concrete foundation wall, about every four feet in height. Drill through with a 3/

The roof extends 12 feet beyond the south wall over the deck.   *Checking the ridgeline for level.*

4" bit, then use a 1 1/2" bit to widen the holes on each side enough to hide the nuts and washers inside the wood. The holes can be plugged later with wood, or caulked over.

Putting the ridgepole up usually requires moving the lifting logs right beside the RPSLs and securing them in place. You do not need to bolt the lifting logs in place. Just secure them to the wall with chains and bolts. A nifty device for tightening the chain is a "chain binder". The chain binder gives you lots of leverage to tighten the chain, and it snaps closed without the need for bolts. .

Raising the ridgepole is a bit of a trick compared to the wall logs, because it has to be lifted over the middle of the house. The best way we found to get the log up is to hoist one end up to the top of the wall with the lifting log positioned there, then tie on with the lifting log from the other end of the house and drag it over the wall. The only problem with this system is that the log eventually crosses its balance point on the wall, at which time it can become a "log missile" that shoots across the house and slams against the other wall. It doesn't cause any harm, but it is kind of exciting, and you have to make sure everyone is well out of the way before hand. Anyway, from there, just lift the nose of the log back up and set the log down suspended on the end walls of the house. Reposition the straps as necessary and hoist the log straight up into position.

Most log house systems put the bow or "crown" of the log up, so that the weight of the roof pushes it back down, but I advise placing the crown down instead. Drill through the ridgepole and put in at least two rebar pins in each end, going straight down into the RPSLs. Afterwards use a hydraulic jack, like you might have in a truck, to lift the middle of the ridgepole until it is level. Use a skinny log or 4 x 4 on top of the jack to reach the log. When the ridgepole is level, just measure from the bottom of the pole down to the floor where the middle support log or logs will sit, and cut the logs to that length. You will probably need to jack up the ridgepole another inch or more to put the new logs in place. Then lower the jack and pin the logs together with rebar.

At this point you are ready to put the roof on, which is detailed in a later chapter. In the meantime, there are some other aspects of log work that must be covered here.

Filling in the Gable Ends

The method we learned for filling in the gable ends of the house was to put the roof on first, and frame in the gables like a conventional wall. There is a good reason for doing the job that way: it's easy. We did not want framed gables on our own house though, so we chose to fill in with additional logs. Putting the logs up is easy, but it helps if the rafters are in place first so you can tell how long each log need to be. We pinned each log to the one below, then pinned through the ridgepole into the top log in the gable. The difficult part of the job is dealing with the log ends that protrude into the rafter space. It took me seven years to get around to covering up the ratty-looking insulation that stuck out of the roof around the logs.

Cutting out Windows and Doors & Trimming the Overdangles

It is kind of fun, once you have built a big log box, to go through with a chainsaw one day and cut out all the windows and doors. The trick to doing a good job is to nail a 2 x 4 to the logs to guide the chainsaw. Measure enough room for the door or window and the framing that goes with it. Mark the width of the opening on the fattest log, then put the 2 x 4 up and use a level to make it plumb.

"Bird blocks" were nailed in between the rafters.

Putting the 2 x 6 tongue-and-groove decking on the roof.

Aesthetically, a window looks best if the top and especially the bottom of the opening occur near the center of a log, so the framing does not stick out of the wall. On the other hand, it is even more important to make sure the tops of the windows are all aligned. I like to align the windows with the doors too. If you achieve all of the above then you are doing really well. Also, the bottoms of the doors should be aligned with the top of the floor, which may take a little figuring if you happen to be working upstairs and there is no floor. In any case, the 2 x frames can be nailed in with any extra large nails, but be sure to use shims where there are gaps, or the nails will bulge out the side of the frame.

We used 2 x 10 frames for our doors and windows, then notched 1 x 4 trim in to the logs around them. The space behind the trim allows heat loss through the 2 x 10 framing, so we filled that space with expanding foam sealant then trimmed the extra off with a knife. A thin coat of Log Jam™ (discussed shortly) over the top makes a beautiful finish.

The overdangles are fun to trim too. Just determine how much of the logs you want sticking out past the end of the house, make a mark, and use a plumb bob to transfer the mark to all the other logs. You may need to have someone tie a rope on the end of the log to help pull the falling pieces away from the house and your ladder, especially when you are working high in the air.

Fiberglass insulation is cut into strips and stuffed between the logs.

Chinking the Walls

Chinking the walls was much like grouting stonework, but a whole lot easier. We were taught to use fiberglass "sill" insulation which comes in long rolls, about six inches wide, but only one inch thick. We cut the insulation into long, narrow strips, a little more than an inch wide, and put one strip in from each side along the gaps between the logs. That left a little additional dead air space in the middle between each strip of insulation. It is important to avoid compressing the insulation, since that reduces the efficiency.

The next step was to hammer the tips of galvanized nails into the logs to hold the fiberglass in place, and more importantly, to provide something for the chinking mortar to grab on to. The mortar does not adhere to wood, but it will flow around the nails and set up rock hard. The nails should be galvanized so they do not rust and discolor the mortar. Hammer a nail in about every three inches along every gap between all the logs. But put the nails only in one log or the other (usually the bottom), instead of both up and down. Otherwise shrinkage of the logs could crack the mortar. A system that works well is to hammer the nails in about half an inch, then bend the tops back into the mortar joint. Finally, use the same mortar and the same tools used for grouting stonework, and trowel it into the joints.

Closed in, but not chinked.

Whew. Time for a break!

This chinking method is both inexpensive and easy, but unfortunately there are some serious problems with it. Both the fiberglass and the mortar are porous, so the wind blows right through them. Sometimes in the winter we have warm, 40-50°F "Chinook" winds that blow down the Rockies and melt all the snow. The temperature warms up outside, but it used to chill our house because the wind went right through the mortar joints.

Our brief, but driving summer rains also blew right through the mortar joints, dampening the inside of the log walls.

In addition, the mortar slumped when applied, and the logs eventually shrunk a little, creating a small gap along the top of the mortar. Little bits of asbestos-like fiberglass filtered through, creating a household hazard.

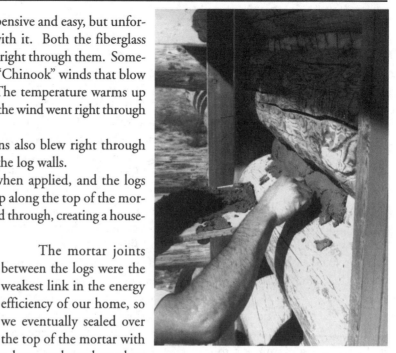

Cement mortar is troweled in along the joints.

The mortar joints between the logs were the weakest link in the energy efficiency of our home, so we eventually sealed over the top of the mortar with a latex and sand product called Log Jam™, which is used for chinking modern log homes. Troweling Log Jam™ over the mortar joints inside and outside the house made a huge difference in the rate of air infiltration. Also, the cement joints were contributing significant quantities of dust to the house. The latex coating solved that problem too.

As for chinking your own home, I would recommend using a mdoern chinking system, which substitutes a "closed-cell" (air-proof) insulation for the fiberglass. The foam wraps used on water pipes is a closed-cell insulation. The same material is also made in long, skinny ropes of many sizes, intended especially for chinking log homes. It is important to use a flexible, rather than sprayed-in hard foam for the insulation, because there will be some shrinkage, and the insulation needs to be flexible to keep the gaps sealed. This system will take less labor than the system we used, but may also be a bit more expensive. Most importantly, it will maximize the energy efficiency of the joints.

Galvanized nails are hammered in every 3" along the walls to give the mortar something to grab on to.

Expanding foam sealant filled in behind the window trim.

Finished!

Building with Bales
It's Cheap, Fast, and Energy Efficient

Strawbale buildings are all the rage in alternative construction today, and with good reason—they are cheap, easy to build, and very energy efficient. Strawbale buildings look similar to adobe, with massive walls, wide window sills and typically rounded corners, but with the added benefit of a higher insulation value. The soft, sometimes curvy edges of strawbale construction can lend a fairy tale look to the finished structures. The fun part of strawbale construction is that anyone can do it. Anyone can help stack the fluffy, oversized bricks in place.

Strawbale homes and outbuildings were first developed by pioneers in the Sand Hills of Nebraska where there was lots of straw, but few trees. The early pioneers built houses of sod, up until the late 1800's when baling technology provided the first compressed, string-tied rectangular bales. The next logical step was to stack those bales like bricks to make warm walls. Strawbale buildings from the early 1900's are still in use and in excellent condition today. Due to publicity in the 1980's and 1990's there are now strawbale buildings popping up all over the world— in wet and dry climates, from hot southern environments to chilling northern extremes.

Overview

Strawbale homes are very well insulated. The orientation of the straw in the bales makes some difference in the **insulation value.** Bales laid flat (with strings running around the top and bottom) rate about R-2.4 per inch while those laid on edge (with strings running around the sides) rate R-3 per inch. However, the bales are usually wider when laid flat than on edge, giving a higher overall R-value. The bales are slightly stronger too, when laid flat.

Bale size varies according to the equipment it is produced on. A typical 3-string bale is 23 inches wide by 16 inches tall, with an R-value of 54.7 when laid flat or R-49.5 on edge. A typical 2-string bale is 18 inches wide by 14 inches tall, with an R-value of 42.8 when laid flat or R-32.1 on edge. Bale sizes in my area run about 18 inches in width and height. Length of the bales is also variable.

Rice straw contains more silica than other **types of straw** like wheat, barley, rye or flax. The silica content makes rice straw more resistant to weathering, but harder on baling equipment, saw blades and other tools. For practical considerations, you will likely use whichever type of straw is available in your area. Avoid using hay, which contains more nutrition (leaves and seeds) to attract pests or turn moldy. Even unprotected strawbales are a haven for rodents and insects, but the stuccoed walls are virtually **vermin** proof. Interestingly, in one strawbale house with termites, only the wooden window frames were attacked, not the straw.

The Sabo house. A conventional footing & slab w/ radiant heat.

A sturdy frame to support the roof. Interior walls are plywood.

Structurally, a properly designed and reinforced strawbale building is very **earthquake** resistant, since the soft bales absorb much of the vibration that would otherwise be transferred to the roof.

Strawbale buildings are also very **fire** resistant. The plaster or stucco surface is virtually fireproof, and there isn't enough air inside the bales to sustain combustion if ignited. Fire tests on strawbale homes indicated they are more fire resistant than standard construction. Accidental fires in strawbale walls typically extinguish themselves. The greatest danger comes from fires ignited in the roof, which may creep down through the tops of the walls.

Moisture problems are a bigger concern, and strawbales are not the most ideal building material in a flood plain, since the saturated bales quickly turn to compost. Most strawbale buildings have been built in arid environments where there is a net loss to evaporation over the course of a year. What this means is that if you set out a bucket half full of water, it will lose more volume to evaporation than it gains from rainfall over the course of time. Eventually the bucket will be completely dry. Environments with net losses to evaporation are ideal for strawbale buildings, because any moisture in the bales naturally moves towards equilibrium with the environment, migrating out of the bales to evaporate. In arid environments builders have even formed stuccoed bale walls around patios, which are completely exposed to the weather. A driving rain may force water right through the stucco, but the bales quickly dry out without damage.

Strawbale buildings have also been built successfully in more humid environments, according to authors of the excellent book, *The Straw Bale House*. The Burritt Mansion built in Huntsville, Alabama, built in 1938 (now a museum) is the best proof that bale structures can withstand long-term exposure to humidity. Newer structures built in the Pacific Northwest and in Quebec have also endured well. Extensive testing by the Canada Housing and Mortgage Corporation showed an average relative humidity of only 13% inside the bales of a Quebec house, much lower than the surrounding environment.

The keys to keeping bale structures dry are 1) make sure the bottom bales are far enough off the ground to prevent saturation, 2) install a moisture barrier to prevent water from wicking up through the masonry footings, and 3) keep the top of the walls dry during the building process. Moisture on the exposed walls from driving rains seems to be far less critical and easy to dry out.

The greatest danger from moisture involves potential **breathability and condensation** problems. One refrigerator built with strawbale walls had a vapor barrier lining the inside of the structure. Moisture migrating through the bales condensed on the bale side of vapor barrier and ruined the straw within a single year. Similar condensation problems may arise in cold, humid climates, where enough moisture could condense on concrete (such as support pillars) to rot the bales.

Ordinary plaster and stucco finishes are very porous, allowing moisture and stale air to migrate slowly out through the bales. Water tight coatings could lead to condensation problems. For more information, be sure to reread the section *About Vapor Barriers* in the chapter *Insulation and Insulation Systems*.

Environmentally, straw is an abundant and renewable resource. There is enough straw produced in this country every year to produce an estimated 5 million homes of 2,000 square feet in size. Much of that straw is otherwise torched as waste in the fields, adding copious quantities of carbon and particulate to the atmosphere.

Bales **cost** about $1 each in my neighborhood, where we have hundreds of acres of wheat and barley crops nearby. The cost per bale rises to $3 or $4 in other parts of the country farther away from suitable crops. Our

Framing in the roof.

After stacking, each bale was strapped to the plywood wall inside.

strawbale chickenhouse (shown in the chapter *Insulation & Insulation Systems*) required one pickup load of strawbales, about $25 worth. Note that good quality strawbales may only be available at certain times of the year, immediately after harvest.

Cost-wise, bale structures can be made about as cheap or as expensive as you want. As with other types of construction, the expensive part is not the walls, but the roof, flooring, doors, windows and other accessories. Most owner-built or contracted strawbale homes cost about as much as their conventional counterparts, but are better insulated and therefore more energy efficient.

Early supporters of strawbale construction had many hurdles to cross when it came to **code compliance**, so the first modern structures were built either quietly, without permits, or in places where building permits and codes did not exist. Today there are so many strawbale homes in existence that it should be relatively easy to get a building permit, though conditions may vary based on the whims of the permitting agencies. The book, *Buildings of Earth and Straw: Structural Design for Rammed Earth and Straw-Bale Architecture* provides professional documentation on the proper application of those building materials. Using that book to properly design your structure and as a source to validate your work, will make it easier to get a permit.

Load-Bearing vs. Non Load-Bearing Walls

There are two types of strawbale houses. One type has load-bearing walls, where the weight of the roof is supported by the bales, while the others are non-load bearing, where the roof is supported by a framework and the bales are filled in afterwards. There are advantages and disadvantages to either approach.

In a load-bearing strawbale building the windows and doors have to be placed carefully to avoid compromising the strength of the walls, and the roof has to be designed to equalize the load distribution to the walls. The size of the building, the height of the walls, and compression and settling of the bales under the weight of the roof and potential snow loads must also be considered. All of these obstacles are overcome when using an independent support structure for the roof.

Typical support structures include conventional lumber framing as well as timber framing, framing with poles or logs, or concrete posts and beams. The support structure holds up the roof, taking the pressure off the bales (and the builder). Besides, a supporting framework enables you to put up the roof first, so that the rest of the work can proceed inside the shelter, protecting yourself, your tools and the strawbales from the weather. That's important since it only takes one rainstorm to soak the tops of the unprotected bales, quickly rotting out your good work.

On the other hand, a supporting framework often requires more lumber than you would use with load-bearing walls, and the framing tends to get in the way of the bales, requiring extra design work to position the framing for minimal interference with the walls, and/or to notch into the bales to fit around the framing. The first sequence of pictures in this chapter is of Jenny and Mark Sabo's strawbale home with structural framing. The interior walls are plywood with a plaster finish. Jenny designed and contracted the home. Mark was one of the carpenters hired to do the finish work. That's how they met!

The method you choose for your strawbale building will depend on many factors. If codes matter in your area then you may have no choice but to use a supporting framework. If you have access to harvestable timber, then you will be able to build an elegant and sturdy support system virtually for free (see the chapter *Log Building Basics*).

Finishing the stucco. Ready for steel roofing.

Warm and cozy in the winter!

Otherwise, load-bearing walls are typically used for small buildings of less than 500 square feet, while supporting frameworks are used for larger structures.

The Zimmerman strawbale shop, featured in the second sequence of photos, is very large for a load-bearing bale building; the slab is 24 feet wide by 48 feet long, but there are only two openings in the entire building, both of them on the ends rather than on the sides that carry most of the weight of the roof. Dave and Janet built a cordwood home at the same time we were building our stone and log home. Over the years they have earned a living with handicrafts such as wooden toys and whirligigs, and now Dave is employed developing better prosthetic devices. Dave needed a large workshop and chose strawbale construction as the fastest, cheapest way to put up a warm building.

Footings & Foundation Walls

A conventional eight-inch wide concrete foundation wall is much too narrow to support strawbale construction, but a bale-width foundation would require too much concrete to get below frost line. To get around this foundation problem, most strawbale homes are built on some type of a concrete slab. Most common may be the monolithic slab-on-grade (see the chapter *Footings, Foundations, and Floors* for definitions). The footing around the perimeter is poured as wide as the bales, but it is rarely more than one foot deep. The Sabo home featured at the beginning of this chapter employed a conventional eight-inch wide foundation which was then filled with gravel and a layer of insulation, more gravel for thermal storage, tubing for radiant heat, and finally a concrete slab. The slab provides the necessary width to support the strawbale walls.

The Zimmerman's used a different approach toward a similar end with their strawbale shop. The location of the site near the creek created some interesting challenges, since the entire building had to be raised above the flood plain. Dave's solution to the problem was to pour a combination footing/slab over blocks of strawbales, thereby raising the floor up two feet with relatively few materials. The spaces between the bales created a honeycomb matrix of short walls to support the slab.

First the site was graded and covered several inches deep in gravel. Dave used our slipforms for the outer form work, then arranged the strawbales inside. The bales were covered with plastic, and rebar was used between the bales for reinforcing. Welded wire mesh was used to strengthen the slab. Originally Dave intended to use bales of shredded waste plastic under the floor, but the contact for that resource fell through. Plastic bales would have been rot-proof and somewhat insulating under the floor. As it is, the strawbales will undoubtedly rot out over time, but they served the essential purpose of forming the raised slab.

The pour required three cement trucks to haul in the concrete, plus a pump truck to reach all the way across the job site. Concrete was poured between the bales first, working in layers to avoid pushing any bales out of place.

The footings and slab formed over bales.

A concrete pump truck and lots of help.

Footings were poured first, then the slab.

Then the slab was poured over the top of the bales and screeded smooth. This pour was not cheap, using 34 yards of concrete, but it was probably one of the most cost effective ways to lift the entire building above the flood plain.

Other foundation systems used with strawbale homes include rubble trenches and sometimes pier blocks or pylons. Another alternative which I think should be considered is a slipformed stone wall, with stone work on both sides and insulation in the core, as illustrated in the chapter *Footings, Foundations, and Floors*.

Note that it is essential to plan the **dimensions of the structure** and **placement of the openings** based on the size of the strawbales, to utilize as many whole bales as possible. Many bales will still need to be cut and re-tied to fit

around doors and windows and other odd spaces, but try to minimize the customized work as much as possible in the design process. Leave a little extra room in the measurements, in case some of the bales are larger than others. It is easier to stuff loose straw into small gaps than to cut and re-tie a bale a little bit shorter.

To anchor the strawbale walls to the footing, short rebar pins should be inserted into the fresh concrete, spaced so that two pins impale each bale on the first layer. The pins should be sized so that 6 inches can be sunk into the concrete, with 12 or more inches sticking up to spear the bales. Here again, you must know exactly how the bales are laid out, even before you pour the footing.

In load-bearing strawbale buildings, it is important to also connect the roof to the foundation, so that

Banding clips were set in fresh concrete along both sides of the walls.

the roof doesn't lift off the bales in a windstorm. There are several means to accomplish this task. One method is to replace some of the rebar in the wall with all-thread bolts, anchored in the concrete and extending all the way to the roof plate. The bolts are used in short sections spliced together with coupling nuts, and spaced about every six feet along the walls, with additional bolts within three feet of the ends. This method slows down the bale-setting process some, since the bales must be impaled on the bolts at just the right points to keep the walls plumb as you go up. A wooden beam is placed on the top of the wall and cinched into place with the bolts and nuts.

An easier and probably less costly method was employed by the Zimmerman's, using banding equipment to tie the roof plate down and cinch it in place. Banding clips were anchored in the fresh concrete of the slab along both sides of the walls. Notice the metal banding in the picture below (added after the roof plate went on).

Building Bale Walls

Before laying any bales, it is important to put down a moisture barrier to prevent water from wicking up through the concrete into the bales. Possible moisture barriers include asphalt emulsion, plastic, roofing felt, rigid insulation, or galvanized metal. Dave Zimmerman used two inch thick sheets of XPS polystyrene insulation board to serve as a moisture barrier, and to lift the bales up off the slab. That protects the bales from accidental water spills on the floor, which might otherwise soak into the walls.

Screeding the slab.

Rigid insulation prevents moisture from wicking into the bales.

The Sabo house was a little different, since the bottom plate of the 2 x 4 framing was attached to the slab, under the bales. In order to level the base, a second run of 2 x 4's was attached to the slab at the outside edge of the wall. Strips of rigid insulation were placed between the two tracks, followed by a layer of asphalt sheeting over the top, as pictured here.

After the moisture barrier is in place, it is time to start stacking bales, by impaling the first row of bales on the rebar pins, being careful to ensure that every bale is properly aligned in the wall. Subsequent layers of bales can be stacked quickly, but you should use a four-foot level to keep the wall plumb every step of the way. When the height of the wall exceeds the length of the level, tape the level to a longer, straight board to extend its reach. Stack each level like bricks, offsetting the bales to bridge the joints of the layer below.

At about the fourth row, rebar (or other reasonable substitutes like bamboo, sharpened sapplings, or wooden stakes) should be driven down through the bales

Asphalt sheeting was installed as a moisture barrier under the bales.

to tie each layer together. At the top row of the wall drive more rebar down into the bales, long enough to reach into or through the other layer that contains rebar. Rebar should be pounded into the ends of the bales at the corners too, the same way it is done when working with logs. After pounding lots of rebar pins through the logs of our house, I was surprised to discover with our chickenhouse that it was almost as difficult to drive rebar through bales of straw.

Note that neither of the buildings featured in this chapter had rebar pins in the slab or rebar reinforcement in the walls. In the Sabo house, each strawbale was simply strapped to the plywood wall. In the Zimmerman shop, Dave used the metal banding and the roof plate to hold the bales in place; he felt the rebar reinforcement was unnecessary. Nevertheless, rebar pins in the concrete may help to prevent strawbale walls from shifting in an earthquake, and rebar throughout the walls can help prevent the bales from blowing out to either side during construction. As you can see, there are many variables to the building process. Building codes in your area may require rebar or a reasonable substitute.

Offsetting the bales necessitates cutting many of them to fill in the half spaces at the ends of each section of wall where there are doors, windows, or support posts. The key to keeping the bale tight when you cut and restring it is to put the new strings on before cutting the old ones. The tricky part is to thread the new strings through the middle of the bale. To accomplish this task it is helpful to make a **needle** long enough to penetrate the bales. A metal

Richard volunteers to heft a few bales.

It's taking shape.

Dave poses with his handiwork.

rod, approximately 5/16 inch in diameter can be hammered flat on one end and ground into a point. A hole is drilled through the flattened point to hold the twine. The other end of the needle may be bent at a 90º angle to make a handle. Feed the twine through the eyelet and push the needle through the bale at the desired point. Tie the bale with the new string, and then it is safe to cut the old ones. A hand saw may be needed to cut through the middle of the bale to better separate the two halves.

Do your best to keep the bale wall straight and plumb as you go. There are always oddities in the bales, but with a little persistence you can make the walls as straight as you want. A little bit of straw may need to be trimmed in places. A **weed eater** is a favored tool for this kind of work.

Bale Needle

Doors, Windows & Roof Plates

If the roof of a strawbale building has an independent support system then the windows can be of just about any size and placed any where in the walls. Note that in the Sabo house, the window frames are attached to the house framing. In a load bearing wall, however, the windows must be kept small, ideally no more than two feet wide, and placed at least a full bale length from any other windows or doors and the corners of the building. The window and door frames should be built very sturdy, much like those used in slipform stone masonry. Door frames should be anchored to the footing, preferably before any bales are stacked.

In a load-bearing wall, the roof plate is cinched down on the bales, **compressing the stack** by up to a few inches. There must be sufficient room above the windows and doors to allow settling of the wall without warping the frame work or excessively compressing the bales below. Adding the weight of the roof, plus any potential snow loads, can lead to further compression of the wall. Wooden shims can be used to make space above the openings and removed as needed during compression.

The **roof plate** is the most effective form of a "lintel" to spread the load evenly across the entire walls. The roof plate is a ladder-like assembly of 2 x 4's or 2 x 6's with plywood or oriented strand board (OSB) on one side. The plate is placed on top of the bales and cinched in place with the aid of the all-thread bolts or a banding system. Note the metal bands wrapping over the roof plate in the accompanying photo. Each of the bands along the wall can be incrementally adjusted to enable equal compression and precise leveling of the roof plate. Additional banding was used horizontally at each end of the Zimmerman shop, to strengthen the corners and to tie the door frames into the walls, also shown in the pictures here. Notice in the photos that the roof plate runs across the bales on the end of the shop, tying the two sides together. The bales below the plate are compressed, while those above it, filling in the gable ends are not compressed.

The roof plate is cinched into place.   *Home-made trusses and a portable winch.*   *Hoisting a truss.*

Putting the Roof On

When the roof plate is in place and cinched in place on the bales below, then it is time for the roof. Dave changed the order a little bit with his shop, completely stacking and partly compressing the bales on one end of the shop before beginning the walls at the other end. This method gave him plenty of room to work with his homemade electric winch to lift the trusses and swing them into place over the other part of the building. He added bales and extended the roof plates as he went along.

The **trusses** Dave made are constructed of 2 x 4's held together with OSB board. The hollow spaces inside the trusses were filled with rigid beadboard insulation. Cross-bracing of the trusses, as shown in the pictures, is critical to tie the truss together. Otherwise the weight of the roof would push outward on the walls, collapsing the building. Notice the unique ridge board used to tie all the trusses together at the top. A notch was left in the peak of each truss so the ridgeboard could be dropped right in place. The roof was finished with more OSB board for sheathing, plus roofing felt and steel roofing. The gable ends were later filled in with bales. The roof was insulated with scraps of insulation from other projects: fiberglass batts, rigid insulation, loose straw and plastic bags full of straw. Dave estimates the total weight of the roof at close to 10,000 pounds. All that weight further contributed to compression of the bales, requiring the bands to be adjusted and tightened over the roof plates. It is important to allow for complete settling of the bales before applying a stucco finish on the walls.

Surfacing the Walls

One of the nicest aspects of strawbale construction is that you can move into it, if necessary, even before the walls are surfaced. Strawbale construction enables you to put up a warm, enclosed structure quickly, and you can deal with the details later. That's important if your project drags into winter and you need a place to live. You can move in, surface the inside first, and wait until spring to finish the outside. It is important to do the outside work in moderate weather, not too hot or cold, not too wet or dry, but somewhere in the middle.

There are many widely different formulas for surfacing strawbale houses, varying from **cement stucco** to traditional **mud or lime plasters**. Mud or lime plasters are easier to work with and may adhere to the straw better, eliminating the need for stuccowire, but the finish isn't as durable and weather resistant as cement stucco. Plasters are still sometimes used in the arid southwest and especially in Mexico, but most new strawbale homes in the U.S. are stuccoed. The wet mortar may not adhere to the wall as easily, but it cures as artificial rock, permanently formed around the straw and stuccowire.

Stuccowire is the matrix that holds the stucco on the wall. Stuccowire looks just like chickenwire, but it is made specifically for stucco work. It must cover all exposed surfaces of the strawbales, wrapped tight enough that it doesn't sag away from the wall, but loose enough that mortar can be worked in between the mesh and the straw. A bale needle, like the one used to re-tie bales at half sizes, can be used to stitch the stuccowire to the bales. Plan to work in pairs, with one person inside and the other outside. The Zimmermans also tied the stuccowire to the metal banding on the walls. The stuccowire should be nailed to the sides of the window and door frames, the roof plate, and any other support structures to better tie the many parts of the house together. The mesh should also be anchored to the footing by attaching it to the banding clips or eyebolts. It would be helpful to include extra attachment points between the banding clips when pouring the footing.

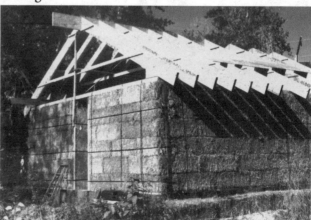

The trusses are in place, now for the ridge piece. *Notice the binding straps on the walls.*

Roofing felt and expanded metal lathe is attached around the windows to make smooth, even corners.

If any wooden members are to be covered with stucco, then it is important to cover them in roofing felt and stuccowire, so that the water in the mortar does not swell the wood and cause cracking. **Expanded metal lathe**, a conventional mesh used for stucco work, can be applied to the corners or any other spaces where you need better control of the shape.

Most strawbale buildings are stuccoed in three coats: a **scratch coat** to fill the voids in the straw, a **brown coat** to even the application over the stuccowire, and a **finish coat** to give a smooth, polished look. The small teeth of a **plaster rake** are helpful to groove the surface of the scratch coat so that the brown coat will have something to grab on to. A **mortar board**, like those used to grout stonework, is helpful to hold the mortar up to the wall, where it can be pushed off the board and onto the wall with the aid of a **rectangular trowel**. Trowels with rounded corners are less-prone to snagging the stuccowire. The stucco should be misted periodically to keep it from drying out before it properly cures, but be careful to avoid completely soaking the wall and potentially rotting the bales. Be sure to read the *Cement Mixing and Measuring Guide* in this book for additional information on working with stucco mortar.

You can stucco a building entirely by hand, but it is probably the most labor intensive aspect of strawbale construction. As with mixing concrete, it is difficult to compete economically with the technology of massproduction. The process can be made much easier using a **pump and sprayer** to apply the mortar for the scratch coat. The sprayer propels the mortar into any voids, creating a tight bond between the mortar and the bales. The brown coat and finish coat can then be applied easily by hand. These brown coat can be applied any time, but sooner is better, preferably the same day or within a few days, to increase the bonding between the coats. The finish coat is usually applied a year later, probably to cover over any hair line cracks that form in the mean time.

Optionally, you should explore the possibility of hiring a **gunnite** applicator. Gunnite mixes the cement ingredients with small amounts of water as it leaves the nozzle, creating an extra hard cement that can be applied in a single coat.

Dave hired an experienced stucco applicator to do his shop, plus two laborers to assist. It took the crew of three only four days and two coats of mortar to stucco the entire outside of the building. One person mixed mortar constantly and kept supply chain going to the other two who applied and troweled the mortar. Most strawbale buildings are also stuccoed on the inside, but Dave put up OSB board instead (secured behind the banding straps and stitched to the bales), so he would have lots of wooden surfaces to nail into. After the stucco work, Dave built a solar hot air system on the long, south-face of the building to collect heat and vent it to the inside.

The roof on and ready for stucco. Note the clerestory windows.

All finished!

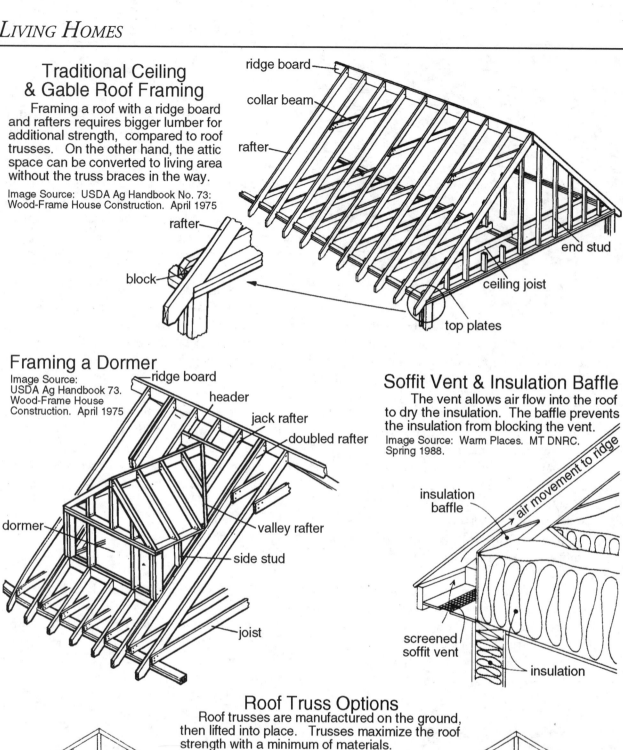

Traditional Ceiling & Gable Roof Framing

Framing a roof with a ridge board and rafters requires bigger lumber for additional strength, compared to roof trusses. On the other hand, the attic space can be converted to living area without the truss braces in the way.

Image Source: USDA Ag Handbook No. 73: Wood-Frame House Construction. April 1975

ridge board
collar beam
rafter
end stud
ceiling joist
top plates

rafter
block

Framing a Dormer

Image Source: USDA Ag Handbook 73. Wood-Frame House Construction. April 1975

ridge board
header
jack rafter
doubled rafter
valley rafter
side stud
dormer
joist

Soffit Vent & Insulation Baffle

The vent allows air flow into the roof to dry the insulation. The baffle prevents the insulation from blocking the vent.

Image Source: Warm Places. MT DNRC. Spring 1988.

air movement to ridge
insulation baffle
screened soffit vent
insulation

Roof Truss Options

Roof trusses are manufactured on the ground, then lifted into place. Trusses maximize the roof strength with a minimum of materials.

Image Source: Warm Places—A sampling of energy-efficient Montana homes. Montana Dept. of Natural Resources and Conservation. Spring 1988.

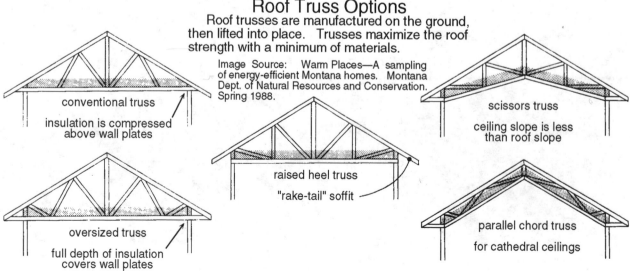

conventional truss
insulation is compressed above wall plates

oversized truss
full depth of insulation covers wall plates

raised heel truss
"rake-tail" soffit

scissors truss
ceiling slope is less than roof slope

parallel chord truss
for cathedral ceilings

Putting the Roof On
The Search for Better Solutions

The roof is often the most expensive and the least energy efficient part of a new house. We have built three houses with three different roofing systems, and I have studied numerous other schemes for putting the lid on, but I have yet to see a system I truly like. Fortunately, understanding the problem at hand—and being thoroughly disgusted with it—is often the first step towards finding a solution!

Traditional roofs are built with sturdy rafters nailed to a central ridge board, as illustrated on the opposite page. Collar beams are used to tie the two sides of the roof together, so that the weight of the roof does not push outward on the walls. If the roof is tall enough, then the space inside the attic can be converted to living area. Dormers may be added for window space and to increase headroom. One style of dormer is illustrated here. An easier way to make a dormer is with a shed roof, by raising a few rafters up enough to frame in the window area. The shed roof eliminates the angle cuts and valley rafters, but isn't quite as fancy either.

Probably the most common method of roofing houses today involves **roof trusses**. There are numerous advantages to roof trusses, since they are cross-braced to give a lot of strength with very little materials. Many lumber yards are set up to quickly and cheaply fabricate custom trusses for any size house. Trusses are easy to put on the house too, so they are a very economical way to frame the roof of a house. In fact, it is relatively cheap and easy to gain a high degree of energy efficiency with a roof-truss system and a flat ceiling. Loosefill insulation like cellulose or fiberglass can be carried into the attic and poured on top of the sheet rock, in between the trusses, and most importantly, it can be poured over the wood framing, to bridge the thermal gap through the wood. A foot or more of cellulose or other insulation can be piled up to guarantee a very warm ceiling.

It is important to keep in mind when insulating a ceiling this way, that moist house air will filter through the sheetrock of the ceiling and migrate up and out through the insulation. Proper attic ventilation is essential, so that air can enter at the eaves, blow across the top of the insulation, and exit at the peak of the house. Otherwise moisture will accumulate and eventually ruin the insulation, the wood, and the sheetrock. Some types of insulation come with paper or foil backing; these may be used for the first layer, but the paper or foil absolutely must not be sandwiched into the middle of a pile of insulation, or it will stop the air-filtration midway, again creating a moisture trap.

In a superinsulated house you have to install a plastic barrier across the bottoms of all the trusses before attaching the sheet rock. The vapor barrier stops air and moisture from migrating through the insulation, but proper ventilation is still required across the top, just in case. Overall, a roof could be easily and cheaply superinsulated using this combination of trusses and loosefill insulation. Aesthetically, however, I passionately dislike flat ceilings in a house, unless of course, there is a room and an open loft overhead.

The biggest disadvantage to roof trusses is that the cross-bracing takes up a lot of space in the ceiling that might otherwise be turned into a usable loft. With a modest additional investment the roof can be raised to a steeper angle to make more room inside, with a ridgepole and rafter system to provide the necessary roof support. That was in fact, our plan with the house featured in the slipforming chapter of this book, until we ran short on money and chopped off the upper story to go with the cheaper and easier trusses.

Fortunately, we were at least able to purchase "scissor trusses", which are braced in such a way that you can make a partial cathedral ceiling. The cathedral ceiling really creates a feeling of spaciousness inside a house. The only problem with the scissor trusses is that there is not enough room to get up in the attic, so we had to stuff batts of insulation up from down below before putting on the sheetrock. We were unable to bridge the thermal gap through the wood trusses, and we could not even inspect the top of the insulation to make sure we put it in place without any gaps. I'm sure we did better than most conventional construction, but I still found it very dissatisfying. Since then I have been determined to rethink roofing systems from scratch to find a better way.

Ridgepole & Rafter Systems

Our house and the Nansel house both have roof systems that include a ridgepole, support logs, and rafters. The ridgepole and support logs were discussed in the chapter *Log Building Basics*. The rafters are discussed in this chapter. Although this method originated with log homes it also works well with stone or strawbale walls and other alternative construction techniques.

Putting the rafters up on this kind of a roof is a matter of bringing one board up from each side to a person sitting right on the ridgepole. They clamp the two rafter boards together, then drill a hole through them and connect the rafters with one bolt. We used 2 x 10 rafters spaced every 24" on most of our house, with 2 x 6 rafters spaced every 16" on the addition. The Nansel's used 4 X 10 rafters spaced every 40" on their roof.

Clamp the rafters together on top of the ridgepole. Then drill through and bolt the rafters together.

All the rafters are hoisted up on the roof, bolted together at the peak, then slid along the ridgepole to the right spot. The rafters are set in place, then leveled using a "string level". A string level is simply a small and lightweight level that slides back and forth on a long string. Hold the string level along the ridge of the house to determine which rafters stick up too far, then move those rafters aside a few inches and chisel or chainsaw away the extra wood, and check again for level. Position all of the rafter peaks exactly how you want them, then level the cap logs.

You will need a point of reference for using the string level across the cap logs, so measure down from the ridgeline and make a mark on one rafter near the cap log, then use the same measurement at the other end of the house, and run the string level from point to point. One convenience of this rafter system is that the single bolt holds the rafters together, but it is also flexible, so you can pick up one end or the other when leveling the cap logs. In fact, the easy way to build a dormer with this method is to simply raise a couple rafters higher than the rest of the roof and frame in the resulting space.

Run a string level right down the ridge to help level and align the rafters. The excess wood at the peak can be sawed off later.

When the rafters are level across the ridgepole and the caps logs, then nail them in place. The large 4 x 10 rafters can be drilled and pinned with rebar to make a virtually indestructible roof system. We simply nailed our 2 x 10's and 2 x 6's in place, but some kind of joist hangers could also be used if a person were in a potential high wind area. In fact, the greatest value of the ridgepole and rafter system is in its strength. A conventional house could easily suffer a great deal of damage from a severe tornado or earthquake, but it would be almost impossible to destroy the supporting components of this kind of roof.

The problem we have had with the ridgepole and rafter system is in figuring out a good solution for the insulation, the ceiling, and the roofing material. The Nansel's used 2 x 6 tongue-and-groove decking on their roof to bridge the forty-inch span between the 4 x 10's (see photos in the log-building chapter). This method made a very sturdy and rustic ceiling, with both the 4 x 10's and the decking showing on the inside. For insulation they put down four inches of polyiso board, then used six inch screws to secure OSB board (like plywood, but made with wood chips) down on top of the insulation. The roof was temporarily protected with rolls of asphalt roofing and later covered with steel roofing.

We did our roof differently, partly to save money, but also because we wanted a white ceiling. We put 1 x 6 "skip sheathing" spaced every 24" across the tops of the rafters, then screwed the metal roofing to the skip sheathing. Later we stuffed 10" fiberglass batts up from underneath, then used sheetrock and texture paint for the ceiling.

For the addition we stuffed 6" fiberglass batts up from underneath (because the rafters were 2 x 6's) then bridged across the bottoms of the rafters with two inches of polyiso board, and finally used three inch screws to attach the sheetrock through the insulation to the rafters.

The methods we used gave us a reasonable R-value at a moderate cost, but there were many drawbacks. First of all, it would be very difficult and expensive to boost the energy efficiency of this kind of roof system enough to make a house that needs no heating or cooling. Total energy efficiency may have

We put skip sheathing down to support the metal roofing, then stuffed fiberglass batts in from below and sheet-rocked the ceiling.

been possible if we sprayed urethane or icynene insulation up between all the rafters to make one continuous and impervious seal, but it was way too expensive for us at the time

Secondly, there are too many separate parts and pieces in the system, between the skip sheathing, metal roofing, fiberglass, polyiso board, and sheetrock. We used enough good nails, screws, caulk, and perfataping, to assemble all the pieces together just like in any kind of conventional construction, but the reality is that each piece will always remain functionally separate and will ultimately require repair or replacement, although perhaps not in our lifetime. In the event of a natural disaster, the roof support system would stand through just about anything, but the parts and pieces tacked on to it could easily fall out or blow away.

The third problem with the roofing system we used is that there are hollow spaces in it for mice, bugs and other vermin. Mice might not be a problem in suburbia where carefully manicured landscapes eliminate all the surrounding habitat for mice, but in the country there may be hundreds of mice living within as many feet from the house, and if there is any way in at all, they will find it. It is truly discouraging to build a house, put the roof on, and hear the "pitter-patter" of mice in the new ceiling. I do not blame the mice. It is not their fault, and I feel bad for killing them when it is our own lack of foresight that caused them to move in. Fortunately the cats keep that problem under control.

Overall, the roof we put on the Nansel house is probably better, or at least more durable, than the one on our house, although it was very expensive and not insulated any better than ours. The cost would be even higher today, as the economic and ecological costs of using lumber continue to rise.

One answer I have found to solve the many problems associated with insulating and finishing framed roofs is customized beadboard panels, as illustrated on the following page. Beadboard panels, press-laminated in a sandwich between two sheets of OSB board, are already used as kind of a "conventional alternative to conventional construction". Six-inch panels are commonly used in the walls with thicker panels for the roof. The R-values of the panels used are usually comparable to conventional framed houses with fiberglass insulation, but the energy bill is significantly lower since the panels virtually eliminate infiltration problems. For the purposes of making a superinsulated house, you would need extra thick panels.

Structural building panels require a support system when used for roofing. Three different support systems are illustrated here. Either standard lumber or glue-lam "I-beams" can be used. The I-beams conserve lumber and minimize the thermal gap though the wood. Beadboard is easily customized at some of the factories, so the panels can be specially cut to your specifications.

Although beadboard between the rafters would greatly reduce energy consumption compared to a similar roof insulated with fiberglass, there is still a potential for heat loss directly through the rafters (if 2 x lumber is used), or more critically, alongside the rafters, if any of the parts are fitted together on site. The beadboard and rafters would need to be press-glued together to completely stop air infiltration.

A better approach to eliminate the thermal gap through the wood, or air infiltration beside the wood, may be to notch the rafters part way into the panels so that the insulation bridges across the tops or the bottoms of the

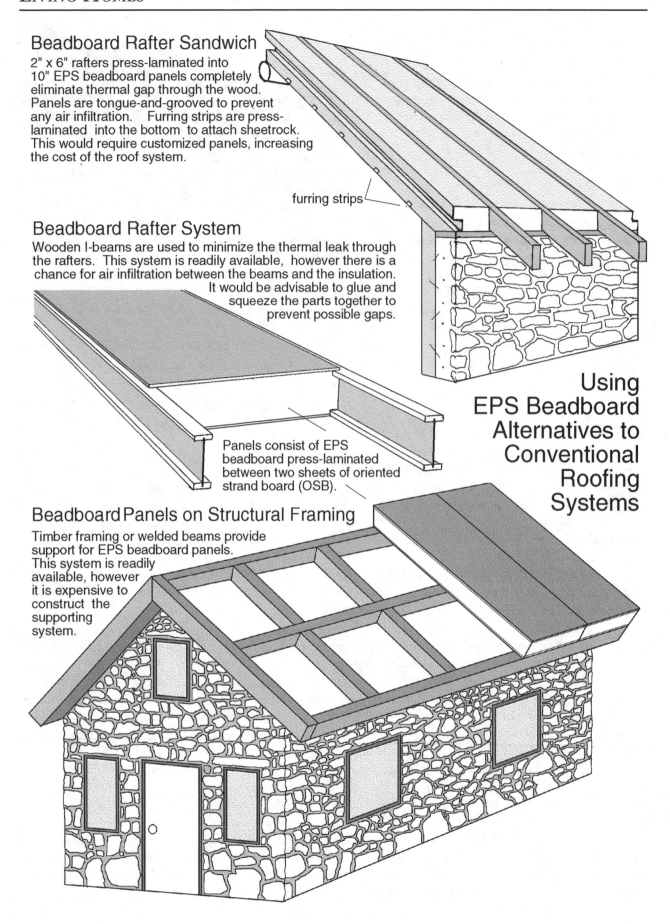

Beadboard Rafter Sandwich

2" x 6" rafters press-laminated into 10" EPS beadboard panels completely eliminate thermal gap through the wood. Panels are tongue-and-grooved to prevent any air infiltration.   Furring strips are press-laminated into the bottom to attach sheetrock. This would require customized panels, increasing the cost of the roof system.

furring strips

Beadboard Rafter System

Wooden I-beams are used to minimize the thermal leak through the rafters. This system is readily available, however there is a chance for air infiltration between the beams and the insulation. It would be advisable to glue and squeeze the parts together to prevent possible gaps.

Panels consist of EPS beadboard press-laminated between two sheets of oriented strand board (OSB).

Using EPS Beadboard Alternatives to Conventional Roofing Systems

Beadboard Panels on Structural Framing

Timber framing or welded beams provide support for EPS beadboard panels. This system is readily available, however it is expensive to construct the supporting system.

rafters.   The example at the top of the opposite page shows 2" x 6" rafters press-glued into 10" beadboard panels, with tongue-and-groove joints in the insulation to eliminate infiltration problems. 1" x 2" furring strips could be press-glued into the bottom surface crosswise to the rafters, to attach sheetrock to the ceiling later.

A press-glued beadboard rafter system would be more expensive than the roof we installed on our own home, but potentially less expensive than sprayed-in urethane or icynene for achieving total energy efficiency in a house. Although I could have a system like this custom-made at the local beadboard manufacturer, I have heard that similar plants in other parts of the country are less flexible in what they will produce.

Papercrete Roofing Systems

In the continuing search for a miracle roofing material, I am now evaluating the possibility of casting roofs from papercrete, as illustrated below. With this system it would be possible to use a cheap, pole-framed roof, with little need for precise leveling. The framework must be more than strong enough to support the weight of the wet papercrete mortar. Stucco wire would be stretched tight over the framework to hold up the papercrete. It might be wise to include additional reinforcement in the middle of the papercrete.

In the spirit of integrated design work, formwork can be used to block out shallow boxes for solar water panels. After the papercrete is dry and the forms are removed, holes are drilled between the panels to connect the piping. Windows are dropped into place on precast notches in the openings.

One potential problem with papercrete is that the fresh mortar would tend to drip on everything below it. That might be okay in a house with stone walls, but it could cause damage to strawbale or other types of construction. Another challenge to papercrete is that it must be protected from wet weather while drying.

When dry, the roof must be sealed to keep out all moisture, since papercrete absorbs water like a sponge. One inexpensive method is to mop a thick layer of tar over the fully dried papercrete. It soaks into every small nook and cranny to form a good bond.

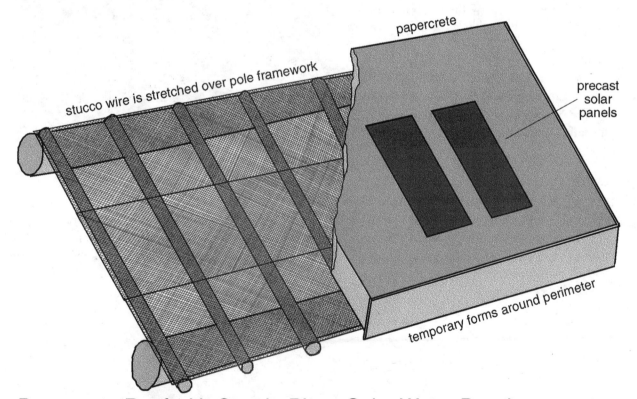

Papercrete Roof with Cast-in-Place Solar Water Panels

A papercrete roof can be cast over a pole-frame support system, with little need to precisely level the wood. There must be more than enough wood to support the wet load of the papercrete mortar, or any other loads that may be placed on the roof, such as snow.   Formwork can be used to block out shallow boxes for solar water panels.   After the papercete is dry and the forms are removed, holes are drilled between the panels to connect the piping. Windows are dropped into place on precast notches in the openings. The roof must be sealed to keep out all moisture.

Another possibility is to stucco or ferrocement the roof, adding additional wire reinforcement. A shingle-like pattern could be imprinted into the mortar to make a really beautiful roof. Concrete dye may be added for color. The cured masonry should be treated with a clear sealant for further protection.

Keep in mind that papercrete is an experimental material, especially in the application proposed here, so it would be important to test the technique on a small outbuilding before using it on a whole house.

Pole Frame Ceilings

For home-builders with access to a woodlot, another potential low-tech, low-cost alternative to the roofing problem may be to utilize lots of small diameter poles laid side-by-side to make a finished ceiling and structural roof. The idea was inspired by the "earthlodge" we once built on our land.

Our earthlodge was patterned after similar structures built by the Mandan Indians on the plains. Post-and-beam construction was used to make a supportive framework. Many small-diameter poles were then laid on top of the framework to make the walls and roof. The earthlodge was then covered with thick layers of straw and dirt. The twenty-three foot diameter lodge cost about $200, including the backhoe work to put the dirt on the roof, plus the cost of the straw. The poles were harvested from the forest. The total labor involved to build such a structure is about two or three weeks.

Unfortunately, because we did not put quite enough straw and dirt on the earthlodge, the rain eventually penetrated through and rotted the poles, bringing the earthlodge to a premature end. We got about five good years out of it.

Although the earthlodge we built did not compare well with a real house, I had to admit that dollar-for-dollar and hour-for-hour, it provided a much greater benefit for the investment. Without too much additional time or money the earthlodge could be converted into a modern home, mostly by adding concrete footings to keep the wood off the ground, plus cement stucco on the outside of the structure instead of dirt. If I had to start all over again I realized I would be better off to develop the earthlodge concept and save myself about $15,000 and five years worth of work to get into a new house.

The earthlodge consists of a pole framework covered with brush, straw and dirt.

Over the years I have grown increasingly interested in dome-shaped homes, simply because domes reduce the need for an expensive support system. Most existing dome homes are ugly, but I think there is great potential, especially where a separate dome is used for each room of a home, as pictured in the chapter *Disaster-Proofing Your Home*. Papercrete shows the most promise out of any material I've seen to be able to mass-produce superefficient and low-cost dome homes. Several domes have been built already with papercrete, although some were not properly waterproofed or reinforced. This is a material I intend to explore much more in the future.

Windows & Doors

Putting a Plug in the Thermos

Building a well-insulated shell without good windows and doors would be like trying to keep chicken soup hot in a thermos with no lid— the insulation of the shell is useless if the openings are not also sealed. Windows and doors account for a fifth to a quarter of the heat loss from the typical home. In a superinsulated structure the heat loss may be proportionately higher, since the rest of the structure is so well insulated. Therefore, if you have taken due care to build energy efficient walls and a roof for you home, then it is important to follow through with high-quality windows and doors too.

Note: the principles of heat gain and loss through windows was covered in the chapter *Solar Input*. The focus of the section is on buying and installing the units. In the ideal world you could simply purchase the best windows and doors available on the market, but in the real world you must balance the long-term energy efficiency with the upfront costs.

Working with Windows

There are two essential rules to follow to save money on window installation: 1) use as many fixed windows (non-opening) as possible, and 2) stick to standard sizes.

You will always need some opening windows in your home, both for ventilation and to provide an escape route from the bedrooms in case of fire. But otherwise, you should design your house with as many **fixed windows** as possible, assuming you are building on a tight budget. Ask your local glass dealer for a list of standard window sizes for glass units without any framing, and add a 1/2" horizontally and vertically when you make the **rough openings**. Don't be stingy with the extra space; the window needs room to expand and contract. You can purchase solid plastic spacers to keep the window up off the framing, plus neoprene padding to cushion around the rest of the window. If the neoprene isn't thick enough to fill the space around the window, then try stuffing in bits of fiberglass or strips of beadboard insulation. Do not use plastic foam insulation to fill the space, because it does not give the glass room to expand. Latex foam, however, remains soft and flexible. None of the padding will show.

Lumber works well for the rough openings, especially for windows in series, as illustrated on the previous

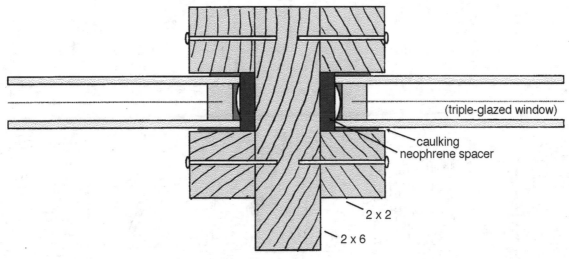

(triple-glazed window)

caulking
neophrene spacer

2 x 2

2 x 6

Framing Fixed Windows in Series

page. Lumber is the obvious choice for framing windows in log houses, while other options should be evaluated for stone or strawbale houses. Aluminum framing is more expensive up front, but it could save money in painting and rot maintenance down the road. To be energy efficient, there must be an insulated space in the framework, so heat doesn't conduct out through the aluminum.

In the chapter *The Art of Slipforming* I also suggested using 2 lb. density beadboard for framing windows. That would work well for individual windows in stone or strawbale houses, but wouldn't be strong enough for windows framed in series.

Opening windows are more complicated to order than fixed windows, so stay alert. Choose your windows early, and make certain you and the dealer both understand the specified measurements for the rough openings. Opening windows are nailed in place with wood framing, but glued in place with concrete or beadboard openings, and the dimensions of the rough openings will vary for these situations. You can always fill in around a window with insulation and trim, if necessary, but it always nice to get it right the first time. The dealer should have installation instructions on hand, and it is a good idea to read them before you frame in the opening.

You can build your own opening windows, but I don't advise trying it unless you are just making single-pane units to separate rooms within a house, as illustrated here. Good quality, tightly sealed windows need to be produced under the exacting conditions of mass-production. It is probably not worth your time to tool up for the job.

Single-Pane Window Framework

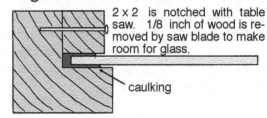

2 x 2 is notched with table saw. 1/8 inch of wood is removed by saw blade to make room for glass.

caulking

We initially built eight opening windows for our house because Renee's family owns a picture frame business, and Renee is highly skilled at that kind of work. We built single-pane windows, which was all we could afford at the time. We couldn't see out the windows much in the winter because of all the ice on the glass, but we survived with that for a few years until we could afford triple-glazed factory-made units. Then we replaced the exterior, opening windows. We kept the original single pane windows which separate the living area from the greenhouse and the laundry room.

Given the time and materials it cost to build and maintain the windows which we later removed and trashed, I think we would have been better to just block the openings with plastic and blankets and waited until we had the money to buy those better windows.

Recycled windows can save you a lot of money in certain situations, but think carefully before you act. You might expect to save a lot of money compared to buying new windows, but the upfront cost of new windows is trivial

Window Types

Image Source: Warm Places: A sampling of energy-efficient Montana homes. Montana Department of Natural Resources & Conservation. Spring 1988.

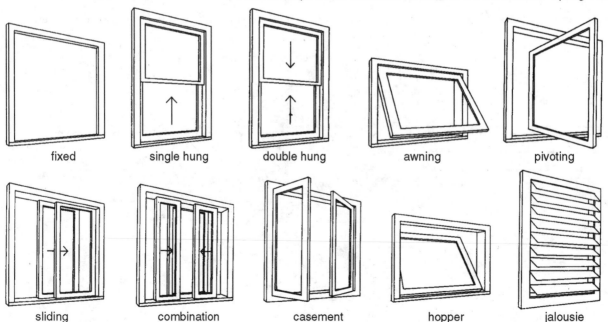

fixed   single hung   double hung   awning   pivoting

sliding   combination   casement   hopper   jalousie

compared to the cost of heat lost through inefficient units. Most secondhand windows are only single-paned, almost useless by today's standards. Nevertheless, the windows can work for seasonal greenhouses, workshops, or other spaces where efficiency isn't required.

Your best bet for recycled glass is double-glazed windows for fixed installations, especially from used patio doors. The silicone seal around the window units gradually deteriorates, and eventually fails. Moist air seeps in between the glass and evaporates, leaving a white film behind. Eventually homeowners have the windows replaced, and sometimes you can purchase the old ones.

Unfortunately, many glass dealers trash old windows at the job site. Partly it is not worth their time to bother bringing the windows back to the shop in one piece, but also, they would rather sell you expensive new units than cheap old ones. A handful of shops bring the old windows back, disassemble them, and sell the individual sheets of glass or build new units. Finding a dealer who will save the old units and sell them to you at a good price requires some persistence. It may help to say that you are using the windows in a greenhouse. Presumably the dealer will recognize that you are not willing to invest as much money in a greenhouse as in a real house, so they will not be losing any business by passing off their secondhand windows for a few bucks.

The quality of secondhand thermopane windows varies widely. We obtained ten patio door windows for our greenhouse at a cost of $10 each (1990 dollars). All were in reasonably good condition, with few mineral stains. The other six custom windows in the greenhouse cost a total of $800 (double glazed with low-E) so we saved a lot by using the patio doors. In order to make our home completely passive solar we will need to eventually replace all the windows triple or quadruple glazed units. Our opening windows were much more expensive.

If you obtain secondhand thermopane windows with mineral stains, it is possible to take them apart, clean the glass and reassemble the units with new spacers. I rebuilt one unit for use on our solar panel. The window sat out in the weather for so long that the glass separated from the spacer. It wasn't difficult, just a bit time consuming for a single unit. Rebuilding several windows at a time would make the process much more efficient.

To **rebuild a thermopane window**, first use a razor blade to cut through the old sealant that holds the panes together. Separate the spacer from the windows and scrape all residue off the glass with the razor blade. The most difficult part to me is wiping the glass clean. I've never mastered that skill. Aluminum spacers, plastic corners and dessicant can be purchased at a glass supply store. The spacers are hollow. Using a hacksaw, cut the aluminum spacers to fit the size of the window, with about 1/8" extra space all the way around. Insert a plastic corner into one end of the spacer and pour the dessicant in from the other end, using a funnel. The dessicant will absorb moisture and prevent condensation inside the finished thermopane. Once the dessicant is opened you should complete the process as quickly as possible, so it doesn't absorb too much moisture before the window unit is sealed.

When the aluminum spacer is filled with dessicant and the plastic corners are inserted to connect the sides together, simply make a sandwhich of the two glass panes and the spacer, then caulk around the outside with 100% silicone sealant. Make sure there are no gaps where moist air could leak in. Allow the silicone to cure for a day to two, and the window is ready to use. The materials cost for me to rebuild one window was $12.

Whether you are buying or building your windows it is helpful to know a little about the glass itself. Most large, rectangular windows of standard sizes are made with **tempered glass**, also known as **safety glass**. The windows are cut at the glass factory, then heat-treated to make the safety glass. Tempered glass is stronger than regular glass, and if broken it will shatter into relatively harmless cube-shaped pieces, instead of angular shards. Tempered glass cannot be cut into smaller pieces without destroying it.

Regular glass, or **plate glass**, can be cut with a simple glass cutter, a straightedge, and some nerve. The glass-cutter should be run only once firmly across the glass. Do not go over a line twice or it ruins the cutter. The glass cutter scores a tiny line on the surface. If done properly then you should be able to snap the glass at that line. You should observe glass-cutting at a dealer and practice on scrap glass before trying it yourself.

In any case, large plate glass windows are made thicker than tempered glass to achieve similar strength. Plate glass poses a potential hazard if used up high where it could break and shatter over head.

Ceramic glass is a very expensive glass used in fireplaces. Cheaper types of glass are sometimes used for this, but they have a limited life under the harsh conditions. Ceramic glass can take very high temperatures without breaking, provided there is sufficient room for expansion and contraction.

Dealing with Doors

Doors, especially exterior doors, must be able to take a lot of abuse. They need to stand up to the impact of people going in and out all day, often slamming or even kicking them shut. Only a high quality door can take that kind of abuse and still seal tightly every time, keeping the warmth in and the weather out. Therefore, as with windows that open, I recommend buying factory-made units, at least for exterior doorways.

I've tried building a number of **exterior doors**, with mixed results. I built the doors with mostly salvaged materials, so the initial cost wasn't high, except in time. The best success is clearly the front door of our house, which is heavily insulated and nearly two inches thick. However, I still have to replace the weather stripping every year or two to keep from freezing the plants in the greenhouse.

Insulated steel doors are remarkably inexpensive, at least compared to the time and materials it takes to build your own. Doors with magnetic weather stripping are more costly, but also more reliable in the long run. Exterior doors are typically 32 to 36 inches wide and 78-80 inches tall. Wider doors help to simplify chores like moving furniture and appliances. You should inquire about rough openings before you build.

This door to our sun room is just under six feet tall because we needed to leave the log above it intact to strengthen that side of the house.

Most **interior doors** are narrower, either 30 or sometimes 32 inches wide and 78-80 inches tall. Factory-made interior doors are very easy to install, and instructions should be supplied with the units. You can also make your own interior doors, or use secondhand doors. Secondhand doors add lots of character to a house. We bought all our downstairs doors at garage sales, and none of them matched exactly, except that all had panels. The old-style doors complement the stonework very well. Working with old doors can save a few dollars, but you won't save any time. The height and width varies widely among used doors, and often they have been trimmed to slightly trapezoidal shapes to fit the sloping floors and walls of older homes.

You might also consider making your own interior doors, especially if you need unusual sizes for special projects. The door to our sun room, shown here, is just under six feet tall because we needed to leave the log above it intact to strengthen that side of the house. We cut secondhand 1/4" thick plate glass to make the window panes.

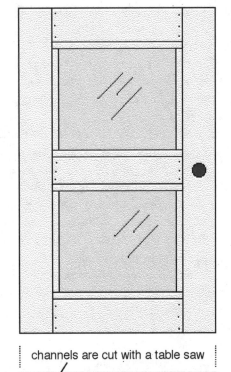

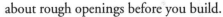

channels are cut with a table saw

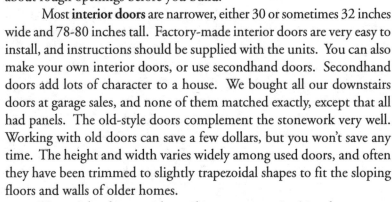

Home-Made Door

Part V
Finishing
The Interior

The Energy Efficient Masonry Fireplace

A masonry stove or fireplace like this one can recover up to 90% of the heat potential in the fuel wood.

Layer-by-layer plans for this fireplace are included at the end of the chapter.

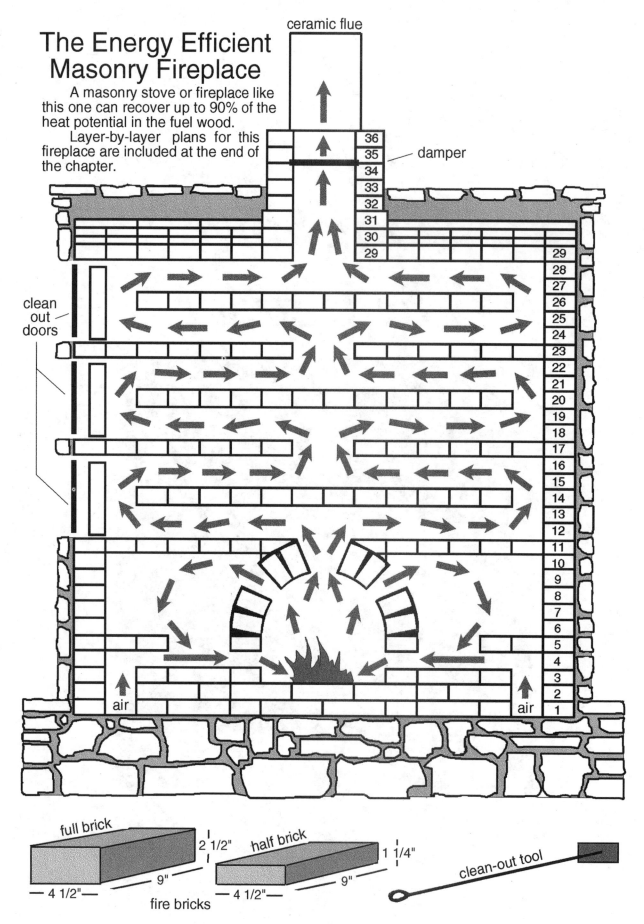

ceramic flue

damper

clean out doors

air

air

full brick

half brick

fire bricks

2 1/2"

9"

4 1/2"

1 1/4"

9"

4 1/2"

clean-out tool

Revival of the Masonry Stove
An Old but Efficient Heating System

Many animals use simple sticks and rocks and leaves as tools, but only humans have learned to use and control fire. It is the one technology that truly sets our species apart. Mastery of fire enabled our ancestors to stay warm and move into new lands, to make pottery, build shelters, manipulate ecosystems and to join hands around the circle of light, singing songs deep into the night.

Today we have a much greater mastery of fire, and we harness it in many forms, using coal, oil, natural gas, and electricity as substitutes for the wood fires of our ancestors. These substitutes effectively power our industries and run our cities. Yet, for the country home with a source of fuel wood, it is still hard to beat the efficiency and aesthetics of a good old-fashioned wood fire.

The aesthetics of the wood fire are an important point. It is for that reason alone, not energy efficiency, that builders still put chincy fireplaces in so many condominiums and apartments today. And although I envision a world of houses so energy efficient that they need no heating system, I would not willingly give up my own wood stove! I

Our masonry stove.

like to stare at the flames and soak up the warmth on those cold winter days, even when the house is already warm.

The type of fireplace we built is traditionally called a "masonry stove". It is also called a "Russian fireplace", but the idea came from eastern Europe more than Russia. The original designs had solid doors like stoves. The type I advocate are made to look like fireplaces yet function as masonry stoves, so they are best described as "masonry fireplaces". I use the terms stove or heater interchangeably, and fireplace to specify stoves with a visible fire.

The essence of a masonry heater is lots of mass to absorb heat from the fire, plus a snakelike flue to extract heat from the exhaust before ventilating to the outside. The masonry warms up slowly, then radiates heat out for hours or days afterwards.

I first learned about traditional masonry stoves while in high-school through an article in *The Mother Earth News* magazine. A house at Mother's Eco-Village in North Carolina included a masonry stove designed by Basilio Lepuschenko of Maine. I eventually wrote away for Lepuschenko's stove plans and studied them intently. Our initial house plans included only the wood cookstove in the kitchen, but later we built an addition to the house and we wanted an efficient fireplace for the new family room.

Evolution of the Masonry Stove

Given my passion for ancient skills, I have spent a large part of my life camped out in makeshift shelters, huddled close to warm fires. In my own way I have retraced some of the history behind our modern stoves.

Most primitive shelters are highly flammable, usually a framework of sticks covered with grasses and leaves. There is often an open fire inside, within a couple feet of a something burnable, either the bedding or the walls, or the pile of firewood. The roof may be covered tight enough that you see no light, but the smoke filters right through the roofing. Such shelters are remarkably efficient and reasonably safe most of the time.

Fire is used in many other ways to heat primitive shelters. It can be used to heat the thermal mass of the ground under a temporary shelter, so that ground radiates warmth long after the fire is out. Rocks are sometimes heated in a fire and transported indoors for heat. Chimneys can be built underneath a shelter to heat the floor. These kinds of techniques have been used by primitive and classical cultures to keep shelters warm.

In Europe it was still common as late as the 1600's to burn open fires inside the house. Our forefathers built squared, wood-stuccoed houses with grass roofs before they built fireplaces or chimneys. The more advanced homes had a raised platform so the woman wouldn't have to bend over to cook, and a few houses had plastered spark arrestors overhead. But still the smoke flowed through the house and filtered out through the grass roofs or gable ends. The methodology was effective, but when one house caught fire it often took the rest of the city with it.

The reason builders did not embrace enclosed fires sooner was simply economics. A fireplace or simple stove with a straight chimney ventilates about ninety percent of the heat to the outside. According to David Lyle, author of *The Book of Masonry Stoves*, sophisticated heaters evolved during the "Little Ice Age", the period between 1550 and 1850 when the climate was unusually cold across Europe. Population increases put more pressure on fuel wood supplies, and tighter housing increased the fire danger. Safe, efficient heaters were developed out of necessity. Efficient heaters were made of thin tiles, cast iron, or heavy masonry, but all shared one characteristic—a series of baffles in the chimney to extract heat out of the exhaust. Although Lyle's book is not a construction manual, I highly recommend it as a source of innovative ideas.

Efficient masonry and tile stoves gradually became popular across eastern Europe, but the idea did not carry over to this continent until very recent times. The knowledge probably wasn't that common yet among immigrants, and there was little need for efficiency anyway, since the New World was full of endless forests of free fuel. American pioneers built inefficient fireplaces and later metal stoves, followed by cookstoves with ovens. Energy efficiency was not an issue in this country until the fuel shortages of the 1970's.

Inventors responded to the energy crisis by making "airtight" stoves. The air supply and exhaust in the stoves was tightly controlled, so the fuel slowly smoldered, giving off an even and steady flow of heat. Airtight stoves increased fuel efficiency to about 60%, but there were serious problems. Much of the remaining heat potential was released in the form of thick smoke, clogging chimney pipes and the atmosphere with unburned, cancer-causing particulate. The particulate built up in chimney pipes and sometimes caught fire, often causing house fires.

Older stoves were much less efficient, but at least they burned the wood more cleanly. The pollution problem in airtight stoves was eventually resolved with the aid of expensive catalytic converters to help burn the particulate in the exhaust. Catalytic converters increased the efficiency of airtight stoves up to 85% or 90%. Unfortunately, the catalytic converters tend to wear out quickly, so the stoves get to be just as bad as airtight stoves after a few years, unless the catalytic converters are replaced.

The energy crisis also led to a new interest in efficient masonry stoves. In recent years a few companies have cast laboratory-tested models into do-it-yourself kits. The quality of the prefabricated units is exceptional, but the cost is astronomical—usually four to six thousand dollars for the core and hardware. Then you still have to add the stone or brick veneer and build a chimney. Masonry heaters burn a hot fire with lots of oxygen, so the exhaust is very clean. A well-designed system extracts up to about 90% of the heat potential before the exhaust is ventilated out.

The reason the commercial units are so expensive is only because of the **refractory cement** used to cast the pieces. Refractory cement is designed for use in high-temperature applications. The cement itself is different from the cement used in regular masonry, and it has bits of steel fibers and broken pottery pieces mixed in for aggregate. You could not buy the cement and cast your own blocks for much less than what you would pay for a factory-made unit. We originally intended to buy a kit stove for our home, just to play it safe with the design, but the commercial units did not fit the available space or our budget, so we designed and built our own.

Homemade masonry stoves are usually built with a core of **fire brick**. Fire bricks are made of clay at a factory and fired like pottery, instead of curing like cement.

The design of our fireplace required the stonework to be completed at the same time, since the baffle system is supported by the stonework around the firebox. I've since refined the design so that the entire heater core can be built first, as shown in the drawings. The stonework can be added afterwards.

The core of our masonry fireplace is built with firebrick. Note the air supply that enters the side of the firebox.

166

Principles of Design

Masonry stoves have taken many different forms over the centuries and you can easily custom design one for your home. As with anything you build, the blueprint is the sum of the criteria. You have to list the criteria, then brainstorm a plan that best fits the criteria. You will no doubt have some specific criteria for your unique situation, but for any masonry stove there are a few universal principles you should consider.

Purpose and Placement: Before you can design a masonry stove or fireplace you must first consider its purpose, and where to put it in the house. Keep in mind that firewood is always messy, and you could save a lot of cleanup work by building the stove along an outside wall, with a loading door inside a garage, workshop, or porch where the firewood is stored. Even with an outside loading door you could still have a glass door in the house to watch the flames. The downside is that you would have to step out of the house to stoke the fire. The stove should be insulated to keep the warmth in the house, unless you also intend to heat the workshop or garage where the loading door is.

All the bricks in the dome of the firebox are keyed together so none can fall out, even if the mortar cracks. The cinder blocks provide ventilation behind the stove to keep the frame wall from getting too hot.

The stove could also be built in a basement, but there should be a door directly to the outside so you can bring the firewood in without crossing the living space. Likewise, if you build the stove in a main living area, with a loading door inside, at least make sure it is close to an outside door (and the woodpile), so you do not have to haul firewood too far through the house. Always minimize the distance from the woodpile to the stove.

In order to equalize heat distribution, the stove should be placed as close as possible to the center of the house. That idea may seem contradictory to putting it on an outside wall, but most houses are longer in one direction. In theory at least, you should be able to put the stove near the center of the house and along an outside wall. This is the principle of integrated design, where you design the stove to fit the house, but also design the house to fit the stove.

One point we failed to consider in our own home was the space immediately in front of our masonry fireplace. The fireplace heats the whole room and the entire house nicely, but we still like to park chairs up next to the hearth. Unfortunately, the main walkway into the house goes right by the stove, so the chairs are always in the way. In your own home you should make sure you have uninterrupted living space around the fire.

The stove must also be placed on a solid footing for support. A masonry stove weighs several tons, and you don't want it sinking into the ground beneath your house! A footing that extends out twelve inches all the way around the heater should be sufficient for most soils. Use plenty of reinforcing bar.

Expansion and Contraction: One of the potential problems with masonry stoves is that expansion and contraction from heating and cooling puts extreme stresses on the masonry. The bricks and rocks and mortar each have unique expansion and contraction qualities, so they don't quite move together. Cracks in the mortar joints may form over time, but fortunately, it is an easily preventable problem. The key is to separate the masonry core from the stone or brick veneer by a about a quarter-inch gap. Then the core can expand without stressing the outer shell. I learned that piece of wisdom just days before I started building our stove from a mason who installs kit stoves locally. He suggested wrapping the core with cardboard to make the gap.

I included room for expansion in our stove, but by then I'd already over-engineered the entire unit to flex without cracking. I was especially concerned about the mortar between the rocks cracking, so I double-bricked the entire core to insulate the rocks better, then added perlite, basically air-expanded volcanic ash, to the mortar to better absorb the shock. I also added fiberglass fibers to the mortar to help tie it together. In retrospect, I think the expansion joint was the critical element, and the fiberglass was a good idea for reinforcement, but the double-bricking and the perlite probably were not necessary. Important: **do not use steel reinforcing** in the heater because it will absorb the heat and expand faster than the surrounding masonry, potentially cracking the mortar.

The arched space on the side of the firebox allows better heat dissipation to reduce expansion-contraction problems. The arches were replaced in the drawings with an extra chamber in that part of the stove.

Chimney Placement: One feature we did not like about masonry stove kits was that the exhaust flues were not centered on top. The stoves were designed to be assembled and connected to an adjacent chimney. The reason the stoves are built separately from the chimney is because of expansion and contraction problems. When a masonry stove heats and expands it lifts the entire chimney with it. Constructing a separate chimney from the ground up is definitely the better option, but not absolutely required. We simply built our chimney so the inner flue could move independently from the outer masonry. The flue tiles are less than an inch thick all the way up, so there isn't a lot of weight involved there. Still, I'm not sure the technique would be sound for taller chimneys. Ours rises only about ten feet above the stove.

Chimney height is an important factor to consider when deciding where to build a masonry heater. The chimney should not be positioned so that the smoke flows past or into an upstairs window, but it is also wise to build the shortest chimney possible, just to save labor and materials. According to code, a chimney should be two feet higher than anything within ten feet of it. Local codes may vary. Masonry heaters are really very fire safe because the sparks seldom make it through all the baffles. If you live in a high precipitation area then you should also design a cap to keep water out of the flue.

Baffles and Clean-Out Doors: A masonry stove needs to be designed with enough baffles to efficiently extract most of the heat from the exhaust, but not so many baffles that it fails to "draw" properly. If the exhaust cools too much then it may stall in the chimney and backdraft into the house. For lack of a degree in engineering, success hinges on a bit of educated guess work. We used Lepuschenko's plans as a guide for designing ours. The total length of the baffles in his stoves is about twenty to twenty-five feet, in up and down series. Our stove has about twenty feet of flue, but it is difficult to compare since it is a split-flue system. The exhaust splits and travels horizontally through about twelve feet of baffles per side, but the baffles are much narrower, so the total surface area is greater. From testing the stove I believe we could have easily added another set of baffles to extract more heat. However, the stove was tall enough already. It would have been out of proportion with the room if it were any taller. The drawings included here utilize the space around the firebox more effectively than our stove. I've also extended the length of the baffles. If necessary, the length could be reduced by the width of a brick (4 1/2") on each side, possibly twice that, without substantially altering the design.

In theory the baffle systems do not require clean-out doors, except on the last run that goes up the chimney. Masonry stoves are designed for hot fires with lots of oxygen, so the smoke is very clean. However, we were not comfortable with the thought of building a system we could not get back into, so we installed three clean-out doors to give access the entire baffle system. I think it was a good choice, especially given the narrow flue-system we used. We use a lot of paper and cardboard to start the fire, and the particulate tends to rise up into the baffle system, so there is always some accumulation. We've also had one of our pet pigeons fly into the chimney from the outside. I don't know how long it was in there, but it was just char when I dragged it out. I recommend that you include clean-out doors in your own designs. It is an interesting challenge to come up with a good design that allows you to install clean-out doors without putting them on the face of the stove.

Firebox Size: Old-style masonry heaters usually had long, skinny fireboxes, sometimes only twelve inches square at the opening, with solid metal doors. The stoves were designed for heating, not for gazing at the flames. We used more of a fireplace style, with a square firebox and an arched door, just barely big enough to put a piece of wood in sideways or lengthwise. We made the firebox as short as we possibly could, so the stove wouldn't take up so much of the room. (I added the width of a firebrick to the stove in the drawings for extra room.) I've heard of other homemade masonry stoves with much bigger fireboxes, but I don't see any advantage to them, unless you are heating a very large space. One feature that is nice about a small firebox is that the heat reflects off the walls right back onto the fuel, creating a sort of "positive feed back loop". Even snow-covered boards seem to instantly combust when placed on the hot coals of the fire.

Air Supply: Fires need to breathe oxygen, and lots of it. You must give the fire all the air it needs, preferably piped in from the outside. The air supply channels a steady wind to the fire, and you will easily feel the vacuum-like suction through the pipe. This is called **sealed combustion**, when the air supply comes from outside and the exhaust is vented back out. A stove that consumes warm air directly from the house must draw cold air in through every little unsealed crack in the walls, roof and floor. I suspect that an otherwise 90% efficient stove would lose more than 15% of its effectiveness when operated on house air.

Sucking the air out of the house also creates negative pressure in the house, if you've made an energy-efficient, airtight house. There is a genuine danger of sucking flue exhaust back into the house to balance the pressure, so it is very important that you install the outside air supply.

The air inlet to our fireplace is simply a half-brick opening in the wall of the firebox. We used flexible 3" aluminum dryer pipe to wind through the base of the fireplace, cast in mortar. Our initial tests, before we extended the pipe outside, indicated there was not quite enough air. We used 4" PVC for the remaining eight feet to the outside. Apparently the difference in pressure outside the house was enough to suck the air in through the four inch and the three inch pipes into the fire. We were very lucky that it worked. I would recommend using at least 4" main supply line for your stove. The supply line could be split into two 3" lines and piped in to both

The air supply pipe to our fireplace sticks out through the wall and the woodpile. We remove the threaded cap when we light the fire.

sides of the firebox. We use a threaded PVC cap to close off the air supply from the outside when the fire has died down to a bed of coals. An indoor-operated valve would be better, but we don't mind the outside jaunt. The pipe is less than ten feet from the door.

Damper: A damper is used to block off the chimney to trap heat inside the mass of the stove. Following Lepuschenko's designs, we used a simple plate of sheet metal that slides straight into the chimney. We simply left a section of firebrick unmortared in front, with recessed mortar around the other three sides as a channel for the plate.

According to information we have found, a fire only produces **carbon monoxide** when the flame is blue. However, our stove has triggered the carbon monoxide detector when we closed the damper and there were still a handful of coals left in the stove. Neither the damper nor the door of the stove are completely airtight, so we now leave the damper open overnight and close it in the morning. But we shut off the air supply before going to bed, to prevent the wind from blowing through and cooling off the mass overnight. Sometimes I also shovel out the last few hot coals out so that we can shut the damper sooner.

Distance to Combustibles: Every commercial metal or masonry stove has a certain setback distance to keep it away from combustible materials. I'm not sure whether the setbacks are determined separately for each stove or if these are just uniform standards, but literature on the commercial models suggested we would need about eighteen inches around our stove to be safe. Given tight space considerations, we built our stove right up against a frame wall, but installed a ventilation system behind the stove with cinder blocks. The hollow cavities of the cinder blocks allow vertical air passage, and we notched the top and bottom rows of blocks to allow horizontal air passage. We thought we would still have to replace the wood studs in the frame wall with metal studs and add wall vents for further protection, but the cinder block ventilation system has worked very well. Our stove has so much thermal mass that the outside never gets unbearably hot. The air through the ventilating system is warm, but well within reason. You will need to evaluate the danger in your own situation and plan accordingly. Be sure to test and monitor the heat output to ensure that your design is safe.

Integral Strength: Stone masons of long ago did not have the benefit of steel reinforcing bar or strong portland cement for their work. Windows and doors had to be arched for strength, or bridged with the aid of a long stone, called a lintel. Due to expansion-contraction concerns, you cannot add steel reinforcing to your masonry stove, so you will need to pay special attention to the integral strength of the masonry work. Firebricks should be fitted together so that they would stay in place even if the mortar between them cracked loose. The stonework needs to be self-supporting. The weight of the stonework above the firebox in these drawings is dissipated via the arch to the masonry pillars in each corner of the stove.

Another point of concern is the top of the stove, where the masonry bridges the core. The top of the core should be built up with half bricks to make a slight dome. Perlite beads can be dumped on top of the core to round out the dome and provide room for expansion. Then a heavy bed of mortar can be laid over the beads to create an arch for strength. The strength is especially important when the top of the stove is supporting the weight of the chimney.

Designing for the Materials: The standard size for a full fire brick is 2 1/4" x 4 1/2" x 9". The bricks are also available in halves (1 1/4" versus of 2 1/4"). The drawings included in this chapter are designed for standard firebricks, with the least possible cutting. Bricks can be cut with a **masonry blade** on a circular saw. The size of the bricks necessarily limits the size of the baffles. For larger horizontal baffles you can cut ceramic flue tile in half, using the U-shaped sections to bridge the tops. Alternatively, some masons use cinder blocks, which come in infinite shapes and sizes, to make the baffle system. However, cinder blocks degrade under the extreme stresses of the fireplace, so the life of the stove would be limited.

A cinderblock wall ventilates heat from behind the stove to protect the wall. Here a half-block was laid on edge for a vent.

Integrated Design: If you incorporate all of the preceding criteria into your design work, then your masonry heater will be well integrated with your home. On the other hand though, the house and the stove still remain two separate pieces: first you build one, then the other. True integrated design work requires that you at least evaluate the possibility of merging the house and the stove together. For example, many older greenhouses included wood heat with the flues imbedded in the walls, running the entire length of the building. The walls of the greenhouse were effectively the walls of the stove too! In most cases this type of integration is impractical, since the walls have to be much thicker, but it is something to consider. You could also run flues under a masonry floor, but then the stove would have to be positioned lower than the floor. The flues should be accessible for cleaning.

Construction of Your Masonry Stove

As you may have sensed by now, designing and building a masonry stove is a complicated and somewhat advanced masonry project. I do not recommend that you build one unless you have already developed confidence with other masonry projects. But when the time is right, then I think you will agree that a masonry stove is a fun and exciting challenge to undertake.

I did the stone and brick work at the same time for our stove, which was required since the masonry supported the baffle system, and because the baffle system was laid entirely without mortar. (Only the firebox was mortared.) Although I think our stove is of sound design, I would still do it different the next time. I would build the entire brick core first, with mortar, then wrap it in cardboard and do the stonework. The illustrations in this chapter show self-supporting brickwork for a "next generation stove". I've included layer-by-layer instructions to build the unit. This design uses about 700 full bricks and 36 half bricks. The baffle system could be shortened by one or two firebricks on each side without substantially altering the design.

The best mortar for the brick work is refractory cement, but it is very pricey. A 50 lb. bag cost us $33.50. We used at least two, maybe three bags just to mortar the little firebox. Mortaring all of the brickwork could easily cost a thousand dollars just for the cement. The cost may be lower if you are closer to the factory. Also, the cost varies with the temperature rating of the cement.

One substitute for refractory cement is called **fire clay**, and it costs half as much. The fire clay probably doesn't bond to the bricks as well as the cement does, but at least it is heat resistant.

You could also use regular Type I & II cement with sand and lime to mortar the baffle system, even though it is more susceptible to cracking. As long as the firebox was mortared with refractory cement then the whole system should still last a lifetime or two.

It is important to **dip the firebricks in water** before applying mortar. The bricks are porous and highly absorbent. A dry brick will suck most of the moisture from the mortar in a few seconds, before it bonds or cures properly. The mortar joints should be flush or slightly recessed. Protruding globs of mortar out of the joints may interfere with expansion and contraction of the bricks. The brick work should be made level and plumb. A thin masonite board makes a good, flexible form for the arch.

The **stone masonry** work would be easiest if slipformed, but we wanted a different look for the stove, and I felt ready for the greater challenge of laying stone freehand. Also, the brick-like layering would provide more integral strength to the stove design.

Freehand masonry is often done with strings as guides, both vertically and horizontally. But I just used the frame wall behind the stove as a guide. Stones on the sides were positioned with the aid of a square off of the flat wall, while those on the front of the stove were checked with a tape measure from the wall. Corners were also checked with a level

Freehand stone work is very different from slip-from masonry. Slip-forms provide a flat plane, and all the rock faces are set behind the plane. Therefore, the plane is always at the outermost edge or bumps on the rocks. In freehand masonry each rock is positioned with the average edge along the plane, with bumps and recesses to either side. If done neatly and carefully, the result is much more beautiful than slipformed masonry. It is also much slower.

The chimney should extend at least two feet higher than anything within ten feet of it.

In slipform masonry the forms hold the rocks from falling out until the mortar has set. In freehand masonry you must take more care to provide a very level mortar bed so that each stone is well-balanced from the start. Many stones require small shims of gravel or split rock to properly level them. I averaged about a foot of height per day on the stone work.

As mentioned earlier, I added perlite to the mortar to better absorb the shock of expansion and contraction, plus fiberglass fibers for reinforcement. These were real fiberglass fibers, from waste fiberglass matting, not the plastic stuff that is often added to concrete. For the **grout** between the stones I used a 1:1:4 mix of cement, lime and masonry sand. The grout mix troweled out smoother and whiter than the other mortar.

Clean-out doors can be purchased at the brick yard, usually in 8" x 8" or 8" x 10" sizes. The plans included here call for three 8" x 10" doors. The framework can be imbedded into the mortar as you go. Positioning the doors plumb, square, and level is tricky, so pay close attention to your technique.

To build the **chimney** I switched from fire brick to **flue tile**. Flue tiles are available in several sizes. The smaller size is 8" x 8" x 12", and that is quite sufficient. Most chimneys today are built with flue tiles inside a special cinder block casing. Stone or bricks are added as veneer. However, the cinder blocks are unnecessary, as long as you provide a space for the flue tiles to expand when heated. Given tight space and economic considerations, both of our chimneys are built without the cinder block casing. We simply wrapped scraps of fiberglass insulation around the flue tile to make an expansion joint, then mortared up against the fiberglass.

Like fire brick, the flue tiles are highly absorbent, so it is important to wet them before mortaring them in place. We used a pre-mixed high-temperature mortar called **Tenax**™ to set the flue tiles. Flue tiles are tricky to level and plumb, so use your level religiously, both horizontally and vertically. Mortar will squish out of the joints as you tap the flue tiles into place; use a gloved finger to smooth it inside and outside.

The masonry should be allowed to **cure** for about a month before using the stove, then start out with paper fires to help dry out any remaining moisture. I poured a temporary door of concrete to test our stove before investing in a more expensive metal and glass door.

There are several companies that make customized fireplace doors. You can expect to pay $400-$600 for a customized arched door and window. We had our door made locally at a welding shop for less than $200. It is a good door, but not as high-quality as we could have got through a more specialized company. We used **ceramic glass** for the window, at a cost of $70. Ceramic wool insulation provides a tight seal between the door frame and the bricks. To install the door we simply drilled holes into the masonry and inserted squared pins flat across the door frame. The ceramic wool insulation pushes the frame out against the pins, so the whole unit could easily be removed by pushing on the frame and removing the pins.

The layer-by-layer plans shown on the next few pages will enable you to build a high quality masonry fireplace. Optionally, it will guide you in designing a unit customized to fit your house plans.

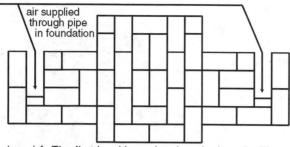

Level 1. The first level is sunken into the hearth. The top of the bricks are flush with the stonework of the hearth.

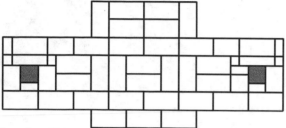

Level 2. This level forms the base of the firebox.

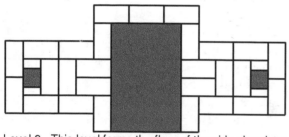

Level 3. This level forms the floor of the side chambers, raised up one brick above the firebox to stay clear of the ashes.

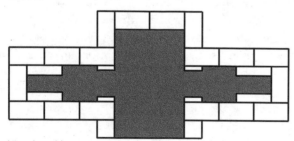

Level 4. Here we make the openings for the air supply to flow into the fire box.

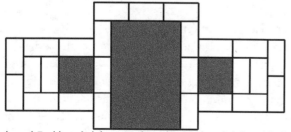

Level 5. Here bricks are placed over the air inlet to help prevent air borne ashes from clogging the air supply.

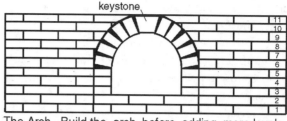

The Arch. Build the arch before adding more levels. The keystones are made of cut bricks placed on edge. See below for details of the brickwork in the arch. This view also illustrates the first 11 levels.

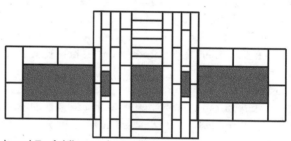

Level 6. Here the brickwork of the walls starts to rise beside the arch.

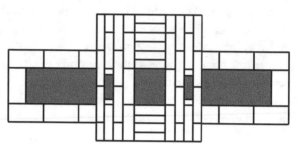

Level 7. Adding to the walls.

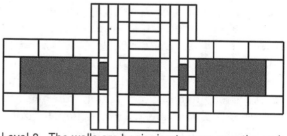

Level 8. The walls are beginning to wrap over the arch. Also look at level 8 in the front view of the arch.

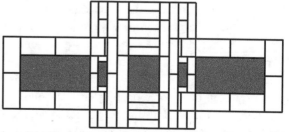

Level 9. The walls reach the level of the opening in the side of the arch that allows heat to circulate through the side chambers.

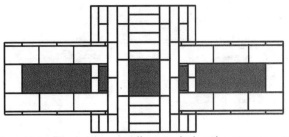

Level 10. The bricks are offset such that the open space can be bridged on the next level.

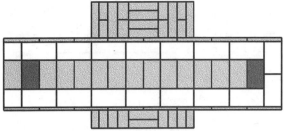

Level 15. Bricks are inset again to form the walls of the baffle system and to allow later bridging.

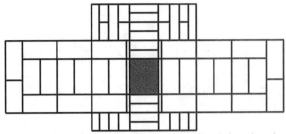

Level 11. The side chambers are bridged, forming the floor for the first set of baffles. The bricks of this level are even with the top of the arch.

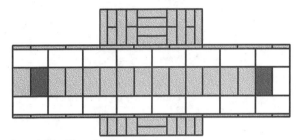

Level 16. More baffle walls.

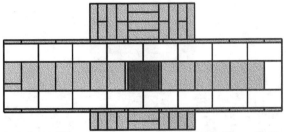

Level 12. Here we form the walls of the baffle system. The bricks are offset so the passage can be bridged later. One end is left open to install a clean-out door.

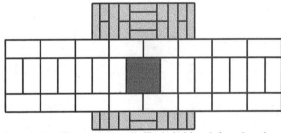

Level 17. The previous baffle is bridged, forming the floor for the next level.

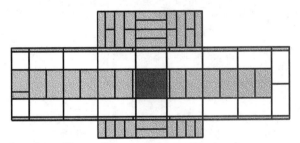

Level 13. The walls are raised another level.

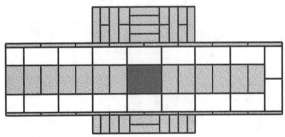

Level 18. More baffle walls.

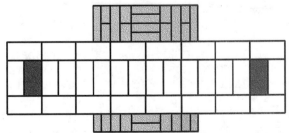

Level 14. Bricks are placed to bridge the passage below, which also forms the floor of the next level.

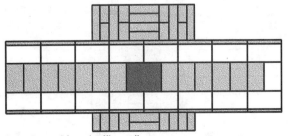

Level 19. More baffle walls.

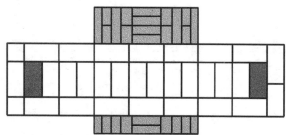

Level 20. Bridging another baffle.

Levels 21 — 29.
Level 21 is the same as level 16.
Level 22 is the same as level 15.
Level 23 is the same as level 17.
Level 24 is the same as level 18.
Level 25 is the same as level 19.
Level 26 is the same as level 20.
Level 27 is the same as level 16.
Level 28 is the same as level 15.
Level 29 is the same as level 17.

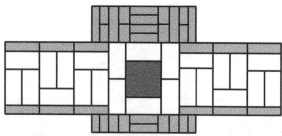

Level 30a. This level is the end of the stove and the beginning of the chimney. Full bricks surround the flue. Half bricks form the beginning of an arch over the baffle system.

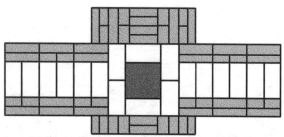

Level 30b. Half bricks taper the arch in a little more.

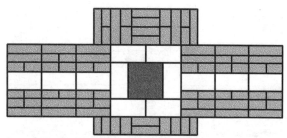

Level 31. Full bricks are added to the flue. One more layer of half bricks finishes the arch. Later, when the stonework is added, beads of vermiculite or perlite are poured over the arch to round it and to give expansion room.

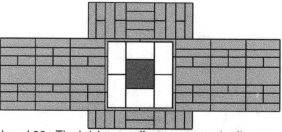

Level 32. The bricks are offset to narrow the flue so that the damper can be bridged with a single brick, and later to support the 8" chimney flue.

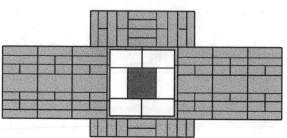

Level 33. Another level of bricks is added to the flue, for the purpose of raising the damper above future stonework.

Level 34. Same as level 32.

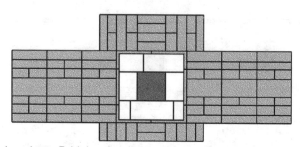

Level 35. Bridging the damper plate. Be sure to recess the grout between levels 34 and 35 to allow the plate to slide through.

Level 36. Sames as level 32. Switch to 8 inch chimney flue above level 36.

—Notes—

A cinderblock ventilation system should be added behind the stove, if it is built against a wall. Glass doors can be installed on both ends of the firebox if it is used as a divider between two rooms.

After the core of the stove is complete, the exterior can be finished with stone masonry or red brick.

The mortar should be allowed to cure for a month before the stove is used. Then start with small paper fires to further dry out the masonry.

On average, we use our stove about one day a week through the winter with pine, or two days a week when burning aspen. We stoke the fire all day to warm the masonry. Then it radiates heat for about three days.

Terra Tiles
Hand-Made Tile Floors from Sand, Cement, Dirt and Dye

There is nothing in the world quite so relaxing as walking and connecting with the natural world. There is something about the feel of real earth underfoot, the soothing sound of birds singing, the many textures and colors, and the whispering of the wind on your cheeks. It is well known that even a walk in a city park can do wonders to help overworked, stressed out people to relax and get a fresh start.

We know that different colors and textures can affect peoples moods too—just imagine painting the inside of your home all blue, or pink, or black, and think about how that might affect you.

I have often thought about the millions of homes and offices in this country and wondered about the psychological effects of all the flat, white walls and ceilings, square corners, and synthetic floorings and furnishings. It seems that the inside of a home should be as real and natural and relaxing as a walk in the park.

I find that the many shapes, colors and textures of our own home are almost hypnotic. I can sit for hours while working on a creative idea, subconsciously reaching out, connecting with every individual stone in the walls and every knot in the woodwork, or noticing the grape leaves gently rustling with the breeze through the greenhouse door, and tracing the contours of the handmade tile floor.

I think the floor is especially important, because we physically come in contact with it every time we move across the house. Carpet or linoleum is too artificial underfoot, and concrete is too hard and unforgiving. I like to feel as if I am touching the earth with every step I take, and the most earthy flooring I know of is literally made from dirt.

Terra tiles are made from a mix of dirt, sand, cement, and dye, troweled smooth and cut into individual tiles.

Imported terra-cotta tiles are nice, but they are also very expensive. Like many other back-to-the-landers, Renee and I had big dreams, but little money. Therefore we were thrilled to discover beautiful, but inexpensive "terra tiles", made from the simple ingredients of sand, cement and dirt.

A soil-cement base , with footings for the interior walls.

Terra tiles are troweled and stamped in small sections.

Terra tiles were developed out of "rammed-earth" technology, where a soil-cement mix is poured into wall forms and tamped or compacted with hand or power tools to make very dense, strong walls. Terra tiles mix is similar, but it is simply troweled into place without being compacted, and the tiles are cut with an oversize "cookie cutter". The idea was pioneered in California in the late 1970's, by David Easton, a rammed-earth contractor.

Through trial-and-error Easton developed a basic process for making terra tiles, including some of what not to do—like trying to mix the sticky mortar in a concrete truck, or trying to tamp it like the drier material used in rammed-earth walls. We learned about terra tiles through articles by Easton (*Popular Science, 1988*) and by an associate of his, Magnus Berglund (*Fine Homebuilding, 1985*). In the course of tiling three houses we have learned more about what not-to-do, as well as more of what really works to make truly beautiful, and very low-cost tile floors.

Preparing the Subfloor

Terra tiles can be poured right over the top of a concrete slab, or they can be made on a tamped, soil-cement base. Concrete slabs are favored in conventional construction because concrete makes such a solid, rigid base. But the inflexible quality of concrete can be a liability too, and I have seen many cracked floors, some with edges high enough to trip a person. A soft, soil-cement slab, on the other hand, has the flexibility to bulge or settle without snapping. Also, the terra tile surface provides an outlet for stress, so that if cracking occurs, it will appear harmlessly in the grout lines between the tiles, rather than splitting across the tiles themselves. Moreover, a soil-cement base costs less than a concrete slab, and repairs are comparatively easy if there are ever plumbing or electrical problems under the floor. I like the soil-cement base just as a matter of principle. It is nice to walk barefoot across an earthen floor, knowing there is no slab of concrete between me and the earth.

Either way, with or without a concrete slab, I recommend installing hot water piping through the floor for radiant heating, at least in the northern climates. Radiant floors are about the nicest heating systems available, but they fell out of favor decades ago due to problems with the copper piping corroding in the concrete. The leaks were difficult and messy to fix. Today, however, there are many new, long-lasting alternatives to copper, so there is a resurgent interest in radiant floor heat. The radiant tubing should be laid out in runs no more than 250 feet long, and spaced about a foot apart across the floor. Ideally you should use a separate loop for each room of the house; then you can control the heat separately to every room. Be sure to read more about radiant systems in the chapter on *Thermal Mass.*

Insulation is normally recommended under the slab in conventional northern construction, but my experience suggests otherwise, provided you have the radiant heat. Foregoing the insulation does not necessarily result in more heat loss, because there really isn't any place for the heat to go. The warmth may sink a few feet into the earth, but that just creates a greater volume of thermal mass to stabilize temperatures inside the house. The added mass can be especially helpful if the system relies on solar heat.

The property we bought for our home had an uninsulated concrete slab, so we adapted our plans to the site and eventually made tiles on the slab. We were not experienced enough at the time with the benefits of radiant floor heating, so we skipped that part and just put the tiles down on the cold floor. Today, even though the house is warm, the floor stays cool. The coolness is a luxury in summer, but hardly helpful in winter. Nevertheless, as we tighten up the rest of the house, the floor seems to get warmer and warmer.

The forms are leap-frogged over each other across the room.

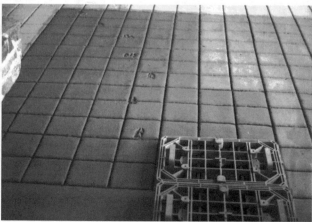

We added deertracks to the walkway through the family room.

To make the subfloor, start by spreading two or more inches of sand or pea gravel between the foundation walls and put down a six-mil plastic vapor barrier to prevent moisture from wicking up from the soil below. This preparation work is necessary in most parts of the country where there are clay soils or significant soil moisture, but can be skipped in much of the arid West, especially where the soil is sandy and holds little moisture.

Easton recommends a five inch soil-cement base under the tiles. He suggests mixing it outside with shovels or a rototiller, then hauling it in and spreading it three inches deep over the plastic layer. The soil cement is then tamped (compacted) to give it strength. The hot water tubing is rolled out on top of that and covered with another two inches of soil mix, and tamped again.

In our projects we had extra soil inside already and no vapor barrier, so we mixed the soil-cement in place. We just spread the cement across the floor and worked it in with a hoe, spraying water over it as we went. Next we used the hoe to dig channels for the tubing. We laid out the tubing, covered it over, and tamped it. Then the subfloor was ready for tiles.

Soil-cement should be kept much drier than other cement mortars. The mix for the subfloor should be damp, but not sticky (the tile mix is much wetter). Ideally the soil should be mostly sandy with some clay, and no topsoil or organic matter. Gravel is okay in the subfloor, but care should be taken to keep sharp rocks away from the hot water tubing, especially if you use a power tamper.

Tamping can be done by hand, or you can rent a pneumatic compactor. A heavy steel plate, at least 4 X 4 inches or larger can be welded to a pipe handle for a good tamper. We once attached handles to five-foot long, eight-inch diameter log and used that for a tamper, with two people lifting it and dropping it. You can tell by the change in sound, a "dull thud" when the soil is sufficiently tamped. We use a hand tamper only if we are doing small sections, otherwise we use a gas-powered pneumatic tamper.

Pneumatic tampers are fast and thorough, but it takes a few minutes to get the feel for it. When the machine is held wrong it jumps around like a mad one-legged kangaroo with a thousand pounds of force under it's foot. Watch your toes! The job is easy once you get control of the demon; then you just steer it around and let it do all the work. When the subfloor is done there should be about an inch of space leftover to allow for the thickness of the tiles. Our tiles are usually about 1 1/4 inches thick.

The Tile Mix

Anyone who knows anything about cement and concrete will let you know you are crazy to mix cement with dirt. Good, strong concrete requires clean sand and gravel, because dirt dramatically weakens the mix. Terra tiles do not require a strong mix, however, just strong enough. The purpose of adding soil to the mix is to create a lighter, more airy tile that is gentle underfoot.

Depending on the site where you build, you may have usable soil leftover from the excavation work, or you may need to haul some in. The important part is to get good subsoil without the dark organic matter of topsoil. The soil should be mostly sandy for strength, but with some clay content for a softer tile. Try dampening a little soil and squeeze it in your hand. It is high in clay if it is sticky-gooey, but high in sand if it just crumbles and falls apart. Easton usually uses a deep red clay, then mixes it with twice as much sand. Our soil is somewhat sandy already, so we use equal portions of each. The soil should be sifted through half-inch screen before use. For a long-lasting surface, it is better to error on the side of too much sand than too much clay.

Tiles are cast in place up against the stoen and concrete walls...   *...and right around any other obstacles.*

We adjust our mix ratio with every project, but usually average about 1 part cement to 2 1/2 parts sand and 2 1/2 parts soil, plus a small amount of dye. In retrospect, I know the tiles in our addition could have used more cement content, since that floor has not held up as well as the rest of the house. We have to sweep the floor religiously, and add fresh coats of sealer often to slow down the wear and tear. On the next project I want to reduce the sand and soil components to test a 1:2:2 ratio for greater resistance against chipping.

As for color, the red clay Easton uses results in a rich earth-tone when mixed with cement and made into tiles. The soils we have used had little color, so our first tiles took on the greenish-gray color of the cement. Since then we have added concrete dyes to create our own colors. We especially like using a bright orange "buff" color that dulls down to earth tones when mixed into the mortar. We also like the iron oxide (rust) dye for brick-red tiles. The dyes can be purchased in powder form from most brickyards. It is advisable to make some test samples to determine the final color. Be sure to create the same drying conditions for the sample as for the floor. We have noticed that the tiles become significantly lighter the faster they dry. In fact, the sections of floor that were tiled under varying drying conditions tended to have much greater differences in color versus the sections where the amount of dye was accidentally doubled or halved.

You can mix the mortar with a hoe and shovel in a wheel barrow, but unless you are doing a very small room or porch, I would advise purchasing or renting a cement mixer. The first batch can be mixed dry before adding the water, but on subsequent batches it is more expedient to put the water in first to clean the mixer, then add the dye, the cement, and alternate portions of sand and dirt. Once you get started you will rarely need to turn the mixer off and fully clean it more than a couple times per day. The soil-cement mix requires more water than concrete does, but add the water slowly and carefully—there is a fine line between too dry and too wet. Good mortar should be sticky like oatmeal, dry enough to stay in a mound if it is dumped on the floor, but wet enough to move easily with a trowel.

Tile-Making Time

Renee and I working together can make about 300 square feet of tiles in one full day. I do the heavy lifting outside to put all the materials in the mixer. She does most of the careful troweling and stamping work.

The Goldblatt Tool Company makes excellent plastic forms for terra tiles work, with several patterns: squares, octagons, or running board (brick-layered). The square pattern is probably the most conventional for tile work, and that is what we use. The forms cost about $80 each, and you need at least two of them to work effectively. The forms measure 16 X 24 inches and cut out 6 tiles at a time. There are cutting edges along one long side and one short side of the form, but not on the opposite sides. This way a form can be left in place temporarily, and the next form set beside it—without cutting the grout lines twice. Also included with the forms are a 1 1/2 inch and 4 inch cutters to hand-cut tiles around obstacles where the larger forms will not fit. The forms can be ordered through most stores that sell other Goldblatt tools. We always spray the forms with WD-40 or some other lubricant before starting work.

Other less expensive forms can also work. Quickcrete™ sells a plastic form for making concrete pavers with a cobblestone pattern. The forms are designed to be filled with mortar, then removed, but the 2 1/2 inch depth is probably thicker than you would want for most terra tiles work. Instead you would need to trowel the mortar smooth on the floor and press the forms in to cut the tiles; then you could make the tiles whatever thickness you wanted. Quickcrete's forms are available at most large home improvement stores.

Excess grout was carefully swept away with a broom....   *...or sometimes a paint brush.*

Start making tiles in the far side of a room, then work your way out the door. It is a good idea to measure the room for square before hand so you do not run into any surprises along the way. If a room is not quite square then you need to decide which walls to square the tiles with. You can also measure out from the wall and mark lines across the floor for guides as you work. Make the lines parallel to the tile rows so you can measure the space from the lines to the edge of the tiles. Measure after each row, and adjust the angle of the forms accordingly during the next row.

We usually make our first row of mortar extra wide, setting the forms out a few inches from the wall, and use the hand tools to go back in and cut the partial tiles along the wall. Setting the forms away from the wall allows for a straight line without bumping up against possible imperfections in the wall, but also we think the partial tiles just look better along the edge. It is also possible to make rows of tiles diagonally across the room, but it would require many more hand-cut tiles around the perimeter.

Terra tiles work is easiest if it is done in rows. Just start laying the mortar out along one wall, trowel it smooth, and stamp from one end to the other before moving on to the next row. Troweling and stamping takes some practice to develop proficiency. The difficult part with troweling is to make each row the same thickness as the one before. It is okay if the finished floor is a little wavy; that just adds to its handmade appearance. But be careful that there are no abrupt edges that could trip a person. If the tiles do not come out quite right, just smooth out the mortar and stamp it again.

The forms do not need to cut all the way through the tiles. Cutting part way through provides the necessary freedom for the tiles to cure and shrink away from each other, with the cracks appearing inside the grout lines. If you put too much weight on, or if the mortar is too soupy, then the forms will sink in deep and imprint the tops of the tiles with the grate that you stand on. Those prints can be carefully touched up with a trowel after the forms are removed.

You must stay in tune with the consistency of the mortar. Wet mortar requires that the cutting forms stay in place longer, or the tiles will sag back into the grout lines. Dry mortar can crumble along the edges when the forms are stamped in and lifted back out. Usually you can trowel the trimmings from one row back into the next row before they dry out.

For added interest you can remove a few tiles from the floor and replace them with tiles of another color. In our rustic-style home we've added interest to the floor with tracks, sometimes on purpose but also accidentally! Cat tracks add an subtle touch to the tiles, and they are all but impossible to keep out anyway. Dog tracks are more dramatic. Most recently we used deer legs to make a trail from door to door across our family room.

We carefully squeezed the wheelbarrow in and out the door all day long to keep the dog out, only to make him so frantic by the end of the day that he finally forced his way past and galloped across the freshly tiled floor into the house. Our two year old son added a few barefoot tracks too, so we had an unmistakable path across the room on the very first day!

Another benefit of terra tiles is that the tiles can be custom sloped to channel water towards a drain, or to gain or lose a small amount of elevation between two rooms. When we replaced the homemade door in our family room with a factory-made insulated steel door, the new threshold was a little lower than before. To get rid of the tripping hazard, I chipped out a few of the old tiles with a pick and replaced them with new tiles, slightly sloping them down to the threshold. It is really handy being able to make tiles of any shape or thickness.

Each tile had to be carefully sponged clean.

On this project we framed the walls after making the tiles.

Grouting the Floor

The most important phase of the terra tiles process may be the part where you do nothing at all. Terra tiles need at least two weeks to cure, dry, and shrink, and you would be wise to be patient during this time. If you grout the floor before the tiles have completely shrunk then you may be plagued with cracks down all the grout lines. Believe me, I know.

Much of the difficulty we have had with grouting was the result of making terra tiles in cool, damp weather when the tiles couldn't dry out. Terra tiles contain quite a bit of clay, and clay shrinks as it dries, so the floor must be completely dry before grouting. Our preferred grout is a simple mix of 1 part cement to 1 part lime to 4 parts 30 mesh silica sand. The sand may be purchased in 50 pound bags from any brickyard. We have also experimented with commercial tile grouts, thinking that the latex ingredient may give the grout lines greater flexibility to withstand cracking. We have since concluded that the commercial preparations cost a lot and contribute little.

We have also experimented with many systems for applying the grout. The greatest challenge to applying the grout is to clean the tiles afterward. We have tested rubber grouting floats, trowels, rubber gloves, reloadable power caulk guns and funnels in the attempt to find the quickest way to grout the floor. Ideally, it should be possible to caulk the grout in neat and clean without any scrubbing, but so far we haven't been able to control the caulk gun enough to produce smooth, even joints. Nevertheless, we have learned a few things along the way.

It especially helps to put one coat of finish across the dry floor before grouting to help stop the mortar from sticking to the tops of the tiles. Then rub the mortar into joints with a grouting float, or even just a pair of rubber gloves. Work only small areas at a time, no more than fifty square feet. Immediately use a trowel to scrape off any excess mortar, and sweep the tiles as clean as you can with a broom, while being careful to avoid sweeping the mortar out of the grout lines. Then it is fairly easy, but still a slow process, to wipe all the tiles clean with a sponge.

Any cracks that do appear in the grout lines can be easily mended by mixing a thin grout, but give it extra strength by adding light gray latex paint instead of water to the dry ingredients.

Finally, finish the floor with several coats of sealer for protection. Acrylic sealers are the available and recommended for porous tile floors, but I've been less than satisfied with the results. A fresh tile floor needs two or three base coats, plus two or three finish coats, which adds up to a lot of work. Then the floor must be maintained with regular sweeping, mopping and additional finish coats, especially in the high traffic areas.

With a gravel driveway, a firewood pile, plus kids and dogs to track it all in, our tile floors are often covered in bits of rock, sand and debris which scratches through the finish coat and can chip the floor tiles. After a good spring cleaning and refinishing we sometimes ban all shoes from the house, at least until the muddy season is over, but shoes or no shoes, it always takes a lot of police work to keep the floors swept clean.

An alternative treatment, which I have tried only in our laundry room, is the concrete floor sealer often used in garages and workshops. It contains toluene and other wonderful carcinogens that require you to wear a respirator during the application. However, it seems to soak into and bond with the tile surface, producing better resistance to chipping. It also has a better shine than the acrylic. If I had a chance to do it all over again, I think I would use the concrete sealer throughout the house. Acrylic sealers can be used over the top of the concrete sealer as necessary to maintain the shine, but not vice-versa. David Easton recommends a traditional paste wax for terra tiles. That should be considered as well.

Natural flooring, cabinetry and stonework make a warm kitchen...   *...and living area.*

Wood Frame Construction
Building Interior Floors & Walls

No matter what type of house you build, whether it is stone, log, straw, rammed earth, or something else, you will always need to fall back on wood frame con-struction for at least part of the work. Slipform stone masonry depends on wood framed forms. Formwork for rammed earth and concrete work usually requires wood-frame construction too. Then there are window and doorways to frame, plus interior floors and walls, and of course the roof. Wood framed outhouses and sheds come in handy too. You may find good substitutes for wood framing on some of these projects, but not all of them.

Small wood frame projects are a great way to de-velop confidence in your construction abilities. Our first

There are still few good substitutes for real lumber.

project when we bought land was to build an outhouse, made from all recycled materials. The construction was a little crude, but adequate for the job. That's one of the things you learn in construction. It doesn't have to be perfect. Just do the best you can. We also used recycled lumber and nails as much as possible building our slipforms. Working with bent-up nails is not terribly efficient, but it is an excellent way to get good and the art of nailing. Essential carpentry tools include a good circular saw, a tape measure, a hammer and nails, and a square.

The problem with wood frame construction is that from an economic and ecological standpoint, good lumber is becoming more scarce and more expensive. Simply put, we've used up all the best old-growth timber that was available. Lumber mills are cutting boards from smaller and smaller trees, and the quality has deterio-rated while the price has risen. To get more mileage out of the available logs, the mills often produce "three-sided" lumber. Boards are cut right to the edge of the log, so one corner is left rounded. Trees that would have been rejected in the past as unacceptable because of insect damage or decay are now being milled and sold as "standard" framing lumber too. According to the economic law of substitutes, as good lumber becomes scarce, the alter-natives become more attractive.

A small project like an outhouse is a great way to develop your abilities in wood frame construction.

There are many alternatives to wood framed exterior walls, including stone, log and straw, as covered through the pages of this book. Unfortu-nately, there are fewer substitutes for interior floors and walls, especially up-per level floors. The laws of physics restrict the possible flooring alternatives to a handful of materials which are able to span long distances and support a load. Wood, it turns out, is an extremely versatile material, and we have yet to engineer any really good alternatives from scratch. For most projects the best substitutes for standard lumber are simply recycled lumber or half-milled logs. Manufactured wood substitutes include glue-laminated lum-ber and TGI beams. Wood frame construction is the primary focus of this chapter. Alternatives to wood are covered at the end.

Sources and Types of Wood

Rough Cut vs. Dressed Lumber: Before you build anything with wood, it is important to understand the differences between rough-cut and dressed lumber. Rough-cut lumber is wood that has been run through the saw, but not planed smooth. The texture is literally rough and you can pick up slivers easily. Rough-cut boards are cut to the specified size: i.e.: a 2 x 4 is legitimately two inches by four inches in size, although actual dimensions may vary a quarter inch either way. Rough lumber is usually only available directly from a sawmill.

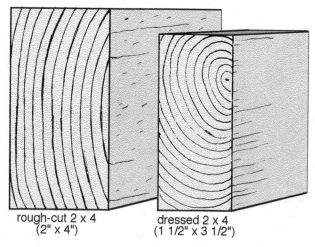

Rough-cut vs. Dressed Lumber

rough-cut 2 x 4
(2" x 4")

dressed 2 x 4
(1 1/2" x 3 1/2")

Dressed lumber is what you get when rough-cut lumber is planed down. A planer smoothes the lumber and makes it consistent in size, but it also removes much of the wood in the process. A dressed 2 x 4 is really 1 1/2 x 3 1/2 inches in size. Larger boards are often reduced even more. A typical 2 x 10 is only 1 1/2 x 9 1/4. Dressed lumber is easier to work with in many applications than rough-cut lumber, since the size is more consistent, but it is not as strong either. A rough-cut 2 x 4 stud has half again as much wood as a dressed stud.

Recycled Lumber: In a lumber-scarce world, salvaging boards from old buildings can be about the most economic and ecological means to build your own place, especially if you have more time than money. Salvaging lumber is also a good way to get high-quality lumber, since older buildings were built with old-growth trees with tight, strong rings. Good wood like that simply isn't available on the market today. Salvaging lumber is also a great way to learn about construction. You can learn a lot about the way buildings are put together just by taking them apart.

We salvaged lumber for our house whenever we lacked the money to buy new wood. Economically speaking, recycled wood is most efficiently used for unseen framing jobs, where you do not need to clean it up. On the other hand, recycled wood is very beautiful when it is properly dressed. You will quickly recover the initial investment in a cheap electric planar and a belt sander, but you really have to watch out for nails.

Finding good salvaged wood for walls, floor joists and beams in the easy part. It is much more difficult to find good, flat wood for decking. Recycled wood makes beautiful and sturdy floors, but you would need a shop-size planer ($1,200+) to uniformly mill the lumber. Again, you have to watch carefully for nails. Planer blades are not cheap.

Half-Milled Logs: Good lumber is becoming scarce, but paradoxically, good timber is still abundant over most of the country. Sawmills cut small logs into smaller boards, but often it would be better to use the logs as beams, either fully round, or half milled so that there are flat sides to nail to. Exposed beams add a touch of nature to the

Floor Joists & Beams

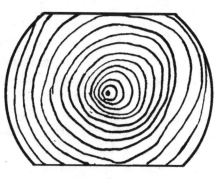

half-milled log

2 x lumber

glue-lam

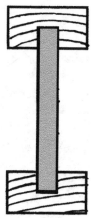

TGI beam

interior of any home. There are hundreds of thousands of small public and private parcels of good trees which are not available to logging companies. In many cases you can get permission or permits to cut a few standing dead trees for your project. Even our cities include vast forests of good timbers. City workers often help residents remove dead trees. The wood is usually cut into firewood, but you may be able to make arrangements to purchase it from the city.

You are best to work with a sawmill to cut the trees to your specifications. The do-it-yourself "chainsaw mills" are usually not efficient enough to bother with. Bandsaw mills are much more efficient with time, fuel, and materials, but also more expensive. You would need to mill enough lumber for an entire frame house, and then some, to recover the initial investment. It might be a good idea if you were building a frame house, but for stone, log, or straw construction you will need only a modest amount of lumber for framing interior walls.

Glue-Laminated Lumber: As good lumber becomes scarce, the timber industry is increasing production of manufactured woods, using glues and presses to convert thin strips or flakes of wood into boards, beams, and sheets. All this cutting, gluing, pressing, and heating makes engineered lumber quite expensive, but it is an economical substitute for some projects, especially if you need very long, squared beams. Door and window companies are also using manufactured lumber on their products, since the quality is always consistent. Laminated beams are stronger than natural wood, since the wood fibers are layered in a more complex pattern. On the other hand, laminated wood can be more susceptible to water damage than natural wood. Commercial builders frequently use laminated beams to span across the center of a house to support the floor joists. (Note the "girder" in the illustration *Traditional Floor Framing* on the next page.) Because engineered lumber is so expensive, the old-fashioned kind is still more economical for most applications other than beams.

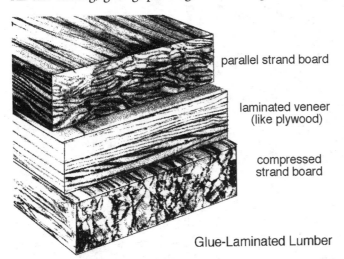

parallel strand board

laminated veneer (like plywood)

compressed strand board

Glue-Laminated Lumber

TGI Beams: The name "TGI beam" presumably stands for "tongue & groove I-beam". I-beams include a top and bottom cap, plus a thin sheet of oriented strand board (OSB) in between them. The beams contain little wood material, yet they are very strong and can be manufactured to almost any length. Nevertheless, TGI beams are expensive, usually used as a substitute for floor joists or rafters only where it is impractical to mill long spans from natural wood. I would be concerned about the performance of TGI floor joists in a fire since there is so little substance to them. Also, the glues in laminated woods produce a very hot fire. Once a fire started under a floor you would have very little time to get across before it collapsed. Fire retardants might be included in TGI beams.

Instead of placing floor joists on top of the beam, you can save space by using metal "joist hangers" to attach them against the beam.

Designing & Building Wood Floors

No matter which materials you build with, the same basic rules of design still apply to all floors: longer spans always require more beams and joists for support than shorter spans. In the illustration on the following page, the joists support the decking, while a girder spanning the house supports the joists. Keep in mind that when a girder or beam is placed below the joists it cuts into the overhead space of the room below. That is okay if the beam will be hidden in a frame wall, but it could be a problem across the middle of a room.

One alternative to save overhead space is to use a **rim joist and joist hangers** to attach the joists against the beam as pictured here. Standard joist hangers are made for dressed lumber (1 1/2" wide) but you can special order wider joist hangers for rough-cut lumber.

Traditional Floor Framing

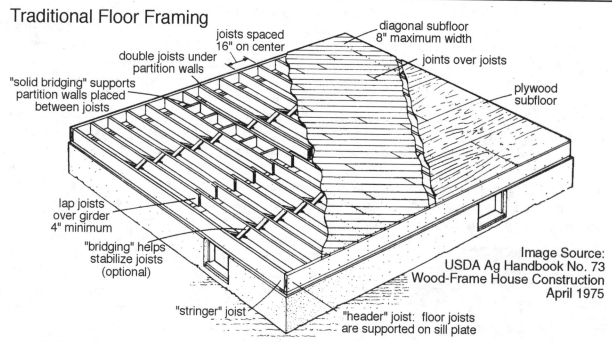

joists spaced 16" on center

double joists under partition walls

"solid bridging" supports partition walls placed between joists

diagonal subfloor 8" maximum width

joints over joists

plywood subfloor

lap joists over girder 4" minimum

"bridging" helps stabilize joists (optional)

Image Source:
USDA Ag Handbook No. 73
Wood-Frame House Construction
April 1975

"stringer" joist

"header" joist: floor joists are supported on sill plate

While longer spans require more support, it is also true that bigger joists, such as 4 x 10's instead of 2 x 10's, can be spaced farther apart. Also, stronger decking materials, like 2 x 6 tongue & groove can allow wider joist spacing. Local building codes may vary on joist size and spacing, but make sure you overbuild and you should be okay. So let's consider the options:

Conventional Flooring: Floors are usually framed with standard lumber, then covered with two layers of subfloor, as illustrated above, before carpet, linoleum or tile is installed. The subfloor can also be used to support a poured gypsum concrete slab. Sheetrock is screwed to the bottoms of the joists to make a ceiling in the lower level.

As good lumber became more scarce, most builders stopped using the diagonal subfloor and substituted thicker, tongue-and-groove plywood. Further scarcity of good wood has since led to a sharp rise in the cost of plywood, so builders have mostly switched to tongue-and-groove OSB board, usually with a softer fiberboard base for the carpet.

The greatest advantage to conventional flooring is that it provides a hidden space to route plumbing and wiring. But these days many health conscious people are seeking alternatives to plywood and OSB board because of concern about formaldehyde outgassing from the glues used in the wood. Another drawback to these materials is that the wood swells apart if wetted, so a minor water problem can evolve into a major house renovation. I do not like conventional framed floors with plywood and carpet simply for aesthetic reasons; they are not "real" enough for me. I would rather have natural wood decking underfoot.

Exposed Beam Floors: A floor with exposed beams and joists does not use any less wood than a conventional floor, but it is a good design for the country-style home. Usually the joists are spaced farther apart, and sturdy **2 x 6 tongue-and-groove** (T&G) decking is nailed or screwed down on top. The good face of the T&G is placed down to make a ceiling. The wood provides a sense of lightness and warmth to the house, and the space between the joists gives the room below an extra feeling of height. The floor surface can be sanded and finished as it is, although dust filters through between the tongue-and-grooves, so it is preferable to add another layer on top. Padding or carpet works well to stop both dust and sounds from above. Optionally, 1 x 4 wood

Exposed beams with 2 x 6 decking..

flooring or wood tiles can be added on top. The 1 x 4 Douglas fir finish flooring my brother used was kiln dried, but there was still a lot of shrinkage after installation. He filled all the cracks with clear epoxy, then sanded the floor smooth.

Keep in mind that 2 x 6 decking is a structural component, so fewer joists may be needed below the floor. We used rough-cut 2 x 10 joists spaced on 24" centers for our floors, but the spans were only twelve to thirteen feet long. The Nansel's used 2 x 10 joists on 16" centers for the lower floor of their log house, and 4 x 10 joists on 48" centers for the upper floor. As pictured, our neighbors used half-milled log beams on 36" centers to support tongue-and-groove decking in their cordwood home. In other words, there is room for flexibility of design. Too many smaller joists make a crowded "busy" ceiling though, so bigger beams are a better choice for aesthetics from below. One big drawback to a floor with exposed beams or joists is that it is difficult to route plumbing and wiring out-of-sight.

Tongue & groove boards tend to warp easily, so you will have to force many of them into place with the aid of a prybar. Make the joints as tight as you can, because the wood will continue to dry and shrink, opening a gap between every board. Joints should always be made right on the joist below, and staggered across the floor.

Tongue & Groove Flooring

Two-by-six tongue & groove decking can be nailed a-cross the joists to make a sturdy floor with a beautiful ceiling below. The floor may be finished as is, but it will allow dust to filter down through the cracks. For a nicer, but more expensive floor, put down a layer of roofing felt to block the dust, then install 1 x 4 flooring (shown here) perpendicular to the decking below.

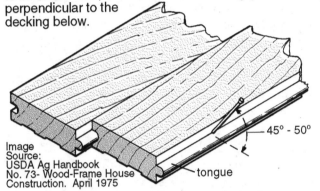

Image Source:
USDA Ag Handbook
No. 73- Wood-Frame House
Construction. April 1975

45° - 50°

tongue

For finish flooring, the nails should be driven through the tongue at an angle into the joist below, so that the nails are hidden in the joints. Nails near the end of the boards may have to be predrilled to avoid splitting the wood. Be sure to use wood glue on the joists to prevent squeaky floors. Do not try driving the nail all the way in with the hammer, or you will likely smash the edge of the flooring. Use a nail punch for the final hit. (For this maneuver the nail punch can be set flat on its side on top of the tongue.) Even better, there are special compressed air tools available at rental shops that slide right up to the groove and blast the nails in at the right angle at just the right spot. The last board can be nailed through the surface, close to the wall where the nails will be hidden under a baseboard.

If the tongue and groove decking is for a sub-floor, then it doesn't matter if the nails show or not.

We screwed all of our 2 x 6 decking down through the tops of the boards into the joists below to make a squeak-free subfloor, with the intention of covering it later with either carpet or finish flooring. That was almost ten years ago, and so far we still haven't installed either one!

Building Frame Walls

When you build your first frame wall you will quickly discover why frame construction is so popular. In very little time you can measure, cut and build an entire section of wall. Since the framing is completely covered up inside the wall, even professional builders work fast and sloppy, often leaving bent and twisted nails smashed in place. A house takes shape very quickly with frame walls, but there are many other steps to go before the walls are completely finished. Two-by-four studs are adequate for most interior walls, but walls with drain pipes require at least 2 x 6 studs.

If you have lots of framing to do, then you may want to purchase precut studs, which are 92 5/8" long for an eight foot wall. That saves the work of cutting each one yourself. The studs are intended to be used with a single bottom plate and a double top plate (1 1/2" each), for a total height of 97 1/8". (The double top plate gives more strength to support a roof or upper floors.) Since sheetrock measures 96" tall, that leaves a gap slightly more than one inch to be covered by flooring material at the base and the ceiling sheetrock at the top. Precut studs are also available for nine and ten foot walls.

Window and door openings in load-bearing walls should be reinforced with headers, using 2 x 6's for small openings and wider boards for larger openings. A supporting stud should be used under each end of the header, as shown in the drawing on the following page..

Frame walls are simple to build. Just space all the studs on 16" centers, so that the sheetrock will line up properly. Measure and mark the top and bottom plates every sixteen inches, and start all the nails in before adding the studs. "Sixteen penny" nails are a good, standard size for framing work.

Framing Stud Walls

Measure and mark every sixteen inches along the top and bottom plates. Drive all the nails part way in first, then turn the plates on edge to attach the studs. Studs are placed "on center" with the marks so that the edges of 4' x 8' sheets of plywood or sheetrock meet in the middle of the studs. Use 16d nails for the job.

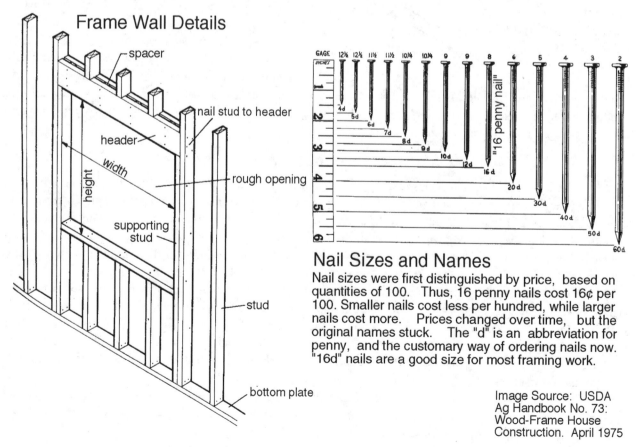

Place studs every 16" on center.

Wall sections can be easily built on the floor, then tilted up into place. After driving all the nails into the top and bottom plates, simply turn them on edge and add the studs. The wood will bounce around quite a bit as you hammer sideways. I usually stand on both pieces to hold them in place while nailing. Optionally, you can butt the wall section up against a solid object, like a stud nailed to the floor, to keep the boards in place while you nail them together.

Level and plumb the walls before securing them in place. A single section of wall should be held in place with a diagonal brace nailed to it and the floor, until other wall sections can be attached. Be sure to use extra reinforcement around doors and windows. Some wall sections may be taller than the sheetrock, or the sheetrock may be installed horizontally. In either case, be sure to use solid wood wherever the edge of the sheetrock will be.

Basic framing skills like this will aid you in many projects, from making slipforms to building walls, rafters and scaffolding. Even after the house is "finished" you will find yourself using similar skills for everything from bookshelves to cabinets and toy chests.

Frame Wall Details

- spacer
- nail stud to header
- header
- width
- height
- rough opening
- supporting stud
- stud
- bottom plate

Nail Sizes and Names

Nail sizes were first distinguished by price, based on quantities of 100. Thus, 16 penny nails cost 16¢ per 100. Smaller nails cost less per hundred, while larger nails cost more. Prices changed over time, but the original names stuck. The "d" is an abbreviation for penny, and the customary way of ordering nails now. "16d" nails are a good size for most framing work.

Image Source: USDA Ag Handbook No. 73: Wood-Frame House Construction. April 1975

Alternatives to Wood Frame Construction

The interior walls and upper floors do not have to be built with wood frame construction, although that is an easy and reliable method. Our own home includes several interior stone walls which we immensely enjoy. Here are some other possible alternatives to consider:

Concrete: Concrete can be made into just about anything you can imagine, although there may be an economic and aesthetic price to pay for it. Formwork can be used to make poured-in-place concrete beams, floors, and walls, or the pieces can be precast on the ground and hoisted into place. There is also a "do-it-yourself" concrete block system, called Spanblock™ that you can assemble into beams and floors without the need for a crane or complicated formwork. The blocks are assembled on site to make "joists", which are connected with reinforcing bar and filled with concrete. The cured joists are light enough to be hoisted in place by hand, then specialized blocks are used to bridge the joists and make a floor on top. The floor is grouted to fill spaces between the blocks.

Although I like masonry floors and walls for houses, even I have my limits. A concrete floor might be all right on the lower level, or even over a full basement, but there is something to be said for wood on upper levels. Partly it is a matter of aesthetics, but also it might just be paranoid survival instinct—there is something disconcerting about having many tons of concrete perched overhead.

On the other hand, thin **gypsum concrete slabs** are often poured over wood-framed floors in apartment buildings, and that might be more desirable in some applications. The concrete is helpful to stop fires or even plumbing problems from spreading quickly between floors. A thin gypsum slab might be a good solution over a floor that was decked with cupped or warped salvaged lumber.

Another alternative is **welded-wire sandwich panels**, as described in the chapter *Insulation and Insulation Systems*. Main beams of concrete or steel are needed for support, but the panels will span several feet. The top and bottom surfaces are shotcreted with concrete.

I would like to experiment with **papercrete** upper floors, similar to the method proposed for roofing with papercrete earlier in this book. Poles would support the floor, and wire mesh would support the papercrete slab. Plumbing and wiring could be embedded in the papercrete. A gypsum slab poured over the top would make a durable floor. At least, that is the theory.

Autoclaved Cellular Concrete: The ideal substitute for wood framing might be some type of lightweight, super strong, foam-like masonry. Autoclaved cellular concrete (ACC) also known as aerated autoclaved concrete (AAC) is a form of concrete that at least partially fills that roll. ACC is a cement mortar made with extremely fine particles of sand, plus a foaming agent to make it rise like a loaf of bread. It is poured as a slab, then cut into sheets or blocks. Autoclaved cellular concrete has a high potential for interior walls, especially in the sheet or slab form, but it would not be strong enough for suspended floors. Labor and wood consumption could be reduced if whole walls of this lightweight masonry were set in place at once, or if large sections of it snapped together. See the chapter on insulation for more information. Another possibility for lightweight interior masonry walls is a mix of straw, sand and cement.

Steel Framing: Steel-framed houses have emerged as a viable industry in recent years, and it is undoubtedly one of the better substitutes for wood, although product availability remains a problem. You can easily order enough steel for an entire house, but for stone, strawbale, or other alternative methods of construction, it is problematic to find the small quantities of steel joists and studs needed for interior work. Aesthetically, steel is hard and cold compared to the warmth and lightness of wood. Steel framing is best used only where it is covered from view.

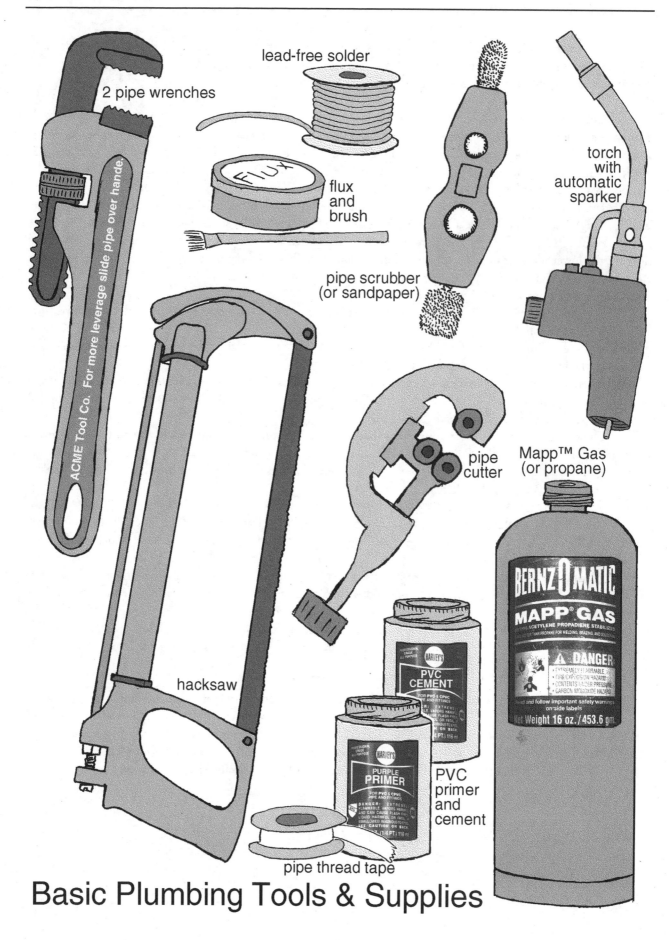

2 pipe wrenches

lead-free solder

FLUX

flux and brush

pipe scrubber (or sandpaper)

torch with automatic sparker

pipe cutter

Mapp™ Gas (or propane)

ACME Tool Co. For more leverage slide pipe over handle.

hacksaw

HARVEY'S PVC CEMENT FOR PVC & CPVC PIPE AND FITTINGS

HARVEY'S PURPLE PRIMER FOR PVC & CPVC PIPE AND FITTINGS

PVC primer and cement

pipe thread tape

BERNZOMATIC MAPP GAS

⚠ DANGER

Net Weight 16 oz. / 453.6 gm.

Basic Plumbing Tools & Supplies

Practical Plumbing
Important Tips I Could Have Used

Its funny, after reading so much about house-building, alternative construction and ecological design, it never occurred to me to read a book about plumbing. I guess I learned a little bit about soldering copper in jewelry class in high-school, and my neighbor gave me a quick lesson about soldering pipe. There were a few greatly simplified drawings in some of my house-building books, so I understood the gist of the idea. The rest of it I figured out by trial and error, plus lots of time spent staring at parts in the plumbing isle of the hardware store. It's no wonder I've plumbed sections of our house twice!

Although most plumbing is remarkably simple, there are enough specialized parts and situations to fill up an entire book. In this text I will cover the basics, including some important tips that you might not find elsewhere. The level of information presented here is intended to enable you to plumb your water supply and waste water lines. I cannot cover the details of hooking up a boiler system or even a well system. Even for the basics, I still recommend that you pick up a book dedicated to household plumbing. Two opinions are always better than one. Just make sure the book is relatively new. Plumbing materials, tools, and codes change surprisingly quickly over the years.

Plumbing Design

In traditional architecture, a house is designed first and the plumbing is routed through afterwards. In smart design the plumbing should be worked out simultaneously with the floor plans and modified as necessary to reduce the required materials and labor. This is a bit of a trick, as you will quickly discover when you try to plan a house with the bathrooms, kitchen, laundry room, solar water heater and boiler all positioned near each other. Outside faucets must also be considered. Meeting all of this criteria is virtually impossible, but the more you can centralize the plumbing fixtures the better.

Note that the expensive part of plumbing is not the pipe, but the fittings and labor. Also keep in mind the **energy and water loss** with a long run of hot water pipes. Water is wasted while waiting for the hot water to reach a faucet or shower. Energy is wasted when the faucet is shut off and the water in the pipes radiates away its heat. Pipe insulation is essential, but it only slows the rate of heat loss. Only smart design can truly stop the waste. In a room with fixtures on both sides, such as the bathroom, try placing the sink and shower closer to the hot water source. The toilet, which needs only cold water, can be placed on the opposite side of the room. On-demand hot water heaters may be placed at the fixtures as an alternative means to get around the problem of heat loss in the pipes.

The design of a house must also include spaces to run the plumbing. In this case, a house with a crawl space and wood-framed floors and walls has a distinct advantage over the alternative modes of construction. It is easy to hide the plumbing in the hollow walls and floors. Just drill holes through the middle of the framing members and pass the plumbing through, being careful to avoid compromising the strength of floor joists. Avoid routing plumbing through exterior walls or the walls of uninsulated rooms like a garage. I've seen houses built over unheated garages where the pipes froze and broke in the ceiling of the garage, soaking all the insulation and sheetrock. These events usually happen in winter when the homeowner turns down the thermostat and leaves on Christmas vacation.

In a house with masonry floors you can easily run the drain lines underneath, provided the septic or other wastewater system is lower than the floor. A tank and pump may be used to lift the wastewater if necessary, but it is preferable to avoid the extra gizmos if possible. Water supply lines can also be routed under the floors. Cross-linked polyethylene (PEX™) tubing is ideal for this application. The tubing can be routed through plastic pipes for added protection, as well as to enable a future homeowner to pull the tubing out and replace it if the need should ever arise. When you route plumbing under a masonry floor you must take extra care and attention to insure that the piping comes up in exactly the right locations. Flexibility is limited when you cast your work in cement!

Note that most stone, log, straw and other alternative homes have framed walls on the interior that make it easier to route the plumbing. With a little forethought you will find it very easy to pick a path and put the piping in place. Framed walls may need to be extra wide, built with 2 x 6's or 2 x 8's to accommodate the plumbing.

Plumbing the Water Supply

In an increasingly urbanized world, most home owners connect to the **city water supply**. The water lines are laid underground along the roads and terminate in a "curb stop" at the edge of each building lot. The curb stop is a valve in a protective box or tube, often deep in the ground and usually operated by a long-handled "key". Connecting to city water involves very little plumbing. Builders usually leave a hole in the foundation wall for the water supply to come through. Plumbers arrive after the frame is up and connect to the water supply at the curb stop, then rough-in the plumbing throughout the house. City water meters are placed in the curb-side box or sometimes in the house.

If you plan to have a masonry floor or simply need the water for your masonry work, then you might want to have the water line ditched from the curb into the house before you pour the footing. Dig around the curb stop by hand, then use a ditch witch or backhoe to dig a trench into the house site. Use flexible copper "K" pipe of the appropriate diameter to connect into the curb stop, usually 1-1/4". Add a valve to the end of the pipe in the house, plus another section of pipe and fittings to connect to a hose. Then you are ready to turn the water on at the curb.

A **gravity-fed spring** like ours is also very simple, but requires a few more parts, since the main line is usually a 1-1/4" or 1-1/2" polyethylene pipe. A **sediment filter** should be added after the main valve to catch any sand or debris coming down the pipe. For plumbing purposes, the objective is to get to copper pipe with soldered fittings in as few steps as possible. A typical hookup is illustrated below. Be sure to use pipe thread tape on the threads.

Connecting to a well or other water supply with a pump is similar, except that the water must be routed through a **pressurization tank** before going to the sediment filter or the rest of the house. A pressurization tank enables water to run upwards throughout a house. An air bladder is compressed inside the tank when water is pumped in from the well. The air bladder pressurizes the water to force it out when a faucet is opened. As the water is used and the pressure drops, the pump kicks on and fills the tank again, so there is always a steady supply. Plumbing and electrical instructions are included with the pressurization tank. You can also install the **well pump** by yourself, but unless you have some experience with this sort of thing already, it is wiser to leave it to the well driller.

Plumbing a house is fast and easy once you get past the threaded joints and into the soldered copper tubing. For simplicity, tee the hot and cold water lines off at the water heater in a centralized location, then run separate hot and cold lines beside each other to fixtures throughout the house. Note that the basic plumbing layout for solar water heaters, homemade boilers, and combinations with conventional water heaters were all included in the chapters on *Solar Input* and *Heating Systems*. When you have plumbed in the water heating system, or left space to include it later, then you are ready to run hot and cold water lines throughout the house.

Interior supply pipes have changed considerably over time. The first household water pipes were mostly made from lead, followed by either brass or galvanized pipe, and eventually thin-wall copper "**pipe**" which is technically called "**tubing**". (I'll call it pipe.) Copper is gradually being replaced by advanced plastic tubings. Polybutylene,

Installing a Main Valve and Sediment Filter on a Gravity Fed Spring

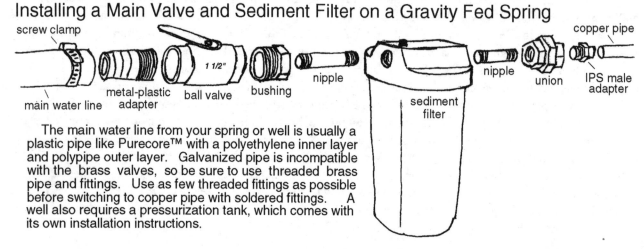

screw clamp · main water line · metal-plastic adapter · ball valve · 1 1/2" · bushing · nipple · sediment filter · nipple · union · IPS male adapter · copper pipe

The main water line from your spring or well is usually a plastic pipe like Purecore™ with a polyethylene inner layer and polypipe outer layer. Galvanized pipe is incompatible with the brass valves, so be sure to use threaded brass pipe and fittings. Use as few threaded fittings as possible before switching to copper pipe with soldered fittings. A well also requires a pressurization tank, which comes with its own installation instructions.

an early contender, went out of favor when there were questions about its longevity. A rigid plastic, CPVC (chlorinated polyvinyl chloride) is still used by some homeowners, but it is brittle and looks cheap and cheesy compared to copper. (Regular PVC is not rated to handle hot water.)

The newer cross-linked polyethylene tubing (PEX™) seems much more promising than polybutylene, but no one can really predict what will happen to it fifty years from now. PEX™ brand tubing is warrantied for 25 years. Personally, I recommend PEX™ tubing as a means to eliminate most of the labor of measuring, cutting, fitting and soldering copper tubing around corners or other obstacles. It should also greatly reduce all those extra trips to the hardware store for those fittings you didn't realize you needed before. Just be sure to give some thought to replacing the tubing, if it should ever become necessary.

Copper lines are used in **branching systems**, usually with a 3/4" diameter main lines, narrowing down to 1/2" diameter lines running to any single fixture. PEX™ plumbing eliminates the branching system in favor of a centralized copper **manifold**. The manifold consists of a 3/4" or larger main line, with separate 1/2" diameter runs to every fixture in the house. This system increases the total amount of tubing in the walls, but still reduces the labor. It also greatly reduces the problems with sudden water pulses that you sometimes experience in the shower when someone turns a faucet on or off elsewhere in the house.

Either way, for a branching system or a manifold, you will still need to learn to solder copper pipe and fittings. Note: do not use secondhand copper pipe, since the soldered joints probably contain **lead**. Just take it to the recycling center and it will be

Soldering Copper Pipe

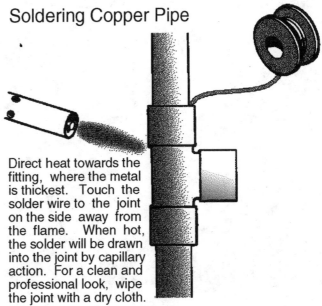

Direct heat towards the fitting, where the metal is thickest. Touch the solder wire to the joint on the side away from the flame. When hot, the solder will be drawn into the joint by capillary action. For a clean and professional look, wipe the joint with a dry cloth.

remanufactured into clean new stock. First however, it would be worthwhile to practice soldering techniques on scrap (or new) pipe until you feel confident with the process. Using the tools pictured at the beginning of this chapter, the soldering process works something like this:

Soldering Check List

- Measure very carefully. Keep in mind that extra pipe is needed to slide inside the fittings.
- Cut pipe with the aid of a pipe cutter. A hacksaw is a poor, but usable substitute.
- Ream the burr out from inside the pipe, using the reamer on the pipe cutter or a rattail file.
- Clean the ends of the pipe and the fittings with a pipe scrubber, emery cloth, or fine sandpaper.
- Assemble as many parts as possible to ensure that the project is coming together as you envision it.
- Disassemble everything in order and brush the contact surfaces with flux. Reassemble.
- Fittings must be propped in the air (not laying on a flat surface) to allow solder to flow around a joint.
- Make sure a pipe or valve is left open to release the expanding hot air.
- Start at one end and solder joints one-at-a-time until you reach the other end.
- Heat the fitting or valve first, where the metal is thickest, then the pipe.
- Touch the solder wire to the joint on the opposite side from the flame.
- When hot, the solder will suck into the joint through capillary action.
- For a clean and professional look, wipe the joint with a dry cloth.
- Avoid jarring your work before the solder has cooled and set.

Flux protects the copper surfaces from oxidation (tarnishing) during heating, and lowers the surface tension of the molten solder so it flows more easily into the joint. It is almost impossible to solder without flux. So take due care to scrub and flux each joint thoroughly. I prefer to assemble most projects prior to fluxing. If I decide to make changes I can disassemble the project and work on it without getting the corrosive flux on my hands. When I am satisfied with the results then I take apart each joint, flux it and put it back together. Heating the flux destroys the corrosive property, rendering it safe. Water-based flux is easier to clean up than oil-based flux.

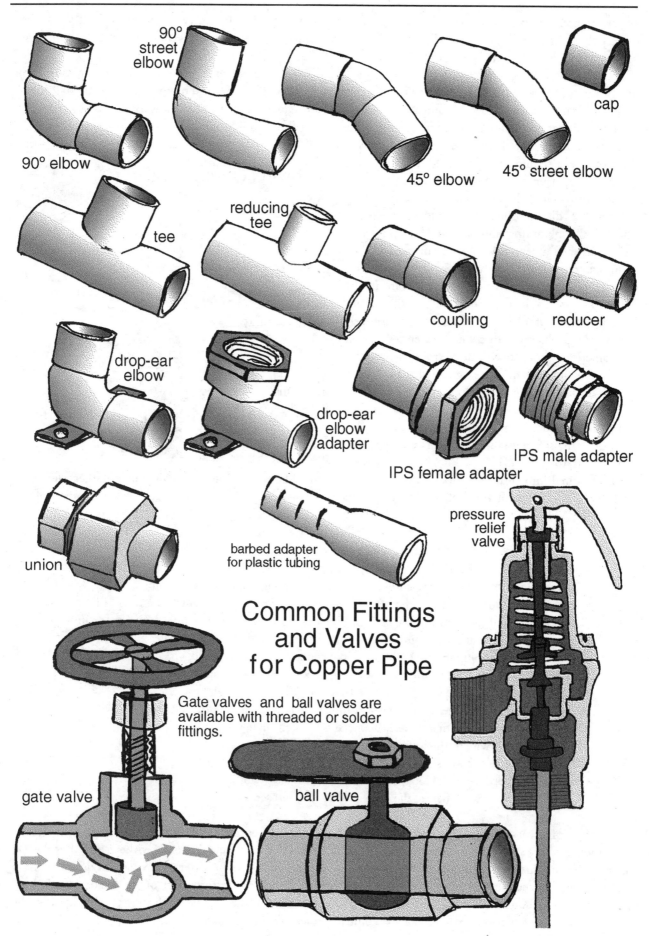

90°
street
elbow

cap

90° elbow

45° elbow

45° street elbow

tee

reducing
tee

coupling

reducer

drop-ear
elbow

drop-ear
elbow
adapter

IPS female adapter

IPS male adapter

union

barbed adapter
for plastic tubing

pressure
relief
valve

Common Fittings
and Valves
for Copper Pipe

Gate valves and ball valves are
available with threaded or solder
fittings.

gate valve

ball valve

Note that solder wicks into joints very easily downward or sideways, but not as easily upwards. Be sure to apply extra heat on the fitting above the joint, to really draw the solder upwards, and drag the solder wire all the way around the joint to suck it up on all sides. Allow the joints a few minutes to cool. Cooling doesn't take long, since the solder sets at a temperature that is still much too hot too touch. Then it is okay to move the pipes or cool them more with water.

Propane is most commonly used for solder work. **Mapp™ Gas** is a slightly different mix with a hotter flame. In either case, the hottest part of the flame is right in front of the blue-white cone.

The moment of truth comes when you open the valve and fill the system. Soldering is truly quite easy, but chances are you will still have one or two leaks in the

A centralized manifold and polyethylene tubing eliminates most of the soldering work. This manifold is ready to connect to the tubing. Sage Mountain Center (www.sagemountain.org).

system. To repair the leaks, drain all the water, open a valve to let out expanding air, reflux the joint and try adding more solder. If that doesn't work, then you will have to heat the joint and take it apart with pliers to clean each surface... or cut the darn thing out and replace it!

The difficult trick to making **repairs** is to get rid of all the water in the pipes. For this reason, it is wise to add a drain in the lowest point of your plumbing system. A small amount of moisture can be steamed away by heating the pipe with a torch, but the job is impossible if more water wicks in to replace it. One trick is to stuff a small chunk of white bread into the pipe to sponge up the extra moisture while you solder. The bread will dissolve into the water and wash out through the tap.

Working with Pipe Fittings & Valves

In plumbing you will inevitably have to use threaded pipe and fittings during some part of the process, such as the main water line and sediment filter, as previously illustrated. Threaded pipe is available in three main types: **galvanized** (with a zinc coating to prevent rust) or **black pipe** (non-galvanized), which is used mostly for interior gas lines, and third: **brass** or **copper pipe**, which are more expensive and less available. I recommend switching from threaded pipe and fittings to soldered copper pipe and fittings as quickly as possible.

Threaded pipes and fittings are expensive and labor intensive to install. And because the pipes are threaded, they come in several different lengths, none of which may fit the job you are working on. To make a custom length you need to cut the pipe and have it threaded at a hardware store or buy a tap and die set to cut the threads yourself. (Threaded pipe uses fittings somewhat similar in form and name to those shown here for soldered copper pipe.)

Another problem is that galvanized pipe is not compatible with brass, which is used in all the valves. In close proximity, brass and zinc react to each other through **electrolysis**. The zinc and brass dissolve, causing the galvanized parts to rust, while also forming pinhole leaks in the brass. Oddly, the brass valves are usually right next to the galvanized pipe and fittings in the hardware store. To purchase threaded brass pipe and fittings that are compatible with the valves, you may have to go to a store dedicated solely to plumbing. I've worked with **gate valves** and **ball valves**, and much prefer the latter, although they are more expensive.

Grades of Copper Pipe

Code	Color	Thickness	Temper	Primary Application	Notes
K	green	heavy	soft or hard	underground service	Used for main line from curb to house.
L	blue	medium	soft or hard	household plumbing	Rarely used any more.
M	red	light	hard	household plumbing	This is your standard grade of copper pipe for most household plumbing.
REF		medium	soft	water supply to refrigerators, plus coil heat exchangers.	Refrigeration tubing is measured by outside diameter, so the 5/8" tubing actually uses 1/2" solder fittings!

Soft-tempered copper comes in coils, usually in 30, 60, or 100 foot rolls. Hard-tempered copper comes in straight lengths, usually 10 or 20 feet long.

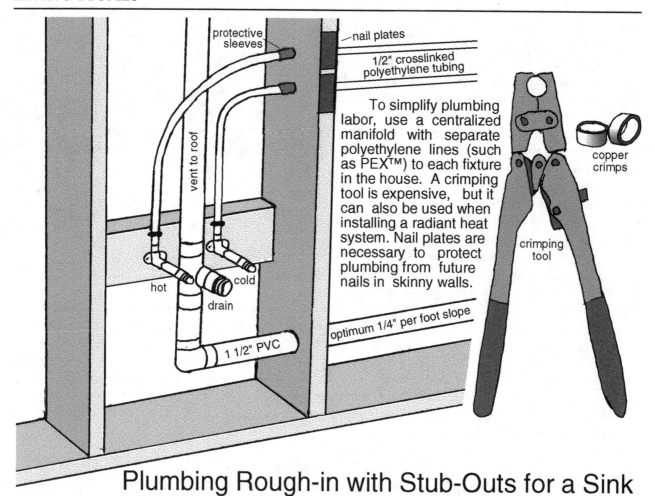

To simplify plumbing labor, use a centralized manifold with separate polyethylene lines (such as PEX™) to each fixture in the house. A crimping tool is expensive, but it can also be used when installing a radiant heat system. Nail plates are necessary to protect plumbing from future nails in skinny walls.

Labels in illustration: protective sleeves; nail plates; 1/2" crosslinked polyethylene tubing; vent to roof; hot; cold; drain; 1 1/2" PVC; optimum 1/4" per foot slope; copper crimps; crimping tool

Plumbing Rough-in with Stub-Outs for a Sink

Pressure relief valves only seem to be available with threads, probably because they are most often used in water heaters and threaded directly into the tank. **Important:** pressure relief valves are designed to deal with increased pressure from water heating and expanding. Beyond a certain threshold, the valves kick open and discharge some of the hot water, which splashes on the floor or is diverted to a drain. In other words, do not make the mistake of installing a pressure relief valve with your water supply flowing in one side and out the other. They don't work that way! Pressure relief valves on conventional water heaters virtually never kick open, but don't dare consider omitting them. If the system overheats, then the valves prevent the tank or pipes from exploding and showering everyone with scalding water. Wood-fired boilers like ours rely on the pressure relief valve much more often, because they lack the thermostatic controls to stop generating heat when the water is already hot. Our system was constantly spitting hot water onto the floor behind the stove—up until we adopted our kids and greatly increased the hot water demand for dishes, baths and laundry!

Once you get beyond threaded fittings and into soldered copper, there are still several different grades of pipe to choose from, as you will see with the accompanying chart. Almost all of your plumbing will be done with "M" pipe, and that is what plumbing shops assume you want, unless you specify otherwise. It is helpful to be aware of the these other types of pipe for special projects, such as building a heat exchanger. The really bizarre thing is that refrigeration tubing is measured by outside diameter, while other grades are measured by inside diameter. Thus the 5/8" refrigeration tubing fits 1/2" soldered fittings!

In a small building or with tightly centralized plumbing, it is reasonable to utilize soldered copper pipe and fittings for all of the water supply lines. In the more typical house, however, I recommend switching from copper over to cross-linked polyethylene tubing, such as PEX™ as quickly as possible, by constructing centralized manifolds for the hot and cold water and running separate lines to each fixture in the house, as shown in the photo. Each run ends in a handful of additional copper fittings, to make a "stub-out" for the fixtures, as illustrated here. A crimping tool and compression rings are used to fasten and seal the tubing onto the copper barb fittings. The crimping tool costs about $160, but you can also use it to install a radiant heat system. This method greatly reduces the labor involved in measuring, cutting, and fitting the piping from point to point through the walls and floor.

There are also a few specialized fittings and valves you should know about, including the **frost-free** or **lawn faucet**. The frost-free faucet has a handle outside the building, but the valve is inside the building, safe from freezing. Ideally the faucets should be placed where they can be exposed but unseen in the house, such as in the laundry room, underneath the stairs, or inside a cabinet below the kitchen or bathroom sink. Optionally, you can hide the faucet within the wall, but it is wise to leave a small void in the insulation, allowing warm house air to protect the valve from freezing in subzero weather. Once in awhile you will have applications where you want to connect a hose directly to a pipe without a valve. For that you can use a **hose adapter** with metal pipe threads on one end and hose threads on the other end.

Another useful part is an air chamber to prevent water hammer and banging pipes in your home. Water hammer is caused when water is racing through the pipes and a valve is suddenly shut off. The water slams into the valve, expanding the pipe and sending shock waves back through the system. Water hammer is most prevalent in homes with high water pressure, quick-shut valves like those found on washing machines, and with long, straight runs of pipe. An air chamber must be installed vertically to trap air in the chamber. The air compresses and absorbs the shock when water slams into the end of the run. **Pipe straps** and hangers are also useful and required to anchor pipe to the surrounding wood or concrete.

Finally, a **check valve** can be useful to make sure water runs in only one direction, and a **stop-and-waste** valve is useful when you want the ability to shut the water off and drain the pipes beyond the valve. Simply unscrew the cap on the side of the valve to release the water. This device eliminates the need for a separate tee and drain valve.

Keep in mind that there are many more useful plumbing parts, and new ones come to market all the time. It will be worth your time to hang out in the plumbing isle for an hour or more, just studying all the parts and how they might be used. Also, many sink and shower fixtures require unique rough-ins, so it is helpful to purchase and study the fixtures beforehand. Installation instructions should be included with the fixtures. Be sure to notice the usually chrome-handled shut-off valves and flexible tubing connectors under the fixtures of the house you are living in now. Simple connector kits are available in the hardware stores.

Other Useful Fittings and Valves

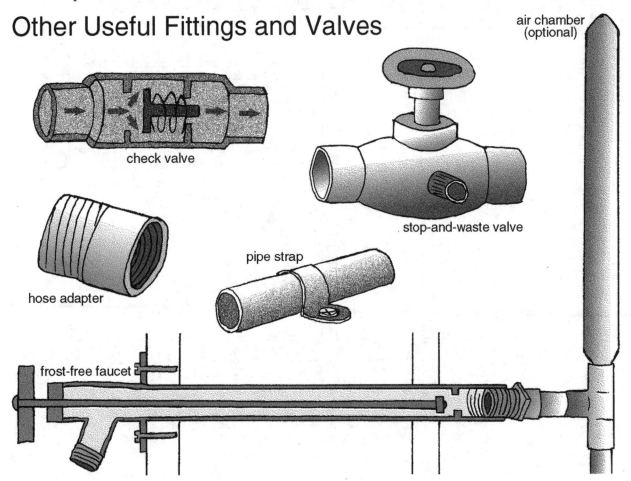

air chamber (optional)

check valve

stop-and-waste valve

hose adapter

pipe strap

frost-free faucet

A Sample Drainage and Vent System

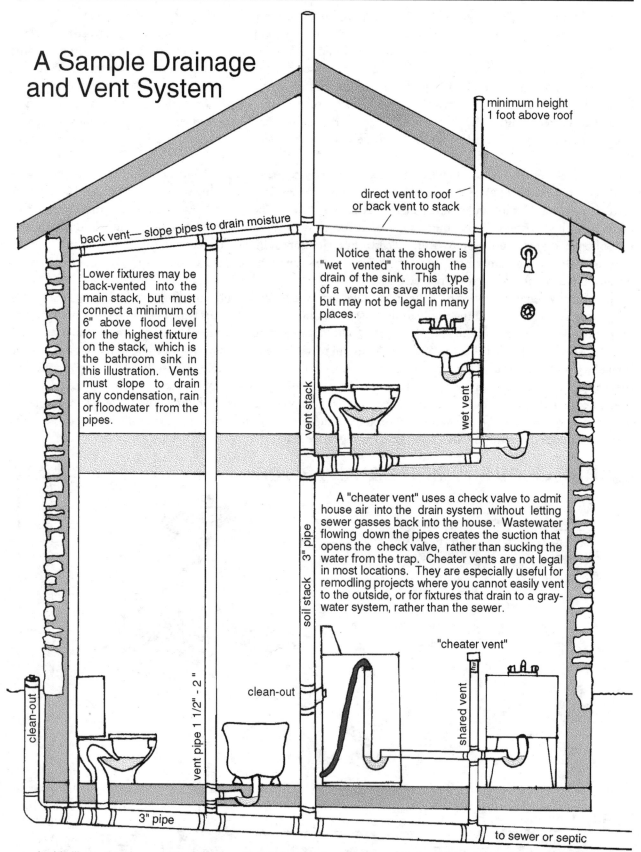

minimum height 1 foot above roof

direct vent to roof or back vent to stack

back vent— slope pipes to drain moisture

Lower fixtures may be back-vented into the main stack, but must connect a minimum of 6" above flood level for the highest fixture on the stack, which is the bathroom sink in this illustration. Vents must slope to drain any condensation, rain or floodwater from the pipes.

Notice that the shower is "wet vented" through the drain of the sink. This type of a vent can save materials but may not be legal in many places.

vent stack

wet vent

A "cheater vent" uses a check valve to admit house air into the drain system without letting sewer gasses back into the house. Wastewater flowing down the pipes creates the suction that opens the check valve, rather than sucking the water from the trap. Cheater vents are not legal in most locations. They are especially useful for remodling projects where you cannot easily vent to the outside, or for fixtures that drain to a gray-water system, rather than the sewer.

soil stack   3" pipe

clean-out

"cheater vent"

clean-out

vent pipe 1 1/2" - 2"

clean-out

shared vent

3" pipe

to sewer or septic

In this illustration the main floor is placed just below the frost-line to avoid the waste of a foundation wall and crawl space. However, the main sewer or septic tank may be higher than the waste line from the house, in which case a tank and pump may be required to lift the wastewater up to the sewer line.

Plumbing the Drain and Vent System

Installing a drain and vent system with PVC or ABS plastic pipe is really easy, just a matter of measuring, cutting, and gluing plastic pipe. The more challenging part of the process is designing it properly. Unlike a pressurized water supply system, where water moves up as easily as down, a drain system must sloped properly for the waste water and gunk to pass through to the disposal system. Equally important, every fixture must be properly vented out the roof of the building to prevent sewer gasses from entering the house.

For proper drainage, horizontal pipes need to be sized and sloped to allow waste to flow easily, without clogging. Approximate **pipe sizes** for various fixtures are shown here. When multiple fixtures are connected to the same drain, then the pipe size must be increased. For example, a bathroom sink and a bathtub together require a 2" drain. A toilet requires a 3" inch drain, while three toilets require a four inch drain. Approximate pipe sizes are indicated throughout the accompanying illustration. Clean-out drains should be placed in convenient locations inside or outside the structure to access the pipes. In many locations code will allow you to use the toilet flange for clean-out access.

Fixture	Pipe Size
bathroom sink	1 1/2
bathtub	1 1/2
shower	2
toilet	3
dish washer	1 1/2
kitchen sink	1 1/2
two sinks w/ one trap	2
washing machine	1 1/2
floor drain	2

For most purposes, drain pipes should be sloped 1/4" per foot. Check the slope with a four foot level. The drainpipe should be an inch lower at one end of the instrument than the other. A more shallow slope of 1/8" per foot is allowed for larger diameter pipes while up to 1/2" per foot is allowed for smaller pipes. A pipe without enough slope may move too slowly to push along the solids, while a pipe with too much slope may allow the water to rush on ahead, leaving the solids behind. When additional slope is needed to make the connections, wait until the end of the run and use a 45º drop to make up the difference. Excessive slope is less of a problem with the slick modern plastic drain pipes than with the older metal, clay or asbestos drain pipes.

The purpose of the **vent system** is to release sewer gasses to the outside, rather than in the house. Besides smelling really bad, sewer gas contains hydrogen sulfide, which can be lethal in sufficient concentrations, plus methane, which is explosive. The **P-traps** used with each fixture are designed to hold water and prevent sewer gasses from coming up through the drains. Toilets have a built in trap. The vent system allows air into the drainpipe within a certain critical distance after each trap, to break the powerful suction of wastewater flowing down the drain. Without the air vent, all of the water in the trap would be sucked out, allowing sewer gasses back into the house. The critical distance is at least two pipe diameters, but no more than 48 pipe diameters between the trap and the vent. Thus, a two inch drain pipe must have the vent pipe at least four inches, but no more than ninety-six inches away from the trap. The **diameter of the drain pipe** should never be smaller than the trap. The **diameter of the vent pipe** is usually the same as the drain, although smaller pipes may be allowed in some locations.

Many of the **fittings** for working with plastic drain pipe are similar to those illustrated for copper pipe, such as elbows, tees, reducers, and couplings. However, there are a few unique aspects to plastic pipe. For example, you have a choice between sharp elbows versus long sweeping elbows. Sharp elbows are useful for tight places, but long sweeping elbows facilitate better drainage and make it easier to clean the lines, if necessary. Also, PVC pipe is sometimes used in pressurized applications (only with cold water), which uses different fittings. The difference is in the sleeve of the fitting that slides over the pipe: drainpipes use "short-sleeved fittings", while pressurized applications require "long-sleeved fittings" for more contact area with the pipe. If you require assistance, then you need to specify fittings for drainpipes or for pressurized applications. The thickness of pipe you want is "**schedule 40**". A thinner "schedule 80" is also available and uses the same fittings, but it breaks very easily. In the near future I hope that recycled plastics will be incorporated into drainpipe systems.

It is helpful to spend sometime staring at the parts in the plumbing isle at the hardware store. If possible, try to get to a construction site after the plumbing is roughed-in, and check it out. It may be helpful to make sketches of the plumbing, in order to help focus your mind on certain details and questions that you might miss otherwise.

Plastic pipe can be cut with just about any kind of saw. I usually use a circular saw, because that is what I have. A potent **primer** (basically lacquer thinner) is used to clean the pipe, which also starts to dissolve the plastic. The **solvent cement** further dissolves the plastic, which then bonds at the molecular level as the solvent evaporates. Once you have glued plastic pipe together, it is virtually impossible to get it apart!

Keep in mind that a composting toilet combined with graywater outlets for each fixture can simplify the drain and vent system and reduce costs. More expensive is a hybrid between graywater and a conventional sewer system, using diverter valves to control which system is in use. Be sure to review those sections of this book.

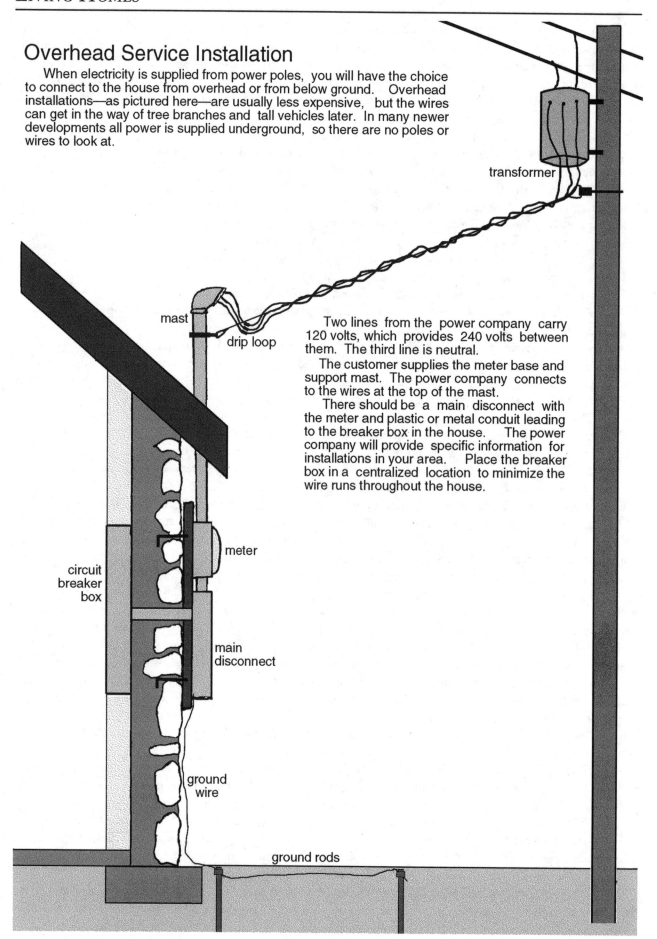

Overhead Service Installation

When electricity is supplied from power poles, you will have the choice to connect to the house from overhead or from below ground. Overhead installations—as pictured here—are usually less expensive, but the wires can get in the way of tree branches and tall vehicles later. In many newer developments all power is supplied underground, so there are no poles or wires to look at.

transformer

mast

drip loop

Two lines from the power company carry 120 volts, which provides 240 volts between them. The third line is neutral.

The customer supplies the meter base and support mast. The power company connects to the wires at the top of the mast.

There should be a main disconnect with the meter and plastic or metal conduit leading to the breaker box in the house. The power company will provide specific information for installations in your area. Place the breaker box in a centralized location to minimize the wire runs throughout the house.

meter

circuit
breaker
box

main
disconnect

ground
wire

ground rods

Electricity
Wiring the Alternative Home

Electricity is magical stuff. It has been studied for centuries, and there is so much we know about it and the way it behaves, plus how to generate it, store it, transmit it, and use it. It can be harnessed to do so many things—to produce light in the middle of the night, to pump water up from hundreds of feet below ground, or used to display sound and video from signals generated hundreds of miles away. Electricity is so well-known and so indispensable, but surprisingly, scientists have yet to determine exactly what it is!

For our purposes, we'll let the quantum theorists haggle over the possibilities, while we remain grounded in the more mundane concerns of wiring lights and outlets to meet code requirements and work properly, without the danger of electrocution or starting a house fire. The more you learn about wiring, the more fun it will become to tinker and make things work. But first, it is helpful to learn a little bit about electricity and how to read your appliances and power bill.

Electricity is similar to plumbing in many ways. Just imagine that the wires are like pipes and the electricity is water. Bigger "pipes" carry more "water", but the quantity is measured in **amperes** (**amps**), often referred to as the current. The force that drives the "water" through the piping is described as voltage or **volts**. The quantity used is measured in **watts**, which are calculated as the amps times the voltage (**amps x volts = watts**). In essence, you take the amount of electricity the pipe holds and multiply it by how fast it is moving through the system.

Household electrical systems in North America are based on a standard force of **120 volts** for common fixtures and appliances and **240 volts** for items that need much more current, such as electric baseboard heaters, water heaters, stoves, dryers and arc welders.

The force or voltage in the wiring is constant, just as water pressure is constant in plumbing lines. Also like plumbing, there are "valves" in the form of fixtures and appliances that can be opened and shut to control the quantity (amps) of electricity passing through. A lightbulb drawing 0.5 amps of current at 120 volts uses only 60 watts of power, while a microwave drawing 12.5 amps of current at 120 volts uses 1500 watts of power.

The utility charges per kilowatt hour of use (**KWh**). A kilowatt hour is 1,000 watts of electricity used for one hour. To determine how much it costs to run an appliance for one hour, simply find the wattage listed on it and multiply that number by the cost per KWh charged by the power company. For example, a 1500 watt microwave oven turned on for one hour uses 1500 watt hours or (1.5 kilowatt hours) of electricity. If the power company charged 10¢ per KWh then you would be billed 15¢ per hour to use it.

Fifteen cents per hour is not too bad for a microwave, which is only in use a little while, but consider a 1500 watt portable electric space heater. Leave it on 24 hours per day for 30 days and your cost for the month is $108! This kind of awareness about how much energy appliances use and how long they are on for is very helpful in building and maintaining a high-efficiency house.

Greater awareness in a grid-connected home will help you to choose better appliances, focusing the most attention on those that use lots of power and stay on for extended periods of time, as was discussed more in the chapter *Rethinking Appliances*.

Home owners with independent power systems especially must count watts, partly to install the most efficient appliances and fixtures, but also to calculate the power system required to run the household. For detailed information, please refer to the *Real Goods Solar Living Sourcebook*.

If you have a choice at your building site, then you should definitely connect to the grid, unless the power company tries to charge thousands of dollars for the hookup. You can still produce your own power if you want, using the grid like a battery. For example, if you install photovoltaic panels, the panels will turn the meter backwards in the daytime when the sun is out, and you can draw that current back from the grid at night.

Photovoltaic power systems independent from the grid are usually over built to produce more than enough power when the sun is out, so that there is at least enough power the rest of the time. In extended sunny weather the batteries will charge, and the rest of the electricity produced is wasted, since there is no place for it to go. So, hook to the grid if you can, and you will have the option of becoming a green energy provider.

Electrical Codes, Permits & Inspections

Laws governing do-it-yourself electrical work vary from state to state. In some places it is illegal to do your own wiring. You must hire a licensed electrician. Such laws are usually advocated for "public safety" but not by consumer groups. It is the electrical contractors and unions that advocate these laws, because it limits competition, creating a bigger market and higher fees. On-the-grid customers have little choice in the matter. You have to hire a licensed electrician to do the work. But be sure to shop around. Costs will vary considerably. Some electricians may even allow you to help them, lowering your costs. If you are not connected to the grid then you may be able to get away without a permit or a licensed electrician, but it depends on how serious the enforcement is in your area.

In many places it is legal to do your own wiring, but you must get a permit from your state before the utility can supply power to your site. The utility can send you the proper forms.

The permit typically allows for a three-step process. First you set up a **temporary power pole**, which must be looked at and approved by a state inspector before the utility provides electricity. Then you have up to one year to build your house and finish the wiring. The electrical inspector must inspect and approve the wiring rough-in, before the sheetrock goes on. Then you complete the house and do the finish wiring and call for a final inspection. Just before or after the final inspection, the utility will hook directly to the house and you can remove the temporary pole. The permit is valid and goes permanently on file. How the permitting and inspection process is enforced varies widely from state to state, and even from one inspector to the next.

Getting a permit and installing a temporary power pole was one of the first things we did after we were married and bought land in 1989. The electrical permit gave us up to one year to finish the house and wiring before we called for a final inspection. But construction proceeded slowly on our place, since we were paying as we went. A year passed and we were still getting ready to put the roof on. We could have renewed the permit, but we didn't get around to it, so it expired. But nothing happened, so we kept building.

At first we lived off of an extension cord, but gradually we wired the house to the best of our abilities and ran all the wires out the west end of the building. There they were tied together in a knot, fed by the single extension cord coming from the temporary power pole. Overloading the circuit wasn't a problem, since we only used it for lights and a few tools. Eventually we replaced that knot of wires with a breaker box. The breaker box was supposed to go on the inside, but we wanted it in the "addition", which was really more of a "completion" to our house. So we installed the breaker box outside on the west wall and weatherproofed it as much as possible, until we could add on to that end of the house. In the meantime, we continued to use an extension cord from the breaker box to the power pole and lived with it that way for a couple years.

Eventually we finished the addition, including the wiring, but there were still a few unfinished electrical projects around the house, as well as some that I wanted to improve, since I developed a better understanding of the code and wiring as we went along. In the meantime, we replaced the extension cord with electrical cable and conduit buried underground from the house to the temporary power pole. In effect, we made a permanent connection to our temporary pole. The plan was to finish all the wiring and put the permanent meter on the house.... eventually.

Then one day I was out looking at a rotten fence post, and I thought about our temporary power pole. This was eleven years after we first hooked up to the utility, and I realized we were running out of time. A week later it blew over in a storm.

After carefully assessing the danger with my brother and the aid of a utility worker who was cutting branches off a nearby power line, we tilted the pole back up and anchored it three ways with ropes, with the base of the pole tied to a metal stake driven into the ground. Getting our final inspection suddenly became a priority!

The bedrock under our home made it impossible to drive the eight-foot ground rods in. Instead of putting the new meter on the wall, we simply replaced the temporary pole with a permanent service pedestal, as pictured on the next page. We paid for a new permit and the power company ran cable underground to the pedestal. Our inspector was very helpful when we called and offered constructive suggestions where needed. Then we got a final inspection of the house and approval from the state.

Service Installations & Breaker Boxes

Chances are you will want electricity on your building site to power all your tools, so you will need to hook up a temporary power pole. The temporary set up includes a meter, main disconnect, a couple breakers and some outlets, all weatherproofed.

If electricity is supplied by power poles to your lot, then you will be able to choose to connect to temporary pole (and later the house) from overhead OR from below ground. Overhead installations are usually less expensive, but the wires can get in the way of tree branches and tall vehicles later. In many newer developments all power is supplied underground so there are no poles or wires to look at. I think these underground installations are highly preferable for aesthetic reasons.

One way you can save a little time and expense is to use an "**early permanent**" service installation. Usually this involves putting up the foundation of the house first, then installing the permanent meter base against the foundation. The trouble with this approach is that you will likely need electricity on site to power saws and tools while working on the foundation. A better solution may be to use a **permanent pedestal** installation, like the one we eventually installed to replace our temporary power pole. A pedestal installation with underground service could be used from the beginning, with weatherproof outlets to power the job site. Then you would be able to dig a ditch from the pedestal to the house when ready, without the need for

We replaced our temporary power pole with a permanent pedestal and underground service.

the utility to come back and remove the temporary service.

Whether the temporary or permanent service installation is overhead or below ground, the customer provides the meter base and main disconnect , plus the ground rods and ground wire. Code requirements change on these items surprisingly quickly, but you can always get up-to-date information locally. The utility will provide illustrated specifications for the appropriate equipment. The local electrical supply store will also be very familiar with the accepted components. Simply tell them what type of installation you want, and they will pick out all the parts you need.

The main disconnect includes a 200 amp circuit breaker which turns on or off all power to the house. Earlier code requirements allowed for smaller breakers, but the plethora of hot water heaters, hot tubs and other energy consumptive products necessitates the larger breaker to handle the maximum load.

After the main disconnect, route the 200 amp wires through 2" PVC conduit to a breaker box in the house. In the illustration at the beginning of this chapter, the box is shown immediately inside the wall, but it doesn't have to be that close to the main disconnect. It is helpful to place the breaker box in a centralized location to minimize the wire runs throughout the house. Note that the breaker box should not be placed behind a sink or any other obstacle. You must be able to walk right up to the breaker box to work on it. Ask the local electrical supply store for an appropriate breaker box and breakers, plus the wire and the necessary conduit.

Inside the breaker box you will install **20 amp 120 volt breakers** for most circuits, with **30 amp, 240 volt breakers** to the specific appliances that require it, such as the electric dryer, stove, hot water heater, or to the garage for an arc welder or heavy duty air compressor. The 240 volt circuits are a combination of two 120 volt lines. Plan on approximately one 20 amp circuit for all the outlets and lights in one room, with at least two 20 amp circuits in the kitchen.

A breaker box is not nearly as complicated as it might look. Here there are two main cables bringing in power from below, connecting to the main breaker. The neutral cable (with the white stripe) wraps around behind the hot cables and connects to the neutral bar on the left.

Individual circuits are split apart as they enter the box. The hot side (black) connects to a breaker in the middle. The neutral side (white) connects to the neutral bar on the left. The ground wires (bare copper) connect to the ground bar on the right.

Wiring Lights and Outlets

Wiring a home for lights and outlets is fun and easy, at least in wood frame construction. Certain types of panel walls are also easy to wire, as long as you can router channels to run the wires in. Wiring a house with solid stone or log walls is more of a challenge, but we'll return to that in a moment.

Most household wiring today is done with **plastic boxes** and "nonmetallic sheathed cable" which is a plastic cable commonly known as **Romex**. Metal boxes are still used for some applications, but they are more expensive, more labor intensive, and usually smaller than their plastic counterparts, so you cannot legally stuff as many wires in them. The following illustrations apply only to plastic boxes and plastic cable. With metal boxes you must also screw or clip the ground wire to the box to ensure good contact.

The first step is to walk through the house and figure out where to place all the outlets and switches and light fixtures. Lamps and other appliances have **six foot cords**, so **outlets** should be no more than twelve feet apart along the walls. Short sections of wall, such as between two doorways, should also have an outlet, in case someone wants to set a small decorative table and lamp there someday. Be sure to put extra outlets in places where an entertainment center or computer might go. Place the bottom of the outlet box about 12" above the finished floor level. The boxes come with nails already in place, so you just set a box next to a wooden stud and drive the nails in with a hammer. The front of the box should be flush with the finished wall, so the box will need to be set forward a little bit to account for the sheetrock. There are guides on the box. Note that if the boxes are notched into insulated panel walls, then they can be secured in place with expanding foam sealant, but only after running the cables.

Next, go through and place all the light fixture boxes where you think they should be. Give some consideration to indirect, versus direct lighting (See the chapter *Rethinking Appliances*). Take your time placing the **switch boxes**. Many houses have lots of lights and lots of confusing switches. Switches should be placed intuitively, preferably so that a person knows exactly where to reach in the dark, even when they have never been in the room before. Avoid lumping too many switches together into one box. Even three switches can be confusing, causing people to turn lights on and off until they find the right one. Besides being an annoyance to figure out which switch is which each time, the on-off cycles tend to shorten the life of the lightbulbs. Four or five switches in a single box is too many!

Keep in mind that any room with a door on two ends should utilize **three-way switches** to control the lights. That way you can turn on the light as you walk in one door and turn it off as you walk out the other. Four way switches are also available if needed. The bottom of a switch box should be placed about 42" above the floor.

After all the boxes are installed, then it is time to run the Romex cable. Standard 20 amp circuits are wired with either **12 gauge or 14 gauge Romex cable**. Twelve gauge is bigger and slightly more expensive, but preferable, since the line can handle a bigger load. Also, the smaller diameter of the 14 gauge wire creates more resistance and power loss through the wire.

You will use "12 - 2 with ground" for most applications, meaning there are two 12 gauge wires (one black, one white), plus a ground wire. You will need a small amount of "12 - 3 with ground" for special applications such as installing 3 way switches. This cable includes one black, one white, and one red wire, plus a ground wire.

Leave enough extra cable in the breaker box to connect the wires later, then run lines through the house to each outlet, switch and light. You will need to mentally install the outlets and switches to make sure there are enough wires in all the critical points. Run about one circuit to each room of the house, with additional circuits in the kitchen. Drill through the studs with a spade bit and run the wires through. If the cable is within two inches of the edge of a stud, then it should be protected with a **nail plate**, like the one illustrated in the plumbing chapter.

When the cable follows the wood, it should be **stapled** down at least every four feet. Poke the cables through the holes of the plastic boxes and leave extra wire to work with. It is easier to cut off the extra later, than to run a replacement wire if the original was too short. This is called "rough wiring". Installing outlets, switches, and light fixtures is considered "**finish wiring**". Wait until after the walls are sheetrocked, taped, and painted before doing the finish wiring. Use the accompanying illustrations as a beginning guide, and always seek out additional information and inquire about the latest code changes.

Also be sure to install "Ground Gault Circuit Interrupter" (**GFCI**) **outlets** in the bathroom and by the kitchen sink. These outlets have their own little circuit breakers that instantly shut the power off in the event that you accidentally drop the hair dryer or some other electrical device in the water. Note that 240 volt wiring for dryers and stoves, etc. is not covered here.

Basic Wiring with Plastic Boxes & Romex Cable

Plastic boxes are suitable for most household wiring. The boxes have attached nails to secure them to wood framing.

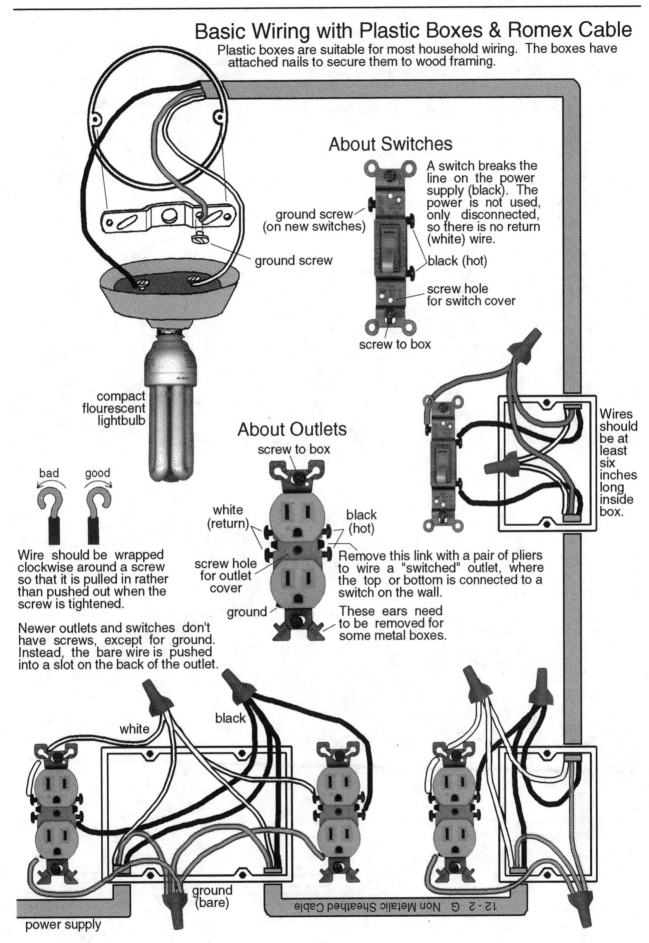

About Switches

ground screw
(on new switches)

ground screw

compact
flourescent
lightbulb

A switch breaks the line on the power supply (black). The power is not used, only disconnected, so there is no return (white) wire.

black (hot)

screw hole
for switch cover

screw to box

About Outlets

screw to box

white
(return)

black
(hot)

screw hole
for outlet
cover

ground

Wires should be at least six inches long inside box.

bad   good

Wire should be wrapped clockwise around a screw so that it is pulled in rather than pushed out when the screw is tightened.

Newer outlets and switches don't have screws, except for ground. Instead, the bare wire is pushed into a slot on the back of the outlet.

Remove this link with a pair of pliers to wire a "switched" outlet, where the top or bottom is connected to a switch on the wall.

These ears need to be removed for some metal boxes.

white

black

ground
(bare)

power supply

12-2 G Non Metallic Sheathed Cable

Switched Outlets

In living rooms it is common to install switched outlets, so that a lamp can be plugged into an outlet and operated by a switch on the wall. To make switched outlets, simply remove the links on the hot side of the outlets, then supply power independently to the tops and bottoms.

Romex cable with 3 wires plus ground is used between the outlet boxes to supply the necessary additional wire.

Notice that power runs up the black wire to the switch then back down the white wire to the outlet. The white wire is wrapped with black electrical tape to signify that it is hot.

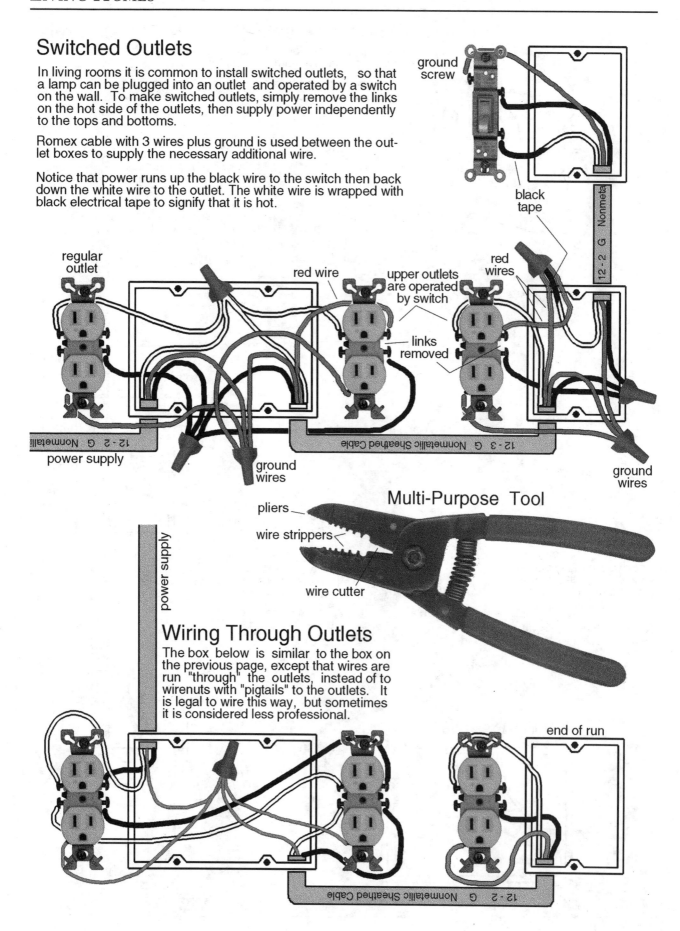

ground screw

black tape

12 - 2 G Nonmeta

regular outlet

red wire

upper outlets are operated by switch

red wires

links removed

12 - 2 G Nonmetalli
power supply

ground wires

12 - 3 G Nonmetallic Sheathed Cable

ground wires

Multi-Purpose Tool

pliers

wire strippers

wire cutter

power supply

Wiring Through Outlets

The box below is similar to the box on the previous page, except that wires are run "through" the outlets, instead of to wirenuts with "pigtails" to the outlets. It is legal to wire this way, but sometimes it is considered less professional.

end of run

12 - 2 G Nonmetallic Sheathed Cable

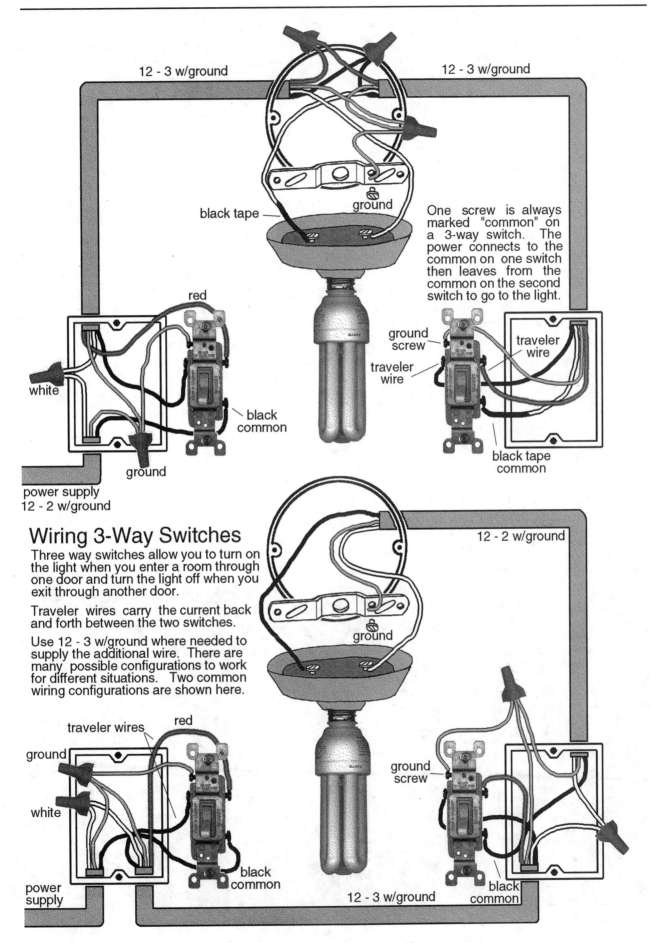

12 - 3 w/ground

12 - 3 w/ground

black tape

ground

One screw is always marked "common" on a 3-way switch. The power connects to the common on one switch then leaves from the common on the second switch to go to the light.

red

ground screw

traveler wire

traveler wire

white

black common

ground

black tape common

power supply
12 - 2 w/ground

Wiring 3-Way Switches

Three way switches allow you to turn on the light when you enter a room through one door and turn the light off when you exit through another door.

Traveler wires carry the current back and forth between the two switches.

Use 12 - 3 w/ground where needed to supply the additional wire. There are many possible configurations to work for different situations. Two common wiring configurations are shown here.

12 - 2 w/ground

ground

traveler wires

red

ground screw

white

black common

power supply

12 - 3 w/ground

black common

Special Wiring Considerations in Stone & Log Homes

Outlets and switches mounted in a support log or on a stone wall lend a fairy tale look to a house, much like the Flintstones or B.C. cartoons. Installing those switches and outlets, however, is no fairy tale. The work is not difficult, just time consuming. The biggest challenge to **wiring stone masonry** is that you have to think ahead to figure out where the wiring should go and how it should work, so that you can mortar the electrical boxes and conduit right into the wall. That is not a big problem in itself, but if you are new to construction work, then you may find it difficult to learn stone masonry and electrical work at the same time. Therefore, I recommend doing the least wiring possible in the stonework and saving the rest for later.

A house with stone on the outside and frame walls or insulation panels on the inside is easy to wire, since virtually all of the wiring runs through the interior walls. Any exterior outlets and light fixtures can be made easily with a **weatherproof box** and a short, straight piece of conduit. Make the unit to fit snugly inside the slipforms, such that the box is pressed against the outside form and the open end of the conduit is pressed against the inside form. Later, you will be able to run a piece of Romex cable straight through into the box while you are wiring the rest of the walls. Use GFCI outlets like the one shown below for exterior outlets.

Interior stone walls require more preparation in advance. We wired sections of our stone walls with metal boxes and metal conduit, much of which as laying around as scrap when we bought our place. The installation was less than perfect and we later mortared over about half the boxes, just because we modified our wiring plans as we went. The metal conduit we worked with was somewhat unwieldy, and mortaring electrical wires directly in the wall is not legal. It would be much easier to wire a stone wall with the aid of **flexible plastic conduit** that you can easily snake back and forth around the rocks and rebar of the wall. If you have to wire a stone wall, then this is definitely the way to go.

If necessary, stone walls can be **surfaced wired**, but the job is more expensive, not as nice in appearance, and it takes as much or more time than it would to lay conduit during the stonework. We routed much of our wiring work through log support posts in our house, completely bypassing the stonework. In other places the wiring runs through grey PVC conduit in out-of-the way corners, or sometimes in the tan-colored boxes and surface mounted conduit, as shown below. Note that the supplies for this type of wiring is about ten times as expensive as regular boxes and conduit.

Wiring through the **logs** was relatively easy, since the trees were fire-killed and quickly dried, causing large "checks" or cracks in the wood. We ran the wires right down the cracks and sometimes opened them a little more with the aid of a router. We outlined the electrical boxes on the surface of the logs, then cut the hole with a spade bit on a drill, plus wood chisels. If the wire came in on the wrong side, then we simply drilled through the log and brought the wire into the back of the box. The support log shown here also has switches on two other sides.

GFCI installed in a weatherproof box.   *Surface wiring is much more expensive.*   *Light switches installed in a log.*

A Primer on Paint
Reuse & Recycling

Nationwide, at least two gallons of paints, stains, varnishes and related materials are manufactured for every man, woman and child every year—more than 500 million gallons all together. Generating all that goop consumes natural resources and energy and costs lots of money. Merely using solvent-based paints further pollutes the air with volatile organic compounds (VOC's), a significant problem in urban areas. Even after they are dry, some paints trigger allergic reactions in people with chemical sensitivities. But that is not the end of it, because most painting jobs end with partial cans of paint, which usually sit on the shelf for years before being illegally poured down the drain or tossed out with the trash, ultimately leaching into the groundwater at the landfill. Clearly we need to rethink the way we make, use and dispose of paints.

The most important step in the process is **redesigning homes** so they require fewer paints and stains to begin with. Alternative building materials, such as stone, log, and straw, require little or no painting or staining, although most people add them anyway. Log houses get the most treatment. Without protection the lignin in the wood oxidizes in the air and sunlight, turning the surface gray. Very old log homes usually have dark, weathered logs. The oxidation process doesn't tangibly hurt the logs, but the graying wood can be unsightly, so most people prevent it with the aid of a stain, urethane or varnish. Stuccoed-strawbale houses do not require any paints on the outside, except for trim, but the stucco can be painted if desired. Stone homes do not require a finish either, although a water repellent can help give the stone more shine and protect it from driving rains. Our own stone and log home has very little paint or stain on the outside and less than average on the inside.

Like most people, we started out with what was available at the hardware or paint store, because that was all we knew about. Today we often use and blend **secondhand paints and stains**—left-overs acquired from friends and relatives, plus a few cans salvaged from the dumpster, but my preferred source of paint is the thrift store.

Thrift stores often get stuck with secondhand paint, even though they do not want it and will not knowingly accept it. Some people drop off new, high quality paints and stains after deciding it wasn't the color they wanted after all. They probably intend well by donating it to the thrift store, but paints are a big, messy problem and thrift stores don't want to deal with it. Other people knowingly drop off unwanted hazardous waste in the night to stick the thrift stores with the disposal problem, including half-full cans of paint, stains and varnish, buckets of printer ink and toner, industrial cleaners, tar, motor oil, pesticides and more. I inquired at one thrift store and they directed me to a free box where they leave the paint in the hopes that someone will carry it away quickly. I carried away about $100 worth of brand new high-quality paints. Now I check the free box for good paints every time I go there.

At another store I was directed to a stockpile out back, which included all the hazardous waste listed above. There are limits to how much of this stuff I can reasonably store and use at a time, but the pile is always there available for use. It is okay to dispose of paint in the dump, but only after it is completely dry. Occasionally the thrift store would dump an entire can of paint on an old, weathered couch (also dropped off in the night), then haul the painted couch off to the dump. They still have to pay disposal fees for the couch.

Many larger communities have **designated drop-off points** for people to get rid of their extra paint. The paints are then available for civic projects, nonprofit groups, and virtually anybody who will take the stuff. Unusable paints are disposed of properly by the city or country program.

To understand the options when working with new and used paints, stains and varnishes we must first divide them into two broad categories, **water-based** finishes and solvent-based finishes. Water-based products cannot be combined with solvent-based products; they are completely incompatible. If you are uncertain which one you have, just look at the clean-up instructions. Water-based finishes use water for cleaning. **Solvent-based** finishes require a solvent like paint thinner, mineral spirits, turpentine or lacquer thinner. A third, smaller category is shellac, which is **alcohol-based**.

Water-Based Finishes

Before the age of synthetics, water-based finishes consisted of various **natural ingredients**, including lime, milk casein, gum arabic, earth pigments and plant dyes. You can still purchase casein paint or "milk paint" from specialty stores, catalogues, and on the web. The new products consist of casein (a milk solid), lime, clay, cellulose, asbestos-free talcum, and salt. Casein is sold as a white powder. Natural earth pigments can be added to create a full spectrum of colors. Casein paints are preferred by people with chemical sensitivities. Natural paints are most effective indoors where they are not exposed to the weather. As a builder, I would seriously consider trying natural paints indoors on future homes.

In modern times, natural water-based finishes have been almost completely replaced by synthetic latex and acrylic paints. Synthetic water-based paints are relatively benign, at least compared to solvent-based paints, discussed later. However, **lead** was used in some brands of white latex paint as late as 1978. Mercury was commonly included in interior latex paint to kill mildew and fungus up until 1990. Many exterior latex paints still contain **mercury** or other **biocides** to keep the paint from molding in the can and to preserve the application on the wall. The danger to the occasional user is probably extremely small, but there may be more concern for people who work with paint all the time. As I said, we worked with conventional paints simply because that's what was available. Nevertheless, we learned a few things along the way that may be helpful to you.

One of our favorite finishes is a "**sand texture paint**"—simply latex paint with fine silica sand mixed in. We bought sand texture paint and used it especially on the poured concrete walls that make up the north and east side of our home, bermed into the hill. We smoothed out the rough spots in the concrete with the aid of plaster and a trowel, then troweled on the sand texture paint to give the walls a hand-plastered look. Our concrete walls are far from flat and even, so the hand-troweled look is appropriate. We used a similar treatment on the sheetrocked ceiling. The only problems with the latex sand texture paint were 1) it is expensive when you apply it by the trowel full, and 2) there are just enough volatile organic compounds in latex paint to make a person dizzy when applying large amounts of it. Be sure to compare the labels to find the brand with the least VOC's.

Later we discovered a much cheaper and more sane alternative. We bought the silica sand at the brickyard and mixed it not with paint, but with ready-mix joint compound. It is easy to mix the ingredients with the aid of a mixing attachment on a standard drill. I applied our **sand texture joint compound** with a trowel to the sheetrock ceiling of the greenhouse, with the intent to give it a thin coat of paint afterwards. As it turned out, however, the sand texture joint compound finish looked so good, we never did paint it! I think it may be possible to finish an entire house that way, although it would be more prone to smudges and chipping. Note that the joint compound makes a very absorbent surface that should be ideal for casein paints.

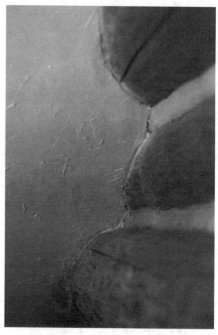

We scribed the sheetrock of the greenhouse ceiling to fit the logs as much as possible. The remaining gaps were filled with expanding foam sealant and trimmed flush. Then we blended silica sand with joint compound and hand-troweled it onto the ceiling. It didn't need to be painted at all.

Much of our painting has been done with **secondhand paints**, only because other people didn't want them, and I tend to attract stuff like that. Partly I just wanted to be helpful, to make sure the paints were disposed of properly instead of being tossed out with the trash. The easiest color to work with is white, for obvious reasons. You can blend a dozen different cans of white and off-white, and get something that is still white and very useful indoors where you want light walls.

One time the kids wanted to repaint their dressers, so we experimented with the available paints from the cellar. Hideous browns and golds were transformed into surprisingly warm colors simply by **mixing** in enough white. It is helpful to make small test batches first, until a desirable color is achieved. When you make up a batch for the final project, be sure to mix more than enough because it is virtually impossible to get exactly the same result twice.

The successes with the kids dressers sent me on a painting frenzy. I blended together blue, blue-gray, and white paints and generated enough material to paint the plywood eves of our chickenhouse. Then I blended a variety of stains and finished all the fence posts around the yard. Three brands of varnish mixed together gave a beautiful finish to the sunroom floor and railing. Another stain worked well for a boot chest I built from scrap lumber. Instead of buying new paints and creating new waste disposal problems, I was able to use up multiple partial cans of old paint. Using old paints is by far the best way to dispose of them. In a matter of a few days, I emptied more than fifteen cans of paint from our cellar and sent the cans off to the recycling center. After many experiences like that, I concluded there was no reasonable need to ever buy another can of paint again!

Over time I discovered that it is easy to work with secondhand paints, provided you are open to a range of possibilities and you have the necessary ingredients on hand to create good blends. It is more difficult to go shopping for specific secondhand paints, as I discovered when Renee brought me a reddish-orange color chip and said she wanted to repaint our doors that color. We were not in a particular hurry, thank goodness, since it took me more than five months of searching and experimentation to reproduce the color! I was more interested in perfecting the process of working with secondhand paints than in actually getting the job done, so I gathered materials every time I went town (once or twice a month) and experimented until I made it work.

This hand-troweled concrete floor was finished with floor quality latex paint. The entire floor was first painted with the darker blue-gray paint. Then white paint was blended in and the new mix was applied with a sponge to create the textured look. Sage Mountain Center (www.sagemountain.org).

First I asked my friends and relatives for their left-over paints, hoping to get lucky. Then I tried the thrift stores, but they didn't have what I needed either. After quite a bit of searching we finally brought the paint to the paint store and asked them to tint it the color we wanted. Normally they will do that sort of thing for a small fee, but there is only so far they can adjust the color, and some stores will only tint the brands they sell. It was hard to tell if they really couldn't make the adjustment or simply wouldn't, so I started inquiring into **paint pigments** and learned that I could buy the pigment by the ounce and do my experimenting at home (bring your own container).

I assumed that white and other light color paints would be easily drowned out by small quantities of colored pigments, but it doesn't work that way. Light paints have powerful pigments in them too, so the paint store was correct in saying that there is only so far they can adjust the color. (I just have to prove those things for myself!) As a rule of thumb, any two colors or shades mixed together in equal quantities will give a result halfway between the two. If you are persistent you may be able to get the color you want, but you might spend more on pigment than on a whole new can of paint, and the end product may not be as durable. In my experimentation I generated a whole bunch of pink paint!

I have also experimented with the **powder pigments** used to dye cement. The powder does not readily dissolve into latex paint, so it is hard to tell what the color is by mixing it with a stick, but you can effectively mix it in place with the paintbrush; it just takes a few extra strokes. Even better, use a blender to mix the latex and mineral pigments. I have my own non-food blender for just these kinds of projects. I finally got the color that Renee wanted, or very close to it, but the final mix was about half pigment and half latex. I added a small amount of water in the blender to thin it out. Obviously a mix like this greatly weakens the original paint, but I blasted one door with the hose and found no immediate problems. All of the painted doors are protected from the weather.

It is okay to **clean-up** water-based paints with soap and water, washing small amounts of paint down the drain, but do not dispose of leftover paint that way. The sewer or septic system will not handle it. If you absolutely have no use for the paint, then let small amounts dry in the can, or spread larger amounts out in a tub and mix it with absorbent kitty litter to set the paint. Stir it for a couple weeks until it is definitely dry, then it can be discarded. At least that is the official line of advice for paint disposal. I suspect that many such projects end up full of rainwater and finally get tossed in the trash in their watered down form.

My preferred method for disposing of latex and acrylic paints, besides blending and using them, is to add them to **stucco mortar** for a smoother quality and better adhesion. It doesn't matter what color the paint is. Small amounts can be diluted into the gray mortar to the point that it is invisible. Larger quantities are okay too, if the stucco work is to be painted anyway.

Note that some businesses are getting involved in **paint recycling** too. Amazon Environmental, with operations in California, Colorado and Minnesota, accepts latex paint and chemically similar materials for recycling. Each container is opened and inspected to determine if the paint is still useable. About 50% of the material received meets their criteria. It is recycled into quality paints, sold at very competitive prices. Amazon Select™ paints are fine strained, filtered, tinted, and viscosity adjusted, with preservatives added. Their standard colors are whipped white, ivory white, tawny beige, grizzly gray, concrete gray and chocolate brown. Color chips are available upon request, and custom colors can be special ordered. Non-reusable paints, including frozen or soured paints, off-colors, "skins" and solidified paints, are manufactured into Processed Latex Pigment, a patented additive used in portland cement. Amazon Environmental paints are available through Dunn-Edwards paint stores across the southwest, or look them up on the internet for contact information. There are several smaller companies doing similar work in other parts of the country.

Finally, I should mention **Polycrylic™** stains which include a mix of acrylic and a water-based polyurethane, used only for indoor projects. Polycrylics contain far fewer volatile organic compounds than their solvent-based urethane cousins, but they are also more pricey. Acrylic is a type of plastic, so this "stain" is more like a plastic coating on top of the wood. We really like the Polycrylic on our bookshelves, windows and doorways, but it has it's limitations where water is concerned, under flower pots, etc. Acrylics are slightly permeable, so water can slowly penetrate through the finish, then lift it right off the wood. Polycrylics are available at most hardware stores. Look for similar finishes manufactured by *McClosky* and *Carver-Tripp*.

Solvent-Based Finishes

The original solvent-based finishes included linseed, hempseed, poppy and walnut oils mixed with pigments and thinned with turpentine (the solvent) distilled from the oleoresin of pine trees. Natural varnish is made of resin, turpentine oil and pigment. Today you can still special order **natural paints, stains, thinners and waxes** formulated from a variety of organic materials such as citrus peel oils and solvents; essential oils and seed oils; tree resins; pigments from earthen materials; inert mineral fillers; bee and tree waxes and lead-free dryers. Linseed oil, tung oil and various oil and water emulsions allow the natural sheen and rich color of the wood to shine through. These are a popular option for people with chemical sensitivities to synthetic finishes. Natural finishes must be applied to raw wood, not over the top of synthetic finishes.

Most solvent-based finishes today consist of a variety of synthetic chemicals derived from petroleum resources, including alkyd resins, epoxy, xylene, toluene and ketones, plus toxic heavy metals. Because these products are so toxic, they must be used with good ventilation, at times when you can leave the windows wide open all day and all night. Products with the least **volatile organic compounds (VOC's)** are the best , because you get less solvent and more finish.

We've used some of these products in our home, especially MinWax™, because that was all we knew about. Today we still use these products, but mostly from secondhand sources, since it is very important that these toxic materials are disposed of (used) properly. Besides, new products are always expensive, and with a little patience you can always find enough free material to complete any project.

It is important to note, however, that while any solvent-based finishes are "mixable" they are not always 100% compatible. It is better to mix urethane with urethane and stain with stain, rather than **blending** them together. I have successfully mixed urethanes, stain, and varnish all together, adding some additional solvent for better penetration, but this kind of mix has to be used very soon. If left for a few days the chemicals react with each other and congeal into a rubber like disk in the bucket. This mix has held up very well inside our greenhouse, even where it gets wet from the hose, but not so well outside where it is exposed to the weather. Keep in mind that these sort of experiments automatically void any warranties on the ingredients or the surfaces you apply them to.

As far as **solvents** go, turpentine is mild, while paint thinner or mineral spirits are more powerful, and lacquer thinner will dissolve just about anything. The more potent the solvent, the more toxic and potentially explosive it is. Rags used to clean up lacquer thinner can **spontaneously combust** if left in a pile. It is important to hang them out to dry before disposing of them. Many finishes also contain enough solvent to sponateously combust if the rags are left in a pile.

Disposing of the solvent can be a problem too, after you've cleaned the brushes. Do not pour it down the drain, as it will likely pass through the septic or sewer untreated and toxic. The most effective method I've found is to dip my paint brush in the solvent and paint out the residue on a piece of wood, rather than swishing the brush around in the solvent. I dip the brush back into the solvent about ten times to clean it, and brush it all onto the shelf wood in our cellar, helping to preserve the wood. (There are canned goods, not vegetables in our cellar.) One batch of solvent lasts a very long time if you clean your brushes this way. If necessary, you can allow the solids to settle out and pour off the clear solvent for further use.

I remember when people still cleaned paint off their hands with paint thinner, basically removing one toxin with another, more penetrating one. Use a citric solvent instead, concentrated from orange peels.

If you do need to dispose of solvent or any solvent-based finish, be sure to do it outside in the open air on a sunny day. The **disposal** system is similar to that for latex paints—just spread it out thin to dry. But keep in mind that anything with solvents in it is potentially explosive. Because solvent-based finishes are toxic and explosive, more and more communities have designated paint collection days for leftover paints. Any good materials are passed on to other people.

Unfortunately it is difficult to remanufacture the ingredients into new products, since there are so many different formulas. Therefore, unusable solvent-based products are usually diverted to **waste-to-energy programs**, such as blending with fuel for cement kilns. Any toxins that survive the burn end up in the air, a "less-bad" alternative to letting them leach into the water supply.

Spray paint will hold its charge for along time in storage. If it fails to spray, it is usually because the directions about shaking before use and cleaning the spray head after use were not followed properly. The can will usually spray again if the nozzle is removed and cleaned thoroughly, and any dried paint particles are removed. It may be necessary to repeat the cleaning process.

Always **recycle steel paint cans**, including those from water-based and solvent based paints, as long as there are no big chunks of solids inside. Scrap cans are heated to 3000° F and reprocessed into pure materials, so a trace of residue won't hurt, even though the cans may later be used for food. Approximately 55% of all steel cans are currently recycled. Spray paint cans may be recycled too, if they are completely emptied first.

Finally, keep in mind that even the best synthetic paints will outgas for some time, possibly years. Be sure to reread the chapter on *Air Quality*, and grow lots of living plants inside your biosphere to scrub toxins out of the air.

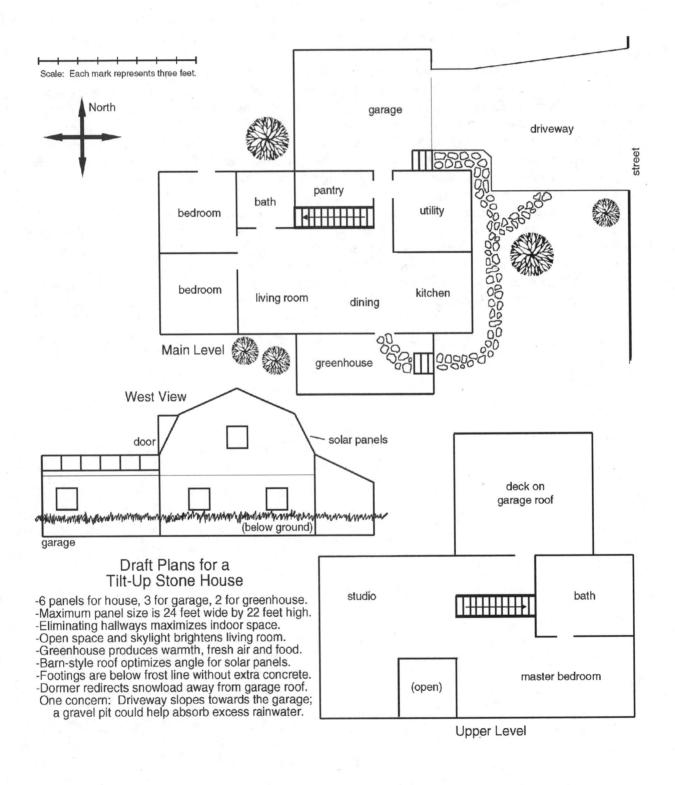

Scale: Each mark represents three feet.

North

garage

driveway

street

bedroom

bath

pantry

utility

bedroom

living room

dining

kitchen

Main Level

greenhouse

West View

door

solar panels

garage

(below ground)

deck on
garage roof

Draft Plans for a
Tilt-Up Stone House

-6 panels for house, 3 for garage, 2 for greenhouse.
-Maximum panel size is 24 feet wide by 22 feet high.
-Eliminating hallways maximizes indoor space.
-Open space and skylight brightens living room.
-Greenhouse produces warmth, fresh air and food.
-Barn-style roof optimizes angle for solar panels.
-Footings are below frost line without extra concrete.
-Dormer redirects snowload away from garage roof.
One concern: Driveway slopes towards the garage;
    a gravel pit could help absorb excess rainwater.

studio

bath

(open)

master bedroom

Upper Level

Conclusion
The End of the Beginning

A blueprint is the sum of the criteria, so each project should be carefully considered from the foundation to the roof based on the specific situation. Instead of building every project with wood frame construction or stone masonry or strawbale, it is wise to apply the most appropriate materials and design for each unique situation. Let me give you some examples, based on some different projects I have in mind. I continue to develop these concepts while working on this book.

The first project is a slipformed stone masonry storage shed beside our house. The purpose of the project is to provide storage space for our bicycles and camping gear. The design criteria is simple. We will use stone masonry to make the structure fit with the rest of our place. It will be bermed into the hill on three sides and at least two feet deep to make the front door level with our driveway and patio. The building will have a roof the proper orientation and slope for a future installation of photovoltaic panels. The shed does not need to be heated, but we will place a window on the south side to provide some warmth. Also we will use the beadboard panel method of slipforming to gain firsthand experience with the technique and to produce a step-by-step video of the process. This will be an expensive project as far as storage sheds go, but the intent is to provide enough information on video so that viewers can apply the technique to a house. We will begin this project shortly after this book goes to print, so be sure to see our website at www.hollowtop.com for details.

Another project we would like to build on our place is a pole-frame strawbale classroom to replace the earthlodge. The framework of the earthlodge was pictured in the chapter *Putting the Roof On*. The new structure will cost very little to build. It will be a circular or oval building with pole framed walls and roof. We will test out the papercrete roofing method proposed in this book. The strawbale wall panels will be added after the roof is finished. The building will have a concrete footing and a terra tile floor.

A similar project I've dreamed of is a two-story bookstore in a nearby town for our publishing company, with pole framing and strawbale infill, but with a rectangular design and a slipformed foundation up to the base of the windows.

I also like to think about building slipformed stone houses in my community where the terrain is too hilly for tilt-up work, or even log houses, if I can buy my own woodlot to sustainably manage. I've also dreamed about retrofitting a few older, inefficient homes, turning them into energy-efficient and elegant stone houses. Can you tell that I dream a lot? Eventually I intend to get back into the construction business, starting with expensive but elegant **tilt-up stone houses**. The purpose will be to make homes that fit mainstream ideas about proper house shape, while introducing ecological design and resource efficiency, plus construction that is built to last for centuries. With only a few well-tuned house plans and reusable formwork, we will be able to make multiple copies of the structures, but spread them out in different subdivisions. A draft house plan for tilt-up construction is illustrated here. It still requires some refinement.

Ultimately I would like to build a small city (okay, a big subdivision) of ultra low cost **papercrete dome homes**, something like the model pictured in the chapter *Disaster Proofing Your Home*. This type of house would not fit anywhere else, except with its own kind. Besides, I would like to design the layout of the subdivision and community center, since I don't like the layout of most existing subdivisions.

The point is that each of these ideas are unique situations with unique criteria and vastly different end products. That is the challenge you face in designing and building your own home. You must pull together the specific criteria appropriate to your situation and create a blueprint that fits that criteria.

My greatest fear in writing this book is that there might be too much information here, to the point that you may be intimidated at the scope of the building process. I hope that is not the case. Keep in mind that design and construction work does not have to be perfect. You just have to do the best you can.

In our house there are sections of stone wall that lean one way or another by an inch, but you cannot tell. The floor in our bedroom is about six inches wider on one end than the other, due partly to the taper of the logs, but no one has ever noticed it. In fact, I know that we made enough mistakes during the design and construction process to fill up several pages of this book. But no matter how glaring the errors seemed when we made them, it is difficult to remember many of them now. I guess the mistakes were not nearly as bad as we imagined at the time!

There are also many projects yet to finish in our home, like staining the woodwork or carpeting the upstairs. And despite all my discussion of energy efficiency, our house was anything but warm when we first built it. Nevertheless, we know this house inside and out and make small improvements to it every year. With each improvement the house becomes more comfortable and we spend less time cutting and hauling firewood.

With the material that I have presented in this text, plus a little day-dreaming on your part, I am confident that your home will be better than ours and even easier to build. I hope you will share your story and photos of your Dream home back with me.

If you have any questions about the content of this book which are not adequately covered in the text, please go to the *Contemporary Living Skills* page of our website at www.hollowtop.com and look for the answers there. At some point we will put up a discussion board for readers to dialogue with each other about the material covered here. In the meantime, you are welcome to send me an e-mail from the website, and I will answer your questions to the best of my ability, although not always in a timely fashion. The feedback from your letters and the discussion board will be incorporated into future editions of this book.

Be sure to return periodically to look for the latest version of the book. This is the fourth edition, and there will always be more to add. Therefore, it is my policy to make a special offer to my readers to "upgrade" to the newest edition of the book at a generous discount. Details will be posted on the website when the next edition is released. I always appreciate your support. Thanks!

HOPS Press
Hollowtop Outdoor Primitive School, LLC
PO Box 697
Pony, MT 59747-0697
www.hollowtop.com

Bibliography

_____. 2.0 Regulation Governing Individual Onsite Wastewater Disposal. Mississippi State Department of Health. Form No. 309. November 1992.

_____. "Air Krete: Cementitious Foam Insulation". Product fact sheet. Nordic Builders: Gilbert, Arizona.

_____. Building with Alternatives to Lumber and Plywood. NAHB Research Center. Home Builder Press: Washington, DC. 1994.

_____. "CABO Okays Frost-free Footings." Builder. March 1995. Page 52.

_____. "A Citizen's Guide to Radon, 2nd Edition." United States EPA. ANR-44. May 1992.

_____. Groiler Multimedia Encyclopedia. Version 11.0. 1999.

_____. Warm Places: A sampling of energy-efficient Montana Homes. Montana Department of Natural Resources & Conservation. Spring 1988.

Alth, Max. Do-It-Yourself Plumbing. Popular Science/Harper & Row: New York. 1975.

Anderson, L. O. Wood-Frame House Construction. USDA. Agriculture Handbook No. 73. July, 1970. April, 1975.

Barnett, Dianna Lopez with William D. Browning. A Primer on Sustainable Building. Rocky Mountain Institute Green Development Services: Snowmass, Colorado. 1995.

Blankenbaker, E. Keith. Modern Plumbing. Goodheart-Willcox Company, Inc.: South Holland, IL. 1978.

Easton, David. The Rammed Earth House. Chelsea Green Publishing Co. White River Junction, VT. 1996.

Eccli, Eugene. Low-Cost, Energy-Efficient Shelter. Rodale Press, Inc.: Emmaus, Pennsylvania. 1976.

Gatchell, John. "Hot Spots." (Montana wildfires) Wild Montana. Montana Wilderness Association. Autumn 2000.

Grady, Wayne. Green Home. Camden House: Camden East, Ontario. 1993.

Heed, Richard & Rocky Mountain Institute. Homemade Money. Rocky Mountain Institute: Snowmass, Colorado. 1995.

Henkenius, Merle. "Radiant Hot-Water Heating." Popular Mechanics. January 1997. Pgs. 78-81.

Jenkins, J. C. The Humanmanure Handbook. Jenkins Publishing: Grove City: PA 1994.

Ludwig, Art. Create an Oasis with Greywater. Oasis Design. Santa Barbara, CA: 1994.

Lyle, David. The Book of Masonry Stoves: Rediscovering an Old Way of Warming. Brick House Publishing Co. Brick House Publishing Co., Inc.: Andover, MA. 1984.

Marinelli, Janet, and Paul Bierman-Lytle. Your Natural Home. Little, Brown and Company: Boston & New York. 1995.

Matthews, Mark. "Home is where the heat is." (Cost of Wildfires) High Country News. August 28, 2000. Page 4.

McCullagh, James C. The Solar Greenhouse Book. Rodale Press: Emmaus, PA 1978.

Parsons, Steve. Stone Houses: A Design & Construction Handbook. Tab Books, Inc.: Blue Ridge Summit, Pennsylvania. 1984.

McPheee, Marnie. "Solar heat with perks." Popular Science. July 1989. Pgs. 76-77.

Pearson, David. The Natural House Book. Simon & Schuster, Fireside: New York. 1989.

Pfarr, Paul & Karyn. Build Your Own Log Cabin. Winchester Press: New York. 1978.

Pratt, Doug (Editor). The Real Goods Solar Living Sourcebook, Tenth Edition. Chelsea Green Publishing Co.: White River Junction, Vermont. 1999.

Sasse, Ludwig. Biogas Plants. Vieweg & Sohn: Braunschweig/Wiesbaden. 1984.

Solberg, Gordon. Building with Papercrete and Paper Adobe. Remedial Planet Communications.: Radium Springs, NM. 1999.

Steen, Athena Swentzell and Bill; David Bainbridge with David Eisenberg. The Straw Bale House. Chelsea Green Publishing: White River Junction, Vermont. 1994.

Wilson, Alex. "Super Bug." (Formosan Termites.) Popular Science. July 2000. Page 31.

VanderWerf, Pieter A. & W. Keith Munsell. The Portland Cement Association's Guide to Concrete Homebuilding Systems. McGraw-Hill, Inc. 1995.

Wilkinson, Todd. "Homes On The Range." Nature Conservancy. July/August 2000. Pgs. 20-26.

Wolverton, B.C. How To Grow Fresh Air. Penguin Books: New York, NY. 1996.

Woodson, R. Dodge. National Plumbing Codes Handbook. McGraw-Hill: New York, NY. 1993.

Index

—Botany in a Day—
Thomas J. Elpel's Herbal Field Guide to Plant Families

Botany in a Day is changing the way people learn about plants! Tom's book has gained a nation-wide audience almost exclusively by word-of-mouth. It is now used as a text and recommended by herbal and wilderness schools, individuals and universities across North America.

Too often people try to learn plants one-at-a-time, without rhyme or reason. But now you can cut years off the process of learning about plants and their uses. Learn how related plants have similar features for identification. Discover how they often have similar properties and similar uses.

Instead of presenting individual plants, *Botany in a Day* unveils the patterns of identification and uses among related plants, giving you simple tools to rapidly unlock the mysteries of the new species you encounter throughout the continent. Tom's book takes you beyond the details towards a greater understanding of the patterns among plants. You will discover that you can learn plants by the dozens—just by looking for patterns.

Most plant books cover only one or two hundred species. *Botany in a Day* includes more than 100 plant families and over 700 genera—applicable to many thousands of species. Understand the magic of patterns among plants, and the world will never look the same again! Exquisitely illustrated with some of the best plant drawings of a century ago.

Botany in a Day

Thomas J. Elpel's
Herbal Field Guide to Plant Families
4th Edition

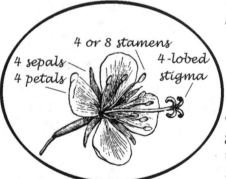

4 or 8 stamens
4 sepals
4 petals
4-lobed stigma

A typical flower of the Evening Primrose Family

"Botany in a Day truly has the potential to become one of the most useful botany and herbal primers ever written."
—Peter Gail, Ph.D.
Goosefoot Acres Center for Resourceful Living. Cleveland, OH

"Botany in a Day has my highest recommendation for anyone beginner or expert interested in plants. Herbalists, naturalists, gardeners, and especially those involved in teaching outdoor and survival skills will wonder how they ever managed without this superb book."
—Susun S. Weed, Director
Wise Woman Center. Woodstock, NY

"Botany in a Day is exactly what I needed for my botany classes. It goes beyond what is available in the standard field key, providing a wealth of information on individual families. Now my students are able to key local flora confidently, knowing they have reached the correct family by referring to Botany in a Day's detailed descriptions and pictures. They can become truly acquainted with the family's characteristics, constituents, medicinal uses, and patterns. I personally love all the stories about the edible plants, which describe in delicious detail how long it takes to collect and prepare each one."
—Garima Fairfax
Rocky Mountain Center for Botanical Studies. Boulder, Colorado

Order on-line at www.hollowtop.com or call HOPS at 406-685-3222.

—Participating in Nature—

Thomas J. Elpel's Field Guide to Primitive Living Skills

"Primitive living is a metaphor we participate in. We journey into the Stone-Age and quest to meet our basic needs. We learn to observe, to think, to reach inside ourselves for new resources to deal with challenging and unfamiliar situations. We return with knowledge, wisdom, and strength to enrich our lives in contemporary society."

—Thomas J. Elpel, Participating in Nature

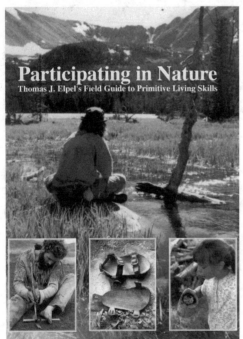

Discover nature by using it! Primitive skills allow you to get closer to nature by experiencing nature directly. Instead of merely hiking through, or camping in nature, primitive living allows you to move in and become part of the process. Learn about nature as you use it to meet your daily needs for shelter, clothing, fire, water, and food. Connect with the land iin an intimate way as you learn about all the plants and trees and rocks and animals, and all their uses.

Tom's guide gives you a direct, hands-on experience of the world around you. With this book you will discover the thrill of staying warm and comfortable without even a blanket! Experience the magic of starting a fire by friction. Learn about the edible plants of the Rocky Mountain region and the techniques to process them, plus "primitive gourmet" cooking skills.

Braintan the hides from your fall hunting trip and manufacture them into durable clothing. Also covered are: sinews, hide glue, backpacking, felting with wool, fishing by hand, stone knives, wooden containers, willow baskets, twig deer, cordage, stalking skills, trapping and tire sandals.

Participating in Nature includes dozens of innovative skills and nearly 200 illustrations, plus an encompassing philosophy. Tom does extensive experiential research. He places an emphasis on publishing new information that is not found in any other source.

"I've read MANY books on survival. Enough that I rarely find fresh ideas in a new one I read. But yours is full of things that I haven't read in many other books. Thanks not only for the fresh ideas, but also for the fresh format. The narrative is wonderfully inspirational. I almost feel like I'm out in the field with you. I don't know if we'll ever meet (I hope we do), but if not I feel like I know you through your writings."

—David W. Attala, AL

Order on-line at www.hollowtop.com or call HOPS at 406-685-3222.

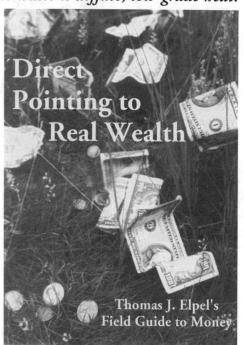
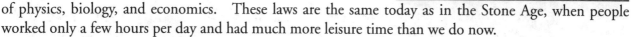